Building Data Pipelines Using Apache Beam

Deliver Unified Batch and Streaming Pipelines for Real-World Production Across Dataflow, Flink, and Spark

Nuzhi Meyen

www.orangeava.com

First Published: April 2026

Published By: Orange Education Pvt Ltd, AVA®

Address: 9, Daryaganj, Delhi, 110002, India

275 New North Road Islington Suite 1314 London,
N1 7AA, United Kingdom

ISBN (PBK): 978-93-49887-87-9
ISBN (E-BOOK): 978-93-49887-52-7

Scan the QR code to explore our entire catalogue

www.orangeava.com

Get a Free eBook

We hope you're enjoying your recent book purchase! Your feedback is incredibly valuable to us and helps other readers discover books that truly make a difference.

If you found this book useful or enjoyable, we'd greatly appreciate it if you could leave a short review with a 5-star rating on Amazon. Your review supports our work and allows us to reach more learners worldwide.

As a thank-you, we're happy to offer you a **free digital copy of this book** plus a **30% discount code** for your next purchase on our official websites:

www.orangeava.com

www.orangeava.in (For the Indian Subcontinent).

☑ How it works:

Leave your review on Amazon, take a screenshot of the confirmation or use the following link to submit the claim and email it to **info@orangeava.com.** Once received the required detail, we will send your rewards within 24 hours, **along with one month free subcription to the book on AVA SkillShelf!**

Claim Form
https://rebrand.ly/4d2477

Thank you for your support–it truly means a lot to us.

Downloading the code bundles and colored images

Please follow the links or scan the QR codes to download the
Code Bundles and Images of the book:

https://github.com/ava-orange-education/Building-Data-Pipelines-using-Apache-Beam

The code bundles and images of the book are also hosted on
https://rebrand.ly/cec00d

In case there's an update to the code, it will be updated on the existing GitHub repository.

Errata

We take immense pride in our work at **Orange Education Pvt Ltd,** and follow the best practices to ensure the accuracy of our content to provide an indulging reading experience to our subscribers. Our readers are our mirrors, and we use their inputs to reflect and improve upon human errors, if any, that may have occurred during the publishing processes involved. To let us maintain the quality and help us reach out to any readers who might be having difficulties due to any unforeseen errors, please write to us at:

errata@orangeava.com

Your support, suggestions, and feedback are highly appreciated.

Dedicated To

My Beloved Parents:

Fahim Meyen and Neumath Rhyhan Meyen.

And

My Sister, Fazla and Her Family.

About the Author

Nuzhi Meyen is a fintech entrepreneur, data scientist, and AI practitioner with a strong foundation in analytics, computer science, and quantitative finance. He is the CEO, Managing Director, and Co-Founder of Helios P2P, where he has led the design and implementation of data-driven financial systems that apply advanced analytics, machine learning, and modern data engineering to real-world challenges in lending, credit risk, and alternative finance.

He holds a Master's degree from the University of Moratuwa and a Bachelor's degree from the University of Colombo, and is a CIMA passed finalist. His professional work spans large-scale data platforms, predictive modeling, and AI-powered decision systems, with hands-on experience across fintech, consumer lending, risk analytics, and data-intensive products. Nuzhi has been closely involved in building production-grade analytics solutions that operate under real operational, regulatory, and scalability constraints, bridging theoretical models with practical implementation.

Beyond fintech, Nuzhi's expertise extends into data engineering and analytics architecture. He has worked extensively with distributed data processing frameworks, cloud-native platforms, and modern data infrastructure. His work emphasizes correctness, scalability, and long-term maintainability– principles that shape his approach to building robust data pipelines and analytics systems.

Nuzhi is also an active contributor to the data and AI community. He writes regularly on data engineering, applied machine learning, analytics architecture, and emerging financial technologies, and has participated at industry forums as well as technical sessions, sharing insights from real-world implementations. Outside his professional work, Nuzhi practices Brazilian Jiu-Jitsu, and enjoys reading non-fiction on technology, finance, history, and behavioral science. He also enjoys traveling and exploring new cultures.

About the Technical Reviewer

Akshay Krishna operates at the intersection of data-driven decision systems, AI-enabled capabilities, and business strategy, with a focus on translating complex operational problems into measurable commercial outcomes. His work centers on building analytical, predictive, and optimization frameworks that directly influence conversion, customer experience, and long-term value creation in digital platforms.

With deep expertise in supply chain strategy and optimization, Akshay has led initiatives across fulfillment optimization, transportation planning, and service-level design, applying machine learning, simulation, and experimentation to balance speed, cost, and reliability. In recent roles, he has been closely involved in designing and operationalizing Estimated Delivery Date (EDD) prediction systems, embedding reliability, delay risk, and customer trust directly into product and fulfillment decision flows.

Across analytics, applied AI, and product strategy roles, Akshay consistently focuses on ensuring that advanced models and AI systems are economically grounded—so that recommendations, promises, and operational actions are aligned with real business outcomes rather than siloed metrics.

Acknowledgments

There are several people whose support made the writing of this book possible, and I am deeply grateful to each of them.

First and foremost, I would like to thank my parents for their constant encouragement, belief, and patience throughout this journey. Their unwavering support gave me the confidence and space needed to see this book through. I am equally thankful to my grandmother for her quiet strength and blessings, which have always been a source of grounding and motivation.

My sincere thanks goes to my sister and her family, including my brother-in-law, Milad for their love and understanding, and especially to my nephew, Aqil and my nieces Hannah and Sofia. Their presence and energy brought welcome moments of balance during long writing stretches. I am also grateful to my extended family for their continued support and goodwill.

I would like to express my appreciation to the technical reviewer, Akshay Krishna, for his thoughtful feedback, technical rigor, and careful scrutiny, which helped improve both the clarity and correctness of this book.

My gratitude also extends to my close friends—Ravi, Shanaka, Lasith, Deeptha and Samadi—for their encouragement, conversations, and quiet support along the way. There are many others who contributed in ways both visible and unseen; naming everyone would take far more space than available here, but your support is sincerely acknowledged and appreciated.

Preface

This book covers many different aspects of building modern data pipelines, and explains the importance of scalable, distributed data processing in today's data-driven industries. It introduces readers to Apache Beam as a unified programming model for handling both batch and streaming data, and highlights why portability, correctness, and scalability are critical in real-world data platforms. The book emphasizes how data pipelines form the backbone of analytics, AI, and decision-making systems across industries.

The book builds a strong foundation in Apache Beam concepts, while keeping a practical, industry-oriented approach. It explains how data is ingested, transformed, processed, and delivered at scale using Beam pipelines that can run on multiple execution engines such as Google Cloud Dataflow, Apache Flink, and Apache Spark. Readers are guided through why a single, portable pipeline model is valuable in environments where platforms, workloads, and requirements continuously evolve.

A key focus of this book is helping readers understand both batch and streaming paradigms using one consistent mental model. It explains how Apache Beam handles event time, windows, triggers, and state, enabling developers to build reliable pipelines for real-time and historical data alike. The book also reinforces the importance of Python and Java as primary development languages for Beam, refreshing core concepts, while applying them directly to data engineering use cases.

This book is divided into nine chapters, organized across designing, developing, and deploying Apache Beam pipelines. The initial chapters introduce Apache Beam fundamentals, pipeline construction, unified batch and streaming processing. Subsequent chapters dive deeper into stateful and stateless processing, event-time semantics, windowing strategies, and triggers, helping readers reason correctly about time and data consistency.

The later chapters focus on building efficient batch and streaming pipelines, using transformations and coders, and applying advanced optimization techniques for large-scale data processing. Readers learn how to improve performance, reuse code, and handle complex scenarios using side inputs, side outputs, and splittable DoFns.

These chapters also address deployment across different runners, monitoring and debugging pipelines, tuning performance, and managing costs in production environments, while the final or last chapter focuses on real word use cases of Apache Beam.

So, by the end of this book, readers will have a clear, practical understanding of how to design, build, deploy, and operate scalable data pipelines using Apache Beam, equipping them with the skills directly applicable to real-world data engineering roles.

DID YOU KNOW

Did you know that Orange Education Pvt Ltd offers eBook versions of every book published, with PDF and ePub files available? You can upgrade to the eBook version at **www.orangeava.com** and as a print book customer, you are entitled to a discount on the eBook copy. Get in touch with us at: **info@orangeava.com** for more details.

At **www.orangeava.com**, you can also read a collection of free technical articles, sign up for a range of free newsletters, and receive exclusive discounts and offers on Print Books and eBooks.

PIRACY

If you come across any illegal copies of our works in any form on the internet, we would be grateful if you would provide us with the location address or website name. Please contact us at **info@orangeava.com** with a link to the material.

ARE YOU INTERESTED IN AUTHORING WITH US?

If there is a topic that you have expertise in, and you are interested in either writing or contributing to a book, please write to us at **business@orangeava.com**. We are on a journey to help developers and tech professionals to gain insights on the present technological advancements and innovations happening across the globe and build a community that believes Knowledge is best acquired by sharing and learning with others. Please reach out to us to learn what our audience demands and how you can be part of this educational reform. We also welcome ideas from tech experts and help them build learning and development content for their domains.

REVIEWS

Please leave a review. Once you have read and used this book, why not leave a review on the site that you purchased it from? Potential readers can then see and use your unbiased opinion to make purchase decisions. We at Orange Education would love to know what you think about our products, and our authors can learn from your feedback. Thank you!

For more information about Orange Education, please visit **www.orangeava.com**.

Table of Contents

CHAPTER 1
Introduction to Apache Beam and Data Processing

Introduction

In today's data-driven world, organizations are no longer choosing between batch or streaming data—they need both, often within the same solution. From processing historical transaction logs to reacting to live events in real time, modern data platforms constantly demand flexibility, scalability, and consistency. Hence, Apache Beam is a powerful response to this need, as it offers a unified programming model that simplifies how data pipelines are designed, executed, and evolved.

Originally developed at Google and later contributed to the Apache Software Foundation, Apache Beam represents a significant shift in how data processing frameworks are approached. Rather than forcing developers to tightly couple their logic to a specific execution engine, Beam introduces a clean abstraction layer that separates *what* the pipeline does from *how* and *where* it runs. Hence, this abstraction allows the same pipeline to execute seamlessly on multiple distributed processing backends, which are referred to as **runners**, such as `Apache Spark`, `Apache Flink`, and `Google Cloud Dataflow`.

Before Apache Beam, developers had to make early, and often irreversible, architectural decisions. Batch processing frameworks like Hadoop MapReduce were well-suited for large, static datasets, but they struggled with low-latency requirements. On the other hand, stream-processing systems like Apache Storm excelled at real-time data, but they required entirely different APIs and mental models. Hence, switching between these paradigms typically meant rewriting large portions of code, retraining teams, and rethinking operational strategies.

Apache Beam addresses these challenges by offering a **single, unified API,** which is capable of handling both bounded (batch) and unbounded (streaming) data. To better illustrate this evolution, the following table contrasts traditional approaches with the Apache Beam model.

Aspect	Traditional Batch Frameworks (for example, Hadoop)	Traditional Stream Frameworks (for example, Storm)	Apache Beam
Processing Model	Batch only	Streaming only	Unified batch and streaming
API Consistency	Batch-specific APIs	Stream-specific APIs	Single, consistent API
Portability	Tightly coupled to engine	Tightly coupled to engine	Portable across multiple runners
Switching Workloads	Requires major rewrites	Requires major rewrites	Requires no rewrites
Developer Focus	Infrastructure-heavy	Runtime-heavy	Business logic–focused

Table 1.1: *Comparing Traditional Approaches with Apache Beam*

Apache's unified API is the core reason that Apache Beam has become a foundational technology in modern data architectures. Hence, by abstracting time, windows, triggers, and execution semantics, Beam allows developers to write pipelines once. Developers can also adapt them to new platforms, scaling requirements, or deployment environments without changing the core logic.

What You Will Learn in This Chapter

By the end of this chapter, you will be able to:

- Understand the fundamental concepts behind Apache Beam's unified programming model.
- Learn how Beam pipelines differ from traditional batch and streaming approaches.
- Set up a basic development environment for Apache Beam.
- Build and run a simple **Apache Beam pipeline**, and gain hands-on exposure from the very beginning.

Reasons to Choose Apache Beam

After examining the limitations of earlier technologies and the operational friction they introduced, Apache Beam stands out as a future-proof choice. It reduces vendor lock-in, supports evolving workloads, and aligns naturally with modern cloud and hybrid architectures. Most importantly, it allows developers and data engineers to focus on *solving business problems*, rather than rewriting pipelines every time infrastructure or processing requirements change.

For these reasons, this book focuses on Apache Beam as a foundational skill for anyone who wishes to build scalable, flexible, and long-lasting data processing systems.

As you progress through the chapters, you will move through simple examples to real-world pipeline patterns. This will help you become more confident about your solutions and their ability to remain relevant, portable, and robust in a dynamic data ecosystem.

Structure

- Key Features of Apache Beam
- Understanding Beam Pipelines
- Unified Batch and Streaming Processing
- `PCollection` and `PTransform : Building Blocks of Beam`
- Building Your First Apache Beam Pipeline

Key Features of Apache Beam

Apache Beam is an open-source, unified programming model designed to simplify the development of large-scale data processing pipelines. It enables teams to build data workflows that work seamlessly across both batch and real-time streaming use cases, while it remains independent of the underlying execution engine. Therefore, by abstracting complex distributed-processing concepts behind a clean, consistent API, Apache Beam allows developers to focus on business logic rather than infrastructure details.

Conceptually, Beam guides users from defining core data processing concepts, to constructing pipelines using transforms, and finally to executing those pipelines on scalable distributed runners. Its cross-language support, portability across multiple runners, and rich ecosystem of connectors make it a powerful foundation for building scalable, future-proof data pipelines that can evolve with changing platforms and workloads. Here are the key features of Apache Beam:

- **Unified Batch and Stream Processing:** With a single API, developers can build pipelines that handle both batch and streaming data consistently.
- **Portability across Runners:** Beam allows you to write pipelines that can run on different execution engines or "runners", without changing the core business logic of the pipeline.
- **Language Support:** Apache Beam offers SDKs for multiple programming languages, including **Python**, **Java**, and **Go**, while providing flexibility for different developer needs.
- **Extensibility and Flexibility:** Through its extensive set of connectors, Beam allows easy integration with numerous data sources and sinks like Google BigQuery, Amazon S3, and Apache Kafka.

Thus, by focusing on simplicity, flexibility, and scalability, Apache Beam empowers developers to build robust data pipelines that can be deployed and run in various environments with minimal adjustments.

For **beginners**, the most important features are the **unified batch and stream processing** and **language support**, which make it easy to get started with a single, intuitive API, while **production users** benefit most from **runner portability** and **extensibility**, which enable scalable, resilient pipelines that can integrate seamlessly with enterprise-grade data platforms.

Apache Beam's Role in the Data Processing Landscape

To understand the significance of Apache Beam, it is important to recognize the current landscape of data processing. Today, data is either bounded or unbounded. Bounded data represents a finite data set, such as a collection of records in a database or log files over a certain period. Unbounded data, on the other hand, refers to an infinite stream of continuously generated data, such as real-time sensor feeds, transaction logs, or social media updates.

In the past, separate frameworks were used for batch and stream processing, each with its own strengths and limitations. For instance, batch processing tools were optimized for working on historical data, where the full data set is available from the start. On the other hand, stream processing tools are designed for real-time data where results need to be computed as new data arrives, and thus requires more immediate feedback.

Apache Beam offers the best of both worlds. Its key value proposition lies in its ability to handle these different data types using a single, coherent programming model. Hence, whether you are processing a batch of logs from the previous day, or are working with a real-time stream of customer interactions, Beam allows you to use the same pipeline definition for both scenarios. This unified approach dramatically simplifies development efforts, and also reduces the cognitive overhead associated with maintaining multiple codebases for different processing needs. The following table summarizes how Apache Beam compares with other batch and stream processing frameworks across different dimensions such as data type to use cases, and so on.

Dimension	Batch Processing Frameworks	Stream Processing Frameworks	Apache Beam (Unified Model)
Data Type	Bounded (Finite Datasets)	Unbounded (Continuous Streams)	Bounded and unbounded
Typical Use Cases	historical analysis, ETL, and reporting	Real-time monitoring, alerts, and event processing	Historical and real-time analytics in a single pipeline

API Model	Batch-specific APIs	Stream-specific APIs	Single, unified API
Pipeline Reuse	Separate codebases required	Separate codebases required	Same pipeline definition reused
Development Complexity	Lower for batch-only needs	Higher due to time/ event semantics	Simplified through unified abstractions
Operational Overhead	Multiple systems to manage	Multiple systems to manage	Reduced via consolidation
Long-Term Flexibility	Limited when requirements evolve	Limited when requirements evolve	Highly adaptable across workloads and runners

Table 1.2: *Apache Bean vs Other Batch and Stream Processing Frameworks Evaluated across Different Dimensions*

For instance, a retail company might use Apache Beam to analyze historical sales data (batch) while simultaneously processing real-time data from its online store to monitor customer activity (streaming). Beyond technical elegance, this unified approach directly enables business value, as teams can detect purchasing trends faster, personalize customer experiences in near real time, optimize inventory levels, and respond immediately to anomalies, such as cart abandonment or fraud. Therefore, by eliminating the need for separate batch and streaming systems, Beam reduces development effort, shortens the time-to-insight, and improves operational agility. The features mentioned allow business stakeholders to act on insights proactively, rather than after the fact.

Industry evidence supports this value-driven positioning. Google Cloud customer case studies using Apache Beam-based pipelines (via Cloud Dataflow) report **30 to 50% reductions in pipeline maintenance effort**, **significant decreases in data latency**, and **faster time-to-market for analytics use cases**, particularly in retail, media, and financial services. A Forrester Total Economic Impact™ study on real-time data platforms highlights that organizations adopting unified batch-and-stream processing architectures achieve **up to 5 to 10x faster insight generation,** as well as measurable improvements in revenue uplift and cost efficiency through real-time decision-making. These outcomes demonstrate how Apache Beam is not just a technical abstraction, but a practical enabler for unlocking tangible business value from data at scale.

Use Cases for Apache Beam

The power and flexibility of Apache Beam make it suitable for a wide range of use cases across different industries. Therefore, the following examples serve as a high-level preview and will be revisited in later chapters as **hands-on case studies**, where each scenario will be explored in detail with concrete Apache Beam pipeline designs, execution strategies, and real-world considerations.

- **Real-Time Data Analytics:** Beam is often used for real-time analytics applications. For instance, financial services firms can leverage Beam to track stock market fluctuations in real time, responding to changes in seconds. Hence, by running the pipeline on a streaming runner, Beam allows analysts to process millions of market events as they happen, and it makes rapid decision-making possible.
- **Data ETL (Extract, Transform, Load):** Data pipelines often need to extract information from various sources, apply complex transformations, and load it into a destination system. Beam simplifies the ETL process by providing built-in transforms for common tasks like filtering, mapping, and grouping data, while also being compatible with various storage systems such as **Google Cloud Storage**, **Amazon S3**, **BigQuery**, and **Apache HBase**.

  For example, an e-commerce platform might need to extract customer purchase data, transform it into a structured format, and load it into a warehouse for future analysis. Beam allows them to implement this as a single pipeline, which is capable of scaling to accommodate huge volumes of data.
- **IoT Data Processing:** In industries like manufacturing and healthcare, the rise of IoT (Internet of Things) has led to the need for tools that can handle vast amounts of streaming data from devices and sensors. Apache Beam's unified approach is ideal for this, allowing companies to monitor and analyze streams of data from IoT devices while incorporating batch processing of historical data for more in-depth analysis.

  For example, in a smart factory, Beam can collect data from machinery sensors in real time, while detecting anomalies like overheating or failure based on predefined thresholds. Simultaneously, historical sensor data could be processed to identify patterns and improve long-term machine maintenance strategies.
- **Hybrid Data Pipelines:** Many organizations deal with both historical data (batch) and real-time data (streaming). Beam excels in environments where hybrid processing is necessary. For instance, social media platforms can process live user data streams to deliver real-time recommendations while running batch jobs to update user models based on historical interactions.

Hence, Beam's hybrid capabilities make it ideal for applications where consistency between batch and real-time results is critical. By eliminating the need to maintain separate codebases for batch and stream processing, Beam provides a consistent, maintainable solution for data engineers and developers alike.

The Portable Nature of Apache Beam

One of the most powerful aspects of Apache Beam is its **portability**, which means that the same pipeline code can run on multiple execution engines (runners) with minimal modifications. Runners are the distributed processing engines responsible for executing a pipeline on clusters of machines. Beam supports a wide range of runners, including:

- **`Google Cloud Dataflow`**: This is a fully managed service optimized for running Beam pipelines in the cloud.
- **`Apache Flink`**: It is a stream-first distributed processing engine, which is commonly used for real-time event processing.
- **`Apache Spark`**: It is another popular distributed processing engine, and is often used for large-scale batch and stream processing.
- **`DirectRunner`**: This is a local runner used for development and testing purposes.

This portability allows teams to build and test pipelines locally using the **`DirectRunner`** and later deploy them on a cloud platform like **`Google Cloud Dataflow`** for full-scale production processing. Apache Beam's flexibility ensures that companies can optimize their resource usage by choosing the best runner for their specific use case, whether for cost, performance, or infrastructure reasons. While Apache Beam provides strong portability, it is also important to note that not all runners support every Beam feature in exactly the same way, and portability should be viewed as *logical portability* rather than a strict lift-and-shift guarantee; the specific capabilities, limitations, and optimization considerations of each runner will be explored in detail in later chapters.

For example, a company might use **`Apache Flink`** for real-time streaming workloads, but they might opt for **`Google Cloud Dataflow`** for large-scale batch processing, all while maintaining a single codebase.

Understanding Beam Pipelines

In Apache Beam, a **pipeline** is the foundational construct used to define the series of operations that process data from input to output. Whether you are handling batch data (for example, historical records) or streaming data (for example, real-time sensor readings), all operations in Apache Beam revolve around pipelines. A pipeline encapsulates the entire end-to-end flow, from data ingestion to transformation and storage.

This section introduces Beam pipelines and explains how they function, while covering their key components such as **`PCollection`** and **`PTransform`**, as well as providing practical examples.

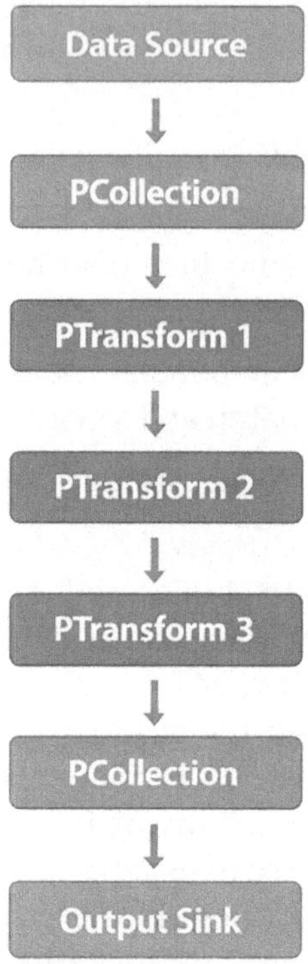

Figure 1.1: *How a Typical Beam Pipeline Looks Like*

Defining a Beam Pipeline

At its core, a Beam pipeline represents a directed acyclic graph (DAG) of data transformations. These transformations, defined using Apache Beam's SDK, are applied to collections of data, which allows users to process both bounded and unbounded datasets in the same pipeline. In a pipeline, the user defines what happens at each stage of the process: data is ingested, transformed, and is ultimately written to an output.

Pipelines are designed to be portable across different execution environments, which implies that you can build a pipeline locally, and run it on distributed clusters with minimal changes to the codebase.

Pipeline Structure

Every Apache Beam pipeline consists of the following stages:

1. **Data Ingestion:** The pipeline starts by reading data from a source. This can be a file, a database, or a real-time data stream.

2. **Transformation:** The data is then transformed using a series of operations (such as filtering, mapping, or aggregation). Each transformation is applied to a **`PCollection`**, which represents the distributed data set in Beam.

3. **Output:** Finally, the pipeline writes the transformed data to an output sink, such as a file or database, or returns it for further analysis.

Simple Pipeline Example

To illustrate how a basic pipeline works, let us walk through an example. The following pipeline reads data from a text file, splits each line into words, and counts the occurrences of each word. The result is then written back to a text file.

To run this example locally, you need to set up a basic Python environment and install Apache Beam. Here are the steps to do so:

1. **Prerequisites**

    a. Python 3.8 or later

    b. pip (Python Package Manager)

    c. A virtual environment is recommended.

    Create and activate a virtual environment through the following command:

    ```
    python -m venv beam_env
    source beam_env/bin/activate        # On Linux / macOS
    beam_env\Scripts\activate           # On Windows
    ```

2. **Install Apache Beam**

    Install Apache Beam with the **`DirectRunner`** (default local runner):

    ```
    pip install apache-beam
    ```

3. **Prepare the Input File**

    Create a file called **`input.txt`** in the same directory as your script through:

    ```
    hello beam
    hello apache beam
    apache beam is powerful
    ```

4. **Save the Pipeline Code**

    Save your pipeline as **`wordcount.py`** through:

    ```
    import apache_beam as beam

    # Define a function to split lines into words
    def split_lines(line):
    ```

```
    return line.split()

# Initialize the pipeline
pipeline = beam.Pipeline()

# Define the pipeline steps
word_counts = (pipeline
               | 'ReadFromText' >> beam.io.ReadFromText('input.
txt')
               | 'SplitIntoWords' >> beam.FlatMap(split_lines)
               | 'PairWithOne' >> beam.Map(lambda word: (word,
1))
               | 'CountPerWord' >> beam.CombinePerKey(sum)
               | 'WriteToText' >> beam.io.WriteToText('output.
txt'))

# Run the pipeline
pipeline.run()
```

5. **Run the Pipeline**

   Execute this from the command line:

   `python wordcount.py`

   Apache Beam will use the **`DirectRunner`**, which will run everything locally on your machine.

6. **Check the Output**

   Beam will generate files such as:

   `output.txt-00000-of-00001`

   Inside, you will see results like:

   a. Each line is split into words using the **`FlatMap`** transform. **`FlatMap`** takes each element of a **`PCollection`** and produces zero or more elements. In this case, each line produces multiple words.

   b. The words are paired with the number 1 using the **`Map`** transform.

   c. The **`CombinePerKey`** transform then sums up all the values for each word (that is, counts the number of times each word appears).

   d. Finally, the result is written to an output text file using **`WriteToText`**.

This simple example illustrates the core concepts of Beam pipelines. Let us now break down the key components in more detail.

In Apache Beam, a **pipeline** is the central construct used to define an end-to-end data processing workflow–from reading data, to transforming it, and writing outputs.

You use the pipeline to describe *what* should happen, while the selected **runner** determines *how and where* it executes (locally, or on a distributed system).

Core Abstractions: `Pipeline`, `PCollection`, and `PTransform`

Every Beam pipeline is built using three key abstractions:

- **`Pipeline`:** A **`pipeline`** is the container for your full data processing job. It acts as the entry point where you define all steps in your workflow.

```
import apache_beam as beam

pipeline = beam.Pipeline()
```

Beam pipelines are portable, which means that the same logical pipeline can be executed in different environments by changing configuration and runner settings (for example, **`DirectRunner`** locally, **`DataflowRunner`** on Google Cloud Dataflow).

- **`PCollection`:** A **`PCollection`** represents a **distributed dataset** in Beam. All data in Beam flows through PCollections, whether the data is:
    - **Bounded**: This refers to finite data (for example, files, database extracts), which is typically found in batch pipelines.
    - **Unbounded**: This refers to infinite or continuously arriving data (for example, Kafka topics, sensor streams), which is typically found in streaming pipelines.

A **`PCollection`** is conceptually similar to a list/array, but is distributed and processed in parallel via the following command:

```
p = beam.Pipeline()
data = p | 'Create' >> beam.Create([1, 2, 3, 4, 5])
```

- **`PTransform`:** A **`PTransform`** is an operation applied to a **`PCollection`**. It can be simple (Map/Filter) or more complex (grouping/aggregation).

Two commonly used **`PTransform`** categories are:

- **Element-Wise Transforms**: These are applied independently to each element (**`Map`**, **`FlatMap`**, and **`Filter`**).
- **Key-Based Transforms**: These operate on key-value pairs (**`GroupByKey`**, **`CombinePerKey`**).

Example:

```
numbers = p | 'Create numbers' >> beam.Create([1, 2, 3, 4, 5])
squares = numbers | 'Square numbers' >> beam.Map(lambda x: x * x)
```

Connecting Beam Concepts to Familiar Tools:

The following parallels help internalize Beam's model:

- **`Pipeline`:** Airflow DAG / Spark job / SQL query plan (defines intent; execution is handled by an engine)
- **`PCollection`**: Spark DataFrame/RDD / SQL table result / Kafka stream (distributed dataset, bounded or unbounded)
- **`PTransform`**: Spark transformations / SQL operations (**`SELECT`**, **`GROUP BY`**) / stream operators

Pipeline Execution and Runners: Once the pipeline is defined, it is executed by a **runner**, which translates the logical DAG of **`PTransforms`** into an execution plan, and schedules work on a target environment.

Common runners include:

- **`DirectRunner`**: Local execution for development/testing
- **`Google Cloud Dataflow`**: Fully managed runner for production-grade pipelines
- **`Apache Flink`**: Optimized for streaming and event-time processing
- **`Apache Spark`**: Supports both batch and streaming at scale

To execute, use the following command:

```
pipeline.run()
```

Note: *Beam pipelines are portable, but* ***not all runners support every Beam feature equally****. Thus, portability is best understood as logical portability, and runner capability differences are covered later in the book.*

Building Blocks of a Beam Pipeline

A practical pipeline typically follows three stages: **ingestion** → **transformation** → **output**.

1. **Data Ingestion**

   Read from files through:

   ```
   p = beam.Pipeline()
   lines = p | 'ReadInputFile' >> beam.io.ReadFromText('input.txt')
   ```

   Read from cloud storage through:

   ```
   lines = p | 'ReadFromCloud' >> beam.io.ReadFromText
   ('gs://bucket-name/input.txt')
   ```

2. **Data Transformation**

   Apply transforms to produce meaningful outputs through:

```
result = (lines
          | 'SplitIntoWords' >> beam.FlatMap(lambda line: line.
            split())
          | 'PairWithOne' >> beam.Map(lambda word: (word, 1))
          | 'CountPerWord' >> beam.CombinePerKey(sum))
```

3. **Data Output**

   Write to a text sink via the following command:

```
result | 'WriteOutput' >> beam.io.WriteToText('output.txt')
Write to a database/warehouse (example: BigQuery):
result | 'WriteToBigQuery' >> beam.io.WriteToBigQuery('project:-
dataset.table')
```

Unified Batch and Streaming Processing

Apache Beam's most powerful feature is its **unified model** for both batch and stream processing. Traditionally, developers needed to use separate frameworks or APIs for handling these types of data. **Batch processing** is optimized for finite datasets, where the full data set is known and available at the beginning of processing. **Streaming processing**, on the other hand, deals with unbounded data streams, processing data in real-time as it arrives. Apache Beam eliminates the need for separate tools, and offers a single, consistent API to handle both scenarios, whether you are processing historical data or real-time data streams. Apache Beam's most powerful feature is its unified model for both batch and stream processing. Traditionally, developers needed to use separate frameworks or APIs for handling these two types of data. Batch processing is optimized for finite datasets, where the full data set is known and available at the start of processing. Streaming processing, on the other hand, deals with unbounded data streams, and processes data in real time as data arrives. Apache Beam eliminates the need for separate tools by offering a single, consistent API to handle both scenarios. Most importantly, the **same business logic is written once and reused without duplication**, which means that developers do not need to maintain separate codebases or introduce additional boilerplate when switching between batch and streaming execution. The pipeline definition remains unchanged; only the execution mode and data source differ, which allows teams to move seamlessly between historical and real-time processing while preserving correctness, maintainability, and development efficiency.

Hence, in this section, we will explore Apache Beam's unified model in detail, while highlighting the key differences between batch and streaming, and demonstrating how Apache Beam handles both through the same API.

Batch Processing: Finite Datasets

Batch processing is the traditional approach to data processing, and is often used for tasks like generating reports, analyzing historical data, or running large-scale ETL jobs. In batch processing, the input data is **bounded**. This means that it is a finite, predefined dataset. The system waits for all data to be available before processing begins, and the goal is to produce a complete result from the entire dataset.

Examples of Batch Processing

- **Daily Sales Reports**: A retailer might process sales data at the end of each day to generate a report summarizing total sales, broken down by store and product.
- **Data Warehousing**: Organizations regularly ingest and process batches of data from transactional databases into their data warehouses to run analytics queries.
- **ETL Pipelines:** Extract, Transform and Load (ETL) processes often run in batch mode to move and transform large datasets from one system to another.

Apache Beam supports batch processing by treating the data as a bounded **`PCollection`** (a fixed-size collection of elements). Once all the data is available, Beam processes it in stages defined by a series of transforms.

Example of a Batch Processing Pipeline

Let us build a simple batch pipeline that processes a set of log files and generates a report of error counts.

```
import apache_beam as beam

# Pipeline to count error messages from log files
def is_error_log(line):
    return ‹ERROR› in line

p = beam.Pipeline()

# Read from a batch data source (for example, a set of log files)
lines = p | 'ReadLogs' >> beam.io.ReadFromText('logs/*.txt')

# Filter lines to keep only error messages
error_logs = lines | 'FilterErrors' >> beam.Filter(is_error_log)

# Count the number of error messages
error_count = error_logs | 'CountErrors' >> beam.combiners.Count.
Globally()
```

```
# Write the count to an output file
error_count | 'WriteOutput' >> beam.io.WriteToText('error_counts.
txt')

p.run()
```

In this pipeline:

- **Bounded Data:** We are reading from a static set of log files (a bounded **`PCollection`**).
- **Transformations:** We filter for lines containing the word **`"ERROR"`**, and then count them.
- **Result:** The total number of error logs is written to an output file, once all the input data has been processed.

Batch processing is a well-suited solution for static, historical datasets that require complete and final results. However, not all data can be treated as bounded. This is where streaming processing comes in.

Stream Processing: Unbounded Data

Stream processing is essential for **handling unbounded datasets** that grow continuously over time. Unbounded data streams, such as website clickstream data, IoT sensor readings, or social media feeds, are infinite by nature. The system does not wait for the data to be "complete" because new data is always arriving.

Unlike batch processing, stream processing requires continuous ingestion, transformation, and analysis of data in real-time. Apache Beam handles stream processing through **unbounded `PCollections`**, which represent datasets that may never be fully complete.

Examples of Stream Processing

- **Real-Time Fraud Detection:** Banks and financial institutions often use streaming data to detect fraudulent transactions in real-time, while analyzing transaction data as it flows in.
- **Real-Time Analytics:** Online platforms like e-commerce websites and social media apps use stream processing to generate real-time analytics for user interactions.
- **IoT Data Processing:** IoT devices constantly generate data (for example, temperature readings, location updates). Stream processing allows this data to be processed as it arrives.

Example of a Stream Processing Pipeline

Let us build a simple streaming pipeline that monitors incoming temperature sensor data and alerts when the temperature crosses a threshold.

```
import apache_beam as beam

# Function to check for high temperatures
def check_high_temperature(reading):
    timestamp, temperature = reading.split(',')
    if float(temperature) > 75.0:
        return True
    return False

p = beam.Pipeline()

# Simulate a streaming data source (for example, from IoT
sensors)
temperature_data = p | 'ReadTemperatureStream' >> beam.io.
ReadFromPubSub(topic='projects/my-project/topics/temperature')

# Filter readings where the temperature exceeds 75.0 degrees
high_temp_readings = temperature_data | 'FilterHighTemp' >> beam.
Filter(check_high_temperature)

# Write the high temperature readings to an alert system
high_temp_readings | 'WriteToAlerts' >> beam.io.WriteToTex-
t('high_temp_alerts.txt')

p.run()
```

In this example:

- **Unbounded Data:** We are reading from a continuous stream of temperature sensor readings (an unbounded **PCollection**).
- **Real-Time Filtering**: Each incoming reading is checked, and if the temperature exceeds 75 degrees, it triggers an alert.
- **Continuous Output:** The pipeline continuously writes alerts to an output sink as high temperatures are detected, without waiting for the entire stream to be processed (since it is unbounded).

Thus, stream processing pipelines like this one are used in situations where time is critical and real-time insights are necessary.

Unified API for Batch and Streaming Processing

The true power of Apache Beam lies in its **unified API**, which allows you to use the same pipeline code for both batch and streaming scenarios. The way Beam abstracts the data as a **PCollection**–whether it is bounded or unbounded–enables the same logic to be applied to both static and dynamic datasets.

- **Bounded PCollection (Batch):** Represents finite datasets where processing occurs after all the data is available
- **Unbounded PCollection (Stream):** Represents infinite datasets where processing happens in real-time as data arrives

This unified API means you can design a pipeline once, and depending on your data source, it can either be a batch job or a streaming job without requiring you to make significant changes to your code.

Here is a breakdown of how Beam achieves this unification:

- **Same Code, Different Sources:** When you write a Beam pipeline, you do not need to worry about whether the data is bounded or unbounded. The runner will adapt the execution based on the source of the data. For example, the same transformation logic can be applied to both a batch of log files (bounded) and a real-time stream of log entries (unbounded).
- **Windowing and Triggers**: In stream processing, since data is unbounded, you often want to group it into windows of time (for example, every 5 minutes, hourly, daily) to apply transformations over manageable segments of data. Windowing becomes mandatory when working with **unbounded PCollections**, because the data stream is infinite and cannot be processed as a complete dataset; windows provide finite, logical boundaries that make it possible to apply aggregations, grouping, and other stateful computations over streaming data. Apache Beam offers rich support for windowing, which allows you to group unbounded data into logical units for processing.
  - **Fixed Windows:** Divide data into fixed-duration windows (for example, 1-minute windows).
  - **Sliding Windows:** Create overlapping windows that slide over time (for example, every 30 seconds, create a 1-minute window).
  - **Session Windows:** Group events into sessions based on periods of activity separated by gaps of inactivity.

Example of a Windowed Streaming Pipeline

```
import apache_beam as beam
from apache_beam.transforms.window import FixedWindows

# Pipeline that processes streaming sensor data with fixed
windowing
p = beam.Pipeline()
```

```
# Ingest data from a streaming source
sensor_data = p | 'ReadSensorData' >> beam.io.ReadFromPub
Sub(topic='projects/my-project/topics/sensor')

# Apply fixed windowing (for example, 5-minute windows)
windowed_data = sensor_data | 'ApplyWindow' >> beam.WindowInto
(FixedWindows(300))

# Perform some transformation (for example, calculate average
reading per window)
avg_readings = windowed_data | 'Average' >> beam.Combine
Globally(beam.combiners.MeanCombineFn()).without_defaults()

# Write the results to an output sink
avg_readings | 'WriteToStorage' >> beam.io.WriteToText('average_
readings.txt')

p.run()
```

- **Triggers:** In streaming pipelines, you may want to control when the results of windowed computations are emitted. This is done using **triggers**. Triggers define when the results should be output, and they are particularly useful when dealing with unbounded data.

  Common trigger types include:

  - **Event Time triggers:** They emit results based on event timestamps.
  - **Processing Time triggers:** They emit results based on system clock time.
  - **Count-Based triggers:** They emit results after a certain number of elements.

Triggers allow you to balance between latency (how quickly you get results) and completeness (how much data you wait for before processing).

Aspect	Batch Processing	Stream Processing
Data Type	Bounded (finite)	Unbounded (infinite)
Processing Model	Processes entire dataset at once	Processes data as it arrives in real-time
Windowing	Not required	Required to group continuous data
Example Use Cases	ETL jobs, historical reporting	Real-time analytics, IoT data processing

Latency	High (results are produced after data is available)	Low (results are produced continuously)
Common Technologies	Apache Hadoop, Apache Spark (batch mode)	Apache Flink, Apache Kafka Streams

Table 1.3: *Batch vs. Streaming- Key Differences*

Apache Beam abstracts away these differences by treating both batch and streaming data as **`PCollections`**, and applying the same pipeline logic. This allows developers to focus on business transformations, while the runner handles whether the data is bounded or unbounded.

`PCollection` and `PTransform`: Building Blocks of Beam

In Apache Beam, **`PCollection`** and **`PTransform`** are the core building blocks for constructing data pipelines. **`PCollections`** represent data, and **`PTransforms`** define the operations applied to this data. These abstractions allow Beam to handle data processing in a consistent and flexible manner, regardless of whether the data is bounded or unbounded, batch or stream.

Therefore, in this section, we will explore both concepts in detail, explaining how they work, how they interact, and how they are used in pipeline development.

`PCollection`: The Fundamental Data Structure

A **`PCollection`** is the central data abstraction in Apache Beam. It represents a distributed dataset that can either be **bounded** (for batch processing) or **unbounded** (for streaming). In practice, a **`PCollection`** is much like a collection in traditional programming languages, except that it is designed to be distributed across multiple machines and processed in parallel.

Characteristics of `PCollection`:

- **Bounded vs. Unbounded Data**
    - **Bounded `PCollection`**: A bounded **`PCollection`** represents a finite dataset where all the data is available from the start. These are typically used in batch processing jobs, where data is static and known in advance (for example, processing a file stored on disk).
    - **Unbounded `PCollection`**: An unbounded **`PCollection`** represents an infinite stream of data. Unbounded **`PCollections`** are typically used in streaming jobs, where data continuously flows in, and it must be processed as it arrives (for example, real-time logs or sensor data streams).

- **Distributed and Parallel Processing: PCollections** are distributed across a cluster, meaning that each element in a **PCollection** can be processed independently in parallel. This makes Beam highly scalable, as it allows pipelines to handle large volumes of data efficiently.
- **Element Types:** A **PCollection** can contain elements of any type (for example, strings, integers, key-value pairs, or complex data structures). These elements are processed individually by Beam transformations.
- **Immutability: PCollections** are immutable, which means that once data is in a **PCollection**, it cannot be changed. Any transformation applied to a **PCollection** results in a new **PCollection**, while ensuring a functional and parallelizable approach to data processing.

Creating PCollections: PCollections can be created from a variety of sources, including reading from text files, databases, message queues, or even in-memory data. Beam provides built-in I/O transforms to ingest data from various sources, and then turn them into **PCollections**.

Example: Creating a PCollection from a List of Elements

```
import apache_beam as beam

# Create a simple in-memory PCollection
with beam.Pipeline() as p:
    numbers = p | ‹Create numbers› >> beam.Create([1, 2, 3, 4, 5])
```

In this example, the Create transform is used to manually create a **PCollection** from a list of numbers.

Example: Creating a PCollection by Reading from a File

```
with beam.Pipeline() as p:
    lines = p | ‹ReadFile' >> beam.io.ReadFromText('input.txt')
```

In this case, the **ReadFromText** transform reads lines from a text file, and stores them as elements in a **PCollection**.

PTransform: Operations on PCollections

A **PTransform** is the operation that you apply to a **PCollection**. These transforms are the building blocks that allow you to process data in Apache Beam. **PTransforms** take one or more **PCollections** as input, apply a transformation to the data, and produce one or more **PCollections** as output.

Types of PTransforms

- **Element-Wise Transforms:** These transforms operate on each element of the input **PCollection** individually. Examples of element-wise transforms include **Map**, **FlatMap**, and **Filter**. These are explained as follows:

- **Map**: It applies a function to each element in the **PCollection**, and returns a new **PCollection** with the transformed elements.
- **FlatMap**: This is similar to Map, but allows the function to return multiple elements for each input element.
- **Filter**: It removes elements from the **PCollection** that do not meet a specified condition.

Example of Map:

```
with beam.Pipeline() as p:
    numbers = p | ‹Create numbers› >> beam.Create([1, 2, 3, 4,
    5])
    squares = numbers | ‹Square numbers› >> beam.Map(lambda x:
    x * x)
```

In this example, the **Map** transform applies a lambda function to generate a square of each number in the **PCollection**.

Example of FlatMap:

```
with beam.Pipeline() as p:
    lines = p | ‹ReadFile' >> beam.io.ReadFromText('input.
    txt')
    words = lines | ‹SplitWords' >> beam.FlatMap(lambda line:
    line.split())
```

Here, **FlatMap** splits each line of text into words and produces multiple elements for each input element.

- **Key-Based Transforms:** Key-based transforms operate on **key-value pairs** within a **PCollection**. These transforms are used for grouping, joining, and aggregating data. Examples include **GroupByKey**, **CombinePerKey**, and **CoGroupByKey**.
  - **GroupByKey**: It groups elements in a **PCollection** by key.
  - **CombinePerKey**: It applies an aggregation function (such as sum or average) to the values grouped by key.

Example of GroupByKey:

```
with beam.Pipeline() as p:
    pairs = p | 'Create pairs' >> beam.Create([('apple', 1),
    ('banana', 2), ('apple', 3)])
    grouped = pairs | 'Group by key' >> beam.GroupByKey()
```

In this example, **GroupByKey** groups elements by their key (for example, all "**apple**" key-value pairs are grouped together).

- **Aggregating Transforms**: Aggregating transforms combine data across the entire **`PCollection`**, or within key groups. Examples include **`Sum`**, **`Count`**, and **`Combine`**.
  - **`Sum`:** Adds up all elements in the **`PCollection`**
  - **`Count`:** Counts the number of elements in the **`PCollection`**
  - **`Combine`:** Applies a custom function to aggregate the elements

Example of Count:

```
with beam.Pipeline() as p:
    elements = p | ‹Create elements› >> beam.Create([1, 2, 3, 4,
5])
    count = elements | ‹Count elements› >> beam.combiners.Count.
Globally()
```

This pipeline counts the total number of elements in the **`PCollection`**.

- **Composite Transforms:** Composite transforms are a combination of multiple **`PTransforms`** into a single reusable operation. They allow you to encapsulate complex processing logic into a single unit, while improving code readability and reusability.

Example of a Custom Composite Transform:

```
class FilterAndSquare(beam.PTransform):
    def expand(self, pcoll):
        return (pcoll
                | ‹Filter Even Numbers› >> beam.Filter(lambda x:
x % 2 == 0)
                | ‹Square Numbers› >> beam.Map(lambda x: x * x))

with beam.Pipeline() as p:
    numbers = p | ‹Create numbers› >> beam.Create([1, 2, 3, 4,
5])
    result = numbers | ‹Filter and Square› >> FilterAndSquare()
```

In this example, **`FilterAndSquare`** is a composite transform that filters even numbers and squares them.

Applying Transforms to `PCollections`: The core idea behind Beam's data processing model is that you define a series of transforms that are applied to **`PCollections`**, which results in new **`PCollections`** at each step. This allows you to chain multiple operations together to build complex data pipelines.

Let us look at an extended example where we chain multiple transforms together:

Example: Processing a Text File to Count Words

```
import apache_beam as beam

with beam.Pipeline() as p:
    # Step 1: Read input from a text file
    lines = p | ‹ReadFile' >> beam.io.ReadFromText('input.txt')

    # Step 2: Split each line into words
    words = lines | ‹SplitWords' >> beam.FlatMap(lambda line:
line.split())

    # Step 3: Assign each word a count of 1
    word_pairs = words | 'PairWordsWithOne' >> beam.Map(lambda
word: (word, 1))

    # Step 4: Group words and sum their counts
    word_counts = word_pairs | 'CountWords' >> beam.Combine
PerKey(sum)

    # Step 5: Write the results to an output file
    word_counts | 'WriteResults' >> beam.io.WriteToText('word_
counts.txt')
```

In this pipeline:

1. **Reading Input**: Data is read from a text file using **`ReadFromText`**, which outputs a **`PCollection`** of lines.
2. **Transformations**: The lines are split into words (**`FlatMap`**), where each word is paired with the number 1 (**`Map`**), and the word counts are summed (**`CombinePerKey`**).
3. **Output**: The results are written to a text file using **`WriteToText`**.

Custom Transforms

One of the strengths of Apache Beam is its ability to let you define **custom transforms** to encapsulate reusable logic. Custom transforms are particularly useful when your pipeline has complex, repetitive logic that can be abstracted into a single unit.

Here is how you can create a custom transform in Beam:

Example: Custom Transform to Filter and Process Data

```
class FilterAndDouble(beam.PTransform):
    def expand(self, pcoll):
        return (pcoll
```

```
                    | ‹Filter Even Numbers› >> beam.Filter(lambda x:
x % 2 == 0)
                    | ‹Double Numbers› >> beam.Map(lambda x: x * 2))

with beam.Pipeline() as p:
    numbers = p | ‹Create numbers› >> beam.Create([1, 2, 3, 4, 5,
6])
    result = numbers | ‹Apply Filter and Double› >> FilterAnd
Double()
```

In this example:

The **FilterAndDouble** custom transform filters even numbers and doubles them. The pipeline, therefore becomes more modular, easier to maintain, and reusable.

Building Your First Apache Beam Pipeline

Now that we have covered the foundational components of Apache Beam, including **PCollections** and **PTransforms**, it is time to put those concepts into practice by building your first complete Apache Beam pipeline. Hence, in this section, we will walk through a step-by-step process of constructing a full pipeline, including data ingestion, transformation, and output. We will also explore how to run pipelines in different environments, whether locally or on a cloud-based runner.

Therefore, by the end of this section, you will understand how to design, execute, and manage a basic Beam pipeline, as well as how to deploy it on various execution engines (runners) such as **DirectRunner**, **Google Cloud Dataflow**, **Apache Flink**, or **Apache Spark**.

Step-by-Step Pipeline Construction

To guide you through the construction of a Beam pipeline, we will build a real-world example that processes data from a CSV file, transforms the data, and then outputs the results to a text file. The example demonstrates how to read data, apply multiple transformations, and write results, while explaining each stage of the pipeline.

Let us break it down into manageable steps.

Step 1: Set up the Pipeline Environment

Every Apache Beam pipeline starts by initializing the pipeline environment, which is done by creating a **Pipeline** object. This object acts as the container for all the transforms that will be applied to the data.

```
import apache_beam as beam

# Initialize the pipeline
```

```
with beam.Pipeline() as p:
    # Your pipeline logic will go here
```

When initializing a pipeline, you can also specify a **runner**. The runner determines where your pipeline will be executed. For local development and testing, the **`DirectRunner`** is typically used. For production workloads, you may use **`Google Cloud Dataflow`**, **`Apache Flink`**, or **`Apache Spark`**.

Example of Specifying a Runner:

```
with beam.Pipeline(runner='DirectRunner') as p:
    # Your pipeline logic
```

For more advanced use cases, you can configure your runner with additional options, such as project credentials for cloud runners.

Step 2: Data Ingestion

The first step in any data pipeline is to ingest the data. Apache Beam provides a wide range of connectors to read data from different sources, including files, databases, message queues, and cloud storage.

For this example, we will read data from a **CSV file**. Beam's **`ReadFromText`** transform allows us to read lines from a text file, and treat them as individual elements in a **`PCollection`**.

Example: Reading from a CSV File:

```
# Read data from a CSV file
lines = p | 'ReadFromCSV' >> beam.io.ReadFromText('data.csv')
```

Here, each line in the CSV file will be represented as a string in the resultant **`PCollection`**. However, before we proceed to transform the data, we need to split each line into individual fields.

Step 3: Transforming Data

Once the data is ingested, the next step is to apply transformations to clean, filter, or process it. Beam's **`PTransform`** functions like **`Map, FlatMap, Filter,`** and others are used to perform these operations.

Let us start by splitting each line from the CSV file into its individual components (for example, splitting the line based on commas).

Example: Splitting CSV Lines into Fields:

```
# Define a function to split each line into fields
def split_line(line):
    return line.split(',')
```

```
# Apply the transformation
split_data = lines | 'SplitLines' >> beam.Map(split_line)
```

The **Map** transform applies the **split_line** function to each element in the **PCollection**, while converting each string into a list of fields. For instance, a line like **"1,John,Doe,25"** will be transformed into **['1', 'John', 'Doe', '25'].**

Applying Multiple Transformations

Once the data is split, we can apply further transformations. For instance, we may want to filter out certain rows, or modify specific fields. Let us filter out rows where the age field is less than 30:

```
# Define a filtering function
def filter_by_age(fields):
    age = int(fields[3])  # Assuming the 4th field is age
    return age >= 30

# Apply the filter transformation
filtered_data = split_data | 'FilterByAge' >> beam.Filter(filter_
by_age)
```

In this example, the `Filter` transform applies the **filter_by_age** function to each element in the **PCollection**, while removing rows where the age is less than 30.

Next, we can map the data to key-value pairs if needed. This is often useful for grouping or aggregating data. Let us convert the data into key-value pairs, where the key is the first field (for example, an ID), and the value is the rest of the fields.

Example: Mapping to Key-Value Pairs

```
# Define a mapping function
def to_key_value(fields):
    return (fields[0], fields[1:])  # ID as key, rest as value

# Apply the map transformation
key_value_data = filtered_data | 'ToKeyValue' >> beam.Map(to_key_
value)
```

Now, we have a **PCollection** of key-value pairs, where the key is an ID and the value is the rest of the fields.

Step 4: Write the Data

Once the data has been transformed, the next step is to output the results. Apache Beam supports a variety of output connectors, including file systems, databases, and cloud services. Hence, for this example, we will write the output to a text file.

Example: Writing to a Text File

```
# Write the processed data to an output file
key_value_data | 'WriteToFile' >> beam.io.WriteToText('output.txt')
```

This will write each element in the **PCollection** to an output file, where each line in the file corresponds to one element in the **PCollection**.

Step 5: Run the Pipeline.

After defining the pipeline steps, the next task is to run the pipeline. When you invoke **p.run()**, Beam processes the data according to the pipeline's transforms. If you are using the **DirectRunner**, the execution happens locally.

```
# Run the pipeline
p.run()
```

If you are using a cloud-based runner, such as **Google Cloud Dataflow**, the pipeline will be executed on a distributed cluster, and you may need to provide additional configuration options, such as project credentials and cloud storage locations.

Building a More Complex Pipeline

Now that we have walked through the basics, let us extend this pipeline to include some more advanced features, such as grouping and aggregation. Suppose, we want to count how many times each unique name appears in the dataset.

- **GroupByKey:** We will use the **GroupByKey** transform to group all entries by name.
- **CombinePerKey**: Then, we will apply **CombinePerKey** to count the occurrences of each name.

Example: Counting Occurrences of Names

```
# Map names to key-value pairs where the value is 1
def to_name_count(fields):
    name = fields[1]  # Assuming the name is in the second field
    return (name, 1)

# Apply the mapping
name_counts = split_data | 'MapNamesToCount' >> beam.Map(to_name_
count)

# Group by name and sum the counts
name_totals = name_counts | 'CountPerName' >> beam.Combine
PerKey(sum)
```

```
# Write the results to a file
name_totals | 'WriteNameCounts' >> beam.io.WriteToText('name_
counts.txt')
```

In this extended example:

- We first map the names to key-value pairs, where the key is the name, and the value is the count (initially 1).
- We then group by name using **`CombinePerKey`**, while summing up the counts for each unique name.
- Finally, the results are written to a file.

Hence, this example showcases how Beam allows you to easily group and aggregate data at scale.

Running the Pipeline on Different Runners

While developing and testing pipelines locally with the **`DirectRunner`** is convenient, you will eventually want to run your pipeline on a distributed execution engine, such as Google Cloud Dataflow, Apache Flink, or Apache Spark. The runner-specific setup and its limitations will be covered in more depth in *Chapter 7: Deploying Apache Beam Pipelines on Different Runners*. Meanwhile, running the pipeline can look like this on different runners:

- **Running Locally with `DirectRunner`**

  `DirectRunner` is ideal for small datasets and local testing. This runner executes the pipeline on your local machine, which allows you to quickly iterate and debug the pipeline.

- **Running on `Google Cloud Dataflow`**

  For large-scale production pipelines, **`Google Cloud Dataflow`** provides a fully managed, scalable service. To use Dataflow, you need to configure additional options, such as the project ID and output paths.

Example of Configuring `Dataflow Runner`:

```
options = beam.options.pipeline_options.PipelineOptions(
    runner=›DataflowRunner›,
    project=›my-project-id›,
    temp_location='gs://my-bucket/temp'
)

with beam.Pipeline(options=options) as p:
    # Your pipeline logic
```

- **Running on `Apache Flink`**

  `Apache Flink` is another popular distributed execution engine for Beam pipelines. To run on Flink, you will need to configure the pipeline for **`FlinkRunner`** and deploy it to a Flink cluster.

Example:

```
options = beam.options.pipeline_options.PipelineOptions(
    runner=›FlinkRunner'


with beam.Pipeline(options=options) as p:
    # Your pipeline logic
```

- **Running on `Apache Spark`**

  Apache Spark can also be used to run Beam pipelines in distributed environments. The process is like configuring for Flink or Dataflow.

Optimizing and Debugging Pipelines

Once your pipeline is running, it is important to monitor its performance and optimize it for efficiency. Beam provides various tools and strategies to help you with this, which are explained as follows:

- **Pipeline Monitoring:**

  Cloud-based runners such as Google Cloud Dataflow provide detailed monitoring and logging for each stage of the pipeline, which helps you track job progress, view error logs, and optimize resource usage.

- **Fusion Optimization:**

  Beam automatically optimizes pipelines by fusing adjacent operations into more efficient execution units. This reduces the overhead of moving data between steps, and improves pipeline performance.

- **Windowing for Streaming Pipelines:**

  When working with streaming data, you can use windowing strategies to manage unbounded datasets, grouping data into fixed-size windows for processing. This allows you to control how data is aggregated over time, and also ensures that your streaming pipelines produce timely results.

Conclusion

In this introductory chapter, we have covered the foundational concepts that underpin Apache Beam, while providing a comprehensive and clear understanding of how Beam serves as a unified model for both batch and streaming data processing. Through the lens of key components like **`PCollection`** and **`PTransform`**, we have explored how Beam abstracts data and operations. These components make Beam a versatile solution for processing bounded and unbounded datasets alike.

We also built a full Beam pipeline step by step, which shows how to:

- Ingest data from various sources.
- Apply transformations using Beam's rich library of transforms.
- Output results to different destinations.
- Execute pipelines locally or on distributed systems such as Google Cloud Dataflow and Apache Flink.

Hence, the power of Apache Beam lies in its ability to handle both batch and streaming data with the same code, while offering flexibility, scalability, and portability across multiple execution engines (runners). Whether you are working with finite data sets (batch), or processing real-time streams, Beam provides the tools to handle these scenarios efficiently and seamlessly.

In *Chapter 2: Stateful and Stateless Processing with Apache Beam*, we will build on these foundational concepts by exploring **stateful and stateless processing in Apache Beam**. You will learn how Beam manages state across streaming pipelines, how stateful operations enable more advanced use cases such as session tracking, anomaly detection, and complex event processing, and when simple stateless transformations are sufficient. Thus, the progression will deepen your understanding of how Beam handles real-world streaming scenarios where context, memory, and time play a critical role in producing accurate and meaningful results.

References

- **Google Cloud**: Apache Beam & Cloud Dataflow Customer Stories: https://cloud.google.com/dataflow/docs/resources/customer-stories
- **Forrester**: The Total Economic Impact™ of Real-Time Data Platforms: https://www.forrester.com/report/the-total-economic-impact-of-real-time-data-platforms/

CHAPTER 2
Stateful and Stateless Processing with Apache Beam

Introduction

This chapter moves beyond the basics of pipeline structure and execution into how Apache Beam handles *memory, context, and continuity* while processing data. In real-world streaming systems, many use cases cannot be solved by treating each event independently; they require awareness of past events, session history, or accumulated metrics over time. Therefore, Apache Beam addresses this through its support for both stateless and stateful processing, while allowing developers to choose between high-throughput transformations, as well as more sophisticated logic that maintains context across events. Hence, by understanding these two paradigms, you will gain the ability to design pipelines that are not only scalable and performant, but also capable of solving complex business problems such as user session tracking, anomaly detection, rolling aggregations, and event correlation in real time.

Structure

In this chapter, the following topics will be covered:

- Stateless vs. Stateful Processing
- Handling State in Apache Beam
- Using Triggers and Timers
- Event Time, Processing Time, and Watermarks
- Assigning Data to Windows
- Use Cases and Implementation Patterns
- Testing and Validation in Practice

Stateless vs. Stateful Processing

When designing data processing pipelines, one of the foundational concepts to master is the distinction between stateless and stateful transformations. Hence, understanding these two processing paradigms guides how pipeline developers handle large volumes of streaming data, respond to dynamic conditions, and build robust, fault-tolerant systems. In Apache Beam, both stateless and stateful processing patterns play a pivotal role. Therefore, knowing when and how to use each approach can help you create more efficient and maintainable pipelines.

Stateful processing is inherently difficult in distributed systems. Data is processed in parallel across many workers, which means that the state must be correctly partitioned, synchronized, and consistently updated without conflicts. As failures are inevitable in large-scale systems, the state must also be durable and recoverable. Additionally, it should ensure that no data is lost or double-counted during restarts. Therefore, as workloads grow, state must scale horizontally, move between workers, and remain performant even under skewed data distributions or "hot keys." Poorly designed stateful systems can lead to race conditions, inconsistent results, memory pressure, and significant operational complexity, which makes them fragile and hard to maintain.

Apache Beam's model exists precisely to address these challenges. It provides a structured and portable abstraction for managing state, timers, and event-time semantics in a way that is safe, scalable, and fault tolerant. Instead of forcing developers to manually manage distributed state, synchronization, and recovery, Beam delegates these responsibilities to the runner and exposes a clean programming model. This allows developers to focus on business logic, confidently apply both stateless and stateful processing patterns, and build streaming pipelines that remain correct, reliable, and scalable even as data volumes and system complexity grow.

Thus, by the end of this section, you will be able to identify when stateless processing is sufficient, when stateful processing is required, and practically implement a **stateful DoFn with state and timers** to build streaming pipelines that handle sessionization, aggregations, and time-dependent logic that is correct and reliable.

Overview of Stateless Processing

Stateless processing operations transform input data into output data without retaining any form of persistent, long-lived state between processing steps. Each input element is handled independently. The output of a stateless transform at a given point in time does not depend on the past inputs it has seen. For example, a simple Map function that converts strings to uppercase is stateless because each input element is processed in isolation. There is no shared memory or contextual information carried forward. Similarly, filtering out data that does not match a criterion is often stateless, since each decision depends solely on the element that is being processed at the time.

Stateless processing aligns closely with the principles of functional programming, where functions always produce the same output for the same input, with no side effects or reliance on external data. It is conceptually simpler, easier to parallelize, and less error prone. Many real-world use cases start with stateless transformations: extracting fields from JSON records, normalizing data formats, dropping unnecessary columns, or performing lightweight computations. Since no history or context is required, stateless transforms scale out horizontally with ease—each worker can process portions of the data independently. This simplicity often translates into more predictable performance and more straightforward debugging.

Despite these advantages, stateless processing also has its limitations. Not all applications can be reduced to independent element-wise computations. For example, consider scenarios like calculating session lengths per user, maintaining running averages, or alerting when a certain threshold of activity is surpassed over a given window of time. Hence, in these cases, the processing logic requires access to previous data or historical context, which stateless transforms cannot easily provide. Therefore, such logic typically calls for stateful operations.

Common Patterns and Use Cases for Stateless Processing

This section describes the typical scenarios where stateless transformations are most effective, focusing on operations that treat each data element independently without relying on past context, and highlights how such patterns form the foundation of simple, highly scalable, and easily maintainable data pipelines.

- **Data Cleansing and Normalization:** Removing null values, trimming whitespace, converting data types, or mapping categorical variables to standardized codes are examples of stateless operations. Each element undergoes the same transformation rules, independently of others.
- **Format Conversions:** Transforming input data from CSV to JSON, or converting timestamps from one format to another, can be stateless if the logic for conversion does not depend on previously processed elements.
- **Filtering and Sampling:** Dropping elements that do not meet certain criteria (for example, incomplete records, out-of-range values), or performing random sampling is stateless, as each decision is made based solely on the current element.
- **Simple Enrichment with Fixed Data:** If a pipeline step enriches incoming data with external constants or configuration values that never change during

runtime, it remains stateless. For instance, appending a static tag or flag to each record does not require tracking history.

Stateless transforms are usually where developers start when learning Apache Beam. They help establish a pipeline's initial shape and logic before introducing more complex capabilities.

Overview of Stateful Processing

Stateful processing involves maintaining some form of user-defined data that persists across multiple processed elements, events, or time intervals. Therefore, it becomes especially essential in streaming scenarios with unbounded data, where events arrive continuously, and meaningful results can only be derived by retaining and evolving context over time, rather than processing each event in isolation. In other words, a stateful transform "*remembers*" information about previously seen data and uses that memory to influence the processing of future elements. This is crucial when calculations or outputs need to reflect aggregates, counts, rolling averages, sessionization, or any logic that spans multiple records or a window of time.

A useful mental model is to think of **state as a small piece of memory that is scoped per key and per window**. This means that for each unique key (such as a user ID) and for each active window, Apache Beam maintains an isolated "memory cell" that stores intermediate values like counters, lists, or aggregates. This memory is automatically created, updated, and cleared as the stream progresses.

Stateful processing allows the pipeline to hold temporary values in state cells (like counters or accumulators), and update them as new data arrives. For example, consider a use case where you need to count the number of times a user clicks a link within a given session. Every new click event for that user updates the count stored in the pipeline's state. Once the session closes, the pipeline can emit a final count. Without stateful processing, it would be challenging to produce such results because the pipeline would have no direct way to recall previous events associated with that user.

In streaming pipelines, stateful processing often pairs with windowing concepts, where data is divided into logical time-bounded segments. Within these windows, the pipeline maintains state and updates it in response to each new event. When the window closes, the aggregated state materialized into a final output. The mechanics of stateful processing closely interact with triggers, timers, and watermarks; these are concepts that handle the dynamics of event time ordering and late-arriving data.

Moreover, stateful processing is more complex to implement than stateless processing. This is because it requires additional considerations for how state is sharded, how state storage scales and performs, and how failures or restarts affect state consistency.

Apache Beam's runtime and its runners handle much of the complexity by providing robust abstractions for state management. It ensures that developers can focus on their business logic, rather than the intricacies of distributed state stores.

Common Patterns and Use Cases for Stateful Processing

Stateful processing becomes indispensable whenever a pipeline must remember past events, accumulate intermediate results, or evolve its output over time based on continuous input. The following patterns represent some of the most common and impactful ways state is used in real-world streaming and hybrid data pipelines:

- **Running Counts and Aggregations:** Stateful processing is required anytime a pipeline needs to keep track of how many events have occurred for a given key, maintain a running total, or sum values over time. For example, a pipeline might track the total sales per user per hour, or maintain a running sum of sensor readings. These counts are typically scoped per key (such as per user, device, or account), and often are further scoped per window, while ensuring that the state remains bounded and does not grow indefinitely. For example, a pipeline might track the total sales per user per hour, or maintain a running sum of sensor readings per device within fixed time windows. This allows accurate aggregation and keeps the state size manageable.
- **Sessionization:** Grouping user events into sessions is a common streaming use case. By holding onto user-related state, pipelines can segment a stream of interactions into bounded sessions. Therefore, session boundaries are typically defined based on **event time and periods of inactivity**, rather than fixed clock intervals. Pipelines use **timers** to detect when no new events have arrived for a key within a specified gap duration, which signals that a session has ended. When the session closes, the pipeline outputs metrics such as session length, number of events, or conversion rates. This event-time-driven approach thus ensures that sessions are formed correctly even when the data arrives late.
- **Complex Pattern Recognition:** Some analytics scenarios require identifying patterns spanning multiple events. For instance, detecting a fraud pattern in a sequence of financial transactions might involve retaining the last few transactions in state to identify suspicious sequences or anomalies.
- **Building Dynamic Machine Learning Features:** Stateful processing can maintain rolling windows of metrics used as real-time features for Machine Learning (ML) models. For example, computing a 10-minute moving average of user clicks or response times can feed directly into predictive models.
- **Incremental Updates to External Systems:** Integrating with external systems that must be updated incrementally can benefit from stateful processing.

Thus, instead of writing an entire dataset to an external database after each batch, a pipeline can keep track of incremental changes, and also apply only the delta to reduce load and latency.

Comparing Stateless and Stateful Approaches

When deciding between stateless and stateful transforms, it is important to recognize that **stateful processing should be used only when it is truly required**, as it introduces additional complexity in terms of state management, scalability, fault tolerance, and operational overhead. Moreover, stateless processing is always preferable when the problem can be solved without retaining historical context. Therefore, you must also consider the following questions:

- **Do You Need Historical Context?** If the logic requires knowledge of previously processed elements, stateful transforms are the natural choice.
- **Is Performance Critical?** Stateless transforms are generally simpler and can be easily parallelized, which often results in higher throughput and lower latency. Moreover, stateful transforms add complexity and overhead; so, they should be used only when necessary.
- **What are the Reliability and Fault-Tolerance Requirements?** While both stateless and stateful processing in Apache Beam are fault-tolerant, stateful processing involves maintaining correct state across restarts and failures. Apache Beam and its runners ensure state consistency, but stateful pipelines may require more careful design to ensure correct semantics during recovery. It is also worth noting that Apache Beam achieves correct recovery for pipelines through **checkpointing and replay mechanisms**, where runners periodically persist state and, in the event of a failure, replay input data from the last consistent checkpoint to reconstruct state accurately. This ensures that even complex stateful computations remain correct and deterministic despite crashes, restarts, or scaling events.
- **How Complex is the Logic?** Stateless transforms are simpler to implement and reason about. If the use case does not demand historical context or dynamic thresholds, stateless transforms keep pipelines more maintainable.

In many real-world pipelines, a combination of stateless and stateful operations emerges naturally. For instance, a pipeline might first apply stateless filters and transformations to clean data and map it into a common format, and then apply stateful operations to aggregate results per key and output summaries. Therefore, integrating both paradigms allows us to build pipelines that are both flexible and efficient, besides leveraging the simplicity of stateless operations, as well as the richer capabilities of stateful operations, wherever required.

Implementation Details in Apache Beam

Apache Beam provides powerful abstractions for both stateless and stateful transforms. Stateless processing is straightforward: developers write simple DoFns, or use built-in transforms like `MapElements`, `Filter`, or `FlatMap`. For more complex pipelines, stateful processing is enabled by Beam's DoFn state API, which allows developers to declare and manage stateful data structures, such as `BagState`, `ValueState`, `CombiningState`, or `MapState`. It is also important to note that the DoFn state API is primarily used in **streaming pipelines with keyed data**, where each key represents an independent scope for state and timers. This enables accurate, scalable, and isolated stateful processing across unbounded data streams.

Key concepts for implementing stateful logic include:

- **DoFn State Declarations:** Within a DoFn, developers can annotate fields with `'@StateId'` to associate them with state cells. Each state cell is keyed by the element's key, and it can store values that persist across multiple calls for the said key.
- **Timers:** Timers integrate tightly with state and operate at the **DoFn level**, which allows developers to register callbacks that fire at a specific event time or processing time for a given key. When a timer fires, it can read or modify state, emit outputs, or clear stored data. In contrast, **triggers operate at the window level,** and control when the aggregated results for a window are emitted. Therefore, timers and triggers together provide complementary mechanisms: timers enable fine-grained, key-scoped control over stateful logic, while triggers govern when windowed computations produce results, both of which are essential for handling event-time semantics and delayed or out-of-order data.
- **State Management by Runners:** The actual storage and retrieval of state are managed by the runner (such as Apache Flink or Google Cloud Dataflow). Runners distribute state across workers, and handle persistence and fault tolerance. Hence, developers do not need to write their own distributed state storage logic, as Beam provides a uniform stateful API that works across runners.
- **Trade-Offs and Performance Considerations:** Storing state for large numbers of keys can increase memory and I/O overhead. Hence, developers must consider key cardinality, state size, and timer frequency, as overly large states can degrade performance and lead to scaling challenges. One important optimization is the use of **State Time-to-Live (TTL)**, which automatically expires and removes state that has not been accessed or updated for a configured duration, which prevents stale or inactive keys from consuming resources indefinitely. Thus, optimizations such as clearing

unused states, compacting stored data, or using combining states can mitigate these issues.

Integration with Other Beam Features

Stateful processing rarely exists in isolation. It often works in tandem with other Beam features such as:

- **Windowing:** Most streaming use cases rely on windowing to group unbounded data into manageable chunks. Stateful operations can be scoped to these windows, and make it possible to maintain counters or aggregations only for the duration of a given window. It then emits the final results when the window closes.
- **Triggers:** While stateful transforms maintain data over time, triggers decide when to produce output based on watermarks, event counts, or processing time. Thus, triggers and state together let you fine-tune when partial aggregates are output, while enabling timely and flexible updates.
- **Side Inputs:** When combining stateful processing with side inputs, the pipeline can utilize additional reference data while maintaining state. For example, look-up tables or configuration parameters can inform how state is aggregated, or when triggers are fired.
- **Error Handling and Dead-Letter Queues:** In complex stateful pipelines, it may be necessary to handle malformed data or unexpected event sequences. A pipeline can rely on side outputs or error-reporting transforms to deal with exceptional cases. Although error handling often remains stateless, the presence of state in the pipeline can influence error resolution strategies.

Therefore, by mastering these concepts, developers unlock the full power of Apache Beam. They can design pipelines that not only process massive streams of data, but also derive meaningful insights over time, handle sessionization, compute aggregates, and respond adaptively as event streams evolve.

Defining State in a DoFn

To use state in a DoFn, developers define stateful fields and annotate them with @ StateId. The annotation binds the field to a named state, and Beam's runtime manages the lifecycle, as well as the persistence of a state on behalf of the pipeline.

Handling State in Apache Beam

State management is a cornerstone of building sophisticated, real-time data processing pipelines. Apache Beam's model allows developers to work with large-scale datasets while maintaining the clarity and simplicity of a unified programming model. Hence, when dealing with advanced scenarios such as session tracking, incremental aggregation, or pattern detection, developers need reliable mechanisms to store and manage state. Apache Beam addresses these needs by offering a set of well-defined APIs and data structures that let pipelines maintain persistent information across events, keys, and time boundaries.

The Role of State in Pipeline Logic

In many streaming applications, each incoming data element is not just another record to process in isolation. Instead, it often contributes to an evolving picture that requires the knowledge of what came before. Therefore, you must consider tracking the cumulative total of purchases per user, maintaining a record of a user's last visit, or identifying the first event that triggered a certain condition. All these tasks involve storing some form of data that persists beyond the immediate invocation of a processing function.

Without state, pipelines could only process events in a self-contained manner. While this works for simple filtering or mapping operations, it falls short when computations depend on previously seen events. State provides the "memory" that streaming applications need to solve real-world problems. Hence, by enabling arbitrary logic that can read, write, and clear stored values, Apache Beam ensures that pipelines are not limited by stateless functional transforms alone.

State Primitives in Apache Beam

To implement stateful logic, Apache Beam provides several state primitives that developers can use inside DoFns. When a DoFn is defined to operate on keyed data (for example, after a **GroupByKey** operation, or on a keyed **PCollection**), the Beam model guarantees that all operations for the same key occur on the same logical worker thread. This isolation allows state to be maintained reliably and consistently per key. Moreover, it is important to note that stateful DoFns **require keyed input**; if a **PCollection** is not keyed, state cannot be correctly scoped, and the DoFn will either fail at runtime, or exhibit incorrect behavior. Therefore, you must always ensure that the data is keyed (for example, using a KV structure and appropriate grouping) before applying any stateful processing logic.

The main state primitives include:

- **ValueState<T>:** This is a single mutable value of type T and the simplest form of state. For example, a **ValueState<Integer>** could hold a running count of how many times a key has been seen. Each time a new element with that key arrives, the pipeline increments the stored integer.
- **BagState<T>:** A mutable collection of values of type T. Unlike a **ValueState** that stores a single value, a **BagState** can hold multiple records. This is useful for collecting elements over a period, then processing them all at once. For

example, a pipeline could accumulate all the events for a user session in a **`BagState<List<Event>>`**, and emit a batch summary once the session ends.

However, **`BagState`** must be used with care: **if it is not paired with windowing, timers, State TTLs, or explicit clearing logic, it can grow unbounded**, leading to excessive memory usage and performance degradation. Hence, it is best suited for scenarios where the lifecycle of stored data is clearly bounded, such as session-based processing or window-scoped aggregations.

- **`CombiningState<InputT, AccumT, OutputT>`**: Designed for aggregations, a **`CombiningState`** keeps track of combined results incrementally as elements arrive. This allows computations like sums, counts, or averages to be updated efficiently on the fly. For instance, a **`CombiningState<Long, Long, Long>`** might store a running sum of values and return their incremental total.

  In practice, **`CombiningState` is generally far more efficient than `BagState` for aggregation use cases**, because it stores only the aggregated result (or a compact accumulator) instead of retaining all individual elements. This significantly reduces memory usage, I/O overhead, and state growth, which makes it the preferred choice whenever raw events do not need to be preserved.

- **`MapState<KeyT, ValueT>`**: Provides a mutable map from keys of type **`KeyT`** to values of type **`ValueT`**. **`MapState`** is useful for more complex aggregations or for scenarios where we need a dynamic data structure keyed by sub-attributes. For example, if tracking inventory counts per product category, **`MapState<String, Integer>`** can maintain a map of product categories to their respective counts.

  Caution: **`MapState`** can develop a **high memory footprint** when the number of sub-keys grows large (for example, high-cardinality categories or per-user-per-item tracking). To keep it efficient, ensure that sub-keys remain bounded, apply windowing or TTL where appropriate, and consider using **`CombiningState`** when only aggregate values are required.

A simple way to choose between these state primitives is to match them to your **access pattern** and the **expected size of stored state**: use **`ValueState`** when you only need a single evolving value (smallest and fastest), prefer **`CombiningState`** for frequent incremental aggregations because it avoids storing all elements, use **`MapState`** when you need random access or updates by sub-key (more efficient than scanning a collection), and reserve **`BagState`** for cases where you truly must retain multiple raw events–keep it bounded with windowing/TTL, as it can grow large and increase memory and I/O overhead.

These state types cover a wide range of scenarios, allowing developers to store counters, sets, lists, and maps of arbitrary complexity. Hence, by mixing and matching these state primitives, complex data transformations can be built that remember historical context and adapt as events flow through the pipeline.

Defining State in a DoFn

To use state in a DoFn, developers define stateful fields and annotate them with **`@StateId`**. The annotation binds the field to a named state, and Beam's runtime manages the lifecycle and persistence of that state on behalf of the pipeline. For example, in the following code in Java:

```
public class StatefulDoFn extends DoFn<KV<String, Integer>,
KV<String, Integer>> {

  @StateId("count")
  private final StateSpec<ValueState<Integer>> countStateSpec =
      StateSpecs.value(VarIntCoder.of());

  @ProcessElement
  public void processElement(
      ProcessContext c,
      @StateId("count") ValueState<Integer> countState) {

    Integer current = countState.read();
    if (current == null) {
      current = 0;
    }
    countState.write(current + c.element().getValue());
    c.output(KV.of(c.element().getKey(), countState.read()));
  }
}
```

In this example, the count state holds a running total for each key. Every time a new **`KV<String, Integer>`** arrives, the function updates this total and outputs the new value. The Beam runtime ensures that values for different keys are kept separate, and that state is correctly managed even if the pipeline scales out horizontally across multiple workers. **This correctness is preserved through runner-managed checkpointing and fault-tolerant recovery—state is periodically snapshotted, and if a worker fails, the runner can replay data from the last consistent checkpoint to reconstruct the per-key state without losing updates, or producing incorrect totals.**

Understanding the Execution Model

When a pipeline runs, keyed data is sharded across multiple workers. Each worker is responsible for a subset of keys, and it manages the associated state. When data arrives for a specific key, the runner ensures that the corresponding state is available to the DoFn. Upon completion, the runner may persist the updated state to disk, cloud storage, or other durable media, depending on the runner and configuration.

If a worker fails, the runner can restore state from a checkpoint or savepoint, thus preserving correctness and consistency.

It is also important to be aware that **uneven key distribution (data skew)** can negatively impact performance, as workers responsible for "hot keys" may become overloaded while others remain underutilized, resulting in higher latency and reduced overall throughput.

Due to this execution model, certain best practices must be followed:

- **Use Keys Appropriately:** State is always scoped to keys. Without keying the data, stateful processing is not possible. To use state, ensure that the pipeline is keyed appropriately, typically using transforms like `KeyBy` (in Flink's terms), or ensuring that the `PCollection` is keyed before applying the DoFn.
- **Choose the Right State Type:** Picking the correct state type (`ValueState`, `BagState`, `CombiningState`, or `MapState`) ensures optimal performance and clarity. Using a `BagState` where a simple counter would suffice can lead to unnecessary complexity. Conversely, using a `ValueState` when you need to store multiple values leads to complicated logic.
- **Be Mindful of State Size:** State is not a replacement for a database. It should be used for intermediate computations and temporary storage. Large states can strain resources. Hence, it is wise to manage state size actively, clearing the state when it is no longer needed, or using accumulation techniques that reduce storage overhead.

  For example, storing an entire customer profile, transaction history, or raw event logs for long periods inside state is a misuse of Beam state; such data belongs in an external database or data lake. State should instead hold lightweight, derived values such as counters, rolling averages, session metrics, or small accumulators that support real-time computation.
- **Handle Timers and Output Correctly:** Often, stateful operations go hand-in-hand with timers that trigger at certain times. When a timer fires, it reads and updates state, emits output, or clears stored values. Therefore, properly integrating timers ensures that the state is used effectively to produce timely and accurate results.

Lifecycle of State

A key aspect of working with state is understanding its lifecycle. The following steps summarize how state typically evolves as data moves through the pipeline:

1. **Initialization**: Before processing any elements, a state cell is uninitialized. Reads from an uninitialized state return null or a default value. The DoFn is responsible for initializing the state, if necessary.

2. **Updates per Element:** Each new element associated with a key can update the state. For example, a running total increments, a set gains a new member, or a timestamp of last event updates to the current event's timestamp.
3. **Periodic Expiration or Clearing:** Not all states should live forever. Once a computation completes–such as after a window closes or a session ends–the state should be cleared to free resources. Hence, clearing state prevents stale data from influencing future computations.
4. **Checkpointing and Recovery:** Runners periodically checkpoint state for fault tolerance. If a failure occurs, the pipeline is restored to a known-good checkpoint. This ensures correctness even in the presence of failures, although at the cost of some runtime overhead.

State and Parallelism

One of the strengths of Apache Beam's stateful model is that it maintains scalability and parallelism. State is always keyed, and keys are distributed across available workers. Thus, by distributing keys, Beam parallelizes stateful operations across multiple threads or machines. For large-scale pipelines, this ability to horizontally scale stateful computations is critical.

However, not all operations parallelize equally well. If a pipeline has a small number of keys with extremely large states, then parallelism may be limited. A more uniform key distribution results in better load balancing and improved performance.

Performance Considerations

Stateful processing, while powerful, introduces overhead. Reading and writing state are more expensive operations than simple in-memory computations because the runner might store state in durable, fault-tolerant systems. Some performance considerations include:

- **State Backends:** Different runners use different mechanisms to store state. For example, **`Apache Flink`** uses its own state backends (for example, memory, **`RocksDB`**) to store keyed state, while Google Cloud Dataflow uses distributed storage. The chosen runner and backend configuration affect performance, throughput, and latency.
- **Batching and Incremental Updates:** Instead of writing every event individually to state, some operations batch updates for efficiency. Using **`CombiningState`** or accumulators can reduce overhead by compacting multiple updates into a single write.
- **Clearing Unused State:** Eliminating unnecessary state data reduces memory and storage costs. For example, once a window closes or a session completes,

clearing the associated state ensures no stale data lingers. Failing to clear state properly can effectively lead to **memory leaks**, where obsolete state continues to consume resources indefinitely. It gradually degrades performance, and potentially causes pipeline instability or crashes. Hence, regularly clearing state is therefore essential not only for efficiency, but also for maintaining the long-term health and reliability of the pipeline.

- **Data Skew and Hot Keys:** If a small number of keys receive a disproportionately large share of the data, the state associated with these "hot keys" might grow large and become a bottleneck. Mitigation strategies include shard splitting (introducing artificial sub-keys), or using techniques to limit state size.

Integration with Timers

State alone cannot effectively handle evolving data streams without a mechanism to time-bound operations. Timers play a critical role because they control *when* state is evaluated and *when* results are emitted, as they allow pipelines to act on accumulated state at precisely defined moments based on event time or processing time. Timers let developers schedule future callbacks that operate on state. For instance, a timer can be set to fire when a certain amount of time has passed since the last event for a key. When the timer fires, the DoFn can read the state, emit results, and clear the state. This combination of state and timers is thus essential for implementing windowing logic, sessionization, or delayed output strategies.

For example, consider sessionization: a pipeline might store user interactions in `BagState` and set a timer to fire after 30 minutes of inactivity. If no new events arrive, the timer fires, the pipeline finalizes the session, outputs the aggregated session data, and clears the state. Without timers, the pipeline would not know when to emit results, which will lead to incomplete or never-ending accumulations.

Debugging and Observability

Working with state can make debugging pipelines more complex; therefore, it is best to start with small, controlled test datasets and use local runners such as the `DirectRunner`, where the behavior is easier to observe, the logs are more accessible, and the state transitions can be validated step by step before scaling to distributed environments Since the final output depends not just on the current input but also on an evolving state, it can be challenging to trace how intermediate values form over time. Observability tools such as logging, metrics, and Beam's built-in counters can help:

- **Logging State Changes:** Developers can add logs whenever state is updated or cleared, while providing a trail of how values evolve. Hence, you must be careful, as overly verbose logging can result in large output and degraded performance.

- **Counters and Distributions:** Beam's metric system can track counts or distributions of state sizes, the frequency of state updates, or how many times a timer fired. These metrics can guide performance tuning and troubleshooting.
- **Runner-Specific Debugging Tools:** Different runners may provide additional debugging capabilities. For example, when using Flink as a runner, Flink's Web UI and checkpoint visualization tools can show the state size per task, which makes it easier to identify hot keys or bottlenecks.

Example Scenarios

- **Running Word Counts over Windows:** A classic example is counting how many times each word appears in a stream over a fixed window. With state, the pipeline can maintain a running sum for each word-key within the window. When the window closes, the pipeline outputs the final count, and then clears the state. The following code in Java illustrates it:

```
// Pseudocode for maintaining a windowed word count
// Assume input: PCollection<KV<String, String>> of (word, "event")
PCollection<KV<String, Long>> wordCounts = input
    .apply(Window.<KV<String, String>>into(FixedWindows.of
(Duration.standardMinutes(1))))
    .apply(ParDo.of(new DoFn<KV<String, String>, KV<String,
Long>>() {
      @StateId("count")
      private final StateSpec<CombiningState<Long, long[], Long>>
countSpec =
          StateSpecs.combiningValue(LongCoder.of(), Sum.
ofLongs());

      @ProcessElement
      public void processElement(
          ProcessContext c,
          @StateId("count") CombiningState<Long, long[], Long>
countState) {
        countState.add(1L);
        // The actual output occurs when the window closes or
triggered
      }

      @FinishBundle
      public void finishBundle(FinishBundleContext c) {
        // On window close, output the accumulated counts
        // This might be handled by a trigger rather than Finish-
Bundle in a real pipeline
```

```
    }
  }));
```

- **Sessionization for Web Events:** Suppose a pipeline tracks user clicks. By using state and timers, the pipeline can accumulate clicks in a **BagState** for each user. When a timer fires indicating 30 minutes of inactivity, the pipeline emits the session summary. This logic might look like:

```
// Pseudocode for sessionization
// Input: PCollection<KV<String, ClickEvent>>
.apply(ParDo.of(new DoFn<KV<String, ClickEvent>, Session
Summary>() {
  @StateId("events")
  private final StateSpec<BagState<ClickEvent>> eventsSpec =
      StateSpecs.bag(AvroCoder.of(ClickEvent.class));

  @TimerId("sessionTimeout")
  private final TimerSpec sessionTimer = TimerSpecs.timer
(TimeDomain.EVENT_TIME);

  @ProcessElement
  public void processElement(
      ProcessContext c,
      @StateId("events") BagState<ClickEvent> eventsState,
      @TimerId("sessionTimeout") Timer sessionTimer) {

    eventsState.add(c.element().getValue());
    sessionTimer.set(c.timestamp().plus(Duration.standard
Minutes(30)));
  }

  @OnTimer("sessionTimeout")
  public void onTimeout(
      OnTimerContext c,
      @StateId("events") BagState<ClickEvent> eventsState) {

    Iterable<ClickEvent> events = eventsState.read();
    // Construct session summary
    SessionSummary summary = ... // aggregate events
    c.output(summary);
    eventsState.clear();
  }
}));
```

This approach shows how combining state and timers enables more complex, temporal logic that can be crucial for real-time analytics.

Testing and Validation

Testing stateful DoFns is more involved than testing stateless transforms because correctness must be validated **over time and across sequences of events**, not just for individual elements. This makes it essential to ensure that state evolution, timer behavior, and recovery semantics remain consistent under all conditions. Hence, developers must verify that state updates occur as expected, that timers fire at the right times, and that clearing state happens correctly. Strategies for testing include:

- **Unit Tests:** Use Beam's **`TestStream`** to simulate inputs and time progression, then assert outputs. By controlling the clock, tests can trigger timers deterministically and verify state changes. **`TestStream`** is primarily intended for validating pipeline logic at the SDK level, and is thus best suited for unit testing; it does not validate runner-specific behaviors such as checkpointing, scaling, or performance characteristics, which must be tested separately on the target runner.
- **`DirectRunner` Execution:** Running pipelines locally with the **`DirectRunner`** lets developers inspect logs and metrics, while ensuring that the state behaves as intended.
- **Integration Tests:** In more complex scenarios, integration tests can run pipelines with sample data against a chosen runner, validating end-to-end behavior, stateful computations, and output correctness. Hence, it is useful to distinguish **functional correctness testing**–verifying that outputs, state evolution, and timer behavior match expectations–from **performance and scalability testing**, which focuses on throughput, latency, resource utilization, and how the pipeline behaves under large volumes, skewed keys, and scaling events in the target runtime environment.

Therefore, by thoroughly testing stateful logic, developers can ensure that their pipelines handle the full complexity of real-time data processing scenarios, without introducing subtle bugs or performance bottlenecks.

Using Triggers and Timers

In Apache Beam, triggers and timers serve distinct but complementary roles–triggers operate at the window level to control when aggregated results for a window are emitted, while timers operate within DoFns to schedule key-scoped, state-dependent actions at specific points in event time or processing time.

Therefore, as pipelines grow more sophisticated, simply reading and writing state is not enough. Developers often need fine-grained control over when results are emitted, how to handle late data, and how to materialize partial aggregates. This is where triggers and timers become essential. In Apache Beam, triggers provide a flexible mechanism to control when windowed results are produced, while timers allow developers to schedule state-dependent actions at future points in event or processing time. Together, they equip pipeline builders with the tools needed to deal with the messy realities of real-world data streams.

The Role of Triggers

A trigger determines when outputs from a window are emitted. While windows group data into temporal buckets, triggers dictate when those buckets are "*closed*" or finalized for output. Without triggers, a pipeline would need to wait until the window boundary is reached and all data is known. However, in a streaming environment, data is often late, out-of-order, or continuous. Triggers help adapt to these conditions, as well as enable pipelines to produce early (partial) results, handle late-arriving data gracefully, and refine previously emitted outputs.

Key Concepts:

- **Early Results:** Sometimes, waiting for a window to fully complete is undesirable. For example, dashboards may need partial, regularly updated aggregates before the window's actual end time. Triggers can emit intermediate results at intervals, or can be based on element counts, while providing timely insights.
- **Late Data:** In an event-time-based system, data can arrive late due to network delays, retries, or batching. Triggers, in combination with watermarks, let pipelines decide what to do when data for a window arrives after the window should logically be complete. A trigger might update previously output results, discard late data, or output a separate "*late*" pane. **Allowed lateness defines how long a window remains open to accept late elements**, and within this period, triggers can fire again to update previously emitted results, emit refined panes, or produce separate "late" panes. Once the allowed lateness expires, any further late data is typically discarded or sent to a side output, which ensures predictable and bounded processing behavior.
- **Refinement and Multiple Panes:** One trigger firing might produce an initial result. Subsequent triggers can refine that result if more data arrives. Beam represents these multiple outputs as multiple panes of the same window, while allowing consumers to handle incremental updates.

Basic Trigger Types

Apache Beam includes several predefined triggers and allows custom triggers to be built. Common trigger types include:

- **Event-Time Triggers:** These triggers rely on the event time progress of the pipeline. They often use watermarks to determine when "*most*" data for a given window has arrived. For example, an event-time trigger might fire when the watermark passes the end of the window by a certain delay, while ensuring that late data can still be considered if it arrives within that delay.

- **Processing-Time Triggers:** Processing-time triggers rely on the system clock instead of event time. This can be simpler but less aligned with the semantics of the data. For example, a processing-time trigger might emit results every 5 minutes of wall-clock time, regardless of the actual timestamps of the events.
- **Element Count Triggers:** These triggers fire after a certain number of elements have arrived in a window. For instance, a pipeline may emit results every time it processes 100 new elements for that window, while providing frequent incremental outputs.
- **Composite Triggers (Early + Late):** Often, pipelines combine triggers. For example, an early trigger might emit partial results every 30 seconds (processing time), while a late trigger fires when the watermark passes the end of the window, besides capturing any straggling data that arrived late.

  Composite triggers are powerful but should be used carefully, as combining early and late triggers significantly increases both cognitive and operational complexity, which makes pipelines harder to reason about, debug, and maintain if their behavior is not clearly documented and thoroughly tested.

Therefore, by mixing and matching event-time, processing-time, and element-count-based triggers, developers can fine-tune when and how results appear. This flexibility ensures that pipelines meet business requirements for timeliness and completeness.

Timers for Fine-Grained Control

While triggers are primarily associated with windowed aggregations, timers offer a lower-level, more granular mechanism for scheduling callbacks in user-defined DoFns. They let you set a specific time in the future, based on either event time or processing time, at which a method in the DoFn is invoked. Within that method, the pipeline can read and write state, emit outputs, and modify logic as needed.

Key Uses of Timers:

- **Session Expiration:** When implementing sessionization, a timer can fire after a certain inactivity period, signaling the end of a session. Upon timer firing, the DoFn might aggregate all session events from state and emits a summary before clearing the state.
- **Delayed Outputs:** A pipeline might wait for a certain period to ensure that most related events have arrived before finalizing an output. A timer set for

the future gives data a "grace period" to show up. When it fires, the pipeline emits the aggregated result.

- **Periodic State Cleanup:** Timers can trigger periodic scans of stored state to remove outdated entries. For example, a pipeline might set a daily timer that cleans up states related to keys that have not been updated for more than 24 hours.
- **Complex Trigger-Like Logic in DoFns:** While triggers are typically defined at the window level using the Beam windowing API, timers allow similar logic to be implemented at the level of a DoFn. For instance, if you need a custom condition–like waiting until both a "start" and an "end" event have arrived–timers can help enforce these rules.

Timers are typically used in conjunction with state. A DoFn might store intermediate data in state and schedule a timer to emit results later. This combination of state and timers makes it possible to implement arbitrary logic that surpasses the capabilities of predefined triggers alone.

Event Time, Watermarks, and Timers

To effectively use triggers and timers, it is important to understand how event time and watermarks interact:

- **Event Time:** The logical time assigned to each event, which represents when it actually occurred, and not when it was processed by the pipeline.
- **Processing Time:** The local time on a processing machine's clock, which can drift and differ between workers. Processing time triggers and timers are simpler, but less semantically aligned with the data.
- **Watermarks:** A watermark is a pipeline's notion of how far along in event time the system has progressed. When the watermark is at time T, it asserts that no events with event times less than T are expected to arrive. This allows triggers and timers to handle late data intelligently. If an event arrives with a timestamp less than the current watermark, it is considered late.

  It is important to note that this assertion is **heuristic rather than absolute,** and depends on the watermark generation strategy of the data source and runner; an imperfect or delayed watermark advancement can cause events that are still in transit to be classified as late.

Therefore, integrating timers with event time and watermarks ensures that pipelines produce results that align with the logical order of events, and not just the order in which they were processed.

Implementing Timers in a DoFn

To use timers in a DoFn, developers declare timer fields and annotate them with **@TimerId**. Timers are associated with keys, much like state. Setting a timer schedules a callback at the specified time. When the timer fires, a method annotated with **@OnTimer("timerId")** is invoked.

For example, look at the following code in Java:

```
public class TimerExample extends DoFn<KV<String, Event>,
KV<String, Long>> {

  @StateId("eventCount")
  private final StateSpec<ValueState<Long>> eventCountSpec =
      StateSpecs.value(VarLongCoder.of());

  @TimerId("inactivityTimer")
  private final TimerSpec inactivityTimerSpec = TimerSpecs.timer
(TimeDomain.EVENT_TIME);

  @ProcessElement
  public void processElement(
      ProcessContext c,
      @StateId("eventCount") ValueState<Long> eventCountState,
      @TimerId("inactivityTimer") Timer inactivityTimer) {

    Long count = eventCountState.read();
    if (count == null) {
      count = 0L;
    }
    eventCountState.write(count + 1);

    // Set a timer for 10 minutes after the current event time
    // If no new data arrives for this key within 10 minutes, the
timer fires
    inactivityTimer.set(c.timestamp().plus(Duration.standard
Minutes(10)));
  }

  @OnTimer("inactivityTimer")
  public void onInactivityTimer(
      OnTimerContext c,
      @StateId("eventCount") ValueState<Long> eventCountState) {

    Long count = eventCountState.read();
    if (count != null && count > 0) {
      c.output(KV.of(c.getKey(), count));
```

```
                // Clear the state after outputting results
                eventCountState.clear();
            }
        }
    }
```

Here, for each key, the pipeline counts events. After the last event for a key arrives, the timer fires if 10 minutes pass with no new data. At this point, the pipeline outputs the count and clears the state. This pattern is common in sessionization and inactivity-based aggregation.

Integrating Triggers with Windowing

Triggers are often defined alongside the windowing logic, usually through **`Window.into()`** transforms. For instance:

```
PCollection<KV<String, Long>> result = input
    .apply(Window.<KV<String, Long>>into(FixedWindows.of
(Duration.standardMinutes(1)))
        .triggering(AfterWatermark.pastEndOfWindow()
            .withEarlyFirings(AfterProcessingTime.pastFirst
ElementInPane()
                .plusDelayOf(Duration.standardSeconds(30)))
            .withLateFirings(AfterPane.elementCountAtLeast(1)))
        .accumulatingFiredPanes()
        .withAllowedLateness(Duration.standardMinutes(5)))
    .apply(Sum.longsPerKey());
```

This configuration:

- Uses a fixed window of 1 minute.
- Triggers once when the watermark passes the window end (the main trigger).
- Emits early results every 30 seconds of processing time after the first element arrives in the pane.
- Emits late results if more data arrives after the main pane, one at a time.
- Accumulates panes, meaning previous results are combined with new data for subsequent trigger firings.
- Allows data that arrives up to 5 minutes late to still update results.

Thus, the combination of triggers and allowed lateness gives granular control over how windows behave. Developers can output intermediate results, refine them as late data arrives, and eventually close out the window for good.

Balancing Complexity and Accuracy

Balancing complexity and accuracy is essential, because while advanced features like state, timers, triggers, and composite windowing enable highly precise results, **simpler pipelines are often more maintainable, easier to reason about, and less error-prone**. These attributes make it important to use additional complexity only when the business requirements truly demand it.

While triggers and timers enable highly responsive and adaptive pipelines, they also introduce complexity. Therefore, developers must carefully consider:

- **Business Requirements for Timeliness:** If the application needs real-time metrics, early triggers ensure prompt results but may produce multiple updates. Hence, downstream systems must handle evolving values.
- **Tolerance for Late Data:** If late data is common, triggers and allowed lateness can re-evaluate results. However, this can produce multiple outputs for the same window, which complicates downstream logic.
- **Performance Implications:** Each trigger firing can cause an expensive recomputation or produce multiple result panes. Overly aggressive triggering may degrade performance. Therefore, balancing timely updates against computation cost is necessary.
- **State Management with Timers:** Timers rely on state to store the necessary data until the timer fires. This means that state usage increases, while possibly raising resource consumption. Hence, judicious clearing of state after timer firings is important.

Debugging Trigger Behavior

Debugging triggers and timers can be challenging because the pipeline's outputs depend on the interplay of event times, watermarks, and trigger conditions. Moreover, this section should be viewed as **advanced guidance primarily aimed at production troubleshooting**, where understanding subtle timing behaviors is critical for diagnosing incorrect outputs, delayed results, or unexpected re-emissions. Some strategies include:

- **Logging Trigger Firings:** Add logs in OnTimer methods, or after triggers fire to trace when events are being output. Although verbose, such logs can reveal if triggers are firing too often, or not at all.
- **Metrics and Counters:** Tracking how many panes each window produces or how many times a timer callback fires can help identify misconfigurations. It is also valuable to establish **baseline metrics** early—such as expected pane count per window, typical late-data rate, watermark lag, timer firing frequency, and

average output latency–so that production runs can be compared against "normal" behavior, and the anomalies can be detected quickly.

- **`TestStreams` in Unit Tests:** Use **`TestStream`** to simulate input data arrival times, control watermarks, and verify that triggers produce the expected outputs at the right times.
- **Runner-Specific Tools:** Some runners offer dashboards or logs for debugging. For example, using Apache Flink as a runner, the Flink UI can help visualize event-time progress, watermarks, and triggered computations.

Example Scenarios

- **Real-Time Dashboard Updates:** A streaming dashboard requires frequent updates. Use an event-time trigger with periodic processing-time-based early firings to continuously update charts. Late data is still accounted for by firing another pane if it arrives.

  Therefore, this setup ensures that the dashboard never goes stale waiting for a window to close fully.
- **Session Finalization after Inactivity:** A session closes after 30 minutes of no user activity. Set a timer on each user key when an event arrives. If the timer fires with no new events, the session ends. This reduces latency compared to waiting for a fixed window boundary, and ensures that sessions are defined by actual user behavior.
- **Periodic Aggregations with Late Handling:** A pipeline computes hourly sales totals. It uses a watermark-based trigger to emit final totals after the hour ends, but also allows a few minutes of lateness. If late sales data arrives, the trigger fires again, updating the previously emitted total. Hence, the final consumer of these results knows to expect possible refinements shortly after the initial output.

Best Practices

The mentioned best practices help strike a balance between correctness, performance, and maintainability, while ensuring that pipelines remain accurate and reliable while avoiding unnecessary complexity that can degrade performance, or make systems difficult to operate and evolve over time. Here are some of them:

- **Keep Trigger Logic Simple Whenever Possible:** Start with default triggers and add complexity only when the business requires it. This is because complex triggers can be harder to maintain and debug.
- **Use Allowed Lateness Sparingly:** Allowing too much lateness can lead to many retractions and refinements. Limit it to what is realistically needed, and factor in data delays.

- **Test with Realistic Data:** Ensure that test data reflects real-world conditions, including late events, out-of-order arrivals, and varying levels of data volume. This validates that triggers and timers behave as intended under production scenarios.
- **Combine with State and Timers Judiciously:** While combining triggers, timers, and state can solve intricate problems, it can also produce complex pipelines. Consider if simpler solutions exist, such as adjusting window sizes or using built-in triggers, before resorting to custom logic.

Assigning Data to Windows

Combine with State and Timers Judiciously

In streaming data processing, the concept of windows is integral to managing unbounded data. Unlike batch processing, where the dataset is finite and fully available before computation, streams are theoretically endless and constantly evolving. Hence, to make sense of streaming data, developers partition it into finite, logical segments called windows. Windows serve as a lens that focuses on subsets of the input stream, while allowing computations like aggregations or pattern detection to be performed on manageable time-bound segments, rather than on an infinite flow of events.

When combined with stateful processing, triggers, and timers, windows form a cornerstone of Apache Beam's unified model. They help define the scope of computations, specifying not just how to compute values, but over what subset of data and time those computations apply. Hence, understanding how to assign data to windows and selecting the right windowing strategy is central to building effective Beam pipelines.

The Purpose of Windowing

Windowing is crucial in streaming scenarios for several reasons, as explained here:

- **Bounded Computations in Infinite Streams:** Without windows, a running average or sum would accumulate indefinitely as data flows in, growing unbounded. Windows let you divide the infinite stream into finite segments–such as every 5 minutes of data–which makes the computation tractable and facilitates the generation of regular outputs.
- **Temporal Context for Analytics:** Many real-world metrics are inherently time-based. For example, tracking hourly sales totals, daily page views, or session lengths requires associating events with specific time intervals. Windows ensure that computations align with these time-based requirements.
- **Handling Late and Out-of-Order Data:** Windows, in combination with triggers and allowed lateness, define when data is considered "on time" or "late", and how to handle elements that arrive after the window's intended boundary.

This allows pipelines to produce timely results, while still correcting those results if late data arrives.

- **Enabling Parallelization:** Each window can be processed independently, enabling parallel and distributed processing of streams. Hence, different workers can handle different windows or subsets of windows, and scale out computations efficiently.

Types of Windows in Apache Beam

Apache Beam supports several types of windows, each suited to different analytical patterns and data characteristics. The most commonly used windowing strategies are:

- **Fixed Windows:** Fixed windows break the timeline into equal-sized, non-overlapping intervals. For example, a pipeline might create 1-minute fixed windows that group all events occurring within that minute. After the minute passes, the window closes, and the pipeline can emit results. Therefore, fixed windows are simple, predictable, and commonly used for regular time-based metrics, such as minute-by-minute or hourly summaries.
- **Sliding Windows:** Sliding windows overlap over time. A sliding window has a fixed size (for example, 5 minutes) and a fixed period at which the window starts (the slide), which could be smaller than the window size. For example, a 5-minute window that slides every 1 minute produces overlapping segments such as:

  1. Window 1: [00:00 - 00:05)
  2. Window 2: [00:01 - 00:06)
  3. Window 3: [00:02 - 00:07)... and so forth.

     As you can see, this overlap allows each element to appear in multiple windows, while enabling computations like moving averages or near-real-time trend analyses, where the pipeline must consider partially overlapping time intervals.

- **Session Windows:** Session windows group events based on periods of activity separated by gaps of inactivity. Instead of using fixed or sliding intervals, session windows are dynamic, and they end when a certain gap passes with no new events. For example, if a session gap is defined as 30 minutes, then all events for a given user that occur within 30-minute intervals of each other belong to the same session. The session closes once 30 minutes pass without a new event. Moreover, session windows model user behavior or other activity-driven patterns more naturally than rigid time boundaries.
- **Custom Windows:** Apache Beam also allows developers to define custom

windowing functions for scenarios not covered by fixed, sliding, or session windows. Hence, custom windows can be tailored to unique business rules, domain-specific patterns, or irregular event flows.

Each window type represents a different way of grouping data. Thus, choosing the right windowing strategy depends on the analysis goals, the nature of the data, and how data timeliness and completeness factor into the pipeline's requirements.

Assigning Windows to Data

In Apache Beam, windows are assigned at runtime based on the event time (unless otherwise specified). When a **`Window.into()`** transform is applied to a **`PCollection`**, it does not immediately produce outputs. Instead, it records the chosen windowing strategy. Subsequent transforms that aggregate or group data (like **`GroupByKey`** or **`Combine`**) use the assigned windows to determine which elements belong together.

For example, to apply fixed windows of one minute, you may use:

```
PCollection<KV<String, Integer>> input = ...;

PCollection<KV<String, Integer>> windowed = input
    .apply(Window.<KV<String, Integer>>into(FixedWindows.of
(Duration.standardMinutes(1))));
```

Now, any subsequent aggregation occurs as per its corresponding 1-minute window. If the pipeline applies a **`GroupByKey`**, each key's values are grouped by their assigned 1-minute window. The runner handles the complexity of assigning elements to windows, and stores them accordingly.

Event Time vs. Processing Time

When assigning windows, the time domain chosen matters. By default, window assignments are based on event time, which is the recommended approach for correctness in most streaming systems. Therefore, the event time represents when the event actually occurred, as embedded in the event's timestamp. Processing time is simply the system time when the event is processed by the pipeline. Relying solely on processing time can lead to inconsistent semantics, if data arrives late or out-of-order.

Event Time Windowing:

- Aligns with the logical occurrence of events
- More stable and deterministic. It ensures that the same set of events always falls in the same window regardless of processing delays.
- Requires a watermark to track how far the pipeline has progressed through event time

Processing Time Windowing:

- Simpler and can be practical for certain real-time dashboards or latency-sensitive computations
- Susceptible to machine load, scheduling delays, and other runtime factors
- Windows assigned by processing time may vary run-to-run if data flow rates or system conditions differ

Hence, in most production pipelines, event time windowing is preferred for stable, correct results. Processing time windows are typically used for quick approximations, or where exact temporal semantics are not critical.

Watermarks and Window Assignment

Watermarks help the pipeline decide when to consider a window complete. Although watermarks primarily influence triggers and how late data is handled, they also affect window assignment. Consider that late data–events whose timestamps occur earlier than the current watermark–are still assigned to the same window they would have belonged to originally, but triggers might have already fired the window's results.

Thus, if late data frequently arrives, developers can configure allowed lateness, while enabling windows to consider these late elements after their initial closure. However, large allowed lateness intervals might mean windows remain "*open*" for reevaluation for extended periods, which can potentially lead to multiple result revisions.

Window Merging

Some window types, notably session windows, involve dynamic merging. As events arrive, the runner may detect that two sessions overlap or should logically combine into one. When this happens, windows merge, and their associated state and triggers must reconcile. Hence, handling merged windows introduces complexity, as the pipeline must gracefully adjust previously considered boundaries. Beam's model and runners handle these details, but developers should remain aware of the implications, which can be:

- Merging windows can produce unexpected results, if they are not carefully considered.
- Sessions grow dynamically, and triggers may fire multiple times as sessions evolve.
- State must be carefully managed, so that all relevant events are accounted for after merging.

Side Inputs and Window Assignment

Side inputs are additional **`PCollections`** that provide reference data to a DoFn, and are also windowed. By default, side inputs use the global window, but they can be assigned to windows if the reference data is time-dependent. This ensures that the side input's contents match the main input's temporal context. For example, if the main data stream is windowed by 1-hour fixed windows, a side input containing hourly exchange rates or configuration parameters can also be windowed. This synchronizes updates, so that each main window can see the correct side input data.

When using windowed side inputs, consider that the side input values must be available when the main input's window is processed. Beam's model ensures that side input data is available when needed, but developers must ensure that the side input's windowing, and that the triggers are aligning logically with the main input's windowing.

Choosing the Right Window Type

Selecting a window type depends on the nature of the data, as well as the desired analysis. Some of these guidelines are as follows:

- **Fixed Windows:**
  - They are best for regular, periodic summaries (for example, compute metrics every minute, every hour).
  - They are simpler to reason about because each window is a fixed interval.
  - They are useful when data is fairly evenly distributed over time, and whenever consistent interval-based reporting is required.
- **Sliding Windows:**
  - They are good for moving averages or trend analysis over a recent time horizon.
  - Each data point contributes to multiple windows, which result in smoother trend curves.
  - They are more computation-intensive due to overlapping windows, but offer finer granularity in real-time metrics.
- **Session Windows:**
  - They are ideal for grouping related events by periods of activity, instead of strict time intervals.
  - They are perfect for user behavior tracking, where sessions naturally start and end based on interaction patterns.
  - Complexity arises from merging windows, but they model real-world patterns more accurately, like user sessions or IoT device bursts of activity.

- **Custom Windows:**
  - They are useful if data patterns do not map neatly to fixed intervals, sliding intervals, or sessions.
  - They can implement arbitrary logic for assigning events to windows, for example, based on key-value signals, custom domain-specific heuristics, or external events.
  - They are generally more complex and less common, but offer maximum flexibility.

Integrating Windowing with Stateful Processing and Triggers

Windowing does not stand alone. It interacts closely with stateful processing and triggers in the following ways:

- **With Stateful Operations:** Each key's state is typically scoped to a window. For example, when computing a sum per hour per key, the state that keeps track of the current sum is bound by the window's boundaries. Once the window closes, the associated state can be cleared, while preventing infinite growth.

  Hence, this scoping ensures that the state is tied to a well-defined temporal segment, while simplifying data retention and cleanup.

- **With Triggers:** Triggers control when partial or final results for each window are emitted. Without triggers, results would only appear when the window closes. Therefore, by combining triggers with windowing, the pipeline can produce early results, handle late data gracefully, and emit final summaries once the window is truly complete.

  For example, a fixed window with a watermark-based trigger and allowed lateness may produce an initial output when the window ends, and then refine that output if additional late events arrive. It finally closes out the window after the allowed lateness period elapses.

Allowed Lateness and Window Persistence

Allowed lateness defines how long after a window's end the pipeline continues to accept late events for the window. By default, once a window is closed and its results are emitted, late arrivals are either discarded or sent to a special "late data" side output. Therefore, with allowed lateness configured, the pipeline can choose to re-open or re-output results for that window, while updating previously emitted values with new information.

This can be powerful, but must be used carefully. For large allowed lateness values:

- The pipeline may emit multiple result panes for the same window over a long period.

- State and resources remain dedicated to old windows, which can potentially increase memory and storage costs.
- Downstream consumers must handle updates, which might complicate their logic.

A balanced approach, therefore will be to choose a small but reasonable allowed lateness. This is because it can ensure timely results with a controlled amount of revisions.

Example Scenarios

- **IoT Sensor Data with Fixed Windows:** Imagine a pipeline that processes temperature readings from thousands of sensors. Assigning 1-minute fixed windows enables computing the average temperature per sensor per minute. Hence, it simplifies downstream analysis, and also allows for timely reporting. Developers might set allowed lateness to a few seconds to account for minor delays, while ensuring that slightly late readings still adjust the computed average before finalizing it.
- **User Behavior Analysis with Session Windows:** A streaming analytics platform tracks user interactions with a website. Events are keyed by user ID, and are then assigned to session windows with a 30-minute gap. If a user clicks at 10:00, 10:05, and 10:25, all these events belong to the same session. If another click arrives at 11:10, that event starts a new session. Hence, by using session windows, the pipeline naturally groups user activity into meaningful sessions without imposing arbitrary fixed intervals. Timers can be used to emit session summaries when sessions close.
- **Rolling Averages with Sliding Windows:** A financial service pipeline might need to compute a 5-minute rolling average of stock prices, updated every minute. Sliding windows of size 5 minutes with a slide of 1 minute let each minute's output reflect the last 5 minutes of prices. Each event contributes to multiple windows, while ensuring smooth transitions in the computed average. Triggers can be used to provide early estimates before all data arrives and refining values as late data comes in.
- **Complex Domain Logic with Custom Windows:** Suppose a streaming data feed represents logs from a manufacturing assembly line. Windows might be defined based on start/stop events in the machinery rather than strict time intervals. A custom windowing function could group all events between a machine "start" event and a corresponding "stop" event. This aligns window boundaries with the domain logic (machine runs) rather than the clock. Hence, such a pipeline might rely heavily on state to track machine states and timers to detect when a machine run ends.

Testing and Validating Windowing Behavior

Testing windowed pipelines can be more involved than testing stateless batch jobs. You can consider the following approaches:

- **Unit Tests with `TestStream`:** Use `TestStream` to inject events at controlled timestamps and manipulate watermarks. By simulating event arrival patterns, late data, and out-of-order events, tests can confirm that windows are behaving as expected, and that triggers are producing correct outputs at the right times.
- **Synthetic Data with Known Patterns:** Feed synthetic data where the timing and values are controlled. This simplifies verifying that windows close as intended, triggers fire appropriately, and late events are handled. For instance, insert a known number of events into a window, and then send an event late to check if the pipeline updates the output.
- **Compare Multiple Windowing Strategies:** In early stages of pipeline design, make sure that you prototype with different windowing options. Compare results from fixed windows versus sliding windows or session windows. You should also analyze performance, complexity, and output semantics to find the best fit for the application's needs.
- **Metrics and Logging:** Add logging that records when windows open, what data they receive, and when they close. Track how many times triggers fire per window. Use Beam metrics to measure the size of windows, or how often late data arrives. This data helps diagnose unexpected behaviors or performance issues.

Performance Considerations

While windowing provides structure and flexibility, it can also affect performance in the following ways:

- **Number of Windows per Element:** In sliding windows, each element belongs to multiple windows, which can increase the computational overhead and memory usage required to store state and produce multiple aggregated results. Therefore, you should balance the window size and slide interval.
- **Session Windows and Merging Overhead:** Session windows require merging, which can be computationally expensive if there are many overlapping sessions. Hence, optimizing the session gap or key distribution can reduce merges. For large, frequent merges, consider whether the complexity of sessions is truly necessary, or if a simpler approach could suffice.
- **Allowed Lateness and State Size:** Allowing significant lateness leads to retaining state for old windows far longer. This can inflate memory usage and

slow down processing. Hence, you must use allowed lateness sparingly, and consider shorter durations if possible.

- **Runner-Specific Optimizations:** Different runners handle windows and state storage in different ways. Some runners may optimize fixed window computations more efficiently than session windows, or provide native support for more advanced indexing structures that speed up merges.

  While Beam's abstraction ensures portability, small adjustments in windowing logic might lead to better performance on a given runner.

Integration with Downstream Systems

Finally, consider how downstream systems consume windowed outputs. If the pipeline produces incremental updates for a window until it finally closes, downstream consumers must handle multiple results for the same time interval or key. This might require either:

- Storing only the latest pane of results, overwriting previous outputs.
- Applying logic to reconcile updates, ensuring the final "late-corrected" result replaces earlier estimates.
- Designing a schema that includes pane information or output versioning, so that consumers can identify final results.

For stable and easy-to-consume outputs, many pipelines produce aggregates on stable boundaries (like hourly or daily fixed windows) and emit a single, final result once the watermark passes the window end. Therefore, this reduces complexity in downstream consumers, though it may introduce some latency.

Use Cases and Implementation Patterns

Having explored the theoretical underpinnings of stateful and stateless processing, handling state, using triggers and timers, and assigning data to windows, the next step is to look at how these concepts are applied in real-world scenarios. Practical implementations of Apache Beam pipelines often involve piecing together multiple features like windowing strategies, stateful transforms, triggers, and timers to solve complex streaming analytics problems. Hence, by examining common use cases, pipeline patterns, and domain-specific solutions, developers gain the insights needed to translate theory into practice.

Common Real-World Scenarios for Stateful and Windowed Pipelines

- **E-Commerce Analytics and Sessionization:** Modern e-commerce platforms generate continuous streams of user interactions such as page views, product clicks, cart additions, and purchases. Their analytics teams rely on session-based metrics to understand user behavior, identify popular products, and measure conversion funnels.

In Apache Beam, session windows naturally model user sessions: a session is created when a user arrives on the site, and is extended as long as the user keeps interacting within a specified inactivity gap. Stateful processing and timers help determine when a session ends. Triggers control when intermediate metrics (for example, items viewed or cart abandonment signals) are emitted. Eventually, the pipeline produces final session summaries that can be fed into recommendation systems, marketing analytics, or predictive models.

- **IoT Device Monitoring and Alerting:** Industrial IoT deployments require continuous monitoring of sensor data to detect anomalies, perform predictive maintenance, and optimize resource usage. Each device may emit a range of metrics (temperature, humidity, pressure) at varying rates. Processing this firehose of data involves aggregating readings over rolling windows, detecting abnormal patterns, and triggering alerts when thresholds are exceeded.

  A pipeline might use fixed windows to periodically aggregate sensor values, while producing hourly averages and min/max readings. Stateful transforms keep track of the running average per device, while triggers might emit early warnings if a threshold is breached before the window closes. Timers can be set to detect prolonged inactivity or sudden spikes. Therefore, late data handling becomes critical if network congestion or intermittent device connectivity delays event arrival.

- **Financial Data Streaming and Fraud Detection:** Financial institutions process continuous streams of transactions that must be analyzed in near real-time to detect fraud and ensure regulatory compliance. Aggregations over short, fixed windows can identify unusual activity patterns, like a sudden spike in high-value withdrawals. Stateful operations store historical transaction counts per account, and trigger emit alerts whenever suspicious criteria are met.

  More sophisticated fraud detection may utilize custom windows aligned with business logic—for instance, considering all transactions that occur between two known events, or dynamically adjusting window sizes based on transaction frequency. Hence, timers schedule checks after certain intervals, while ensuring that delays or out-of-order events do not leave potential fraudulent activity undetected.

- **Digital Advertising and Campaign Performance Tracking:** Online advertising platforms measure the performance of ad campaigns in terms of impressions, clicks, conversions, and engagement over sliding time windows. By using sliding windows, pipelines continuously update metrics, such as a rolling

30-minute click-through rate updated every 5 minutes. Stateful operations track user interaction sequences, session windows group related events for each user's interaction, while triggers ensure timely updates of campaign performance dashboards.

Therefore, late data handling is crucial since conversion events (like a purchase) might be reported long after the initial click due to attribution models. Beam's model allows re-emitting refined metrics when conversions appear late, while ensuring that advertisers receive accurate performance statistics.

- **Healthcare and Medical Device Data Streams:** Healthcare providers increasingly rely on streams of patient data from wearable devices, hospital sensors, and medical equipment. Thus, analyzing this data in real-time can improve patient outcomes, detect early warning signs, and optimize resource allocation. Pipelines might window data by patient, and use custom triggers that fire when critical thresholds are exceeded (for example, heart rate or blood pressure anomalies). The state is used to accumulate patient metrics over time, while timers send alerts to clinicians if conditions persist beyond a certain duration.

  Session windows model periods of patient activity or attention windows (such as time spent in a hospital wing). Therefore, allowed lateness can handle delayed reporting from remote sensors, while ensuring that medical staff always have the most updated and accurate readings.

Pattern-Based Implementations

Instead of looking at use cases by domain, another approach is to consider common pipeline patterns that apply across industries. Some of these patterns are:

- **Rolling Aggregations with Sliding Windows:**

  Pattern: Compute a rolling statistic (for example, average, sum, percentile) over a recent period.

  Implementation:

  i. Assign sliding windows over the chosen time horizon.

  ii. Use `CombiningState` to maintain running aggregates for each key.

  iii. Set triggers for early and repeated firing as windows slide forward.

  iv. Clear state when the window is complete or after a certain period.

  Example: A pipeline that computes a 10-minute rolling average CPU load for each server, is updated every minute. Each server key maintains a sliding window. A trigger fires every minute, producing a refined average. If late data arrives, it updates the average before finalizing the window.

- **Sessionization with Timers:**

  Pattern: Group data into sessions based on activity gaps and produce results after sessions end.

  Implementation:

  i. Use session windows with a defined gap duration.

  ii. Store user events in **`BagState`** keyed by user ID.

  iii. Set a timer that fires after the session gap elapses.

  iv. On timer firing, aggregate the collected events, output session metrics, and clear state.

  Example: A web analytics pipeline tracking user clicks. If no click occurs for 30 minutes, the session ends. The timer firing event triggers output of the session's aggregated metrics.

- **Alerting on Threshold Breaches:**

  Pattern: Identify if a metric exceeds a threshold within a certain time frame, and emit an alert.

  Implementation:

  i. Use fixed windows for periodic evaluation, or rely on event-time timers for dynamic timeframes.

  ii. Maintain stateful counts or sums per key (device, user, or account) in a **`ValueState`**.

  iii. If the state surpasses a threshold, output an alert. Optionally, set a timer to reset the state or revert conditions after a cool down period.

  Example: A pipeline that monitors financial transactions per account in a 10-minute window. If total withdrawals exceed a certain limit, emit a fraud alert. A timer might reset counts after action is taken.

- **Complex Pattern Recognition via State Machines:**

  Pattern: Detect event patterns that span multiple windows or depend on specific sequences.

  Implementation:

  i. Represent the pattern as a state machine, where each state is stored in **`ValueState`**, and transitions occur on specific event types.

ii. Use timers to progress the state machine if events don't arrive on time.

iii. Windowing may be fixed or session-based, but the key idea is that stateful logic tracks the partial matches. Once a pattern is complete or a timeout occurs, emit a result.

Example: Fraud detection might require seeing a sequence like "`login followed by large withdrawal within 5 minutes, followed by an account detail change`". A pipeline uses state to track where in the pattern the user is and triggers outputs when a full match occurs.

- **Data Enrichment with State and Side Inputs:**

  Pattern: Enhance streaming data with reference data that changes over time. **Implementation**:

  i. Window both the main data stream and the side input.

  ii. Use state to store partial aggregates and timers to refresh reference data from side inputs as they evolve.

  iii. Combine these features to produce fully enriched output records.

  Example: A pipeline that merges a stream of log messages with a slowly updating mapping of IP addresses to user accounts. The mapping might be updated hourly; therefore, you must use a timer to reload side input data and store it in `MapState` keyed by IP. As log events arrive, look up the current user in the map state and attach that user info.

Testing and Validation in Practice

Practical applications demand robust testing. Real data streams are often messy, and pipelines may operate continuously for long periods. Therefore, ensuring correctness and performance under production conditions should be your topmost priority. To initiate testing and validation in practice, you must consider these tips:

- **Test Multiple Aspects of the Pipeline:**
  - **Functional Tests:** Validate that the pipeline produces correct aggregations, session metrics, and alerts. Use `TestStream` to simulate input streams with varied timestamps, out-of-order elements, and late data.
  - **Performance and Load Tests:** High data rates can stress stateful operations. Use synthetic workloads to ensure that the pipeline maintains low latency and high throughput under peak conditions.
  - **Fault Tolerance Tests:** Intentionally introduce worker failures. Confirm that the state is restored correctly and timers still fire as expected.

Validate that outputs remain consistent, and that no data is lost or double-counted.

- **Mocking External Systems:** Many practical pipelines integrate with external systems like databases, APIs, or storage services. Mock these systems during testing to ensure that the pipeline handles delays, partial failures, or slow responses gracefully.
- **Replay and Regression Testing:** As Beam pipelines are event-time aware, it is possible to replay historical data streams to test how changes in windowing strategy, triggers, or state logic affect outputs. Therefore, regression testing ensures that modifications do not introduce correctness regressions or performance regressions.

Operational Considerations

Building the pipeline is only part of the story. Running, monitoring, and maintaining a Beam pipeline in production, therefore involve the following operational best practices:

- **Choosing the Right Runner:** The choice of runner (for example, Dataflow, Flink, Spark) influences state storage options, performance characteristics, and available observability tools. For large-scale applications, a runner with robust state backends and advanced checkpointing (like Apache Flink), or auto-scaling capabilities (like Dataflow) may be preferred.
- **Scaling State and Managing Resources:** Large states require careful resource management. If the session windows generate massive state for active users, consider strategies like partial aggregations, splitting sessions by sub-keys, or using combining states that reduce memory footprint. Additionally, do not forget to monitor metrics to identify bottlenecks and hot keys.
- **Cloud and On-Premise Deployments:** Deploying pipelines in the cloud often integrates with managed services for storage and monitoring. On-premise deployments may rely on self-managed distributed storage for state. Therefore, you must ensure that stateful operations are tuned for the underlying infrastructure, and that triggers and timers behave consistently across environments.
- **Monitoring and Observability:** Use Beam's metrics to track the number of elements processed per key, the average size of states, how often triggers fire, and how many late events arrive. Combine these metrics with logs and runner-specific dashboards to gain a complete picture of pipeline health.
- **Upgrades and Schema Evolution:** Pipelines may run for months or years. Over time, data schemas can change, and windowing strategies may need to be adjusted. Implement robust versioning and schema evolution strategies to

ensure backward compatibility. Write data in formats that tolerate missing fields or additional attributes over time.

Advanced Techniques

As developers gain experience, they may experiment with advanced patterns that blend multiple concepts:

- **Chaining Stateful Transforms:** A pipeline might apply several stateful transforms in sequence. For example, first, group events into windows to compute intermediate aggregates, and then apply a sessionization transform on top of those results to identify user-level patterns. Each transform can maintain its own state, triggers, and timers to form a layered approach to data refinement.
- **Dynamically Changing Windows or Triggers at Runtime:** While not a common scenario, some advanced use cases may adjust window sizes or trigger parameters dynamically based on observed traffic patterns. This requires careful coding and testing, as dynamically changing window assignments or triggers can complicate state management and consistency.
- **Machine Learning (ML) Integration:** Stateful pipelines can maintain feature aggregates and feed them into online ML models. Timers trigger model evaluations or updates. For example, a real-time fraud detection model might rely on stateful aggregations of user behavior, and ends up triggering that update to the model's inputs every few minutes. Windowing thus ensures that the features reflect recent activity, while state maintains historical baselines.
- **Multi-Stage Windowing and Sessionization:** Complex scenarios might involve applying different windowing strategies at different stages. For instance, first apply fixed windows to batch events into daily partitions, then within each partition, apply session windows keyed by user to find meaningful sessions. This hierarchical approach can simplify data management and reduce memory pressure.

Integration with Other Framework Features

Stateful processing, windowing, triggers, and timers are powerful tools within Beam's ecosystem, but they also interact with other Beam capabilities such as:

- **Side Outputs and Error Handling:** Complex pipelines often need to separate normal results from error conditions. Late data that arrives too late for even allowed lateness might be sent to a side output. Similarly, corrupted records might be redirected to an error handling **`PCollection`**. State can track how many errors occurred per key, and triggers might emit alerts if too many errors accumulate within a window.

- **Stateful Splittable DoFns:** Splittable DoFns allow pipelines to handle large or infinite sources in a parallelizable manner. Therefore, you can combine splittable DoFns with state and timers to handle backpressure or rate-limiting scenarios. For instance, a pipeline reading from an external streaming API could use a splittable DoFn to manage checkpoints and reassign work as needed, while timers periodically poll for new data, and also update state to maintain progress counters.
- **SQL Transforms:** Apache Beam SQL allows developers to write queries over streaming data. Under the hood, SQL transforms translate to Beam primitives involving windowing, grouping, and stateful aggregations. Understanding how state, triggers, and timers work at a low level aids in reasoning about the behavior of SQL-based pipelines, and optimizing their performance.

Retrospectives and Post-Production Analysis

Even after a pipeline is in production, continuous improvement is possible. Analyze historical metrics to see if windowing configurations are optimal. Are certain windows producing too many updates due to late data? Are triggers firing too frequently, causing performance overhead? Could session windows be refined with a different gap size to capture user behavior more accurately?

Therefore, you must regularly revisit and refine pipeline logic to ensure that it remains aligned with evolving business requirements and data characteristics. Adjust triggers to emit fewer redundant updates, tweak allowed lateness to reduce churn, or experiment with a different window type if usage patterns change.

Handling Complexity and Maintaining Pipeline Quality

As pipelines grow in complexity, managing their logic, performance, and maintainability becomes crucial. Hence, you must consider these best practices:

- **Modularization:** Break complex pipelines into well-defined components. For example, separate the logic for window assignment from the logic for stateful aggregation. This improves readability, testability, and reusability.
- **Documentation:** Document why certain windowing strategies, triggers, or stateful patterns are chosen. Additionally, include examples of typical

input/output behaviors, handling of late data, and expected performance characteristics.

- **Version Control and Continuous Integration (CI):** Keep pipeline code in version control and run CI pipelines with automated tests. Verify that changes to windowing or triggers do not produce unexpected regressions.
- **Incremental Rollouts and Canary Testing:** When changing windowing strategies or adding stateful computations, roll out changes incrementally. Test with a small portion of the data stream to validate correctness and performance before applying them to the entire pipeline.

Example End-to-End Pipeline

To tie these concepts together, consider a simplified end-to-end scenario:

- **Use Case:** A global news aggregator collects headlines from various sources, calculates trending topics, and emits these trends every 5 minutes for dashboards and alerts.

  Approach:

  1. **Input and Keying:** Each event is a headline with a timestamp and category tags. A key is determined by topic or keyword.
  2. **Windowing:** Assign data to fixed 5-minute windows based on event time.
  3. **Stateful Aggregation:** Maintain a count of how often each keyword appears in the current window using a `CombiningState`.
  4. **Triggers:** Use a watermark-based trigger that fires after the window end, along with an early trigger every 1 minute for preliminary trends. Allowed lateness of 1 minute handles slightly delayed headlines.
  5. **Timers (Optional):** If a keyword suddenly stops appearing, a timer might be set to check if it should be dropped from the trending list after some inactivity period, while clearing state and resources.
  6. **Outputs:** When triggers fire, output current trending keywords. Late arrivals may update previously emitted results if they appear before the allowed lateness period expires.
  7. **Monitoring:** Track the number of panes emitted per window, the volume of late data, and the size of the state per keyword to ensure that the performance is stable.
  8. **Refinement:** If too many updates are emitted, reduce the frequency of early triggers or shorten allowed lateness. If data arrives too late, consider

adjusting watermark generation, or providing a slightly longer allowed lateness to improve accuracy.

Hence, this scenario demonstrates multiple concepts like windowing for time-based segmentation, stateful aggregations for counting, triggers for timely outputs, and allowed lateness for handling real-world data delays integrate. This demonstrates how a global news aggregator can use Apache Beam to collect headlines from multiple sources, and analyze the topics which are trending and publish them.

Conclusion

The discussed scenario brings together the core ideas of stateful stream processing in Apache Beam, while showing how windowing enables time-based segmentation; how stateful logic maintains evolving context; how triggers control when results are emitted, and the way allowed lateness ensures correctness in the presence of delayed or out-of-order data. Together, these capabilities illustrate how Beam provides a robust, scalable, and fault-tolerant model for solving complex real-world streaming problems while still allowing developers to write clear and expressive business logic. Hence, by understanding how to balance stateless and stateful processing, managing state safely, and using timers and triggers effectively, you will be now able to design pipelines that are both powerful and maintainable.

In *Chapter 3, Handling Event Time, Windows, and Triggers*, we will explore the foundations that make these mechanisms work. You will explore event time versus processing time in detail, learn how different windowing strategies shape pipeline behavior, and understand how triggers and watermarks work together to control correctness, latency, as well as the completeness of results in streaming pipelines.

CHAPTER 3
Handling Event Time, Windows, and Triggers

Introduction

Streaming data pipelines introduce unique challenges around time because events may arrive late, out of order, or at irregular intervals. Therefore, it is essential to distinguish when an event actually occurred from, and when it is processed by the system. Apache Beam addresses these challenges through a powerful and consistent model built around event time processing, windowing, watermarks, and triggers. These concepts allow developers to reason about time correctly, produce accurate aggregations, and handle real-world imperfections in streaming data such as network delays and retries.

Hence, in this chapter, you will learn how to differentiate between event time and processing time, and understand why that distinction is critical for correctness. You will also explore how windowing groups data into meaningful time-based segments using fixed, sliding, and session windows, and how triggers control when results are emitted, including early and late outputs. Additionally, you will see how watermarks track progress in event time and enable reliable handling of late data. Through practical examples and code samples in both Python and Java, this chapter will provide you a hands-on foundation for building robust, time-aware streaming pipelines in Apache Beam.

Structure

In this chapter, we will cover the following topics:

- Event Time vs. Processing Time
- Windowing Concepts

- Fixed Windows (Tumbling Windows)
- Sliding Windows
- Session Windows
- Trigger Mechanisms
- Event-Time Triggers
- Processing-Time Triggers
- Data-Driven (Count) Triggers
- Composite Triggers
- Accumulation vs. Discarding Modes
- Watermarks
- Late Data Handling
- Allowed Lateness
- Real-World Applications of Windows and Triggers
- Monitoring and Debugging Windowed Pipelines

Event Time vs. Processing Time

In streaming systems, there are two different "times" to consider for each data element, which are:

- **Event Time:** This is when the event actually occurred, as recorded by the event itself (often a timestamp in the data).
- **Processing Time:** This refers to when the event is observed and processed by the pipeline (the time according to the system that processes the data).

These two times can differ significantly. Moreover, there is some lag between an event happening and it being processed; as a result, events might arrive out of order.

For example, if a user's phone goes offline and later sends events, the *event time* might be when the user performed an action, whereas the *processing time* is later when the data finally reaches the server. In any realistic scenario, **event time and processing time rarely align perfectly**–this can be seen in network delays, offline devices, or system lags that cause events to be processed later than they have occurred.

Thus, understanding this difference is crucial. If we only use processing time (that is, when the data is seen by the pipeline) to group and analyze events, our results can be incorrect when the data arrives late. Hence, Apache Beam by default uses **event time** for computations (especially windowing), so that results reflect the actual time of events, and not just the arrival order. Beam attaches a timestamp to each element (the event time), and uses this timestamp for time-based groupings like windows.

Meanwhile, processing time is used for driving certain triggers or background timers, but not for the primary event grouping, by default.

Reasons This Matters: Consider an example where we want to count user clicks in 1-minute intervals. If a click from 9:01 AM arrives only at 9:05 AM (due to delay), an event-time approach will still count that click in the 9:01-9:02 AM window (where it belongs by event time). A processing-time approach without special handling would count it in the 9:05 AM window, or it might miss the intended window entirely. Therefore, by using the event time, Beam's model ensures that **late-arriving data can still be processed in the correct window** (with some limitations that we will discuss in the section addressing watermarks and lateness).

Beam's programming model attaches timestamps to each element. Many data sources (like messaging systems) can provide an event timestamp for each element. In Apache Beam, every element is associated with a timestamp that represents its event time. In most cases, this timestamp is automatically provided by the I/O connector. For example, messaging systems such as Kafka or Pub/Sub typically attach event timestamps as part of the message metadata, and Beam propagates these timestamps into the pipeline without requiring any extra work from the developer. Therefore, before assigning timestamps manually, you should always chcck the documentation of the chosen I/O connector to understand how timestamps are populated by default.

Manual timestamp assignment is usually required only when the source does not supply meaningful event times, such as when reading raw files, logs, or byte streams, or when the true event time is embedded inside the data payload itself (for example, as a field in a JSON record). In such cases, Beam provides explicit mechanisms to set timestamps. In Java, this is done using the **`WithTimestamps`** transform, while in Python you can use **`beam.window.TimestampedValue,`** or apply a **`ParDo`** that emits elements with assigned timestamps. This ensures that event-time processing, windowing, and triggering operate on the correct logical time, rather than on ingestion or processing time.

If your source does not provide one (for example, reading from a log file of events), you should assign event timestamps in your pipeline. Beam provides transforms to assign timestamps manually. In Java, you can use the **`WithTimestamps`** transform; in Python, you can use **`beam.window.TimestampedValue`** or apply a **`ParDo`** to set timestamps.

For example, suppose we have a **`PCollection`** of events (each event has a field timestamp which is the event's occurrence time in milliseconds since epoch). We can assign event time timestamps as follows:

```
// Java: Assign event timestamps to each element (assuming Event
has getTimestamp())
PCollection<Event> events = p.apply("ReadEvents", ...);
PCollection<Event> eventsWithTs = events.apply("AssignEventTime",
```

```
        WithTimestamps.of((Event e) -> new Instant(e.getTimestamp()))
            .withAllowedTimestampSkew(Duration.ZERO));

# Python: Assign event timestamps using TimestampedValue
import apache_beam as beam
from apache_beam import window

events = p | "ReadEvents" >> beam.Create([...])  # or read from
source
# Assuming each event is a dict with a 'timestamp' field (Unix ep-
och seconds)
events_with_ts = events | "AssignEventTime" >> beam.Map(lambda e:
window.TimestampedValue(e, e['timestamp']))
```

In the Java example above, **`WithTimestamps.of(...)`** takes a function to extract the event time from each element. We use **`Duration.ZERO`** for allowed skew to ensure that we do not assign timestamps far in the future (for safety, Beam requires specifying allowed timestamp skew if event timestamps might be significantly behind or ahead of processing time). In the Python example, we wrap each element 'e' in a **`TimestampedValue`** with the event's timestamp. After this step, each element in the **`PCollection`** has its event timestamp attached in Beam's records.

Now that the events have proper event-time timestamps, we can use Beam's time-based transformations correctly. Next, we will see how to group events by time into **windows** using these timestamps.

Windowing Concepts

Windowing is the mechanism that allows grouping unbounded, continuous data into finite chunks based on time. Instead of waiting for all data (which is infinite in streaming) to arrive, we divide the data by time, so that we can compute aggregates on each chunk. Hence, Beam's model supports different windowing strategies to cover common patterns of grouping by time.

In Beam, each element belongs to one or more windows, determined by its event timestamp and the windowing function. All elements in the same window are processed together for aggregations (like counts, sums, and so on). Beam's default, if you do nothing, is a single **global window** (all data ends up in one window). For bounded (batch) data, the global window is often fine because the data is finite. However, for unbounded (streaming) data, a global window would never "finish" (since data keeps coming); therefore, you can almost always apply a finite windowing strategy for streaming.

Types of Windows in Apache Beam

- **Global Window:** This is a single window that contains all elements and the default one for a bounded **`PCollection`.** In streaming, using a global window requires triggers to periodically emit results, since it never ends by itself. In a streaming pipeline, the Global Window has no natural end, so the default trigger (which waits for the watermark to pass the end of the window) will never fire because the end time is effectively infinite **(`MaxTimestamp`)**. As a result, your pipeline may appear to "hang", and will produce no output at all. Therefore, to make a Global Window usable in streaming, you must define a custom trigger, such as **`Repeatedly.forever(AfterProcessingTime…),`** so that the results are emitted periodically based on processing time and other conditions.

- **Fixed-Time Windows (Tumbling Windows):** Windows that represent non-overlapping, consistent time intervals (for example, every 5 minutes, on the minute). Each event falls into one fixed window based on its timestamp, and the windows do not overlap.
- **Sliding Windows:** These are windows that have a fixed duration but can overlap. A sliding window is defined by a window duration and a slide (or period) interval. For example, if there are 10-minute windows that slide at every 5 minutes, an event may belong to multiple overlapping windows (which allow repeated counting in multiple periods).
- **Session Windows:** Windows that represent periods of activity separated by gaps of inactivity. A session window has a gap duration (inactivity threshold). Events are grouped into the same session if each consecutive event arrives within the gap duration from the previous one. If there is a longer pause than the gap, a new session starts. Session windows can vary in size, and are great for capturing user sessions or bursts of activity.

Now, let us dive deeper into the three main types (Fixed, Sliding, Session) of windows, and see how to use them in practice.

Fixed Windows

Fixed windows (also known as tumbling windows) divide the timeline into equal-length, back-to-back intervals. For example, we might window events into 1-minute intervals at 00:00–00:59, 01:00–01:59, 02:00–02:59, and so on (assuming time in seconds and minutes). Thus, an event with timestamp 10:02:15 falls into the 10:02:00–10:02:59 window. Fixed windows **do not overlap**, as each moment in time belongs to exactly one fixed window.

Use Case: Fixed windows are useful for periodic reporting, such as "compute the number of clicks per minute", or "average sensor reading every hour". They provide a simple, regular time-based grouping.

Apache Beam Implementation: To apply fixed windowing in Beam, you use the **Window** transform (Java) or **WindowInto** (Python) with a **FixedWindows** windowing function.

- ***Java***: Use **Window.into(FixedWindows.of(Duration))** to specify the window length. For example, **FixedWindows.of(Duration.standardMinutes(5))** for 5-minute windows.
- **Python**: Use beam.WindowInto(beam.window.FixedWindows(window_size)). The window size is typically given in seconds for the Python SDK (for example, **FixedWindows(300)** for 5 minutes).

```
// Java: Apply a fixed window of 5 minutes to a PCollection of
events
import org.apache.beam.sdk.transforms.windowing.FixedWindows;
import org.joda.time.Duration;

PCollection<Event> events = ...;  // assume this is our stream of
events with timestamps
PCollection<Event> windowedByFixed = events.apply(
    Window.into(FixedWindows.of(Duration.standardMinutes(5)))
);

# Python: Apply a fixed window of 5 minutes (300 seconds)
import apache_beam as beam

events = ...  # PCollection of events with timestamps
windowed_by_fixed = events | beam.WindowInto(beam.window.Fixed
Windows(300))
```

After this transform, the **PCollection windowedByFixed** is partitioned into 5-minute windows. If we now perform a grouping or aggregation (like **a .apply(Count.perKey())** or **CombineGlobally**) on **windowedByFixed**, it will be computed separately for each 5-minute window rather than over the entire collection. For instance, counting on this **PCollection** will produce one count per window (and per key, if a key is involved), such as "**Window [10:00-10:05) count = X, Window [10:05-10:10) count = Y**", and so on.

Sliding Windows

Sliding windows also have a fixed duration, but they "slide" by a specified interval, which can be smaller than the window duration. This means windows can overlap. An element can belong to multiple sliding windows if windows overlap at that timestamp.

A sliding window is defined by two parameters: **window duration** and **window period (or slide interval)**. For example, consider 10-minute windows that start every

5 minutes. The first window might cover 0–10 minutes, the second window 5–15 minutes, the third 10–20 minutes, and so on. Hence, an event at time 12 minutes would belong to the window [10–20), as well as to [5–15), since those windows overlap that timestamp. In general, with window duration D and slide P, an event will fall into ⌈D/P⌉ windows.

This mathematical property has important performance implications. As each element belongs to multiple overlapping windows, Beam must internally replicate that element (or its contribution) for every window it falls into. In practice, this means that an element is duplicated approximately ⌈D / P⌉ times in internal state. If the window duration D is large and the slide interval P is small—such as a 1-hour window sliding every second—each event would be copied into thousands of windows, and will lead to a significant increase in state size, memory usage, and computation cost. For this reason, sliding windows should be chosen carefully, as they can help you balance analytical needs against resource consumption.

Use Case: Sliding windows are useful for computing moving averages or trends, where you want overlapping analyses. For example, a sliding window can produce an update every minute for the last 5 minutes of data (this is common in dashboarding, to see a rolling window of activity).

Apache Beam Implementation: In Java, use **`SlidingWindows.of(Duration windowSize).every(Duration period)`**. In Python, use **`beam.window.SlidingWindows(window_size, window_period)`**.

Example: Sliding Windows in Code

```
// Java: 10-minute windows that slide every 5 minutes
import org.apache.beam.sdk.transforms.windowing.SlidingWindows;

PCollection<Event> events = ...;
PCollection<Event> windowedBySliding = events.apply(
    Window.into(SlidingWindows.of(Duration.standardMinutes(10))
                              .every(Duration.standardMin-
utes(5)))
);

# Python: 10-minute windows sliding every 5 minutes
windowed_by_sliding = events | beam.WindowInto(beam.window.
SlidingWindows(600, 300))
# 600 seconds = 10 minutes window, 300 seconds = 5 minutes slide
```

Session Windows

Session windows group events by *periods of activity* separated by inactivity gaps. Unlike fixed or sliding windows, session windows do not have a fixed length, but they **dynamically expand** based on data. You define a *gap duration*, which is the maximum allowed time between consecutive events in a session. Hence, Beam will create a new session window, whenever it sees a gap in events that is larger than the gap duration.

For example, suppose the gap duration is 30 minutes. If a user has events at 10:00 and 10:10, they are within 30 minutes, so they are a part of the same session (the session starts with the 10:00 event and remains open because the 10:10 event arrives within the 30-minute gap). If the next event from that user arrives at 11:00 (50 minutes later), it is beyond the gap, so the first session closes (after the 10:10 event, the session is considered active until 10:40; if no further event arrives before then, the session closes), and a new session starts at 11:00. If another event comes at 11:20, it is 20 minutes after 11:00, which is still within the 30-minute gap, so it extends that session to 11:20. If no more events arrive, the session will close after waiting out the gap.

Session windows are particularly useful for grouping user interactions or any events that naturally cluster in time with idle periods in between.

Use Case: These windows can be found in clickstream sessions, machine active periods, rides in a taxi app (from start to end of a ride), and so on.

Apache Beam Implementation: In Java, use **`Sessions.withGapDuration(Duration)`**. In Python, use **`beam.window.Sessions(gap_duration)`**.

Example: Session Windows in Code

```
// Java: Session windows with 30-minute gap
import org.apache.beam.sdk.transforms.windowing.Sessions;

PCollection<Event> eventsByUser = ...; // assume it is keyed by
user or we will key it
PCollection<Event> windowedBySession = eventsByUser.apply(
    Window.into(Sessions.withGapDuration(Duration.standard
Minutes(30)))
);
# Python: Session windows with 30-minute gap (1800 seconds)
windowed_by_session = events | beam.WindowInto(beam.window.
Sessions(1800))
```

Typically, session windows are applied on a per-key basis, where you first key your **`PCollection`** by some entity (like user ID) using **`beam.GroupByKey`** or similar, and then apply session windowing, so that the sessions are computed per key. In Java, you might do **`.apply(Window.into(Sessions...)).apply(GroupByKey.create())`** for keyed collections. In Python, if you use **`beam.GroupByKey()`** after windowing, Beam will group elements by key and window (therefore, you get the session grouping behavior).

Important: Session windows can merge. If two separate session windows end up touching or overlapping (say, if an event arrives just at the boundary of the gap), Beam will merge those sessions into a single one. The windowing function handles this merging under the hood.

Now, we have seen how to define windows. However, when do we get the results for each window, especially in a streaming context where data might arrive late or out of order? This is where **triggers** and **watermarks** come into play. By default, Beam will wait until it believes that it has seen all data for a window before producing the output for that window. However, you might want earlier results, or need to handle late data arriving after the fact. Hence, we will explore triggers, which give us fine-grained control over when to emit the results of each window.

Trigger Mechanisms

A **trigger** in Apache Beam determines **when to emit the aggregated results of a window**. In batch (bounded) processing, the default behavior is to emit results when the window (often global or fixed interval) is complete, which for bounded data is the occasion when all the data is processed. In streaming (unbounded data), since data keeps coming, Beam's default trigger for time windows is based on the **event-time watermark**—essentially, it will output the window result when Beam estimates that no more events will arrive for that window (we will discuss watermarks soon). This default is an *event-time trigger at end of window.*

However, depending on your use case, you might not want to wait until all data has arrived and might want:

- **Early results** (speculative results) before the window is fully complete, to get low-latency updates.
- To **handle late arrivals** by emitting updates if data arrives after the window's first result was given.

Triggers let you configure these behaviors. With triggers, we can emit multiple times per window (multiple "panes" of results); for example, one early pane, one on-time pane, and optional late panes for late data. Or, we can simply change the conditions of when a result is produced.

Beam provides several types of triggers:

- **Event Time Triggers:** These operate on the event-time progress (the watermark). The default trigger in Beam is event-time based, which fires once when the watermark passes the end of the window (that is when Beam believes that the all on-time data for that window has arrived).
- **Processing Time Triggers:** These operate on processing time (wall-clock time). For example, a trigger that fires every 1 minute of *processing time* regardless

of event time. These are useful for early results (for example "give me updates every minute in real time").

- **Data-Driven Triggers (Count-Based):** These trigger based on properties of the data itself, such as a certain number of elements have arrived. For instance, fire after every 100 elements in the window.
- **Composite Triggers:** Combinations of the above triggers. You can create complex logic like "fire after 1 minute of processing time *or* 100 elements, whichever comes first", or "fire early after 1 minute, and always fire once at end-of-window". Beam also has helper triggers like **`AfterAny`**, **`AfterAll`**, Repeatedly, and so on, to combine triggers.

Hence, by configuring triggers, you trade-off between **completeness** of results and **latency**. A very slow trigger (like waiting for all data) gives complete results but high latency, whereas a fast trigger (for example, every few seconds) gives low latency. However, the results might be partial, and would need updates.

Default Behavior: If you do not set a trigger, Beam uses a default event-time trigger that emits once per window when the watermark passes the window's end, and it will discard any late data (late data is dropped by default). This yields one output per window containing all the on-time data. There are no early results, and the late data is ignored.

Therefore, to obtain a different behavior, we must set a trigger explicitly. When we set a trigger in Beam, we also need to consider some other settings such as:

- **Allowed Lateness:** This refers to the time you have to wait for the late data after a window closes (we will elaborate more about it in the next section, but for now, you should know that it essentially keeps the window open for late events).
- **Accumulation Mode:** This refers to if you would accumulate the data across trigger firings, or discard it after each firing. Here is a brief description of each mode:
  - **Discarding Mode**: Each trigger firing outputs the data for that pane, and then forgets those elements (the next firing will only include new elements).
  - **Accumulation Mode**: It controls how the *contents of each pane* are produced when a trigger fires. It does not delete or lose window data arbitrarily; instead, it determines whether each pane represents a **delta** or a **snapshot** of the window's current state.
- **Discarding Mode (`DiscardingFiredPanes`):** In this mode, the trigger firing outputs only the elements that have arrived since the previous firing. After emitting a pane, those elements are "forgotten" for future panes. This is best understood as producing **deltas**. However, it does not mean that

the data is lost; it simply means that each pane contains *only new changes.* This mode is useful when writing incremental updates, for example:

- Inserting new rows into a database
- Appending records to a log
- Applying incremental updates to downstream systems

- **Accumulating Mode (`AccumulatingFiredPanes`):**

  In this mode, every trigger that fires outputs all the elements seen so far in the window, including those emitted in the previous panes.

  This produces **snapshots** of the current window state. Each new pane represents the latest total.

  This mode is useful when:

  - We are updating a database row with the latest aggregate (for example, `UPDATE count = latest_value`).
  - We are maintaining dashboards where values should always reflect the full current total.
  - We are emitting corrected results as late data arrives.

A simple mental model looks like this:

Mode	**Pane Meaning**	**Typical DB Action**
Discarding	Delta	INSERT/APPEND
Accumulating	Snapshot	UPDATE/UPSERT

***Table 3.1**: Comparison of Accumulating and Discarding Modes*

Hence, this framing helps us avoid the misconception that "discarding" implies data loss. Instead, it is about whether each pane contains *only what changed* or *the full current result.*

Now, let us look at an example of using triggers in Beam. Suppose that we have a streaming pipeline with a 5-minute fixed window, but we want to emit an early result for each window every 1 minute of processing time, and then also handle late data up to 5 minutes late. We can achieve this by:

1. Setting an event-time trigger to fire at the end of window (this happens by default with `AfterWatermark`).
2. Adding an early trigger on processing time (at every minute).
3. Allowing lateness of 5 minutes, and then adding a late trigger (for example, fire each time late data arrives, or you could fire once after the end of allowed lateness).

In Java, we might configure this with the Window transform's trigger API, which might look like this:

```
import org.apache.beam.sdk.transforms.windowing.AfterWatermark;
import org.apache.beam.sdk.transforms.windowing.AfterProcessing-
Time;
import org.apache.beam.sdk.transforms.windowing.AfterPane;
import org.apache.beam.sdk.transforms.windowing.AccumulationMode;
import org.joda.time.Duration;

PCollection<Event> events = ...;
PCollection<Event> windowed = events.apply(
    Window.<Event>into(FixedWindows.of(Duration.standardMin-
utes(5)))
        .triggering(AfterWatermark.pastEndOfWindow()
            .withEarlyFirings(AfterProcessingTime.pastFirst
ElementInPane()
.plusDelayOf(Duration.standardMinutes(1)))
            .withLateFirings(AfterPane.elementCountAtLeast(1)) )
        .withAllowedLateness(Duration.standardMinutes(5))
        .accumulatingFiredPanes()
);
```

Now, let us break down what this Java code does:

- **`FixedWindows.of(5 min)`**: We window the data into 5-minute chunks.
- **`triggering(...)`**: We set a custom trigger:
    - **`AfterWatermark.pastEndOfWindow()`** is the core event-time trigger that waits until the watermark passes the window end (that is, all on-time data likely received).
    - **`.withEarlyFirings(AfterProcessingTime.pastFirstElementInPane().plusDelayOf(1 min))`** adds an early firing trigger. **`pastFirstElementInPane()`** means that the timer starts when the first element in that window is seen; then **`.plusDelayOf(1 min)`** means to fire 1 minute after that. Essentially, this will give an early emission of about a 1 minute into the window with whatever data that has arrived by then. It will repeat for each pane if we used '**`Repeatedly`**', but in this configuration, Beam will fire once every minute because after firing, the pane remains open for more data. The pane remains open because we used the accumulating mode.
    - **`.withLateFirings(AfterPane.elementCountAtLeast(1))`** means that if the late data arrives after the window has closed (watermark passed), fire output for each late element, or each batch of late elements. This is a simple way to say, "Whenever late data comes, output it immediately."

- **withAllowedLateness(5 min)**: Keep the window open for 5 minutes after it would normally close. This is done to accept late data up to 5 minutes late.
- **accumulatingFiredPanes()**: Use the accumulating mode, which means that each firing will include all the data we have seen so far. Hence, the on-time pane will have all the on-time data. If a late element comes up, the late pane output will include both the on-time data and the late element (that is, the count would be final count). This is often used so that the final pane represents the true final result.

In Python, trigger syntax is similar but uses the **beam.trigger** module. The Python Beam SDK requires specifying **allowed_lateness** and **accumulation_mode** when setting a trigger (just like in Java). Here is how we could do the same in Python:

```
import apache_beam as beam
from apache_beam import trigger

windowed = ( events
    | beam.WindowInto( beam.window.FixedWindows(300),  # 5 min-
utes in seconds
        trigger=trigger.AfterWatermark(
            early=trigger.AfterProcessingTime(60),      # fire
early after 60 sec of first element
            late=trigger.AfterCount(1)                 # fire
whenever 1 late element arrives
        ),
        accumulation_mode=trigger.AccumulationMode.ACCUMULATING,
        allowed_lateness=300 )  # 5 minutes lateness
)
```

Tip:

*Be careful when using **AfterCount(1)** as a late trigger in production systems. If your pipeline receives a large number of late events (for example, 10,000 late elements for a single window), this configuration will cause the window to fire 10,000 separate times, which might overwhelm downstream systems such as databases, message queues, or dashboards. This can create significant backpressure and operational instability.*

*In real-world deployments, it is often safer to batch late updates by using a time-based trigger (such as **AfterProcessingTime(30)** wrapped with **Repeatedly**) or a higher count-based trigger (for example, **AfterCount(100)**), so that the late data is emitted in controlled groups, rather than in one event at a time.*

In this Python snippet:

- We set a 5-minute window **(FixedWindows(300) seconds)**.

- The trigger is **`AfterWatermark`** with **`early=AfterProcessingTime(60)`** seconds (which is one minute) and **`late=AfterCount(1)`**.
- Use **`accumulation_mode=AccumulationMode.ACCUMULATING`** to accumulate results.
- Use **`allowed_lateness=300`** seconds to keep window open for late data that can come until 5 more minutes.

Note: *In Python, **`AfterProcessingTime(60)`** will fire once 60 seconds of processing time by itself after the first element in the window. If we wanted it to fire repeatedly at every 60 seconds until the window closes, we could wrap it with **`trigger.Repeatedly(trigger.AfterProcessingTime(60))`**. In our example, one early firing per window is enough. Also, **`AfterCount(1)`** as a late trigger means that we will get an output immediately for each late element; if you prefer to wait and gather possibly multiple late elements, you could use a higher count or a time-based late trigger.*

With these triggers, how will the output look? For each window, we can get:

- An early pane at roughly 1 minute into the window (processing time) will fetch us partial results.
- The on-time pane is the official window result with all on-time data, when the watermark passes the window end (around the 5-minute mark, or whenever Beam is convinced that it has all the data up to that time).
- If any late events (up to 5 minutes late) arrive, each triggers an output (since we used **`AfterCount(1)`** late trigger). If multiple late events arrive close together, Beam may also bundle them depending on runner optimizations. However, logically, we allow outputs for each late event.
- After 5 minutes of allowed lateness, the window is closed for good; any data later than that is dropped.

Different Trigger Patterns: The example above combined event time, processing time, and data-driven triggers (making use of composite trigger capabilities). You can also use simpler triggers like:

- **`Processing` Time Trigger Only:** For example, **`Repeatedly.forever(AfterProcessingTime(x))`** on a global window to get periodic outputs every *x* time. This effectively ignores event times, and gives you just a pulse output.
- **`Count` Trigger:** for example, **`AfterCount(100)`** to emit results each time 100 elements have arrived in the window.
- **`AfterAll/AfterAny`:** For example, **`AfterAll.of(AfterProcessingTime(30 seconds), AfterCount(100))`** fires only when *both* 30 seconds have passed and 100 elements ARE seen (whichever comes last in practice), whereas **`AfterAny`** would fire when *either* condition is met (whichever comes first).

- **`OrFinally`:** In Java, the **`OrFinally`** is used to have a final condition that will fire and close the window.

For a beginner-friendly approach, the main triggers to remember are:

- **Default (Event Time) Trigger**: One output when the window is complete (watermark)
- **Early Trigger (Processing Time or Element Count)**: For speculative early results
- **Late Trigger**: To handle late data after the event-time closure
- **Accumulation vs. Discarding**: To decide whether to keep adding, or reset for each pane

Hence, triggers provide for a lot of flexibility in streaming. However, they work closely with the concept of the **watermark** and allowed lateness, which define the point when Beam considers a window "complete". In the example cited previously, we mentioned watermarks and allowed lateness without defining them. In the next section, we will clarify what watermarks are, and how Beam handles late data.

Watermarks and Late Data Handling

In streaming pipelines, since data can arrive late or out of order, we need a way to measure progress in event time. A **watermark is Beam's mechanism** to track how far along in event time the pipeline is, and to estimate when all data for a certain timestamp (or window) has likely arrived.

A watermark is often described as a timestamp T such that the system believes that it has seen all the events with event times less than T. In other words, when the watermark for a **`PCollection`** reaches time X, Beam assumes that there will be no more elements with the timestamp < X. Watermarks are usually provided by the data sources, or assigned in the pipeline. For example, if reading from Kafka or Pub/Sub, the source might advance the watermark as messages come in, or if reading from a file, the watermark might jump to end when file read is done.

Beam's default trigger (event-time trigger) uses the watermark; when the watermark passes the end of a window, Beam fires the window's output, as it considers that the window complete. However, what if this assumption is wrong, and some straggler event arrives late? Beam allows us to handle it through **late data** mechanisms.

Late Data: Any element that arrives with an event timestamp **less than the current watermark** is considered late. More concretely, if the window for 10:00–10:05 is closed at watermark time 10:05, and then an event with the timestamp 10:03 arrives afterward, the event is late for its window. By default, Beam will drop late data (it will not include it in the window computation), to avoid endlessly updating results.

However, you can choose to accept and process late data by setting an **allowed lateness** on the window.

Allowed Lateness: This is a windowing property that tells Beam to keep the window open for a certain amount of additional time (in event time) beyond the window's end to accept late arrivals. If late data arrives within this lateness interval, Beam will still process it (possibly by emitting a late pane via triggers). If the data arrives after the allowed lateness has passed, it is considered **droppable late data,** and is discarded.

For example, if the allowed lateness is 5 minutes for a window that ends at 10:05, Beam will accept late events timestamped up to 10:05 + 5min = 10:10. The watermark reaching 10:10 (window end and allowed lateness) is often considered the point of final closure for that window. Past 10:10, any data for the 10:00–10:05 window is dropped.

More precisely, Beam will continue to accept late events for the 10:00–10:05 window **as long as the pipeline's watermark has not yet advanced past 10:10**, which is the window end time plus the allowed lateness. It is not the event's timestamp alone that determines acceptance, but whether the *current watermark* is still below 10:10. Once the watermark passes 10:10, the window is considered fully closed, and any further elements for that window are dropped, regardless of their event timestamps.

It is thus important to note that allowed lateness is a trade-off; keeping windows open for longer consumes more memory/state, and the late data complicates output. You should set it based on how late data can arrive in your scenario and how much you are willing to deal with the updates. Some pipelines with strict latency requirements might set allowed lateness to 0 (drop all late data), while others with important accuracy needs might allow a generous lateness (minutes or hours).

Using Allowed Lateness in Codes:

- In Java, as shown earlier, you specify **`.withAllowedLateness(Duration)`**, when you are configuring the Window transform.
- In Python, you pass the **`allowed_lateness`** parameter to **`WindowInto`**.

If you set allowed lateness, but do not specify triggers, Beam's default behavior (without a late trigger) will be to drop late data anyway. Effectively, to make use of allowed lateness, you should also have a trigger that can fire to emit late data. One common approach is using the default event-time trigger for on-time data, and then adding a late trigger for late data (like **`.withAllowedLateness(...)`** + **`.withLateFirings(...)`** in Java, or using **`trigger.AfterWatermark(late=...)`** in Python as we saw). If you do not specify any late trigger, but allow lateness, the late elements will be collected in the window. However, they will be never emitted unless you have something like `.withClosingBehavior(FIRE_ALWAYS)` (in some Beam SDKs) to force a final pane at window closure.

Watermark Propagation: The watermark advances as the sources inject data. For example, if reading from multiple input sources, the overall watermark is the minimum of the sources (to avoid declaring completeness until all sources catch up). Runners like Dataflow often visualize watermark progress. Hence, if an event is extremely late (beyond allowed lateness), it is often dropped by default; you might choose to send such data to a side output or logging, if needed, but it is beyond the basic scope.

To summarize late data handling:

- **On-Time Data:** It arrives before the watermark (that is, before the window is closed) and is handled by default.
- **Late Data within Allowed Lateness:** It can be included in results, if allowed lateness and triggers for late data are set. It often produces *late panes* of output.
- **Late Data beyond Allowed Lateness:** It is dropped (ignored) by the pipeline.

Hence, Beam's design, with watermarks and allowed lateness, ensures that the windows eventually finish, and you can trade-off between waiting for all the data versus timeliness. The watermark is a heuristic (it might sometimes be wrong, as data can still arrive later), which is why allowed lateness exists as a safety net.

Finally, how do these concepts apply in real-world scenarios? Let us explore a few practical examples of pipelines, as well as how they use event time, windows, triggers, and watermarks.

Real-World Applications

Now that we have covered the mechanics, let us put them in context. Here are some typical real-world applications of event time windowing and triggers in Apache Beam, and how you could handle time in each case:

- **Real-Time Metrics and Reporting (Fixed Windows with Early Results):** Imagine that you run a website and want to update a dashboard every minute with the number of page views in the last minute. You would thus use a **fixed window of 1 minute** for page view events. To get low-latency updates, you might set an **early trigger** to emit results periodically (say, every 10 seconds processing time) before the minute is over. Late data is not a huge concern if most events arrive on time (perhaps allowed lateness of a few seconds to account for minor delays). This setup ensures that the dashboard gets a near-real-time count that updates continuously, and at the end of the minute the count finalizes. In Beam, you might do the following:

a. Window into 1-minute fixed windows.

b. Trigger after processing the time every 10 seconds, and the default event-time at end of the window. Accumulate counts, so that each update is incremental.

c. Allowed Lateness will be small (or 0), if you prefer to ignore very late events.

d. This provides frequent updates (early panes), as well as a final accurate count at the end of each minute window.

- **User Session Analysis (Session Windows):** Suppose you are analyzing user sessions on a platform. A session is a period of continuous activity by a user, and you want to compute the total actions per session or the session duration. To do so, you can use **session windows** keyed by the user ID, with a gap duration that defines inactivity (for example, 30 minutes as in our example). Hence, all the events for a user that occur within 30 minutes of each other will be grouped into the same window/session. If an event arrives late (out of order), as long as it is within the allowed lateness, it can still be merged into the session. Here, you would likely allow some lateness (since maybe logs could arrive late), but maybe not too long. Triggers might simply be default (emit when session is complete according to watermark), and might fire once finally at the end of allowed lateness for any stragglers. The result is an output per session with aggregated information. For example, you might output when the user's session is over (no events for 30 minutes)—the watermark will eventually pass the end of that session window, and trigger the output. If an event was delayed, but arrives 10 minutes late, it can still be added to the session if it is within allowed lateness, and will then update the session output.

- **IoT Sensor Data with Out-of-Order Events (Handling Late Data):** Consider the example of IoT sensors sending temperature readings to a central system. Network issues might delay some readings. You want to compute the hourly average temperature. Here, you would use **fixed windows of 1 hour** for the event times. However, because readings can be late, you set an allowed lateness (perhaps 2-3 hours) to accept late readings. You might not need early triggers in this case if you are content with the hourly results, but you want to include late arrivals to improve accuracy. Beam will use the watermark (based on sensor timestamps or ingestion times) to trigger the initial hourly result at roughly the hour boundary. If some readings come in a few minutes late, a late trigger can recompute or adjust the average. The implementation looks like:

a. **Window**: 1 hour fixed

b. **Allowed Lateness**: For example, 5 minutes

c. **Trigger**: Could be **`AfterWatermark`** with **`.withLateFirings(AfterCount(1))`** and accumulating mode, so that any late reading causes a recomputed average. Or, you could choose to emit only once at end of allowed lateness (to avoid multiple outputs).

d. This way, you get one output per hour on the hour, and if any stragglers arrive shortly after, you get an updated output including them.

e. If a sensor reading arrives days late (beyond allowed lateness), it will be dropped, and will be logged as too late.

- **Complex Event Processing (Multiple Triggers and Windows):** In more complex pipelines, you might combine windowing with triggers to detect patterns. For example, detecting fraud might involve a session window per user, and a trigger that fires early if suspicious activity is detected (data-driven trigger). Or a pipeline might use a **global window with processing-time triggers** for cases where event time is not relevant (rare, but for some periodic synchronisation jobs, it would make sense to just emit every X minutes using the processing time triggers).

  Hence, in all these scenarios, the key is to pick a windowing strategy that matches the problem's time frame, and triggers to balance timeliness with completeness. You should also tune allowed lateness based on how delayed data can be. If you know that your data sources have at most a 2-minute delay, setting allowed lateness a bit above that (say, 5 minutes) ensures that you capture almost all data. If the data is nearly always on time, you might not allow lateness at all.

- **Monitoring and Debugging:** When building Beam pipelines with windows and triggers, it is helpful to log or inspect how windows and panes are firing. For instance, Beam's **`org.apache.beam.sdk.transforms.windowing.PaneInfo`** (Java), or simply logging in a DoFn in Python can tell you if an element is in an early/late pane. In practice, you will test with sample (or real) streaming data to ensure that your trigger behavior meets your expectations.

Conclusion

Time-based processing is one of the most powerful features of Apache Beam, as it allows out-of-order and late data to be handled gracefully. Hence, by using event time, your computations can reflect the real world timing of events. Windowing lets you break infinite streams into manageable chunks like "per minute" or "per session", while watermarks provide a heuristic for completeness, and triggers give you control over when to emit results (early results for low latency, and additional results to account for late data). With these tools, you can implement robust streaming analytics that produce accurate results even in the face of out-of-order, late, or bursty data.

Therefore, this chapter provided a practical overview of how Apache Beam handles event time, windows, and triggers, while showing how these concepts work together to produce accurate and timely results in streaming pipelines. Hence, by mastering event time semantics, windowing strategies, watermarks, and trigger configurations, you can gain precise control over correctness, latency, and completeness, even when data arrives out of order or significantly late.

In the next chapter, we will explore how these mechanisms are implemented and tuned in real pipelines. We will also focus on advanced windowing patterns, detailed trigger configurations, and practical strategies for handling late data at scale. You will learn how to choose the right window types, design efficient trigger policies, and balance accuracy with system performance, which will allow you to build production-grade streaming pipelines that are both reliable and efficient.

CHAPTER 4
Building Pipelines with Apache Beam

Introduction

Apache Beam is an open-source unified programming model that allows you to build both batch and streaming data pipelines using the same concepts, and often the same code. Hence, in this chapter, you will learn how to design and implement pipelines from scratch in a beginner-friendly and hands-on manner, even if you have no prior experience in stream processing. We will begin by introducing core Beam concepts such as bounded and unbounded data, pipeline architecture, and how Beam's unified model enables code reuse across batch and streaming workloads. You will then build your first batch pipelines step by step, while covering environment setup, creating `PCollections`, applying transformations, and running pipelines.

The chapter also guides you through building streaming pipelines, while focusing on essential concepts such as windowing, triggers, and handling out-of-order or late data. Code examples for both Python and Java are provided via simple and generic use cases to clearly demonstrate Beam's APIs and transforms. You will see how a batch pipeline can be adapted to streaming with minimal changes, while reinforcing Beam's portability and reusability. Finally, the chapter introduces practical integrations with Apache Kafka as a streaming source, and Apache Flink as a runner, which will culminate in an end-to-end example. Hence, by the end of this chapter, you will be comfortable building and running both batch and streaming pipelines, understanding core Beam abstractions, and deploying pipelines on different execution engines.

Structure

In this chapter we will cover the following topics:

- Apache Beam Core Concepts
- Building Batch Pipelines Step-by-Step
- Building Streaming Pipelines Step-by-Step

- Integrating Apache Beam with Apache Kafka and Apache Flink
- Trigger Mechanisms
- Watermarks and Late Data Handling
- Real-World Applications

Apache Beam Core Concepts

Before diving into code, it is important to understand the key concepts and terminology in Apache Beam's programming model. Apache Beam provides a *portable* and *unified* API, which means that the same concepts apply whether you are doing batch or streaming processing. Here, we will break down the fundamental ideas:

- **`Pipeline`:** A Beam pipeline is essentially a **Directed Acyclic Graph (DAG)** of data processing steps that you construct in your code. It encompasses the entire workflow from input to output. As the pipeline is a directed *acyclic* graph, data always flows forward and never loops back to a previous step. This is intentional, as iterative or feedback-based logic cannot be modeled by graph cycles, and must instead be implemented using state, timers, or external storage, which allows Beam to execute pipelines safely, deterministically, and in parallel at scale. You can think of the pipeline as the blueprint of your data processing job–it does not do anything until you run it, but it defines *what* will be done. Therefore, in Beam, a pipeline is represented by the Pipeline class (in both Python and Java). The pipeline object is the container for the series of transformations that you will apply to your data.
- **`PCollection`:** A **`PCollection`** is Beam's core data abstraction, which represents a collection of data elements. The "P" stands for parallel, since **`PCollections`** are designed for parallel processing. You can imagine a **`PCollection`** as "an array or multiset of data in Beam's world". This could be a finite set of records (if it is a batch pipeline) or an infinite, growing stream of records (for a streaming pipeline). Every data set in Beam is a **`PCollection`**, whether it comes from reading a file, querying a database, or subscribing to a real-time data stream. **`PCollections`** are *immutable*, since if they are created, you will not be able to modify a **`PCollection`** in place; instead, transforms take one or more **`PCollections`** as input, and then produce new **`PCollections`** as output.
- **Bounded vs. Unbounded `PCollections`: `PCollections`** can be **bounded** (with a fixed number of elements) or **unbounded** (potentially infinite, growing over time). This distinction is crucial. A bounded **`PCollection`** (for example, data from a file or a finite database query) can be processed in a batch mode, where the pipeline reads all data, processes it, and eventually finishes. An unbounded **`PCollection`** (for example, data from a pub/sub topic or Kafka topic) represents an ever-growing stream that *never ends*, and thus requires

streaming processing–the pipeline runs continuously, while processing elements as they arrive. In Beam's unified model, the same transforms and APIs apply to both bounded and unbounded data, but how the pipeline executes (batch vs streaming) will differ based on this property. We will discuss later how Beam handles unbounded data via windowing and triggers.

- **`PTransform`:** A **`PTransform`** (parallel transform) is the operation or step in the pipeline. Transforms in Beam take input **`PCollections`**, perform some processing, and output new **`PCollections`**. They are the workhorses of your pipeline. Core Beam transforms include element-wise operations like **`Map/FlatMap`** (collectively done via **`ParDo`** in Beam's model), grouping operations like **`GroupByKey`** (to collect all values with the same key, which are often combined with aggregation like counting), and composite operations that may combine multiple steps. For example, a **`ParDo`** transform allows you to apply a user-defined function to each element in a **`PCollection`** (similar to a "map" operation in other frameworks). Transforms can be simple (one input **`PCollection`** to one output **`PCollection`**) or complex (some have multiple inputs or outputs). You can also create your own composite transforms that bundle multiple processing steps into one reusable unit.
- **Runner:** Beam pipelines are *portable*, which means that the Beam code you write is independent of the execution engine. A **Runner** is the component or backend that actually takes your pipeline, and then executes it on a specific engine. There are various Beam runners available, such as the **`DirectRunner`** (which runs pipelines locally on your machine, useful for development and testing), the **`Apache Flink`** Runner (to run Beam pipelines on a Flink cluster), **`Apache Spark`** Runner, and **`Google Cloud Dataflow`** Runner, among others. For example, if you choose the **`Flink`** Runner, Beam will translate your pipeline into a Flink job and run it on an Apache Flink engine. The key point is that you write your pipeline once using Beam's API, and you can execute it in different environments by simply switching runners (often with a configuration change). This is a powerful feature because it allows you to develop and test on a small scale (for example, using **`DirectRunner`** locally), and then run at large scale on a distributed system (like Flink or Dataflow) without changing your pipeline code. It is thus important to understand that what is portable is the **pipeline logic and programming model**, and not the performance characteristics or resource assumptions. While the same pipeline code can run on different runners, a pipeline that works on the **`DirectRunner`** may fail or behave poorly on Flink or Dataflow if it relies on assumptions such as all data fitting in local memory, low key cardinality, or minimal parallelism. In distributed runners, the state must scale, keys are sharded, and memory is limited per worker, so that locally acceptable designs may expose performance bottlenecks or correctness issues at scale.
- **Apache Beam's Unified Model:** Beam's model unifies batch and streaming. In

traditional systems, you might have had to use different APIs, or even different frameworks for batch versus stream processing. Beam avoids that split. As noted, a **`PCollection`** can be bounded or unbounded, but the way you interact with it in code is mostly the same. You use the same classes and transforms for both finite and infinite data. This unified approach means you can often start with a batch pipeline (because it is simpler to test on a fixed dataset), and later adapt it to streaming when the data needs to be processed in real time, without a complete rewrite. Beam's model, sometimes called the **Beam Model**, provides built-in mechanisms to handle streaming concerns (like out-of-order data) under the hood, while letting you reuse your business logic on either type of data. In summary, Beam's philosophy is "*write once, run anywhere (any runner), on any data (bounded or unbounded)*". We will see this in action when we compare batch and streaming versions of a pipeline.

- **Pipeline Architecture:** Putting it all together, a Beam pipeline reads data from one or more **sources** (for example, reading from a file, a database, or a messaging system), applies a series of **transforms** (**`PTransforms`**) to that data (which create intermediate **`PCollections`**), and writes the results to one or more **sinks** (for example, writing to files, databases, another messaging system). The path from sources through transforms to sinks forms the pipeline's directed acyclic graph structure. For example, a simple pipeline might have: one **`PCollection`** as input -> a transform to parse or clean the data -> a transform to aggregate or analyze -> an output **`PCollection`** written to a results sink. More complex pipelines can have branching (a **`PCollection`** goes into two different transforms in parallel) or merging (two **`PCollections`** are combined). However, fundamentally, everything is still a graph of **`PTransforms`** operating on **`PCollections`**. Hence, the separation of *what* the pipeline does (your code) from *how/where* it runs (the runner) is a key architectural aspect.

Thus, with these core concepts in mind, we are ready to start building pipelines. We will start with batch pipelines (which operate on bounded data) as they are easier to grasp and test, and then move on to streaming pipelines (for unbounded data). Remember, however, that the concepts largely overlap thanks to Beam's unified model; therefore, what you learn in batch will carry over to streaming, besides a few additional considerations.

Building Batch Pipelines Step-by-Step

Batch pipelines process a finite dataset and eventually produce a result (and then terminate). In this section, we will walk through the creation of a simple batch pipeline using Apache Beam. We will cover setting up your environment for Beam, defining the pipeline, creating `PCollections` from input data, applying transforms to process the data, and then writing the output to a sink. All steps will be illustrated in both Python and Java (as Beam supports multiple languages; we focus on these two as they are commonly used).

Let us assume our task for this batch pipeline is something straightforward and generic, such as counting the occurrences of words in a static text file (the classic "word count" example). This example is easy to understand, as it demonstrates many important concepts like reading input, transforming each element (splitting lines into words), grouping and aggregating (counting words), and writing results. We will build this pipeline step by step.

Step 1: Setting up the Development Environment

Before writing any Beam code, you need to set up your development environment with the Apache Beam SDK.

For Python: Make sure that you have Python 3 installed. You can install the Beam SDK for Python using **`pip`**. It is recommended to do this in a virtual environment. For example, you might do the following in your terminal:

```
# Create and activate a virtual environment (optional but
recommended)
python3 -m venv beam-env
source beam-env/bin/activate

# Install Apache Beam
pip install apache-beam
```

This will install the core Apache Beam Python SDK. You can now write Beam pipeline code in Python. You do not need any separate "Beam server"—the Direct Runner (which runs pipelines locally) is included. If you plan to use other runners (like Dataflow or a portable runner), additional setup might be needed, but for now, this is enough for local batch execution.

In practice, you will often install Apache Beam with extra dependency sets depending on the features or runners you plan to use. The base command **`pip install apache-beam`** installs only the core Beam SDK, which is sufficient for local development with the **`DirectRunner`**. However, additional components are required for cloud runners, interactive notebooks, and certain I/O connectors.

For example:

```
pip install apache-beam[gcp]
```

This installs the extra dependencies needed to run pipelines on Google Cloud

Dataflow, and to use Google Cloud services such as BigQuery, Pub/Sub, and Cloud Storage. This is required if you plan to deploy Beam pipelines to GCP.

```
pip install apache-beam[interactive]
```

This installs dependencies for using Beam in Jupyter notebooks, including visualization tools and interactive pipeline execution. It is useful for experimentation, teaching, and debugging pipelines step by step.

You can also combine extras if needed through this command:

```
pip install apache-beam[gcp,interactive]
```

Hence, using these optional dependency groups ensures that all required libraries are installed upfront, and avoids runtime errors caused by missing packages when you start using specific runners or I/O connectors.

For Java: Ensure that you have JDK (Java Development Kit) installed (Java 8 or previous, as Beam supports Java 8+). Apache Beam provides Maven artifacts for easy inclusion in Java projects. You can either use Maven or Gradle to manage dependencies, or even use the Beam provided **Maven Archetype** to generate a starter project. The simplest way to set up is using Maven. In your project's pom.xml, add the Beam SDK dependency. For example, to use Beam 2.x (replace with the latest version as of this writing), include:

```
<dependencies>
  <dependency>
    <groupId>org.apache.beam</groupId>
    <artifactId>beam-sdks-java-core</artifactId>
    <version>2.xx.x</version> <!-- use latest Beam version -->
  </dependency>
  <!-- You might also include a runner dependency here; for local
testing, DirectRunner is built-in -->
</dependencies>
```

If you intend to run on a specific runner, you will also add the dependency for that runner (for example, beam-runners-direct-java for `DirectRunner`, or beam-runners-flink for `Flink` Runner, and so on, but for now we can proceed without explicitly adding `DirectRunner`, since it is a part of the core).

You can also use the **Beam Quickstart**. For instance, Beam's quickstart guide suggests using Maven to run an example pipeline. However, since we want to write our own pipeline, ensure that you can compile and run a Java program with Beam dependencies.

At this point, Beam is ready to use. We will now proceed to use the Direct Runner (the default) for running our batch pipeline locally.

Step 2: Creating the Pipeline and Reading Input (`PCollections`)

Now, we will create our pipeline and define the input source. In a batch pipeline, input is typically a bounded source like a file or a set of files, a database table, and so on Apache Beam has many I/O connectors (for files, BigQuery, JDBC, and so on), but for simplicity, we will use a text file as input in this example.

In Beam, reading the data is done via transforms as well. For example, Beam Java SDK provides **`TextIO`** for reading from text files, and Beam Python SDK provides **`ReadFromText`**. These are built-in transforms that produce a **`PCollection`** of elements (each element would be one line of text from the file, in our case).

Let us say we have an input file input.txt that contains text lines (for example, a few sentences). We will read this file into a **`PCollection`** of strings (each element is a line), as shown here:

Python:

```
import apache_beam as beam

# Create a Pipeline using Beam's DirectRunner
with beam.Pipeline() as pipeline:
    # Read from a text file into a PCollection of strings (each
element is one line)
    lines = pipeline | beam.io.ReadFromText('path/to/input.txt')
    # (We will add transformations on 'lines' in the next steps)
```

Java:

```
import org.apache.beam.sdk.Pipeline;
import org.apache.beam.sdk.io.TextIO;
import org.apache.beam.sdk.options.PipelineOptions;
import org.apache.beam.sdk.options.PipelineOptionsFactory;

// Create PipelineOptions and the Pipeline
PipelineOptions options = PipelineOptionsFactory.create();
// We can set options like runner or config here if needed. Using
DirectRunner by default for local run.
Pipeline pipeline = Pipeline.create(options);

// Read from a text file into a PCollection of strings
PCollection<String> lines = pipeline.apply(TextIO.read().from
("path/to/input.txt"));
// (We will add transformations on 'lines' in the next steps)
```

In these snippets, we constructed a pipeline, and then applied a source transform to read the input file. In Python, using the | syntax is a convenient way Beam allows chaining transforms (it is syntactic sugar, where **`pipeline | beam.io.ReadFromText(...)`** means to "apply the `ReadFromText` transform to the pipeline"). In Java, we call **`pipeline.apply(...)`** with **`TextIO.read()`** configured with the file path.

After this step, we have a **`PCollection`** called lines that contains the lines of the file. This is a bounded **`PCollection`**, as it comes from a finite file. Note that at this point, nothing has actually executed yet; we have just built the pipeline structure. Beam uses *lazy evaluation*–the pipeline will run when we execute **`pipeline.run()`** (in Java), or when the with **`beam.Pipeline()`** block executes (in Python, the pipeline runs at the end of the with block, or when you call **`pipeline.run()`** explicitly).

Step 3: Applying Transformations to the `PCollection`

With our input **`PCollection`** in place, we can now apply transformations to process the data. In our example of counting words, we need to:

1. **Parse the Lines into Words**: Take each line (string) and split it into individual words. This can be done with a **`FlatMap`** transform (because one line will produce multiple words, so it is one-to-many). In Beam, this is often done with **`beam.FlatMap`** in Python or **`FlatMapElements/ParDo.of(...)`** in Java.
2. **Filter out Any Empty Results**: Depending on how we split, we might get empty strings (for example, if there are extra spaces or punctuation). However, we can filter them out.
3. **Count Each Unique Word**: We need to count occurrences, which involves grouping identical words together and summing up. Beam provides convenient transforms for this common pattern, such as **`Count.perElement()`**, which counts the occurrences of each distinct element.

We will go into this step by step. First, we will split the lines into words:

Python (Splitting into Words and Filtering):

```
# Continuing from previous Python snippet inside the pipeline
context
    words = lines | beam.FlatMap(lambda line: line.split())  # split
on whitespace by default
    # Filter out empty strings (if any word is empty after splitting)
    words = words | beam.Filter(lambda word: word != '')
```

Here, **FlatMap** takes a function that returns an *iterable* (list) of results for each input. **The lambda line: line.split()** will produce a list of words for each line, while **FlatMap** will flatten these lists into a single stream of words (**PCollection** of individual words). We will then apply a Filter to drop any empty strings (just in case).

Alternatively, we could use a regex to split on non-word characters to handle punctuation, but for simplicity, **.split()** is fine (it splits on whitespace). This is a generic example pattern of mapping and filtering.

Java (Splitting into Words and Filtering):

```
import org.apache.beam.sdk.transforms.FlatMapElements;
import org.apache.beam.sdk.transforms.Filter;
import org.apache.beam.sdk.values.TypeDescriptors;

// Split lines into words
PCollection<String> words = lines.apply(FlatMapElements
    .into(TypeDescriptors.strings())  // Beam needs to know the
type of elements (String)
    .via((String line) -> Arrays.asList(line.split("\\s+")))  //
split on whitespace regex
);

// Filter out empty words
PCollection<String> filteredWords = words.apply(Filter.by((String
word) -> !word.isEmpty()));
```

In Java, this **TypeDescriptors.strings()** line is required because of **type erasure**. Java removes most generic type information at compile time. Therefore, at runtime Beam cannot automatically infer what type of elements are flowing through the pipeline. Beam needs this information to choose the correct **coder** (serializer) and to validate pipeline structure.

Therefore, this line is:

```
.into(TypeDescriptors.strings())
```

This is essentially telling Beam that:

"The output of this transform is a collection of String objects. Please use the appropriate encoding and type handling for Strings."

Without it, Beam cannot reliably determine how to serialize, distribute, and process the data, and you will often see confusing runtime errors related to missing coders or type inference failures.

Thus, a simple mental model is:

- Python keeps type information dynamically, so that Beam can usually infer types.

- Java erases generic types, so Beam must be explicitly told what the element type is.
- That is why beginners frequently run into issues when skipping **TypeDescriptors**, especially when using transforms like **FlatMapElements, MapElements**, or custom lambdas.

  In short:

  Java deletes type information at runtime, so Beam needs **TypeDescriptors** to know how to encode and move your data safely through the pipeline.

Hence, this single line prevents a whole class of subtle and frustrating errors.

In Java, we used **FlatMapElements.into(TypeDescriptors.strings())** to specify the output element type, and provided a lambda to split each line into a list of words. We split on \\s+ (one or more whitespace characters). Then, we filtered with **Filter.by(...)** to remove empty strings. We could also chain these, but it is clearer to separate the steps.

Now, we have a **PCollection** of individual words (non-empty). The next step is to count the occurrences of each unique word.

Beam offers a transform **Count.perElement()** that does a combination of grouping by the element and counting, all in one step. Under the hood, it is doing a **GroupByKey** and sum, but we can use it directly for convenience.

Python (Counting Each Word):

```
word_counts = words | beam.combiners.Count.PerElement()
    # word_counts will be a PCollection of (word, count) tuples
(as a beam type KV<word, count>)
```

Java (Counting Each Word):

```
import org.apache.beam.sdk.transforms.Count;

PCollection<KV<String, Long>> wordCounts = filteredWords.
apply(Count.perElement());
```

After this transform, **word_counts** (Python) or **wordCounts** (Java) contains a collection of key-value pairs, where each key is a word and the value is the count (as a Long in Java, or typically an 'int' in Python, which Beam will treat as a Int64, since Beam's Count returns 64-bit count). In Python, **Count.PerElement()** yields a tuple (word, count) for each distinct word. In Java, it yields a **KV<String, Long>** object (Beam's generic key-value container).

However, you must note that the **Count.perElement()** is a composite transform that will handle the necessary grouping and summing for you. If we were not using it, we would manually do something like **.apply(WithKeys(word -> word))**, and then

.apply(GroupByKey()) then **.apply(ParDo.of(sum counts))**. However, Beam's combiners like Count make it simpler.

At this point, we have done the main processing: we read the lines, broke them into words, and counted the words. These are standard patterns: reading input, using a **FlatMap** (one-to-many transform), possibly filtering, and finally, aggregating by key.

Beam also has other useful transforms, which are:

- **Map:** One-to-one mapping (in Python, **beam.Map(lambda x: ...);** in Java can use **MapElements.via())**
- **ParDo with DoFn:** A lower-level way to define any processing logic; useful for more complex or stateful processing, but for basic cases the lambda transforms cover it.
- **Combine:** Combining elements with a custom function (summing numbers, and so on)
- **Flatten:** Merging multiple **PCollections**
- **Partition:** Splitting one **PCollection** into many by some function. We will not go into all of these now, but know that Beam's transform library is rich. Our pipeline currently sticks to basic ones suitable for beginners.

Step 4: Writing the Output to a Sink

After processing data in a pipeline, we typically want to output the results to some external storage or system—for example, writing to files, a database, and so on. Hence, in batch processing, a common sink is writing to an output file (or files). For our word count example, we can write the counts to a text file.

Beam provides **WriteToText** in Python and **TextIO.write()** in Java for writing **PCollections** to text files. We will use them. However, we might need to format the **(word, count)** pair into a nicely readable string (since by default it may output as Python tuple or Java KV object string). In our example, we can format it like **"word: count"** for each pair.

Python (Writing Output):

```
    # Format the (word, count) pairs into a string
    formatted_results = word_counts | beam.Map(lambda pair:
f"{pair[0]}: {pair[1]}")
    formatted_results | beam.io.WriteToText('path/to/output.txt')
```

We applied a **beam.Map** transform to turn each (word, count) into a single formatted string (for example, ("hello", 3) becomes "hello: 3"). Then, we use **WriteToText** with a file path. Beam will create the file (actually, possibly multiple files if the **PCollection** is distributed, by default Additionally, Beam may produce one file per parallel worker, but since we are likely using the **DirectRunner** on a small input, it might just be one file; otherwise, you can specify a file name prefix and Beam will add suffixes like -00000-of-00001). Here, we gave **'path/to/output.txt'** as a prefix; Beam will typically produce files like output.txt-00000-of-00001 and so on. For simplicity, you can think of it as writing to an output file.

Thus, when using **WriteToText**, Beam may generate multiple output files (one per parallel shard). For batch pipelines, you can force a single output file during development and testing by setting the number of shards to one:

This is very convenient for debugging and validation because it produces exactly one file instead of many. However, this should be used only in small-scale or local test runs. Setting **num_shards=1** forces all output data to be written by a single worker, which removes parallelism, and quickly becomes a serious performance bottleneck in production pipelines. For large datasets, it can slow down the pipeline significantly, and even cause memory or I/O pressure on that single worker.

Therefore, a good rule of thumb is:

- Use **num_shards=1** for local testing, demos, and unit validation.
- Let Beam manage sharding automatically in production to preserve scalability and throughput.

This reinforces an important Beam principle: convenience settings that simplify development often trade-off against performance and scalability in real deployments.

Java (Writing Output):

```
import org.apache.beam.sdk.transforms.MapElements;
import org.apache.beam.sdk.transforms.SimpleFunction;
import org.apache.beam.sdk.values.KV;
import org.apache.beam.sdk.values.TypeDescriptors;

// Format the results as "word: count" strings
PCollection<String> formattedResults = wordCounts.apply(MapElements
    .into(TypeDescriptors.strings())
    .via((KV<String, Long> wordCount) -> wordCount.getKey() + ": " +
wordCount.getValue()));

// Write the output to a text file (could also specify .withSuffix or
.withNumShards, etc.)
formattedResults.apply(TextIO.write().to("path/to/output.txt"));
```

Here, we used **MapElements** to convert each **KV<String, Long>** into a string of the desired format. Then, we applied **TextIO.write()**. In Java, **TextIO.write().to("file")** will create files with that prefix (for example, file-00000-of-00001 and so on). Hence, if you want exactly one output file, you could specify **.withNumShards(1)** and perhaps a suffix like **.withSuffix(".txt")**, but for simplicity we will not dive into that here.

Now our pipeline is complete: it reads from an input text, processes the data, and writes out results to an output text.

Step 5: Running and Validating the Pipeline

With the pipeline constructed, we need to actually run it. In Python, if we have used the with **beam.Pipeline()** as pipeline: context, the pipeline will run automatically when the block exits (or you could manually call **pipeline.run().wait_until_finish())**. In Java, after building the pipeline, you call **pipeline.run()**. If running locally with **DirectRunner**, you might also call **.waitUntilFinish()** to wait for completion (especially in an interactive or batch script).

Python:

When the with block completes, Beam will run the pipeline. You should then find the output file(s) with the word counts. If you were not using the with statement, you could do:

```
pipeline = beam.Pipeline()
# ...construct pipeline...
pipeline.run().wait_until_finish().apache.beam.sdk.transforms
```

This will explicitly run the pipeline and wait for it to complete, since in batch, it will finish when it is done.

Java:

```
pipeline.run().waitUntilFinish();
```

By default, with the **DirectRunner**, this will run the pipeline in your local JVM, and the program will exit when done (especially if you **waitUntilFinish**).

At this point, you can open the output text file to verify the results. For example, you might see the following (if these were the counts of each word in the input).:

```
hello: 3
world: 2
Beam: 1
```

Hence, this simple example has walked through all the typical steps of a batch pipeline, which are:

1. Setting up Beam
2. Creating a pipeline and defining the input source
3. Transforming the data with one or more transforms (**map**, **filter**, **group+count**)

4. Writing the output
5. Running the pipeline and getting results

Even though our example was word count, these steps apply broadly:

- If you wanted to do an ETL job (extract-transform-load), you might read from a database, apply transformations, and then write to another database.
- If you wanted to process log files, you would read the logs, parse them, filter interesting events, aggregate statistics, and then write out a report.

The Beam model stays the same; you would just use different I/O connectors or different transform logic for your domain. The code structure will be very similar to what we have done.

Before moving to streaming, make a quick note on **pipelines with multiple transforms**; Beam allows you to have multiple outputs or even multiple inputs. For instance, you can branch: `PCollection` -> Apply two different transforms -> Get two results. Or, you can merge using Flatten. These are beyond the simple linear pipeline, but the idea is that your pipeline is a flexible graph. Hence, you must always ensure that you end the pipeline with some outputs (if you do not use a `PCollection`, it is fine, but typically, you will have a '`Write`', or some terminal operation to actually do something observable).

Now that we have a handle on batch pipelines, let us explore streaming pipelines, which handle unbounded data. We will see that much of what we learned carries over, with the addition of a few new concepts to manage the continuous nature of the streaming data.

Building Streaming Pipelines Step-by-Step

Streaming pipelines deal with **unbounded** data sources–data that continues to arrive and does not have a fixed end. Examples include messages from a Kafka topic, events from IoT sensors, or user interaction logs being sent continuously from a website. In streaming, you often cannot wait until "all the data is in" (since theoretically the data could keep coming forever), so the approach to processing and emitting results is different from batch. Apache Beam's model provides tools like **windowing** and **triggers** to handle this.

Despite these differences, the structure of a Beam pipeline for streaming is similar to batch; you still create a pipeline, apply transforms, and write results. The big differences come in how you read the input (unbounded source), and how you make sense of infinite data (by windowing it into finite chunks, for example).

In this section, we will construct a streaming pipeline that, conceptually, does something similar to our batch example (counting occurrences), but now in an ongoing real-time context. For instance, imagine we have a stream of text lines coming in (maybe from a messaging system like Kafka or Pub/Sub), and we want to continuously count words in a time-windowed manner (say, every minute). We will focus on the new streaming aspects like windowing the data, deciding when to emit the results (triggers) or the considerations of latency (handling late-arriving data).

Reading from Unbounded Sources

In a streaming pipeline, the source can produce an infinite stream of data. Common unbounded sources in Beam include:

- **Messaging Systems**: For example, Apache Kafka topics, Google Cloud Pub/Sub subscriptions, RabbitMQ, and so on
- **Socket or Text Streams**: For example, reading lines from a TCP socket
- **`GenerateSequence` or `TestStream`**: Synthetic sources that generate data for testing or demo

To keep things simple without requiring a complex external setup, let us assume our streaming input is coming from a Kafka topic (since we will cover Kafka integration in detail later). We will conceptually use a Kafka source in code. (If you do not have Kafka, imagine using any other streaming source–the idea is similar.)

In Beam **Java**, there is a KafkaIO transform for reading from Kafka. In **Python**, Beam uses a cross-language transform to call Kafka IO from the Java SDK (it is also possible, though requires Java setup underneath). Hence, we will show an example of using Kafka as the source in both languages. (We will discuss the setup required for Kafka in the integration section, but for now assume that the environment is prepared with Kafka accessible.)

Suppose we have a Kafka topic named "**`text_stream`**" that continuously receives lines of text (similar to our batch file lines, but in real time). We now want our pipeline to read from this topic as an unbounded **`PCollection`** of strings.

Python (Reading from Kafka Unbounded Source):

```
import apache_beam as beam
from apache_beam.io import ReadFromKafka

# Pipeline for streaming (with a runner that supports streaming,
for example, Flink or DirectRunner in streaming mode)
pipeline_options = beam.options.pipeline_options.PipelineOp-
tions(streaming=True)  # ensure streaming mode
with beam.Pipeline(options=pipeline_options) as pipeline:
    # Read from Kafka topic "text_stream"
    kafka_config = {"bootstrap.servers": "localhost:9092"}
# Kafka broker
```

```
    lines = pipeline | ReadFromKafka(
        consumer_config=kafka_config,
        topics=['text_stream'],
        key_deserializer='org.apache.kafka.common.serialization.
ByteArrayDeserializer',
        value_deserializer='org.apache.kafka.common.serialization
.StringDeserializer'
    ) | beam.Map(lambda kv: kv[1].decode('utf-8') if isin-
stance(kv[1], bytes) else kv[1])
    # The ReadFromKafka returns key-value pairs (key, value). We
only need the value (the text line).
    # Now 'lines' is an unbounded PCollection of strings (lines
of text).
```

In this code, **ReadFromKafka** is used to subscribe to the topic. We provided a bootstrap server (adjust as appropriate), the topic name, and deserializers for key and value. Kafka messages have keys and values as byte arrays; we specified the value deserializer to be String (so, we will get strings out). The result of **ReadFromKafka** in Python is a **PCollection** of key-value pairs (in Beam Python, these are just tuples). We then used a **beam.Map** to extract the value (the text) and ensure it is a string. After that, lines are a **PCollection** of strings, just like in our batch example–but crucially, it is unbounded (as data keeps coming from Kafka). We also set **PipelineOptions(streaming=True)** to indicate that we are running a streaming pipeline (some runners need this flag).

Java (Reading from Kafka Unbounded Source):

```
import org.apache.beam.sdk.io.kafka.KafkaIO;
import org.apache.kafka.common.serialization.StringDeserializer;
import org.apache.beam.sdk.values.KV;
import org.apache.beam.sdk.values.PCollection;

PipelineOptions options = PipelineOptionsFactory.create();
options.setJobName("streaming-wordcount");
// If using a specific runner like FlinkRunner, you would set:
options.setRunner(FlinkRunner.class);
options.as(org.apache.beam.sdk.options.StreamingOptions.class).
setStreaming(true);
Pipeline pipeline = Pipeline.create(options);

// Create Kafka IO read transform
PCollection<KV<String, String>> kafkaMessages = pipeline.ap-
ply(KafkaIO.<String, String>read()
    .withBootstrapServers("localhost:9092")
    .withTopic("text_stream")
    .withKeyDeserializer(StringDeserializer.class)
    .withValueDeserializer(StringDeserializer.class)
```

```
        .withoutMetadata()  // we drop Kafka metadata, we get
    PCollection<KV<key, value>>
    );
    // Extract the message values (lines of text) from the Kafka
    messages
    PCollection<String> lines = kafkaMessages.apply(org.apache.beam.
    sdk.transforms.Values.<String>create());
```

By default, **KafkaIO.read()** produces a **PCollection<KafkaRecord<K, V>>**, where each element contains not only the key and value, but also Kafka-specific metadata such as topic, partition, offset, and timestamp. Hence, when you add **.withoutMetadata()**, Beam discards this extra information and converts each element into a simpler **PCollection<KV<K, V>>**, which contains only the key and the value.

This distinction is important because it directly affects the type you see in your IDE and the type your downstream transforms must handle. Without **.withoutMetadata()**, your transforms must work with **KafkaRecord<String, String>** objects. With **.withoutMetadata()**, you can work directly with **KV<String, String>**, which is often simpler and matches most examples that operate on key–value pairs.

In short:

- Without **.withoutMetadata()** → output type is **PCollection<KafkaRecord<K, V>>**
- With **.withoutMetadata()** → output type is **PCollection<KV<K, V>>**

This makes it much easier for readers to understand compilation errors, as well as align their transform signatures with what Beam is actually producing.

In the Java snippet, **KafkaIO.read()** is configured with bootstrap servers and topic, and deserializers for both key and value (here we assume the key is a string or not used, and value is string). **.withoutMetadata()** tells Beam that we only care about the key/value, not Kafka metadata like offsets (hence, it outputs KV<key, value> pairs). Then, we use **Values.create()** transform to get just the values (the lines of text) as a **PCollection<String>**. Now, lines is our unbounded **PCollection** of strings from Kafka.

(If you are not actually running with Kafka, you could imagine using a ***GenerateSequence*** *as an unbounded source, but Kafka is a realistic example.)*

At this point, for a streaming pipeline, we have lines which are continuously receiving new elements. If we applied the same transforms as the batch example (split into words, count), what would that mean? Without windowing, an unbounded aggregation like "count of word X" would theoretically keep growing forever, and will never be final (since more occurrences could always come in the future). That is why we introduce **windowing** in streaming.

Windowing: Dividing the Infinite Stream into Finite Chunks

Windowing is the mechanism by which Beam (and stream processing in general) cuts an infinite stream into manageable, finite pieces based on time. Instead of computing aggregates over an unbounded dataset (impossible to finish), you compute them over each window. For example, you might want to count words per minute of event time, or sum metrics per hour, and so on. Hence, the windows can be based on processing time or event time, but the Beam encourages event-time windows (the time associated with each data element, typically when the event happened).

Some common window types are:

- **Fixed Windows (Tumbling Windows):** Each window covers a fixed duration (for example, 1 minute windows, or 5-minute windows), and they do not overlap. For instance, 0:00–0:59 is window1, 1:00–1:59 is window2, and so on.
- **Sliding Windows (Hopping Windows):** Windows of a fixed duration that slide by a given interval, which can overlap. For example, a 5-minute window that slides every 1 minute–this means that a new window starts at every minute, while covering the next 5 minutes of data. Thus, an event can belong to multiple overlapping sliding windows.
- **Session Windows:** These are windows that group the events occurring in temporal proximity, albeit with a gap duration. For example, a session window with a gap of 30 minutes means that if data pauses for 30 minutes, the session window will be cut off. Hence, it is useful for grouping user activity sessions.
- **Global Window:** This is a giant window that contains all data (essentially no windowing, which only makes sense with appropriate triggers and allowed lateness, and not for unbounded data, unless you intend to never actually get the final results). By default, if you do not specify the windowing in a streaming pipeline, Beam uses a global window for the `PCollection`.

Hence, for our scenario (streaming word count), a reasonable choice is to use fixed time windows, which might be, say, about 1 minute long. This means that we will count the words for each minute's worth of data separately. Every minute, we would like to output the count of each word that occurred in that minute.

Thus, to implement windowing in Beam, we use the Window transform. We also need to consider the notion of event time versus processing time, which are explained as follows:

- **Event time** is the time when the event actually happened (or a timestamp attached to the data element).
- **Processing time** is the time when the data element is processed by the pipeline.

Beam by default attaches timestamp to each element–for a Kafka source, the event timestamp might come from Kafka (for example, Kafka message timestamp, or the log append time). If not, it might default to processing time. Thus, for correct event-time windowing, each element's timestamp is used to assign it to a window. We will not manually set timestamps here, but you must be aware that in some cases you might need to assign timestamps (using **WithTimestamp** transform) if your source does not have them.

Now, let us apply a fixed window of 1 minute to our lines **PCollection** before counting, as shown here:

Python (Applying Windowing):

```
from apache_beam.transforms import window

    # Apply a fixed 1-minute windowing to the PCollection of lines
    windowed_lines = lines | beam.WindowInto(window.Fixed
Windows(60))  # 60-second windows
```

Java (Applying Windowing):

```
import org.apache.beam.sdk.transforms.windowing.FixedWindows;
import org.apache.beam.sdk.transforms.windowing.Window;
import org.joda.time.Duration;

PCollection<String> windowedLines = lines.apply(Window.into
(FixedWindows.of(Duration.standardMinutes(1))));
```

This takes each element in lines, and assigns it to a 1-minute window based on the element's timestamp. Now, any further aggregation like Count will be done per window. In other words, Beam will maintain separate counts for each window.

If we now perform the same transforms (split into words, count per element) on **windowed_lines**, we will get windowed counts. The code is almost the same as batch, but we just do it on **windowed_lines**, instead of the original lines. This is shown here:

Python (Continued Streaming Pipeline Transforms):

```
    # Assuming we applied WindowInto as above
    words = windowed_lines | beam.FlatMap(lambda line: line.
split()) | beam.Filter(lambda w: w != '')
    word_counts = words | beam.combiners.Count.PerElement()
    # Format and write out (we might write to some sink or just
log for this example)
    formatted = word_counts | beam.Map(lambda pair: f"{pair[0]}:
{pair[1]}")
    formatted | beam.io.WriteToText('path/to/output_counts', file_
name_suffix='.txt', shard_name_template='-SSSS-of-NNNN')
```

In a real streaming scenario, writing to a single file like this is tricky, as the file would be constantly appended. Beam's file writing for streaming usually requires windowed file sinks or using a database sink. However, for simplicity, we show **`WriteToText`** with a suffix–Beam will create rolling output files for each window, or set of windows (the actual behavior: by default, **`WriteToText`** in streaming mode will create files with window information in the name to avoid constantly reopening the same file). Here, we added a **`file_name_suffix='.txt'`** and a shard template. In practice, a more common streaming sink might be writing to another Kafka topic or a database. We will cover Kafka sink soon, but for now, assume that writing to text is illustrative.

Java (Continued Streaming Transforms):

```
PCollection<String> words = windowedLines.apply(FlatMapElements
        .into(TypeDescriptors.strings())
        .via((String line) -> Arrays.asList(line.split("\\s+"))))
    .apply(Filter.by((String word) -> !word.isEmpty()));
PCollection<KV<String, Long>> wordCounts = words.apply(Count.
perElement());

// Format results
PCollection<String> formatted = wordCounts.apply(MapElements.
into(TypeDescriptors.strings())
    .via((KV<String, Long> wc) -> wc.getKey() + ": " + wc.get
Value()));

// Write to an output (In a real streaming pipeline, consider an
appropriate sink)
formatted.apply(TextIO.write().to("path/to/output_counts").with-
WindowedWrites().withNumShards(1));
```

Therefore, writing streaming results to text files is primarily for debugging. Production pipelines almost always write to a message bus (Kafka) or a database.

In the Java snippet, note the use of **`.withWindowedWrites()`** on the **`TextIO.write()`**. This tells Beam that we are writing windowed data, and it should handle file naming for windows (it will include window timestamps in file names to ensure uniqueness per window). We also set **`withNumShards(1)`** just to simplify the output to one file per window (optional).

With the windowing in place, our pipeline will output results for each minute. For example, if the pipeline is running and processing data, after each window (say the window covering 12:00:00 to 12:00:59), once Beam determines it has received all data for that window (we will discuss how it decides that via watermarks and triggers next), it will emit the counts for that window (for example, counts of each word seen in that minute).

Handling Late Data and Triggers in Streaming

In streaming processing, a significant challenge is that data may arrive late or out-of-order. For instance, suppose that an event actually happened at 12:00:30 (so, it logically belongs in the 12:00-12:01 window by event time), but because of network delays or retries, it might not arrive at our pipeline until 12:05. Hence, by default, our pipeline windowing would not include that event in the 12:00-12:01 window if its results have already been emitted by then. Hence, Beam uses a concept called the **watermark** to track progress of event times, and **triggers** to decide when to emit output for a window.

- **Watermark:** The watermark is an estimate of how far along in event time the pipeline has processed. This is essentially Beam's guess that "no events older than time T will arrive in the future". The watermark is typically provided by the source (for example, KafkaIO has heuristics for watermarks). When the watermark for a window passes the window end, Beam considers that window as complete (which means that all on-time data should have arrived).
- **Allowed Lateness:** Beam allows you to specify a tolerance for late data. For example, you can say that if data is up to 5 minutes late beyond the window, Beam will still accept and process it (possibly updating results), but it will drop it beyond that. This is set via windowing API (for example, `.withAllowedLateness(Duration)` in Java, or an argument in Python `WindowInto`).
- **Triggers:** By default, Beam uses a trigger that waits for the end-of-window (that is, the watermark passes window end) to output the aggregated result, and then discards the late data. However, you can configure triggers for different behaviors. Triggers determine *when* to emit results for a window, and whether to emit early results or handle late data in a specific way. Some common triggers are:
    - **Event Time Trigger (The Default)**: Emits when watermark passes the end of window (that is, when Beam thinks all data for that window has arrived)
    - **Processing Time Trigger**: Emits results based on processing time (for example, it emits partial results every 1 minute of processing time, regardless of event times)
    - **Data-Driven Trigger**: Emits when a certain count of elements arrives in a window
    - **Repeated Triggers or Composite Triggers**: For example, emits early, as well as at end of window. After end-of-window, you can also have a trigger to handle late data if it comes (for example, output a new result if late data arrives).

Therefore, for a beginner, it is enough to understand that:

- By default, Beam will emit one result per window if it thinks that window is complete, and late data will be ignored (or rather, it will not re-open the window by default).
- If you need to account for late data, you can allow lateness, and then use triggers to emit updates.

For example, if we want to ensure we capture data that might be late by up to 5 minutes, we could set allowed lateness to 5 minutes. If we want to emit early results before the window closes (to reduce latency), we could add an early trigger. However, keep in mind that handling late data means possibly updating results (or emitting multiple results per window).

In our simple streaming word count example, let us not complicate triggers too much. We will go with default behavior, which is: the pipeline will output the count when it thinks the window is done. If some events come late, they will be considered late data, and will be dropped by default (we could log or count dropped data if we set allowed lateness with accumulation mode, but that is an advanced concept).

However, it is worth mentioning the effect on **latency**. If we wait for the perfect time when all data is in, we might wait for too long, and not show the results quickly. If we emit too early, we might miss some data. Hence, triggers are used to balance this trade-off in the following ways:

- **Low Latency, Approximate Results:** Use early triggers (for example, emit every X seconds of processing time) to get partial counts quickly, and a final count at window end. This way, results appear faster, but they might not have all data initially.
- **High Accuracy, Higher Latency:** Use the default end-of-window trigger with perhaps a bit of allowed lateness. You will get one output per window that has (almost) all data, but you wait until that window's watermark passes, which could be late if the data is delayed.

We will not code a custom trigger here, but know that you can do something like in Java:

```
Window.into(FixedWindows.of(...))
       .triggering(AfterProcessingTime.pastFirstElementInPane().
plusDelayOf(Duration.standardSeconds(30)))
       .withAllowedLateness(Duration.standardMinutes(5))
       .accumulatingFiredPanes();
```

This would, for example, emit results every 30 seconds of processing time, and also handle late data up to 5 minutes late (accumulating counts). In Python, similar options exist in '**`WindowInto`**' via arguments.

For now, our pipeline will use Beam's default event-time trigger at the end of the window to discard late data. This is okay if we assume that the data mostly arrives on time (or we are not too worried about a small delay).

Example: A Complete Streaming Pipeline (Pseudocode)

Let us summarize a complete streaming pipeline scenario in pseudocode (mixing the steps we described):

1. **Source:** Read from unbounded source (Kafka in our case).
2. **Window:** Window the incoming **`PCollection`** into fixed windows of 1 minute.
3. **Transform:** Split lines into words, and filter the empties.
4. **Aggregation:** Count occurrences per window.
5. **Sink:** Write the results somewhere (for demo we said text files; realistically, it might be another Kafka topic or database).

We already showed code fragments for each part. Here is how it might look when it is assembled:

```
Pipeline p = ... (streaming pipeline)
PCollection<String> lines = p.readFromKafka("text_stream")

PCollection<String> windowedLines = lines.windowInto(Fixed
Windows.of(1 minute))

PCollection<String> words = windowedLines.flatMap(splitIntoWords).
filter(notEmpty)

PCollection<(String, Long)> counts = words.countPerElement()

counts.writeTo(...)  (for example, write to text files or another
sink, with windowing support)
```

This pipeline will continuously run. It does not terminate on its own because the source is infinite. If you run this on a runner like Flink or Dataflow, it will keep running, while outputting new results every window. If you run it on **`DirectRunner`**, it will also attempt to keep running (**`DirectRunner`** can do streaming, but it will run until you forcefully terminate the job in a local context).

One important note to make for streaming pipelines is that when you run them on a distributed runner, you typically do not use **`waitUntilFinish()`** without a timeout, as that would mean waiting forever. Instead, you often deploy the pipeline and let it run. In local testing, you might run with a small timeout, or have some termination condition for test purposes.

Latency Considerations: By using a window of 1 minute and default trigger, our latency is around the size of the window (we will get results roughly every minute, assuming data arrives promptly). If the data arrives exactly on time, the results come at the window boundary. If some data is late, but arrives before the watermark, the runner can wait a little until it is confident that the late data is in (depending on watermark). If you need faster results, you can shorten the window, or add early triggers. However, you may have to deal with possibly incomplete data in each result.

Exactly-Once Processing: Beam (with a runner like Flink or Dataflow) strives for *exactly-once delivery of results*, meaning that each element should be reflected in the output exactly once, even if retries happen, and so on, thanks to checkpointing and deduplication. This is an advanced detail, but it is useful to know that Beam is designed to avoid double counting in failures.

We have now built a streaming pipeline and covered windowing and triggers conceptually. The key takeaways for streaming in Beam are thus explained as follows:

- Always window unbounded data before aggregation (like count) to get finite groupings.
- Use event-time windowing, so that results reflect the time events occurred, and are able to handle out-of-order via watermarks/triggers.
- Decide on triggers based on latency needs–default is simplest (one result when complete).
- Understand that streaming pipelines run continuously; therefore, you typically need to manage the job (stop it when needed, and so on).

Next, we will discuss how one might transition a pipeline from batch to streaming, and then we will cover integrating with systems like Kafka, as well as running on Flink in more detail, which will strengthen the concepts with real-world touches.

Transitioning from Batch to Streaming Pipelines

One of the powerful aspects of Apache Beam's unified model is that you can often take a pipeline that was written for batch processing and, with minimal changes, run it as a streaming pipeline (or vice versa). This is not to say that *no* changes will occur; streaming does have extra considerations as we saw, but your core logic will remain the same. Hence, for beginners, it is useful to see how similar the code looks and understand what needs to change when it is "going to streaming."

Let us use our word count example as the basis. Imagine that we wrote a batch pipeline (like we did in the earlier section) to count words in a file. Now we have a use case where words are coming in real-time (say, tweets or chat messages), and we want to count them per hour continuously. How would we transition our pipeline then?

Therefore, the differences between batch and streaming in Beam are:

- **Data Source:** Batch uses a bounded source (for example, `ReadFromText` or a finite dataset). Streaming uses an unbounded source (for example, `ReadFromKafka`, `ReadFromPubSub`, and so on). Thus, you will likely switch out the I/O transform you use for input. For example, the file input will become a Kafka subscription in streaming.
- **Windowing:** In batch, if you did any grouping or global aggregation, it would be across the entire dataset (global window by default for batch). In streaming, you will usually need to add windowing for any aggregations to get results periodically. If your logic was purely element-wise (like mapping or filtering each element independently), you can actually reuse that as-is. This is because Beam does not force you to window data if you are not aggregating, but if you want periodic results, you will have to window. Essentially, any unbounded `GroupByKey/Combine` in streaming must have a window (the system will actually default to a global window with possible infinite accumulation, which is not what you would want in most cases).
- **Triggers/Latency:** In batch, results come when processing is done. In streaming, you might configure triggers if needed. However, if you are okay with waiting until each window is complete (like batch-like completeness for each chunk), you can stick to default triggers.
- **Pipeline Termination:** A batch pipeline ends when data is done. A streaming pipeline runs until cancelled. This means that you will handle it differently in your program or deployment. For example, if you run streaming from your IDE, you might let it run indefinitely or for some test duration. If deploying, you run it as a service or job on a runner.
- **Runners:** Not all runners support streaming. For instance, Beam's `DirectRunner` supports streaming for testing, but is not meant for production streaming (it is single-machine). Runners like Flink, Spark (in newer versions), and Dataflow support streaming. Therefore, transitioning to streaming might involve changing the runner or runner configuration (for example, you might develop batch with `DirectRunner`, but also run streaming on Flink.).

Reusing Code via Modular Design

This is a good place to introduce the concept of a **composite transform**. In Apache Beam, the idiomatic way to reuse pipeline logic is to wrap multiple related transforms into a single reusable unit by creating a class (or function) that extends `PTransform`.

A composite transform therefore groups several steps, such as parsing, filtering, and counting, into one logical operation that can be applied like any other Beam transform. Therefore, it makes pipelines cleaner, improves readability, and allows the same business logic to be reused across both batch and streaming pipelines without duplication.

Hence, to illustrate code reusability, consider separating your pipeline into logical parts. For instance, you could write a function or transform for "process lines to word counts" that is agnostic to batch or streaming. Then, apply it in either pipeline.

In Python, you might have a function like this:

```
def count_words(pcoll):
    return (
        pcoll
        | beam.FlatMap(lambda line: line.split())
        | beam.Filter(lambda w: w != '')
        | beam.combiners.Count.PerElement()
    )
```

Note: *This functional style is very natural and effective in Python, and it works well for keeping pipelines concise and readable. In larger or production-grade pipelines, however, this logic is often wrapped inside a class that extends* ***`beam.PTransform`****. Hence, it makes the transform easier to unit test, configure, and reuse across multiple pipelines and projects.*

This function also takes a **`PCollection`** of lines (could be bounded or unbounded), and returns a **`PCollection`** of (word, count). In batch usage, the **`PCollection`** might be from a file read; in streaming, the **`PCollection`** might be after windowing the stream. You could use this function in both scenarios, as shown here:

```
# Batch usage
lines = pipeline | beam.io.ReadFromText('file.txt')
counts = count_words(lines)
counts | beam.io.WriteToText('output.txt')

# Streaming usage
lines = pipeline | ReadFromKafka(... etc ...)
windowed = lines | beam.WindowInto(FixedWindows(60))
counts = count_words(windowed)
counts | beam.io.WriteToText('out', file_name_suffix='.txt', shard_
name_template='...')  # or to Kafka
```

In both examples, notice that the **`count_words`** transform does not care whether pcoll is windowed or not, bounded or unbounded. It just applies the transformations element-wise and then does count per key. This is a simple example of making your pipeline logic modular, so that it can be reused.

In Java, you can similarly create a reusable **`PTransform`**. For example, define a **`PTransform<PCollection<String>, PCollection<KV<String, Long>>>`** that encapsulates the steps of splitting and counting. Then, apply it in both pipelines. (Beam's official **`WordCount`** examples actually do this–they create composite transforms for each part).

Switching from Batch to Streaming in Code:

1. Change the source transform (for example, **`TextIO`** -> **`KafkaIO`**).
2. Add windowing before any aggregation.
3. Adjust the sink (or maybe, writing to a different type of output suitable for streaming).
4. Set the pipeline options to streaming, and then choose a streaming-capable runner.

As a concrete mini example, here is how a snippet might change:

Batch Version (Java):

```
PCollection<String> lines = pipeline.apply(TextIO.read().
from("inputs/*.txt"));
PCollection<String> words = lines.apply(ParDo.of(new Extract
WordsFn()));
PCollection<KV<String, Long>> counts = words.apply(Count.per
Element());
counts.apply(TextIO.write().to("outputs/counts"));
pipeline.run().waitUntilFinish();
```

Streaming Version (Java):

```
options.as(StreamingOptions.class).setStreaming(true);
options.setRunner(FlinkRunner.class);  // for example, use Flink
runner for streaming
Pipeline pipeline = Pipeline.create(options);

PCollection<KV<Long, String>> kafkaRecords = pipeline.apply
(KafkaIO.<Long, String>read()...);
PCollection<String> lines = kafkaRecords.apply(Val-
ues.<String>create());
PCollection<String> windowedLines = lines.apply(Window.into
(FixedWindows.of(Duration.standardMinutes(1))));
PCollection<String> words = windowedLines.apply(ParDo.of(new
ExtractWordsFn()));
PCollection<KV<String, Long>> counts = words.apply(Count.per
Element());
// Write to a streaming sink, for example, Kafka or file with
windowed writes
```

```
counts.apply(MapElements.into(TypeDescriptors.strings())
                .via(kv -> kv.getKey() + ": " + kv.getValue()))
      .apply(TextIO.write().to("outputs/counts").withWindowed-
Writes().withNumShards(1));

pipeline.run(); // For streaming, typically do not waitUntilFin-
ish indefinitely
```

Here, the core logic `ExtractWordsFn` (which splits lines into words) and the `Count.perElement()` part are reused exactly. We just had to bolt on the Kafka source and windowing, and then adjust the writing.

- **Code Reusability Tip**: If you anticipate needing both batch and streaming, design your transforms in a way that they can be applied on either type of `PCollection`. Avoid hard-coding assumptions like "I will only ever get one global window" in your logic. Instead, lean on Beam's abstraction–for example, a DoFn (function in `ParDo`) does not need to know if it is in streaming or in batch; it just processes element by element.
- **Testing with Batch, Deploying as Streaming**: A common approach is to use batch pipelines on sample data to ensure the logic works, and then shift to streaming on live data. Beam helps because you might first test your `count_words` logic on a static input to verify correctness, and then integrate it with the streaming source knowing that the logic is solid.
- **Allowed Lateness**: If your batch logic assumes all data is present, consider how to handle late data when moving to streaming. You may set an allowed lateness, so that if something straggles in a little late, you still count it. Or, if exact counts per window are not crucial, you can ignore late events beyond a threshold.
- **Resource Considerations**: A streaming job will run continuously; hence, you must ensure that you provision resources accordingly. A batch job might just use resources for a short time. This is more operations-focused, but note that a streaming pipeline on Flink will occupy the cluster as a continuously running job.

In summary, transitioning from batch to streaming primarily involves:

- Changing I/O (source/sink)
- Introducing windowing
- Configuring the pipeline for streaming execution

The core transform logic can often remain unchanged. Thus, this is a testament to Beam's unified model, and it encourages you to write pipelines in a modular way. Start with as pure of a function as possible for the data processing, and then plug it into either a bounded or unbounded pipeline harness.

Now that we have both batch and streaming pipelines under our belt, let us look at integrating external systems that are common in real-world data pipelines: Apache Kafka for messaging, and Apache Flink as a runner for execution. This will give you the complete picture of how Beam works in a production-like environment.

Integrating Apache Beam with Apache Kafka and Apache Flink

In real-world scenarios, you would rarely have a self-contained pipeline that just reads local files and writes them. Therefore, you would often need to interact with other systems like message queues, databases, and run on distributed processing engines. Apache Beam makes this easier by providing connectors (IOs) for many systems, and by allowing pipelines to run on different runners.

Two important technologies to know in the context of streaming data pipelines are **Apache Kafka** and **Apache Flink**:

- **Apachc Kafka** is a popular distributed messaging system (a durable log for events), which is often used to collect and distribute high-volume data streams. You might use Kafka as the source of events for your Beam streaming pipeline, or use Beam to process data, and then write results back to Kafka for other consumers.
- **Apache Flink** is a powerful stream processing engine (and also supports batch). It can serve as a runner for Beam pipelines. Thus, running a Beam pipeline on Flink means that Flink takes care of parallel execution, state management, fault tolerance, and so on, while Beam provides the pipeline logic. Flink is known for its event-time processing and exactly-once guarantees, which complements Beam's model.

Now, let us break down the integration into two parts—using Kafka with Beam (as source and sink), and using Flink as the runner to execute Beam pipelines.

Apache Kafka Integration (Source and Sink)

Setting up Kafka: To use Kafka, you need a running Kafka cluster (which consists of one or more Kafka brokers, as well as Zookeeper, if you are using older Kafka, although the newer versions can work without Zookeeper for certain functions). For our purposes, let us assume that Kafka is running at localhost:9092 (a common default for a local single-broker setup). You will also need a topic created (for example, "input-topic", and maybe "output-topic").

Using Kafka in Beam (Java): The Beam Java SDK has a built-in I/O connector for Kafka, `KafkaIO`. We saw how to read using `KafkaIO.read()`. Similarly, there is `KafkaIO.write()` for writing to Kafka. Beam's `KafkaIO is` an *unbounded source/sink*, meaning that it is meant for streaming use. You can technically use **KafkaIO** in a batch pipeline (reading a bounded range of offsets), but typically it is for streaming.

KafkaIO Read Example (Recap) Java:

```
PCollection<KV<String, String>> kafkaRecords = pipeline.apply
(KafkaIO.<String, String>read()
    .withBootstrapServers("localhost:9092")
    .withTopic("input-topic")
    .withKeyDeserializer(StringDeserializer.class)
    .withValueDeserializer(StringDeserializer.class)
    .withoutMetadata());
PCollection<String> lines = kafkaRecords.apply(Values.<String>
create());
```

This will continuously read messages from "input-topic" as they come. If you wanted to bound it (like read up to a point), you would have to manually handle offsets or stop conditions; however, streaming jobs run continuously.

KafkaIO Write Example

If we want to send results to Kafka, say to an "output-topic", we can use **KafkaIO.write()**. Kafka expects key-value pairs on write as well. We might not care about keys for results, so we can use a null or empty key. **KafkaIO** in Beam can be used in two ways– by writing **KV<key, value>**, or via only values. The API provides a way to write just values by **calling .values()** on the transform.

For example, writing just values (with default null keys) will look like:

```
// Assume resultStrings is PCollection<String> of the final output
lines to publish
resultStrings.apply(KafkaIO.<Void, String>write()
    .withBootstrapServers("localhost:9092")
    .withTopic("output-topic")
    .withValueSerializer(org.apache.kafka.common.serialization.
StringSerializer.class)
    .withKeySerializer(org.apache.kafka.common.serialization.
VoidSerializer.class)
    .values()  // this indicates we're providing just values,
Beam will use Void for keys
);
```

In the previous example:

- We parameterized **KafkaIO.write** with **<Void, String>** because key is **void** (none) and the value is '**String**'.
- We set the serializers for key and value. Kafka clients need serializers to turn our objects into bytes. **StringSerializer** is provided by Kafka for string

values. For the key, since we used Void, we will now use **VoidSerializer** (which writes no key).

- **.values()** is called because we are giving it a **PCollection<String>** (just values). If we had a **PCollection<KV<String,String>>**, we would not call **.values()**, and instead provide both the serializers.

After this transform, Beam will connect to Kafka, and will start producing messages to "output-topic" for each element of **resultStrings**.

Using Kafka in Beam (Python): The Beam Python SDK does not implement **KafkaIO** natively in pure Python, but it leverages the **KafkaIO** from Java via cross-language. The Beam team provides **apache_beam.io.ReadFromKafka** and **WriteToKafka** in Python (in newer Beam versions), which internally launch a tiny expansion service to use the Java **KafkaIO**. We used **ReadFromKafka** earlier. Similarly, **WriteToKafka** exists.

A Python example to write to Kafka will look like:

```
from apache_beam.io import WriteToKafka
from apache_beam.coders import ByteArrayCoder

# Suppose we have a PCollection of strings called result_strings
# We need to provide bytes for key and value to Kafka (or use
specific coders)
result_strings_kv = result_strings | beam.Map(lambda s: (None,
s.encode('utf-8')))
# We map each string to a (key, value) tuple. Using None for
key (which will translate to null key in Kafka), and encode the
string to bytes.

result_strings_kv | WriteToKafka(
    producer_config={'bootstrap.servers': 'localhost:9092'},
    topic='output-topic',
    key_serializer='org.apache.kafka.common.serialization.Byte
ArraySerializer',
    value_serializer='org.apache.kafka.common.serialization.By
teArraySerializer'
)
```

In this Python snippet:

- We turned our **result_strings** into **(None, b"value")** pairs. Kafka expects byte arrays for keys and values; therefore, using **ByteArraySerializer** on both ends means that it will just take the bytes we give. We used **encode('utf-8')** to get bytes for the string. The key is None which will be treated as null.
- We call **WriteToKafka** with a producer configuration (where we specify at least the bootstrap server) and topic. We also give the serializer classes (by their fully

qualified Java class name) to use for key and value. The **`ByteArraySerializer`** just sends raw bytes.

Hence, under the hood, Beam will use the expansion service to tap into Java **`KafkaIO`** for writing.

Kafka Integration Considerations:

- **Parallelism:** **`KafkaIO`** can be parallelized by partitions. If your Kafka topic has multiple partitions, Beam can read from all of them in parallel across workers. Similarly for writing, multiple workers can write to Kafka (Kafka will partition by key if key is set, or round-robin, if the key is null by default).
- **Checkpoints and Exactly-Once:** Beam (especially with certain runners like Flink, Dataflow) will manage Kafka offsets so that if a failure happens, it does not reprocess data more than once or skip data. **`KafkaIO`** in Beam supports checkpointing offsets as part of Beam's checkpoint state, while enabling exactly-once delivery of messages in many cases. This is a complex topic, but it suffices to say that Beam's **`KafkaIO`** is built to work with Beam's model of checkpointing (it uses the Kafka Consumer API, which is designed for at-least-once, but Beam's processing and deduplication via state/watermarks can help achieve exactly-once in output quite effectively).
- **Watermark in KafkaIO:** By default, KafkaIO uses record timestamp (Kafka messages have a timestamp field, which could be set by producer as event time or log append time). It uses that for watermarks, or if none, it can use processing time. There are ways to provide custom timestamp functions, but it is usually okay by default.
- **Starting Offsets:** KafkaIO by default will start reading from the latest offset if no checkpoint is present. You can override to read from earliest by setting **`ConsumerConfig`** properties via **`.updateConsumerProperties(...)`** (for example, set **`auto.offset.reset`** to "earliest" if you want to read from beginning for new subscriptions, or provide a specific offset). Hence, for a new pipeline on an existing topic, decide if you want historical data (earliest) or just new data (latest).

In summary, integrating Kafka:

- Uses **`ReadFromKafka/KafkaIO.read`** for sources
- Uses **`WriteToKafka/KafkaIO.write`** for sinks
- Provides necessary configs (servers, topics, serializers)
- Ensures that your Beam pipeline is running with a runner that can maintain the streaming (**`DirectRunner`** is fine for tests, while Flink/Dataflow works for production)

- You may need to have Java available if you are using Python due to cross-language (Beam will automatically handle it if Java is installed).

Apache Flink Runner Integration

Apache Flink is a distributed computing engine for stateful computations over data streams (and also capable of batch processing). It has a robust model for event-time processing, windowing, and exactly-once state consistency. Flink can be seen as an alternative to frameworks like Spark or Storm, but it is particularly strong in streaming. Beam can use Flink as an execution engine through the Flink Runner.

Using Flink with Beam: If you have an existing Flink cluster or you need the scalability and features of Flink, you can still write your pipeline in Beam, besides running it on Flink. This also means that you are not tied to one runner; Beam code could run on Flink, or on Google Cloud Dataflow, and so on, without code changes (just configuration).

Setting up Flink for Beam: To run Beam on Flink, you need a Flink installation (Flink cluster or Flink local instance). The Flink Runner in Beam has two modes–the classic (for Java only) and the portable (for multiple languages, including Python).

For Java pipelines, if you include the Flink Runner library, you can run the pipeline directly on Flink by submitting your program to a Flink cluster:

- **Include Dependency**: For example, beam-runners-flink-2.xx in Maven.
- **Set Runner**: `options.setRunner(FlinkRunner.class);`.
- If you are running it on a Flink cluster, you might package your pipeline as a JAR, and then use the Flink run command to submit it.

For Python pipelines, Beam uses the portable Flink runner. This typically means that:

- You need a **Flink Job Server** that can accept Beam jobs. Beam provides a job server jar (for Flink) that you can launch, or if you run on Flink with certain flags, it starts one. In practice, using Python with Flink might involve running something like: `python pipeline.py --runner=PortableRunner --job_endpoint=localhost:8099 --environment_type=LOOPBACK`, where a Flink job server is running on 8099. However, newer Beam versions might have simplified ways, and some distributions like **Apache Beam Playground** or others can run Python on Flink easier. For Python users, using a managed service (like Dataflow) or the **`DirectRunner`** is recommended for learning. Hence, running Python on self-hosted Flink requires an advanced infrastructure setup (Job Service), which is outside the scope of this chapter.
- Alternatively, you can use Docker to run Beam Python on Flink (the Beam community provides docker images for Flink job server for Beam).

For simplicity, let us focus on Java where integration is straightforward:

Running a Beam Pipeline on Flink (Java):

1. Add the Flink Runner dependency (matching your Beam version and Flink version compatibility–check Beam docs for Flink runner compatibility).
2. In **`PipelineOptions`**, specify **`FlinkRunner`**, as shown here:

Java:

```
PipelineOptions options = PipelineOptionsFactory.create();
options.setRunner(FlinkRunner.class);
// If running on a remote Flink cluster, you might specify master
URL, and so on, via FlinkPipelineOptions
FlinkPipelineOptions flinkOptions = options.as(FlinkPipeline
Options.class);
flinkOptions.setParallelism(4); // for example, use 4 parallel
threads/tasks
```

3. Construct your pipeline as usual (batch or streaming).
4. Run the pipeline. However, you should also note that:
   i. If you run it as a normal Java program with **`FlinkRunner`**, it will actually start an embedded Flink cluster (if not provided a cluster address), and run on it before exiting. This can be alright for testing.
   ii. For long-running streaming, you likely want to submit to a Flink cluster. In that case, you might not call **`pipeline.run()`** in code, but instead use the compiled JAR with Flink's CLI:

```
mvn package  (produce an uber-jar including Beam and your
pipeline code)
./bin/flink run -c com.example.YourMainClass yourpipeline-bundled.
jar --runner=FlinkRunner --parallelism=4 ...
```

5. The Flink Runner will pick up those options, and then execute on the cluster.

Flink-Specific `PipelineOptions`: There are options like **`FlinkPipelineOptions`** (for setting parallelism, and so on), as well as **`StreamingOptions`** (for setting streaming mode true/false which usually is inferred by runner if unbounded source is present, but they can also set manually).

Exactly-Once and Checkpoints: When running on Flink, Beam leverages Flink's checkpointing mechanism to provide fault tolerance and exactly-once processing semantics. However, it is important to note that checkpointing must be explicitly enabled in the Flink configuration (for example, in **`flink-conf.yaml`**), or via Beam's **`PipelineOptions`**. It is not guaranteed to be active by default in every Flink setup.

Hence, without checkpointing, state and source offsets cannot be reliably persisted, and exactly-once guarantees do not hold.

Hence, when checkpointing is enabled, Flink periodically snapshots the pipeline's state, including window state and source progress such as Kafka offsets. For example, KafkaIO stores its consumer offsets inside Flink's checkpoints. Thus, if the job fails and restarts, it resumes reading from the exact position where it left off. This avoids both data loss and duplicate processing.

Integration Example (Kafka + Flink + Beam): A likely real scenario is using Beam to tie Kafka and Flink together, while essentially using Beam as the glue:

- **Source**: Kafka (incoming events)
- **Processing**: Beam pipeline logic (windowing, aggregations, and so on)
- **Sink**: Maybe Kafka (outgoing processed events)
- **Runner**: Flink (to execute this continuously and at scale)

Let us outline such an example in Java (while combining a few bits from the explained integration example section):

Java:

```
PipelineOptions options = PipelineOptionsFactory.create();
options.setRunner(FlinkRunner.class);
options.as(StreamingOptions.class).setStreaming(true);
options.as(FlinkPipelineOptions.class).setParallelism(4);
Pipeline pipeline = Pipeline.create(options);

// Read from Kafka "input-topic"
PCollection<KV<String, String>> kafkaInput = pipeline.apply
(KafkaIO.<String, String>read()
        .withBootstrapServers("broker:9092")
        .withTopic("input-topic")
        .withKeyDeserializer(StringDeserializer.class)
        .withValueDeserializer(StringDeserializer.class)
        .withoutMetadata());

// Extract values (assuming key is not important)
PCollection<String> events = kafkaInput.apply(Values.create());

// Window into 5 minute windows, allowing 1 minute lateness
PCollection<String> windowedEvents = events.apply(Win-
dow.<String>into(FixedWindows.of(Duration.standardMinutes(5)))
        .withAllowedLateness(Duration.standardMinutes(1)));

// Process events (for example, count occurrences of each event
type)
```

```
PCollection<KV<String, Long>> counts = windowedEvents
        .apply(FlatMapElements.into(TypeDescriptors.strings()).
via((String e) -> Arrays.asList(e.split(",")))) // just an
example parsing
        .apply(Filter.by(e -> !e.isEmpty()))
        .apply(Count.perElement());

// Format results as strings "key=count"
PCollection<String> formatted = counts.apply(MapElements.into
(TypeDescriptors.strings())
        .via(kv -> kv.getKey() + "=" + kv.getValue()));

// Write results to Kafka "output-topic"
formatted.apply(KafkaIO.<Void, String>write()
        .withBootstrapServers("broker:9092")
        .withTopic("output-topic")
        .withValueSerializer(StringSerializer.class)
        .withKeySerializer(VoidSerializer.class)
        .values());
```

This code sets up a streaming pipeline on Flink that reads from input-topic, does a windowed count (with some dummy parsing logic for demonstration), and writes results to output-topic. The **`.withAllowedLateness(Duration.standardMinutes(1))`** means that if data is up to 1 minute late to a window, Flink will still include it (Beam will emit an update for that window, if it is not already emitted; if it is already emitted it might have to use a trigger that allows late data–by default, actually, Beam would discard late data unless you specify a trigger to emit late data; **`.withAllowedLateness`** by itself does not output late data unless you also set **`.accumulatingFiredPanes()`** or similar, but it goes deeper. Thus, to keep it simple, assume **`.withAllowedLateness`** might work with default trigger to extend waiting period before closing the window).

When you run this on a Flink cluster:

- The pipeline will be deployed as a Flink job. Flink's Web UI will show the job as running.
- It will read from Kafka in parallel (Flink will create tasks, each reading some partitions).
- It will maintain the window state, and then count (by using Flink's state backend to store partial counts, until the window is complete).
- At every 5 minutes (or whenever each window triggers), it will output the counts and send them to Kafka output-topic.
- If a machine fails, Flink will restart the job from the last checkpoint; Beam's logic on Flink ensures that it picks up from last read offset on Kafka, and uses

the saved state for windows to not lose counts, achieving exactly-once output in the end.

- You can cancel or stop the job via Flink's CLI or UI when you want to stop streaming.

Monitoring: With Flink runner, you can use Flink's monitoring tools to see throughput, watermarks, and so on Beam does not abstract that away; you can still introspect via Flink.

Using Flink for Batch: You can also run batch pipelines on Flink. For example, if you have a large batch of data and a Flink cluster, you might choose to run it on Flink for efficiency. You can still set FlinkRunner, but not the streaming mode (to disable streaming mode set streaming=false). Flink will handle it similarly to how it does batch jobs.

Flink vs. DirectRunner vs. Dataflow vs Others: DirectRunner is single-machine, which is mainly used for development. Dataflow is Google's cloud service (fully managed). Flink requires you manage the cluster (or use a managed Flink service). Spark runner could run on Spark clusters similarly (though Spark's streaming model differs slightly). The good part is that Beam lets you swap these out. For example, the pipeline we wrote previous for Flink could run on Dataflow by just changing the runner and some configurations (and Dataflow has its own KafkaIO integration, or via cross-language perhaps).

Finally, always ensure that the versions are compatible; the Beam Flink runner version must match the Beam SDK version, and the Flink cluster version must be compatible as per the Beam release notes. Usually, Beam tries to support a range of Flink versions.

Summary of Kafka and Flink Integration

- **Kafka**: Beam pipelines can consume from and produce to Kafka topics. This makes Beam a good choice to build streaming data processing in a Kafka-centric architecture (for example, using Kafka as the source of truth for events).
  - We saw how to use **`ReadFromKafka/KafkaIO`** with the necessary configurations.
  - We format data appropriately (keys/values and their serialization).
  - For beginners, the key is to understand that Kafka provides the continuous data, and Beam reads/writes it in a scalable way.
  - Make sure to install Java if you are using Python for Kafka, as it uses Java under the hood.
- **Flink**: Beam can run on Flink to leverage distributed processing.
  - We need to specify the **`FlinkRunner`** in options, and also provide any cluster configuration.

- Flink offers high throughput and low latency streaming, as well as exactly-once guarantees.

Therefore, running Beam on Flink inherits these properties.

- If you have a Beam streaming pipeline (like our word count example), running it on Flink will allow it to scale out (parallelize) and handle faults robustly. For instance, Flink can maintain the state of window counts in a fault-tolerant manner (using snapshots to disk).
- From a beginner perspective, deploying to Flink is one extra step beyond writing the code; you might run a command or use Flink's interface to submit the job. However, your Beam code largely stays the same aside from pipeline options.

In practice, many streaming applications might use **Kafka, Beam, and Flink** together; Kafka as ingress, Beam (on Flink) to process, and Kafka (or a database) as egress. Hence, this trio allows you to build complex streaming data processing pipelines (Beam for logic, Flink for execution, Kafka for data distribution), without tying yourself to a single vendor or a single programming model.

Fixed Windows

Fixed windows (also known as tumbling windows) divide the timeline into equal-length, back-to-back intervals. For example, we might window events into 1-minute intervals at 00:00–00:59, 01:00–01:59, 02:00–02:59, and so on (assuming times in seconds or minutes). An event with timestamp 10:02:15 falls into the 10:02:00–10:02:59 window. Fixed windows **do not overlap**, as each moment in time belongs to exactly one fixed window.

Use Case: Fixed windows are useful for periodic reporting, such as "compute the number of clicks per minute" or "average sensor reading every hour". They provide a simple, regular time-based grouping.

Apache Beam Implementation: To apply fixed windowing in Beam, you use the **`Window`** transform (Java) or **`WindowInto`** (Python) with a **`FixedWindows`** windowing function.

- **Java:** Use **`Window.into(FixedWindows.of(Duration))`** to specify the window length. For example, **`FixedWindows.of(Duration.standardMinutes(5))`** for 5-minute windows.
- **Python**: Use **`beam.WindowInto(beam.window.FixedWindows(window_size)).`** The window size is typically given in seconds for the Python SDK (for example, **`FixedWindows(300)`** for 5 minutes).

```
// Java: Apply a fixed window of 5 minutes to a PCollection of
events
import org.apache.beam.sdk.transforms.windowing.FixedWindows;
import org.joda.time.Duration;
```

```
PCollection<Event> events = ...;  // assume this is our stream of
events with timestamps
PCollection<Event> windowedByFixed = events.apply(
    Window.into(FixedWindows.of(Duration.standardMinutes(5)))
);

# Python: Apply a fixed window of 5 minutes (300 seconds)
import apache_beam as beam

events = ...  # PCollection of events with timestamps
windowed_by_fixed = events | beam.WindowInto(beam.window.Fixed
Windows(300))
```

After this transform, the **`PCollection windowedByFixed`** is partitioned into 5-minute windows. If we now perform a grouping or aggregation (like a **`.apply(Count.perKey())`**, or **`CombineGlobally`**) on **`windowedByFixed`**, it will be computed separately for each 5-minute window, rather than over the entire collection. For instance, counting on this **`PCollection`** will produce one count per window (and per key if a key is involved), such as "Window [10:00-10:05) count = X, Window [10:05-10:10) count = Y", and so on.

Sliding Windows

Sliding windows also have a fixed duration, but they "slide" by a specified interval, which can be smaller than the window duration. This means that the windows can overlap. An element can belong to multiple sliding windows, if the windows overlap at that timestamp.

Hence, a sliding window is defined by two parameters: the **window duration** and the **window period (or slide interval)**. For example, consider 10-minute windows that start at every 5 minutes. The first window might cover 0–10 minutes, the second window 5–15 minutes, the third 10–20 minutes, and so on. An event at time 12 minutes would belong to the window [10–20) and also to [5–15), since those windows overlap that timestamp. In general, with window duration D and slide P, an event will fall into $\lceil D/P \rceil$ windows.

Use Case: Sliding windows are useful for computing moving averages or trends, where you want overlapping analyses. For example, a sliding window can produce an update every minute for the last 5 minutes of data (it is common in dashboarding to see a rolling window of activity).

Apache Beam Implementation: In Java, **use `SlidingWindows.of(Duration windowSize).every(Duration period)`**. In Python, use **`beam.window.SlidingWindows(window_size, window_period)`**.

Example of Sliding Windows in Code:

```
// Java: 10-minute windows that slide every 5 minutes
import org.apache.beam.sdk.transforms.windowing.SlidingWindows;

PCollection<Event> events = ...;
PCollection<Event> windowedBySliding = events.apply(
    Window.into(SlidingWindows.of(Duration.standardMinutes(10))
                              .every(Duration.standardMinutes(5)))
);

# Python: 10-minute windows sliding every 5 minutes
windowed_by_sliding = events | beam.WindowInto(beam.window.
SlidingWindows(600, 300))
# 600 seconds = 10 minutes window, 300 seconds = 5 minutes slide
```

Session Windows

Session windows group events by *periods of activity* separated by inactivity gaps. Unlike fixed or sliding windows, session windows do not have a fixed length; they **dynamically expand** based on data. You define a *gap duration*, which is the maximum allowed time between consecutive events in a session. Therefore, Beam will create a new session window whenever it sees a gap in events that is larger than the gap duration.

For example, suppose that the gap duration is 30 minutes. If a user has events at 10:00 and 10:10, they are within 30 minutes, so they are a part of the same session (window from 10:00 start until at least 10:10). If the next event from that user arrives at 11:00 (50 minutes later), that is beyond the gap, so the first session closes (it might be considered 10:00–10:30 or 10:00–10:10 depending on when no more events came), and a new session starts at 11:00. If another event comes at 11:20, that is 20 minutes after 11:00, still within the 30-minute gap, it extends that session to 11:20. If no more events arrive, the session will close after waiting out the gap.

Session windows are particularly useful for grouping user interactions or any events that naturally cluster in time with idle periods in between.

Use Case: For example user clickstream sessions, machine active periods, rides in a taxi app (from start to end of a ride), and so on.

Apache Beam Implementation: In Java, use **`Sessions.withGapDuration(Duration).`** In Python, use **`beam.window.Sessions(gap_duration)`**.

Example of Session Windows in Code:

```
// Java: Session windows with 30-minute gap
import org.apache.beam.sdk.transforms.windowing.Sessions;
```

```
PCollection<Event> eventsByUser = ...; // assume it is keyed by
user or we will key it
PCollection<Event> windowedBySession = eventsByUser.apply(
    Window.into(Sessions.withGapDuration(Duration.standard
Minutes(30)))
);
# Python: Session windows with 30-minute gap (1800 seconds)
windowed_by_session = events | beam.WindowInto(beam.window.
Sessions(1800))
```

Typically, session windows are applied on a per-key basis: you first key your **`PCollection`** by some entity (like user ID) using **`beam.GroupByKey`** or similar, and then apply session windowing so that sessions are computed per key. In Java, you might execute **`.apply(Window.into(Sessions...)).apply(GroupByKey.create())`** for keyed collections. In Python, if you use **`beam.GroupByKey()`** after windowing, Beam will group elements by key and window (so that you get session grouping behavior).

Important: Session windows can merge. If two separate session windows end up touching or overlapping (say an event arrives just at the boundary of the gap), Beam will merge those sessions into a single one. The windowing function handles this merging under the hood.

Now, we have seen how to define windows. However, when do we get the results for each window, especially in a streaming context where data might arrive late or out of order? This is where **triggers** and **watermarks** come into play. By default, Beam will wait until it believes it has seen all the data for a window before producing the output for it. However, you might want earlier results or need to handle late data arriving after the fact. Therefore, we will explore triggers next, which give us fine-grained control over when to emit the results of each window.

Trigger Mechanisms

A **trigger** in Apache Beam determines **when to emit the aggregated results of a window**. In batch (bounded) processing, the default behavior is to emit results when the window (often global or fixed interval) is complete (which for bounded data means that when all data is processed). In streaming (unbounded data), since data keeps coming, Beam's default trigger for time windows is based on the **event-time watermark**—essentially, it outputs the window result when it estimates that no more events will arrive for that window (we will discuss watermarks soon). This default is an *event-time trigger at end of window.*

However, depending on your use case, you might not want to wait until all data has arrived and:

- You might want **early results** (speculative results) before the window is fully complete to get low-latency updates.

- You might also want to **handle late arrivals** by emitting updates if the data arrives after the window's first result was given.

Triggers let you configure these behaviors. With triggers, we can emit multiple times per window (multiple "panes" of results); for example, one early pane, one on-time pane, and optional late panes for late data. Or, we can simply change the conditions of when a result is produced.

Beam provides several types of triggers, which are:

- **Event Time Triggers:** These operate on the event-time progress (the watermark). The default trigger in Beam is event-time based, firing once when the watermark passes the end of the window (that is when Beam believes all on-time data for that window has arrived).
- **Processing Time Triggers:** These operate on processing time (wall-clock time). For example, a trigger that fires every 1 minute of *processing time* regardless of event time. These are useful for early results (for example "give me updates every minute in real time").
- **Data-Driven Triggers (Count-Based):** These trigger based on properties of the data itself, such as a certain number of elements have arrived. For instance, fire after every 100 elements in the window.
- **Composite Triggers:** Combinations of the previous triggers. You can create complex logic like "fire after 1 minute of processing time *or* 100 elements, whichever comes first", or "fire early after 1 minute, and always fire once at end-of-window". Beam has helper triggers like **`AfterAny`**, **`AfterAll`**, Repeatedly, and so on, to combine triggers.

Therefore, by configuring triggers, you trade-off between **completeness** of results and **latency**. A very slow trigger (like waiting for all data) gives complete results, but gives out high latency, whereas a fast trigger (for example, every few seconds) gives low latency, but the results might be partial, and will therefore need updates.

Default Behavior: If you do not set a trigger, Beam uses a default event-time trigger that emits once per window when the watermark passes the window's end, and it will discard any late data (late data is dropped by default). This yields one output per window containing all on-time data. There are no early results, and the late data is ignored.

To get different behavior, we must set a trigger explicitly. When we set a trigger in Beam, we also need to consider two other settings, which are:

- **Allowed Lateness:** How long to wait for late data after a window closes (more on this in the next section, but essentially it keeps the window open for late events).

- **Accumulation Mode:** Whether to accumulate data across trigger firings or discard after each firing.
  - **Discarding Mode**: Each trigger firing outputs the data for that pane and then forgets those elements (the next firing will only include new elements).
  - **Accumulating Mode**: Outputs keep accumulating all elements seen so far (the next firing's result will include previous ones again). Accumulating mode is useful if you want each successive pane to include corrections (for example, final count includes earlier elements and late ones, and not just the late ones by themselves).

Let us look at an example of using triggers in Beam. Suppose that we have a streaming pipeline with a 5-minute fixed window, but we want to emit an early result for each window every 1 minute of processing time, and also handle late data up to 5 minutes late. We can achieve this by:

1. Setting an event-time trigger to fire at the end of window (this happens by default with **`AfterWatermark`**)
2. Adding an early trigger on processing time (every 1 minute)
3. Allowing lateness of 5 minutes and adding a late trigger (for example, fire each time late data arrives, or you could fire once after end of allowed lateness)

In Java, we might configure this with the Window transform's trigger API, which is:

```
import org.apache.beam.sdk.transforms.windowing.AfterWatermark;
import org.apache.beam.sdk.transforms.windowing.AfterProcessing-
Time;
import org.apache.beam.sdk.transforms.windowing.AfterPane;
import org.apache.beam.sdk.transforms.windowing.AccumulationMode;
import org.joda.time.Duration;

PCollection<Event> events = ...;
PCollection<Event> windowed = events.apply(
    Window.<Event>into(FixedWindows.of(Duration.standard
Minutes(5)))
        .triggering(AfterWatermark.pastEndOfWindow()
            .withEarlyFirings(AfterProcessingTime.pastFirst
ElementInPane()
                                                   .plusDelayOf
(Duration.standardMinutes(1)))
            .withLateFirings(AfterPane.elementCountAtLeast(1)) )
        .withAllowedLateness(Duration.standardMinutes(5))
        .accumulatingFiredPanes()
);
```

Now, let us break down what this Java code does:

- **FixedWindows.of(5 min)**: We window the data into 5-minute chunks.
- **triggering(...)**: We set a custom trigger, where:
    - **AfterWatermark.pastEndOfWindow()** is the core event-time trigger that waits until the watermark passes the window end (that is, all on-time data likely received).
    - **.withEarlyFirings(AfterProcessingTime.pastFirstElementInPane().plusDelayOf(1 min))** adds an early firing trigger. **pastFirstElementInPane()** means that the timer starts when the first element in that window is seen; then **.plusDelayOf(1 min)** means fire for 1 minute after that. Essentially, this will give an early emission of about 1 minute into the window with the data that has arrived by then. (It will repeat for each pane if we used a Repeatedly, but in this configuration, the Beam will fire once every minute because after firing, since we use accumulating mode, the pane remains open for more data.)
    - **.withLateFirings(AfterPane.elementCountAtLeast(1))** means that after the window has closed (watermark passed), if late data arrives, fire output for each late element (or each batch of late elements). This is a simple way to say "whenever late data comes, output it immediately".
- **withAllowedLateness(5 min)**: Keep the window open for 5 minutes after it would normally close to accept late data up that might come up till 5 minutes later.
- **accumulatingFiredPanes()**: Use accumulating mode, which means that each firing includes all data seen so far. So, the on-time pane will have all on-time data. If a late element comes, the late pane output will include both the on-time data, as well as that late element (that is, the count would be final count). This is often used so that the final pane represents the true final result.

In Python, trigger syntax is similar, but it uses the **beam.trigger** module. The Python Beam SDK requires specifying **allowed_lateness** and **accumulation_mode** when setting a trigger (just like in Java). Here is how we can do the same in Python:

```
import apache_beam as beam
from apache_beam import trigger

windowed = ( events
    | beam.WindowInto( beam.window.FixedWindows(300),  # 5 minutes
in seconds
        trigger=trigger.AfterWatermark(
            early=trigger.AfterProcessingTime(60),      # fire early
after 60 sec of first element
```

```
            late=trigger.AfterCount(1)                  # fire whenever
  1 late element arrives
        ),
        accumulation_mode=trigger.AccumulationMode.ACCUMULATING,
        allowed_lateness=300 )  # 5 minutes lateness
)
```

In this Python snippet:

- We set a 5-minute window (**`FixedWindows(300)`** seconds).
- The trigger is **`AfterWatermark`** with **`early=AfterProcessingTime(60)`** seconds (or 1 minute) and **`late=AfterCount(1)`**.
- **`accumulation_mode=AccumulationMode.ACCUMULATING`** is used to accumulate results.
- **`allowed_lateness=300`** seconds is used to keep the window open to admit late data for 5 minutes.

Note: *In Python,* ***`AfterProcessingTime(60)`*** *by itself will fire once 60 seconds of processing time after the first element in the window. If we wanted it to fire repeatedly at every 60 seconds until the window closes, we could wrap it with* ***`trigger.Repeatedly(trigger.AfterProcessingTime(60))`****. In our example, one early firing per window is enough. Also,* ***`AfterCount(1)`*** *as a late trigger means we will get an output immediately for each late element; if you prefer to wait and gather possibly multiple late elements, you could use a higher count or a time-based late trigger.*

With these triggers, how will the output look? For each window, we can get:

- An early pane at about 1 minute into the window (processing time), which will generate partial results.
- The on-time pane when the watermark passes the window end (around the 5-minute mark, or whenever the Beam is convinced that it has all data up to that time); this is the official window result with all on-time data.
- If any late events (up to 5 minutes late) arrive, each triggers an output (since we used AfterCount(1) late trigger). If multiple late events arrive close together, Beam may also bundle them depending on runner optimizations, but logically we will allow outputs for each late event.
- After 5 minutes of allowed lateness, the window is closed for good; any data that comes up later than that is dropped.

Different Trigger Patterns: The example previous combined event time, processing time, and data-driven triggers (making use of composite trigger capabilities). You can also use simpler triggers like:

- **`Processing Time` Trigger Only:** For example, **`Repeatedly.forever(AfterProcessingTime(x))`** on a global window to get periodic outputs every *x* time. This effectively ignores event times, and gives you just a pulse output.

- **`Count` Trigger:** For example, **`AfterCount(100)`** to emit results each time 100 elements have arrived in the window.
- **`AfterAll/AfterAny`:** For example, **`AfterAll.of(AfterProcessingTime(30 sec), AfterCount(100))`** fires only when *both* 30 seconds have passed and 100 elements are seen (whichever comes last in practice), whereas **`AfterAny`** would fire when *either* condition is met (whichever comes first).
- **`OrFinally`:** In Java, there is **`OrFinally`** that provides a final condition that will fire, and then closes the window.

For a beginner-friendly approach, the main triggers to remember are:

- **Default (Event Time) Trigger**: One output when window is complete (watermark)
- **Early Trigger (Processing Time or Element Count)**: For speculative early results
- **Late Trigger**: To handle late data after the event-time closure
- **Accumulation vs. Discarding**: Whether to keep adding or reset for each pane

Triggers give a lot of flexibility in streaming. However, they work closely with the concept of **watermark** and allowed lateness, which define when Beam considers a window "complete". In the previous example, we mentioned watermarks and allowed lateness without defining them. Thus, in the next section, we will clarify what watermarks are and how Beam handles late data.

Watermarks and Late Data Handling

In streaming pipelines, since data can arrive late or out of order, we need a way to measure progress in event time. A **watermark** is Beam's mechanism to track how far along in event time the pipeline is, and to estimate when all data for a certain timestamp (or window) has likely arrived.

A watermark is often described as a timestamp T, such that the system believes that it has seen all events with event times less than T. In other words, when the watermark for a `PCollection` reaches time X, Beam assumes there will be no more elements with timestamp < X. Watermarks are usually provided by the data sources, or are assigned in the pipeline. For example, if reading from Kafka or Pub/Sub, the source might advance the watermark as messages come in, or if reading from a file, the watermark might jump to end when file read is done.

Beam's default trigger (event-time trigger) uses the watermark; when the watermark passes the end of a window, Beam fires the window's output, while considering that the window is complete. However, what if this assumption is wrong and some straggler event arrives late? Beam allows us to handle that through **late data** mechanisms.

Late Data: Any element that arrives with an event timestamp **less than the current watermark** is considered late. More concretely, if the window for 10:00–10:05 is closed at watermark time 10:05, and then an event with timestamp 10:03 arrives afterward, that event is late for its window. By default, Beam will drop late data (it will not include it in the window computation), to avoid updating results endlessly. However, you can choose to accept and process late data by setting an **allowed lateness** on the window.

Allowed Lateness: This is a windowing property that tells Beam to keep the window open for a certain amount of additional time (in event time) beyond the window's end to accept late arrivals. If late data arrives within this lateness interval, Beam will still process it (possibly emitting a late pane via triggers). If data arrives after the allowed lateness has passed, that data is considered **droppable late data,** and is finally discarded.

For example, if allowed lateness is 5 minutes for a window that ends at 10:05, Beam will accept late events timestamped up to 10:05 + 5min = 10:10. The watermark 10:10 (window end and allowed lateness) is often considered the point of final closure for that window. Any data for the 10:00–10:05 window is dropped if it exceeds 10:10.

It is also important to note that allowed lateness is a trade-off: keeping windows open longer consumes more memory/state, and the late data complicates output. You should set it based on how late data can arrive in your scenario and how much you are willing to deal with updates. Some pipelines with strict latency requirements might set allowed lateness to 0 (drop all late data), while others with important accuracy needs might allow a generous lateness (minutes or hours).

Using Allowed Lateness in Code:

- In Java, as shown earlier, you specify **`.withAllowedLateness(Duration)`** when configuring the Window transform.
- In Python, you pass the **`allowed_lateness`** parameter to **`WindowInto`**.

If you set allowed lateness, but do not specify triggers, Beam's default behavior (without a late trigger) is to drop late data anyway. Effectively, to make use of allowed lateness, you should also have a trigger that can fire to emit late data. One common approach is using the default event-time trigger for on-time data, and then adding a late trigger for late data (like **`.withAllowedLateness(...)`** + **`.withLateFirings(...)`** in Java, or using **`trigger.AfterWatermark(late=...)`** in Python as we saw). If you do not specify any late trigger, but allow lateness, the late elements will be collected in the window. However, they will never be emitted unless you have something like **`.withClosingBehavior(FIRE_ALWAYS)`** (in some Beam SDKs) to force a final pane at window closure.

Watermark Propagation: The watermark advances as the sources inject data. For example, if you are reading from multiple input sources, the overall watermark is the minimum of the sources (to avoid declaring completeness until all sources catch up). Runners like Dataflow often visualize watermark progress. Therefore, if an event is extremely late (beyond allowed lateness), it is often dropped by default; you might choose to send such data to a side output or logging, if needed, but that is beyond the basic scope.

To summarize late data handling:

- **On-Time Data:** It arrives before the watermark (that is, before the window is closed) and is handled by default.
- **Late Data within Allowed Lateness:** It can be included in results if allowed lateness and the triggers for late data are set. It often produces *late panes* of output.
- **Late Data beyond Allowed Lateness:** It is dropped (ignored) by the pipeline.

Thus, Beam's design, with watermarks and allowed lateness, ensures that the windows eventually finish, and you can trade-off between waiting for all the data and the timeliness. The watermark is a heuristic (it might sometimes be wrong, data can still arrive later), which is why allowed lateness exists as a safety net.

Finally, how do these concepts apply in real-world scenarios? Let us explore a few practical examples of pipelines, and how they use event time, windows, triggers, and watermarks.

Real-World Applications

Now that we have covered the mechanics, let us put them in context. Here are some typical real-world applications of event time windowing and triggers in Apache Beam, and how you would handle time in each case:

- **Real-time Metrics and Reporting (Fixed Windows with Early Results):** Imagine that you run a website and want to update a dashboard every minute with the number of page views in the last minute. You would use a **fixed window of 1 minute** for page view events. To get low-latency updates, you might set an **early trigger** to emit results periodically (say every 10 seconds processing time) before the minute is over. Late data is not a huge concern if most events arrive on time (perhaps, an allowed lateness of a few seconds to account for minor delays). Hence, this setup ensures the dashboard gets a near-real-time count that updates continuously, and the count finalizes at the end of 1 minute. In Beam, you might use/do:
    - **Window** into 1-minute fixed windows.

- **Trigger**: After processing time every 10 seconds, and default event-time at window end. Accumulate counts so that each update is incremental.
- **Allowed Lateness**: Small (or 0), if you prefer to ignore very late events. This provides frequent updates (early panes), as well as a final accurate count at the end of each minute window.

- **User Session Analysis (Session Windows):** Suppose that you are analyzing user sessions on a platform. A session is a period of continuous activity by a user, and you want to compute something like total actions per session or session duration. You can use **session windows** keyed by user ID, with a gap duration that defines inactivity (for example, 30 minutes as in our example). All events for a user that occur within 30 minutes of each other will be grouped into the same window/session. If an event arrives late (out of order), as long as it is within the allowed lateness, it can still be merged into the session. Here, you would likely allow some lateness (since maybe logs could arrive late), but maybe not too long. Triggers might simply be default (emit when session is complete according to watermark), and maybe let out a final fire at the end of allowed lateness to catch any stragglers. The result is that you get an output per session with aggregated information. For example, you might output when the user's session is over (no events for 30 minutes)—the watermark will eventually pass the end of that session window, and trigger the output. If an event is delayed, but it arrives 10 minutes late, it can still be added to the session if it is within allowed lateness, and will be updated in the session output.
- **IoT Sensor Data with Out-of-Order Events (Handling Late Data):** Consider IoT sensors sending temperature readings to a central system. Network issues might delay some readings. You want to compute the hourly average temperature. Here, you would use **fixed windows of 1 hour** for the event times. However, because readings can be late, you set an allowed lateness (perhaps 5-10 minutes) to accept late readings. You might not need early triggers in this case, if you are content with hourly results, but you do want to include late arrivals to improve accuracy. Beam will therefore use the watermark (perhaps based on sensor timestamps or ingestion times) to trigger the initial hourly result at roughly the hour boundary. If some readings come in a few minutes late, a late trigger can recompute or adjust the average. The implementation is therefore:
  - **Window**: 1 hour fixed
  - **Allowed Lateness**: For example, 5 minutes
  - **Trigger**: Could be simply `AfterWatermark` with `.withLateFirings(AfterCount(1))` and accumulating mode; hence, any late reading causes a recomputed average. Or, you could choose to emit only once at end of allowed lateness (to avoid multiple outputs).

This way, you get one output per hour on the hour; if any stragglers arrive shortly after, you get an updated output that includes them.

If a sensor reading arrives days late (beyond allowed lateness), it will be dropped, and will be logged as too late.

- **Complex Event Processing (Multiple Triggers and Windows):** In more complex pipelines, you might combine windowing with triggers to detect patterns. For example, detecting fraud might involve a session window per user, and a trigger that fires early if suspicious activity is detected (data-driven trigger). Or, a pipeline might use a **global window with processing-time triggers** for cases where event time is not relevant (rare, but for some periodic sync jobs it could make sense to just emit every X minutes using processing time triggers).

In all these scenarios, the key is to pick a windowing strategy that matches the problem's time frame, and triggers that balance timeliness against completeness. You should also tune allowed lateness based on how delayed data can be. If you know that your data sources have at most a 2-minute delay, setting allowed lateness slightly before that (say 5 minutes) ensures that you capture almost all data. If data is nearly always on time, you might not allow lateness at all.

Monitoring and Debugging: When building Beam pipelines with windows and triggers, it is helpful to log, or inspect how windows and panes are firing. For instance, Beam's `org.apache.beam.sdk.transforms.windowing.PaneInfo` (Java), or simply logging in a DoFn in Python can tell you if an element is in an early/late pane. Hence, in practice, you can test with sample (or real) streaming data to ensure that your trigger behavior meets your expectations.

Conclusion

This chapter delivered a practical, end-to-end view of how Apache Beam enables unified development for both batch and streaming pipelines. We explored core concepts such as pipelines, bounded and unbounded data, and how Beam's programming model allows the same business logic to be reused across processing modes. Through hands-on examples in Python and Java, we built batch pipelines, evolved them into streaming pipelines using windowing and triggers, and learned how thoughtful design makes this transition straightforward. We also saw how Beam integrates naturally with real-world systems, such as Apache Kafka for data ingestion and output, and Apache Flink as a powerful runner that provides scalability, state management, and fault tolerance, while enabling complete production-ready data flows.

We then focused on time-based processing, one of Beam's most important strengths for streaming analytics. Thus, by using event time instead of processing time, pipelines reflect the real timing of events rather than when they happen to arrive. Windowing breaks infinite streams into meaningful chunks, while watermarks act as heuristics for progress and completeness, and triggers provide precise control over when results are emitted, while supporting early results, on-time results, and late data corrections. Together, these concepts make it possible to build streaming systems that are both responsive and accurate, even in the presence of out-of-order, delayed, or bursty data. Hence, with this foundation, you will be well prepared to design pipelines that are robust, scalable, and aligned with real-world data behavior.

In the next chapter, we will explore how data is manipulated and represented inside pipelines. You will also learn how Beam's core transformations work in detail and how coders define the serialization of data, which is critical for performance, correctness, and interoperability across runners.

CHAPTER 5
Transformations and Coders in Apache Beam

Introduction

Using Apache Beam transforms and coders allow you to build efficient data pipelines. Hence, in this beginner-friendly chapter, we will explore how to manipulate data with core **transformations,** and how **coders** handle data serialization in Apache Beam. By the end of this chapter, you will know how to apply common transforms (like `Map`, `Filter`, and `FlatMap`), how to group and partition data, and how to optimize your pipeline with custom coders. We will also provide step-by-step examples in both **Python** and **Java**, and show you how to run pipelines locally (using the `DirectRunner`) on Google Cloud Dataflow.

Using Apache Beam transforms and coders allow you to build **efficient** data pipelines, where efficiency refers not only to correctness and scalability, but also to performance and portability across execution environments. Beam's unified programming model means that you can write the same logic once, and run it on diverse runners like Flink, Spark, or Google Cloud Dataflow without changing your code, which is a distinguishing characteristic of maintainable, flexible architectures. The Beam model and its transforms simplify parallel execution; therefore, coders will be able to ensure that data is correctly serialized as it flows between workers, which is essential for achieving performance and scalability in distributed systems.

In practice, efficiency in Beam pipelines is tied to how well they leverage runner capabilities and serialization choices. For example, when pipelines are run on distributed engines such as Apache Flink or Dataflow, Beam's abstractions allow horizontal scaling to handle growing workloads while keeping your pipeline logic stable and portable across environments. Case studies published on the official Apache Beam site show real-world impact; companies like LinkedIn, HSBC, and Booking.com have reported substantial performance improvements, cost reductions, and processing scale gains by adopting Beam's unified model for data processing.

(https://beam.apache.org/case-studies/)

Beam's programming model centers around **`PCollections`** (parallel collections of data) and **`PTransforms`** (operations on that data). Therefore, the transforms discussed here are applied to **`PCollections`** using the Beam SDKs. In the Python SDK, you will often use the pipe | operator to chain transforms, whereas in Java you will use the **`apply()`** method. Now, let us dive into the fundamental transformations first.

Structure

- Introduction to Key Transformations (**`Map`**, **`Filter`**, and **`FlatMap`**)
- Grouping and Partitioning Data (**`GroupByKey`**, **`Partition`**, **`CoGroupByKey`**)
- Understanding Coders in Beam
- Optimizing Serialization with **`PCollection`** Coders
- Example Pipeline Implementations

Introduction to Key Transformations (`Map`, `Filter`, and `FlatMap`)

Element-wise transformations in Beam let you process elements in a PCollection independently. The most common ones are **`Map`**, **`Filter`**, and **`FlatMap`**. These transforms are similar in spirit to their counterparts in other data processing frameworks. In summary:

- **`Map`**: This applies a function to each element and outputs a single transformed element for each input element.
- **`Filter`**: This retains only elements that satisfy a given condition (predicate) and discards others.
- **`FlatMap`**: This is similar to Map, but the function can output **zero, one, or many** elements for each input. Moreover, the results are flattened into a single collection.

These transformations are *parallelizable*, and can operate independently on elements (as no knowledge of other elements is needed). Under the hood, these are convenience transforms that are built on Beam's lower-level **`ParDo`** (parallel Do) transform. Hence, as a beginner, you can use **`Map`**, **`Filter`**, and **`FlatMap`** for simplicity. Moreover, you must know that Beam will handle the parallel execution for you.

One important requirement in Beam is that **your element-wise functions must be**

serializable (so that they can be shipped to workers), and should be **idempotent / side-effect-safe**. Beam runners may retry user code due to failures, scaling, or checkpoint recovery, and the model does not guarantee that your function will run exactly once per element. This is why transforms should avoid non-idempotent side effects (for example, writing to an external database, calling an API, or even relying on `print()` for correctness). Therefore, if you perform side effects, use proper sinks/connectors or design the operation, so that repeated execution does not produce incorrect results (for example, deduplication, transactional writes, or idempotent updates).

Decision Table 1: `Map` / `Filter` / `FlatMap` vs. `ParDo`

What You Need to Do	Use This	Reason
Apply a simple 1→1 transformation (no side outputs, no state/timers)	`Map`	Most readable for element-wise mapping
Keep/drop elements based on a predicate	`Filter`	Purpose-built and clear intent
Turn 1 element into 0..N elements (tokenize, explode arrays)	`FlatMap`	Designed for fan-out; output is automatically flattened
Need side outputs (main + "errors"/"late"/"dead-letter")	`ParDo`	It supports tagged outputs and richer control flow.
Need state, timers, or per-key memory	`ParDo` (stateful DoFn)	`Map`/`FlatMap`/`Filter` do not expose state/timers APIs.
Need access to element metadata (timestamps, windows, pane info)	`ParDo`	DoFn context provides these details.
Complex logic, multiple steps, or shared setup/teardown	`ParDo`	Cleaner encapsulation, as well as easier testing and reuse

Table 5.1: *Decision Table on How to Use Map/Filter /FlatMap vs ParDo*

A rule of thumb here will be to start with `Map/Filter/FlatMap` for straightforward element-wise logic, and then graduate to `ParDo` when you need richer pipeline control (context, side outputs, state/timers, or complex processing).

Decision Table 2: When to Avoid GroupByKey and Prefer Combine.perKey

Goal	Prefer	Avoid	Why
Sum/count/min/max/mean, or any associative aggregation	`Combine.perKey(...)` / built-ins like `Count.PerKey()`	`GroupByKey()`	To combine pre-aggregates ("combines") before shuffle, reducing network/memory pressure
You only need a compact summary per key (for example, running totals).	`Combine.perKey`	`GroupByKey`	`GroupByKey` materializes *all* values per key, which can blow up memory for hot keys.

Large key cardinality or "hot key" risk	**Combine.perKey** + windowing	**GroupByKey** everywhere	Minimizes shuffle volume and per-key fan-in load
You truly need the full list of values per key (for example, join-like behavior, or a full-session event list).	**GroupByKey** (carefully, usually windowed + bounded)	–	It is sometimes unavoidable, but must control state size (windows/TTL/cleanup).

Table 5.2: *Decision Table on When to Avoid GroupByKey and When to Prefer Combine.perKey*

Anti-Pattern to Avoid: Using **GroupByKey()** as a default for "aggregation". In production, it is one of the fastest ways to create memory spikes and long shuffles; reach for **Combine.perKey()**, unless you explicitly need *all* raw values.

Now, let us look at each transform in detail with examples in Python and Java. However, before running any code, ensure that you have Apache Beam set up (for example, **pip install apache-beam** for Python, or adding the Apache Beam SDK dependency for Java).

Map Transform

The **Map** transform applies a user-defined function to each element in the input **PCollection** and produces a new element as output. It is a 1-to-1 transform–one output for every input element. Use Map when you want to *transform* or *enrich* each element independently.

- **Python:** In the Python SDK, you can use **beam.Map(func)** with a lambda or function. For example, to square each number in a **PCollection** of integers, use:

```
import apache_beam as beam

# Sample input: PCollection of numbers
with beam.Pipeline() as p:
    numbers = p | beam.Create([1, 2, 3, 4])
    # Use Map to square each number
    squares = numbers | beam.Map(lambda x: x * x)
    # Print results (for local runner demonstration)
    squares | beam.Map(print)
```

In this example, we first create a **PCollection** of numbers with the elements [1, 2, 3, 4]. Then we apply **beam.Map(lambda x: x * x)** to produce a new **PCollection** of squares where each number is replaced by its square. The final **beam.Map(print)** will print each squared number (when running locally with the **DirectRunner**).

Note: *Using* ***beam.Map(print)*** *is convenient for quick local demonstrations with the* ***DirectRunner****, as the output is printed directly to your console. However, on distributed* *runners (such as Dataflow, Flink, or Spark), this behaves differently. The* ***print()*** *function executes on remote worker machines; therefore, its output goes to the worker logs, and not to your local terminal. Additionally, since* ***print()*** *returns None, the elements flowing out of this transform will become None, which usually makes the downstream pipeline incorrect or unusable.*

In real pipelines, avoid using **print()** as a processing step. Instead, use proper logging (for example, Python's logging module) for debugging, and Beam **metrics** (counters, distributions, gauges) to observe pipeline behavior in a structured way. For final results or debugging output, write data to a sink such as files, databases, or monitoring systems, rather than relying on print().

- **Java:** In Java, you can use the **MapElements** transform with a type descriptor for the result type, or use **ParDo** with a DoFn. The Beam Java SDK also allows using Java 8 lambdas for concise mapping. For example, to square each integer:

```
import org.apache.beam.sdk.Pipeline;
import org.apache.beam.sdk.transforms.MapElements;
import org.apache.beam.sdk.values.TypeDescriptors;
// ... (other necessary imports)

Pipeline p = Pipeline.create();
PCollection<Integer> numbers = p.apply(Create.of(1, 2, 3, 4));
// Use MapElements with a lambda to square each number
PCollection<Integer> squares = numbers.apply("SquareNumbers",
    MapElements.into(TypeDescriptors.integers())
              .via((Integer x) -> x * x)
);
// You could further use the squares PCollection, for example,
print or write to output.
p.run().waitUntilFinish();
```

Here, **MapElements.into(TypeDescriptors.integers())** tells Beam the output type (Integer), and the **.via((Integer x) -> x * x)** part provides the lambda function to apply. Hence, each element from numbers is processed to produce the corresponding square in the squares **PCollection**. If we run this pipeline, squares would contain [1, 4, 9, 16]. (In a real pipeline, you might write the results to an output sink, rather than printing them to the console.)

Explanation: The **Map** transform is handy for simple transformations like scaling numbers, converting types (for example, parsing strings to objects), or extracting a field from a more complex element. Map operations do not change the number of elements in the collection (just their content). If your mapping function needs to drop or produce multiple elements, consider using **Filter** or **FlatMap** instead (as we will see next).

Filter Transform

The **Filter** transform allows you to include or exclude elements from a **PCollection** based on a predicate (a condition). It is used to *filter out* unwanted data and let only certain elements pass through. Each element is tested against a predicate function; if the function returns true, the element is kept, otherwise it is discarded.

- **Python:** Use **beam.Filter(predicate).** For example, to keep only even numbers from a **PCollection**:

```
with beam.Pipeline() as p:
    numbers = p | beam.Create([1, 2, 3, 4, 5, 6])
    evens = numbers | beam.Filter(lambda x: x % 2 == 0)
    evens | beam.Map(print)  # This will print 2, 4, 6
```

The **lambda x: x % 2 == 0** is the predicate that returns True for even numbers and False for odd numbers, so evens will contain [2, 4, 6]. In Python, you can also define a standalone function instead of a lambda for more complex conditions. The Filter transform does not modify the elements, it only selects a subset of them.

- **Java:** In Java, Beam provides a Filter transform with static methods or you can use **Filter.by(...)** with a predicate. For example, to filter a **PCollection** of strings keeping only those longer than 3 characters, as shown here:

```
import org.apache.beam.sdk.transforms.Filter;
import org.apache.beam.sdk.values.PCollection;
import org.apache.beam.sdk.transforms.Create;

PCollection<String> words = p.apply(Create.of("hello", "hi",
"world", "beam"));

PCollection<String> longWords = words.apply(
    "FilterLongWords",
    Filter.by((String word) -> word.length() > 3)
);

// longWords will contain: "hello", "world", "beam"
```

We can demonstrate filtering even numbers in Java as well, such as:

Java:

```
import org.apache.beam.sdk.transforms.Filter;

PCollection<Integer> numbers = p.apply(Create.of(1, 2, 3, 4, 5, 6));
PCollection<Integer> evens = numbers.apply("KeepEvens",
    Filter.by((Integer num) -> num % 2 == 0)
);
// evens will contain 2, 4, 6
```

In this Java example, we filter the numbers collection, while keeping only those that satisfy the predicate (**num % 2 == 0**). The result evens will contain [2, 4, 6]. Beam allows using lambda expressions (because **Filter.by** expects a **SerializableFunction**) for conciseness. You can also use predefined filters like **Filter.greaterThan(3)** for numeric comparisons, or implement the **SerializableFunction/Predicate** interface for more complex logic.

Explanation: Use **Filter** when you need to remove unwanted data early in your pipeline. This helps reduce the volume of data processed by subsequent transforms. Filter does not change the data itself, only the *set* of elements. When it is combined with Map, you can first narrow down to relevant data, and then transform it.

FlatMap Transform

The **FlatMap** transform is a generalized form of Map that can output **zero, one, or many elements** for each input element. This is useful for tasks like splitting a single element into multiple parts. For example, splitting sentences into words produces multiple outputs per input. **FlatMap** can also drop elements (by outputting none for some inputs); therefore, it can be used for filtering as well, though Beam provides Filter for that specific purpose as we saw.

- **Python:** In the Python SDK, use **beam.FlatMap(func)**. The function returns an *iterable* (list, generator, and so on) of results for each input. Beam will flatten these iterables into the output **PCollection**. For example, let us split lines of text into words:

```
with beam.Pipeline() as p:
    lines = p | beam.Create([
        "Apache Beam is unified",
        "Beam supports batch and streaming"
    ])
    # FlatMap: split each line into words
    words = lines | beam.FlatMap(lambda line: line.split(" "))
    words | beam.Map(print)
```

In this example, the input **PCollection** lines contains two strings. The **FlatMap** transform uses **line.split(" ")** to split each line into a list of words. The Beam then flattens these lists–the resultant **PCollection** words contains all the individual words from all the lines. For the given input, words would output "**Apache**", "**Beam**", "**is**", "**unified**", "**Beam**", "**supports**", "**batch**", "**and**", "**streaming**" (each as a separate element). Notice that for each input line, multiple outputs (the words) are produced. If a line were empty or the split found no words, the function could return an empty list, and **FlatMap** would simply not add any elements for that input (hence, zero outputs for that input, which is allowed).

You can also define **FlatMap** functions using a generator. For example:

Python

```
def split_words(line):
    for word in line.split(" "):
        yield word

words = lines | beam.FlatMap(split_words)
```

This yields the same result. The key is that **FlatMap** expects an iterable of results from the function.

- **Java:** In Java, the equivalent is **FlatMapElements**. We provide a function that returns an iterable for each element. For example, splitting lines into words in Java will look like:

```
import org.apache.beam.sdk.transforms.FlatMapElements;
import java.util.Arrays;
// ...

PCollection<String> lines = p.apply(Create.of(
    "Apache Beam is unified",
    "Beam supports batch and streaming"
));
PCollection<String> words = lines.apply("SplitLines",
    FlatMapElements.into(TypeDescriptors.strings())
                   .via((String line) -> Arrays.asList(line.
split(" ")))
);
// words PCollection will contain each word as a separate element.
```

Here, for each input line (a String), the lambda returns a **List<String>** of the words. Beam flattens these lists into the output **PCollection** words. The result is similar to the Python example, which is a **PCollection** of individual words. We also used **Arrays.asList** to easily create a list from the array returned by **line.split(" ")**.

Explanation: Use **FlatMap** when a single input should result in multiple outputs. Common use cases include splitting records (for example, parsing logs into individual events), expanding hierarchical data, or emitting alternative representations of data. **FlatMap** can also be used to combine the effect of Map and Filter; if the function returns an empty list for some inputs, those inputs effectively get filtered out. However, for clarity, it is often better to use Filter explicitly for conditional removal, and reserve **FlatMap** for true one-to-many expansions.

Note: *The **Map**, **Filter**, and **FlatMap** transforms we discussed are all special cases of Beam's general **ParDo** transform. **ParDo** (Parallel Do) is the most flexible element-wise transform that allows writing custom DoFn (Do Functions) with setup/teardown, emitting multiple outputs (including side outputs), and so on For many simple use cases, **Map/Filter/***

`FlatMap` are sufficient and more concise. You can think of `Map` as a `ParDo` with one output per input, `Filter` as a `ParDo` that conditionally emits the input, and `FlatMap` as a `ParDo` that can emit multiple items per input. Beam also provides other convenience transforms (like `.apply(Filter.greaterThan(x))` or `.apply(MapElements.via(func))`) that we have touched on. Now, let us move on to transforms that deal with grouping data by keys and partitioning collections.

Grouping and Partitioning Data (GroupByKey, Partition, CoGroupByKey)

Many data processing tasks require grouping data by some key or partitioning a dataset for separate processing. Apache Beam provides transforms to group keyed data and to partition a **`PCollection`** into multiple **`PCollections`**. Key grouping is essential for aggregations (like count or sum by key) and joins, while partitioning is useful for splitting data into parallel streams.

In Beam, **grouping** is done on key/value pairs. This means elements must be in the form of **(key, value)** to be grouped by key. For joining multiple datasets on a key, Beam provides **`CoGroupByKey`**. On the other hand, **partitioning** splits a single **`PCollection`** into fixed sub-collections according to a function (not necessarily by key, just by some condition or hash).

Let us summarize the transforms in this category:

- **`GroupByKey`**: It groups the values of a **`PCollection`** by their key. Input must be key-value pairs. The output is a **`PCollection`** of (**`key`**, **`iterable_of_values`**) for each unique key.

Important Caution for `GroupByKey`: `GroupByKey` is one of the biggest performance and scalability determinants in a Beam pipeline, as it triggers a **distributed shuffle,** and then **materializes all values for each key (and typically per window in streaming)** as an iterable. It means that if you have **hot keys** (a few keys receiving huge volumes) or high-cardinality/high-volume data, the per-key value lists can grow very large, and might cause excessive shuffle traffic, worker memory pressure, as well as out-of-memory failures.

Whenever your goal is an **aggregation** (sum, count, min/max, average, and so on), prefer **incremental combiners** that avoid materializing all raw values:

- Use **`Combine.perKey(...)`** for general aggregations.
- Use built-ins like **`Count.perKey()`** / **`Count.PerElement()`** for counts.
- Use other combiners (for example, **`Sum.perKey()`**, **`Top.perKey()`**), wherever applicable.

These combiners can often **pre-aggregate** before the full shuffle, which reduces both network transfer and memory footprint, while still producing the correct per-key results. Therefore, you should reserve **GroupByKey** for cases where you truly need the *full set of values per key* (for example, certain join-like patterns or when emitting complete grouped lists), and control growth with windowing, allowed lateness, and careful handling of skew within those cases.

- **CoGroupByKey**: It is like **GroupByKey**, but for *multiple* input collections. It groups by key across all inputs simultaneously (essentially implementing a join on the key). The output for each key contains the collection of values from each input **PCollection**.
- **Partition**: This splits the elements of one **PCollection** into N separate **PCollections**, according to a user-defined partitioning function. Each element is routed to one of the N output partitions.

We will discuss each of them and provide corresponding examples. Meanwhile, keep in mind that having a *deterministic key coder* is important for **GroupByKey** and **CoGroupByKey** (we will explain coders in the next section). For now, using simple keys like strings or numbers is the best way.

A critical fact here is that in Python, many complex objects use **PickleCoder** by default, and **PickleCoder** is **not deterministic**. This makes such objects unsafe to use as keys for **GroupByKey** or **CoGroupByKey**, as different workers may serialize the same logical object differently, which may cause incorrect grouping or runtime errors.

For example, the following example is problematic:

```
# BAD: using a dict as a key
data = p | beam.Create([
    ({"user": "alice"}, 10),
    ({"user": "alice"}, 20),
])
grouped = data | beam.GroupByKey()
```

Even though the two dictionaries look identical, their serialized form is not guaranteed to be stable across processes; therefore, Beam cannot reliably group them.

The correct approach is to use **simple, stable, primitive keys**, such as strings, integers, or tuples of primitives, as shown here:

```
# GOOD: use a stable primitive key
data = p | beam.Create([
    ("alice", 10),
    ("alice", 20),
])
grouped = data | beam.GroupByKey()
```

Or, if your key is embedded inside a complex object, extract a deterministic field with:

```
# GOOD: extract a stable field from a complex structure
data = p | beam.Create([
    ({"user": "alice", "region": "EU"}, 10),
    ({"user": "alice", "region": "EU"}, 20),
])

keyed = data | beam.Map(lambda x: (x[0]["user"], x[1]))
grouped = keyed | beam.GroupByKey()
```

Rule of Thumb:

- The keys must be **deterministic, immutable, and small**.
- Prefer str, int, float, or small tuples of these.
- Avoid dict, set, custom Python objects, or anything that relies on **PickleCoder**, unless you explicitly define a deterministic coder.

This is why the note about coders is so important; key coders directly affect correctness, and not just performance.

GroupByKey

GroupByKey is used to collect all values associated with the same key. This is the foundation for aggregations per key. For example, you might group clicks by user ID, or sensor readings by sensor ID, before computing some statistics per group.

Warning for Streaming (Unbounded) Data: On an unbounded **PCollection**, **GroupByKey** (and **CoGroupByKey**) must be paired with **non-global windowing** (and often an appropriate trigger). Otherwise, the pipeline may fail validation (for example, an **IllegalStateException** in some runners), or it may **never emit results**, because grouping over an infinite stream without windows has no natural completion point.

Hence, a safe pattern is to window the stream *before* grouping will be:

```
import apache_beam as beam
from apache_beam import window, trigger

# events: PCollection[KV[user_id, click]]
grouped = (
    events
    | "WindowInto1Min" >> beam.WindowInto(
        window.FixedWindows(60),
        trigger=trigger.AfterWatermark(
```

```
                early=trigger.AfterProcessingTime(10)  # optional:
emit early updates
            ),
            accumulation_mode=trigger.AccumulationMode.ACCUMULATING,
            allowed_lateness=60
        )
        | "GroupByUser" >> beam.GroupByKey()
)
```

In this example, the infinite stream is broken into **1-minute windows**, so **GroupByKey()** groups values **per key per window**, which allows Beam to produce results continuously as windows close (and optionally emit early updates).

Thus, before you can apply **GroupByKey**, your **PCollection** elements must be structured as key/value pairs (in Beam's Java SDK this is KV<K, V>; in Python, a tuple (key, value) is typically used). Often, you will have to map your data into (key, value) form using a Map or **FlatMap** before grouping.

- **Python:** In Python, the transform is **beam.GroupByKey()**. Suppose we have a **PCollection** of key-value pairs (for example, fruits with their quantity sold in a day), and we want to group quantities by fruit. Therefore, it will look like:

```
with beam.Pipeline() as p:
    sales = p | beam.Create([
        ("apple", 3),
        ("banana", 4),
        ("apple", 5),
        ("banana", 2),
        ("orange", 7)
    ])
    grouped = sales | beam.GroupByKey()
    grouped | beam.Map(print)
```

The input sales **PCollection** contains tuples of fruit names and some numbers. After **GroupByKey**, the grouped **PCollection** will contain one element per unique key (**fruit**). Each element is a tuple of the form (**key, list_of_values**). For the above data, the output printed might be:

```
('apple', [3, 5])
('banana', [4, 2])
('orange', [7])
```

The order of values in the lists is not guaranteed, but all values for the same key are gathered together. In this example, "**apple**" had two entries (**3** and **5**) which are now in a list, "**banana**" had **[4,2]**, and "**orange**" had **[7]**. Typically, after **GroupByKey** you would apply another transform to each (key, values) pair, such as summing the values or finding an average. We could, for instance, easily compute total sales per fruit by mapping (**fruit**, **values_list**) -> (**fruit**, **sum(values_list)**). We will also see an example of aggregation after grouping in the **WordCount** example later.

- **Java:** In Java, **GroupByKey** is available via the **GroupByKey.create()** transform. The input must be a **PCollection<KV<K, V>>**. Let us do a similar example in Java, while grouping some data by a string key:

```
import org.apache.beam.sdk.transforms.GroupByKey;
import org.apache.beam.sdk.values.KV;
// ...

PCollection<KV<String, Integer>> sales = p.apply(Create.of(
    KV.of("apple", 3),
    KV.of("banana", 4),
    KV.of("apple", 5),
    KV.of("banana", 2),
    KV.of("orange", 7)
));
PCollection<KV<String, Iterable<Integer>>> grouped = sales.
apply(GroupByKey.create());
```

After this transform, grouped will be a **PCollection** of **KV< key, Iterable<Integer> >**. In our example, it would contain:

- **KV("apple", Iterable[3, 5])**
- **KV("banana", Iterable[4, 2])**
- **KV("orange", Iterable[7])**

The iterable holds all values for that key. If we wanted to sum the values per key, we could apply another **ParDo**, or combine transform to the grouped **PCollection** (for example, using a **Combine.perKey** with sum, which Beam provides).

Important: **GroupByKey** is often an implicit part of other composite transforms (like **Combine.perKey** or **Count.perKey**, which do a **GroupByKey** internally). Hence, you must directly use **GroupByKey** when you need to explicitly gather data for further custom processing. Also, note that **GroupByKey** is a *per-key shuffle* operation; it might be an expensive step, as it involves moving data across workers by key. Beam's optimization and runners handle this, but it is something to be aware of while designing pipelines.

From an execution perspective, **GroupByKey** triggers a **shuffle** operation. This means that all elements are redistributed across workers based on their keys; hence, every value for the same key ends up on the same worker. In distributed systems, shuffles are typically dominated by **network and disk I/O**, not CPU. As a result, **GroupByKey** often becomes the most expensive step in a pipeline in terms of latency, cost, and resource usage.

Due to this, a few practical rules are critical when designing pipelines, which are:

- **Reduce Payload Size before the Shuffle.**

  Apply filtering, projection, or transformation steps *before* `GroupByKey`, such that only the minimum necessary data is moved across the network. Smaller records mean less network traffic and faster shuffles.

- **Avoid Skewed (Hot) Keys.**

  If one key receives a disproportionate amount of data (for example, "`unknown`" or "`default`"), that worker becomes a bottleneck, and can run out of memory. Hence, you should always examine key distributions, and also consider re-keying, salting, or hierarchical aggregation if skew is unavoidable.

- **Prefer Combiners Whenever Possible.**

  Use `Combine.perKey`, `Count.perKey`, or other combiners instead of `GroupByKey` when your goal is aggregation. Combiners perform partial aggregation *before* the shuffle, which drastically reduces the amount of data that must be transferred and stored.

- **Use GroupByKey Only When You Truly Need Raw Grouped Values.**

  For example, when implementing custom join logic, session materialization, or complex event correlation that requires full access to all values per key.

In short, `GroupByKey` is a powerful but heavy operation. It defines a major scalability boundary in your pipeline, and thoughtful design around it often determines whether a pipeline performs well in production, or if it becomes expensive and unstable.

CoGroupByKey

`CoGroupByKey` is the transform for performing **joins** across two or more `PCollections` sharing the same key type.

Important: Window Alignment Requirement

Before using `CoGroupByKey`, ensure that *all* input `PCollections` are windowed in a compatible way. This means that they must use the same windowing strategy (for example, fixed, sliding, or session windows), the same window size and parameters, and compatible trigger and allowed-lateness configurations. Beam only joins elements that fall into the *same window*. If one input uses 1-minute fixed windows, and another uses 5-minute fixed windows, or if one is unwindowed while another is windowed, the pipeline will fail validation at the construction time with an error. This is one of the most common pitfalls that you might encounter while working with joins in streaming pipelines.

If you have multiple datasets and you want to merge or compare them based on keys, **CoGroupByKey** is the tool to use. It generalizes **GroupByKey** to *multiple inputs*. For each key that appears in any of the inputs, the output will contain that key and all values from each input associated with that key.

Let us say that we have two datasets:

- One is a **PCollection** of (user, age) pairs.
- Another is a **PCollection** of (user, city) pairs.

We want to join these so that we get age and city information for both the users.

- **Python:** In Python, **CoGroupByKey** expects a dictionary mapping tag names to **PCollections**. Each **PCollection** should consist of key/value pairs (tuples). The result will be a **PCollection** of (**key**, **value_dict**), where **value_dict** maps each tag to a list of values from the **PCollection** for the key. For example:

```
with beam.Pipeline() as p:
    ages = p | "CreateAges" >> beam.Create([
        ("Alice", 25),
        ("Bob", 30)
    ])
    cities = p | "CreateCities" >> beam.Create([
        ("Alice", "NY"),
        ("Charles", "LA")
    ])
    # CoGroupByKey requires a dict of PCollections
    grouped = ({'ages': ages, 'cities': cities}
               | beam.CoGroupByKey())
    grouped | beam.Map(print)
```

In this example, we have two input **PCollections:**

- **ages: Contains ("Alice", 25), ("Bob", 30)**
- **cities: Contains ("Alice", "NY"), ("Charles", "LA")**

We pass a dictionary **{'ages': ages, 'cities': cities}** to **CoGroupByKey()**. The output grouped will be a **PCollection** of **(key, {'ages': [...], 'cities': [...]})**. If we run this, it would print something like:

```
('Alice', {'ages': [25], 'cities': ['NY']})
('Bob', {'ages': [30], 'cities': []})
('Charles', {'ages': [], 'cities': ['LA']})
```

Let us interpret this result:

- "**Alice**" is in both **PCollections**. In the output, the key "**Alice**" has **'ages': [25]** and **'cities': ['NY']**.

- "**Bob**" appears only in the ages **PCollection** (with 30), and not in cities. In the output, "**Bob**" has **'ages': [30]** and **'cities': []** (an empty list for cities because "**Bob**" had no entry in the cities **PCollection**).
- "**Charles**" appears only in the cities **PCollection** (with "**LA**") and not in ages. The output shows "**Charles**" with **'ages': []** and **'cities': ['LA']**.

Hence, **CoGroupByKey** essentially performed a **full outer join** on the key "**user**". Every user from either dataset appears once, with missing values represented by empty lists. If we wanted an inner join (only keys present in both), we could follow up with a filter to drop entries where one side is empty. Similarly, left or right joins could be emulated by filtering, as and when needed. However, the raw **CoGroupByKey** gives you everything.

After **CoGroupByKey**, you typically will process the results to a more convenient form. For example, for each (**user**, **info_dict**), you might want to combine the information into a single object or tuple. In our case, for "**Alice**" we would want to produce ("**Alice**", **25**, "**NY**"), for "**Bob**" maybe ("**Bob**", **30**, **None**) if there is no city, and so on. You can do this with a simple **Map** on the grouped **PCollection**. The structure {'ages': [...], 'cities': [...]} is how Beam represents the multiple value streams in Python. Therefore, you can access them by the same keys you provided.

- **Java: CoGroupByKey** in Java is a bit more involved due to static typing. You use **CoGroupByKey** via a builder called **KeyedPCollectionTuple**. You also need to define *tuple tags* to identify each collection's values in the result. Here is how you could join two **PCollections** in Java:

```
import org.apache.beam.sdk.values.TupleTag;
import org.apache.beam.sdk.values.CoGbkResult;
import org.apache.beam.sdk.values.KeyedPCollectionTuple;
// ...

// Assume these are our input collections:
PCollection<KV<String, Integer>> ages = p.apply(Create.of(
    KV.of("Alice", 25),
    KV.of("Bob", 30)
));
PCollection<KV<String, String>> cities = p.apply(Create.of(
    KV.of("Alice", "NY"),
    KV.of("Charles", "LA")
));

// Define tuple tags for each collection
final TupleTag<Integer> ageTag = new TupleTag<>();
final TupleTag<String> cityTag = new TupleTag<>();
```

```
// Build the KeyedPCollectionTuple and apply CoGroupByKey
PCollection<KV<String, CoGbkResult>> grouped = KeyedPCollection-
Tuple
    .of(ageTag, ages)
    .and(cityTag, cities)
    .apply(CoGroupByKey.create());
```

Let us break this down:

- We have two **PCollection<KV<String, ...>>**: one for ages (key type String, value type Integer), and the other for cities (key type String, value type String).
- We create two **TupleTag** objects, one for each value type. These tags serve as identifiers for the value lists in the result.
- We then use **KeyedPCollectionTuple.of(tag1, coll1).** and **(tag2, coll2). apply(CoGroupByKey.create())** to join them.

  The result grouped is a **PCollection<KV<String, CoGbkResult>>**. Each element has a key and a **CoGbkResult** object, which holds the values from each input for that key. Hence, you can retrieve the values by this tag:

Java:

```
grouped.apply("ProcessResults", ParDo.of(new DoFn<KV<String,
CoGbkResult>, String>() {
    @ProcessElement
    public void processElement(ProcessContext c) {
        String user = c.element().getKey();
        CoGbkResult result = c.element().getValue();

        Iterable<Integer> ageValues = result.getAll(ageTag);
        Iterable<String> cityValues = result.getAll(cityTag);

        Integer age = ageValues.iterator().hasNext() ? ageValues.
iterator().next() : null;
        String city = cityValues.iterator().hasNext() ? city
Values.iterator().next() : null;
        // Now we have at most one age and one city since our
data had at most one per user.
        String output = user + ": age=" + age + ", city=" + city;
        System.out.println(output);
        c.output(output);
    }
}));
```

This DoFn processes each joined KV. We get the key (user name) and the **CoGbkResult**. From the **CoGbkResult**, **getAll(ageTag)** gives an **Iterable<Integer>** of all ages for that user, and **getAll(cityTag)** gives an **Iterable<String>** of all cities for that user. In our simple data, each iterable will have at most one element. We extract those (if present), and then format a string. The **System.out.println** will execute on workers (so it will show up in local runs; on Dataflow, it would go to worker logs). We also call **c.output(output)** to emit the formatted string to the next stage (if we had one).

If we ran this pipeline, we get an output similar to the following:

```
Alice: age=25, city=NY
Bob: age=30, city=null
Charles: age=null, city=LA
```

This matches the earlier Python example logically (using "null" for missing in Java versus empty list in Python).

As you can see, **CoGroupByKey** in Java requires some boilerplate code with **TupleTags** and **CoGbkResult**. It is powerful, though, as it allows you to join multiple collections (more than two if needed by chaining more **.and()** calls with more tags). The pattern here is: prepare keyed **PCollections**, use **KeyedPCollectionTuple** to combine them, apply **CoGroupByKey**, then interpret the results. For beginners, it is fine to start with joining two collections. As an exercise, you can extend it to three by adding another **TupleTag** and **.and()** clause. Use **CoGroupByKey** when you need to perform joins. Always ensure that the **PCollections** you are joining have the same key type and an appropriate coder for the key (Beam must be able to group them, more on coders soon). As a result, **CoGroupByKey** will shuffle and group data similar to **GroupByKey**, but across multiple sources. However, keep in mind that if one of the collections is significantly larger than the other, it will influence performance (just as in any join operation). Beam (and the runner) handles the mechanics of grouping and matching keys. After the **CoGroupByKey**, you typically use a **ParDo**/DoFn or **Map** to merge the results into the final form you need.

Partition

Partition is different from the above key-based transforms. Partitioning is about splitting a single **PCollection** into fixed number of parts, using a function to decide which part each element goes to. This is useful when you have categories or shards you want to separate data into *without grouping by key*. For instance, you might partition a dataset into a training set and a test set (common in ML scenarios), or route events to different paths based on some attribute.

Therefore, when using Partition, you must specify the number of output partitions (N) upfront. The partition function will assign each element an output index from **0 to N-1**, and each index corresponds to a separate output **PCollection**.

So if N = 3, valid partition indices are 0, 1, and 2. This zero-based indexing is important to remember, as returning N or any value outside this range will result in a runtime error.

- **Python:** In Python, **beam.Partition(fn, N)** is used, and it returns a tuple of N **PCollections**. For example, let us partition a **PCollection** of numbers into evens and odds (2 partitions):

```
with beam.Pipeline() as p:
    numbers = p | beam.Create(list(range(10)))  # 0,1,2,...9
    def partition_fn(x, num_partitions):
        # Return 0 for even numbers, 1 for odd numbers
        return 0 if x % 2 == 0 else 1

    even_part, odd_part = numbers | beam.Partition(partition_fn, 2)
    # even_part will contain [0, 2, 4, 6, 8]
    # odd_part will contain [1, 3, 5, 7, 9]
    even_part | beam.Map(lambda x: f"even: {x}") | beam.
Map(print)
    odd_part  | beam.Map(lambda x: f"odd: {x}")  | beam.
Map(print)
```

In the above code, **Partition(partition_fn, 2)** returns each element x in numbers. If **partition_fn** returns 0, the element goes to the first output (index 0, which we assign to **even_part**); if it returns 1, the element goes to the second output (**odd_part**). We then separately process **even_part** and **odd_part** (here just printing them with labels). The output would be lines labeled "**even:**" and "**odd:**" accordingly.

A few things to note here are:

- The partition function **partition_fn(x, num_partitions)** takes the element and the total number of partitions (here 2), and returns an integer in [0, num_partitions-1]. Any value outside that range or other irregularities will cause an error.
- The number of partitions (2 in this case) must be known when constructing the pipeline graph (you cannot decide to have a dynamic number of partitions at runtime).
- After partitioning, you get multiple **PCollections** which you can handle independently. They are still a part of the same pipeline and will execute in parallel.
- **Java:** In Java, use **Partition.of(N, partitionFn)**. This returns a special object **PCollectionList<T>** which contains N **PCollections**. You then retrieve each partition by index. Let us do the same even/odd partitioning in Java:

```
import org.apache.beam.sdk.transforms.Partition;
import org.apache.beam.sdk.transforms.Partition.PartitionFn;
import org.apache.beam.sdk.transforms.MapElements;
```

```
import org.apache.beam.sdk.values.TypeDescriptors;
import org.apache.beam.sdk.values.PCollectionList;

// ...

PCollection<Integer> numbers = p.apply(Create.of(0, 1, 2, 3, 4,
5, 6, 7, 8, 9));

PCollectionList<Integer> partitions = numbers.apply(
    Partition.of(2, (PartitionFn<Integer>) (Integer x, int
numPartitions) ->
        (x % 2 == 0) ? 0 : 1
    )
);

PCollection<Integer> evens = partitions.get(0);
PCollection<Integer> odds  = partitions.get(1);

// For demonstration, multiply evens by 2 and odds by 3 (different
processing for each partition):
PCollection<Integer> processedEvens = evens.apply(
    MapElements.into(TypeDescriptors.integers())
               .via(x -> x * 2)
);

PCollection<Integer> processedOdds = odds.apply(
    MapElements.into(TypeDescriptors.integers())
               .via(x -> x * 3)
);
```

In this code:

- We create a **PCollection** of numbers 0 through 9.
- We call **Partition.of(2, partitionFn)**. The partition function lambda returns 0 for even numbers and 1 for odd, which is similar to the Python example.
- The result is a **PCollectionList<Integer>** containing two **PCollections**. We obtain them with **partitions.get(0)** and **partitions.get(1)**.
- We then show that you can continue processing each partition separately; maybe the even numbers go through one set of transformations, while the odd numbers go through another. In this example, we arbitrarily multiply evens by 2 and odds by 3 (just to illustrate independent processing). Hence, if we collected results, **processedEvens** would contain [0, 4, 8, 12, 16] (doubles of even inputs), while **processedOdds** would contain [3, 9, 15, 21, 27] (triples of odd inputs).

Explanation: Partition is useful when you want to **split** a single stream of data into multiple streams. Unlike **`GroupByKey`**, it does not group multiple elements together or depend on keys; each element stays separate, but is routed to a different output. Partition is a *static* split based on conditions you define. Some common scenarios can be:

- You may split data into train/test sets (for example, 80% vs. 20% partition)–you could generate a random number for each element, and partition it by threshold.

  Warning: A "random per element" split is often *not reproducible* in distributed Beam runners. Different workers, retries, or re-runs can produce different random values, which may cause the same record to land in train in one run and test in another. This makes experiments hard to compare, and can introduce subtle data leakage.

  A more reliable approach thus is a **deterministic split** using a stable identifier (for example, user ID, transaction ID, or a concatenated natural key). Hash the stable key and route based on a fixed rule (for example, hash(key) % 100 < 80 for an 80/20 split). This keeps train/test partitions consistent across workers, retries, and re-runs, which is especially important in production and ML workflows.

- You may separate data by type or category (if you had a field that indicates type, you could partition into different **`PCollections`** per type).
- You may implement logic where different subsets of data need to go through different processing branches in your pipeline.

Here, it is worth noting that you could achieve similar results using multiple Filters (one filter for each condition). For example, to split evens and odds, you could do two filters. However, that would read the input **`PCollection`** twice (once for each filter transform). Partition reads each element once, and then decides the output, which can be more efficient especially if you have many partitions.

You will also observe that you can achieve similar results using multiple Filter transforms (one filter for each condition). In that case, each element is evaluated against multiple predicates, which can add overhead. While runners may optimize and fuse transforms, so that the source is not literally read multiple times, each filter still performs its own condition check.

Partition, on the other hand, routes each element exactly once by computing a single partition index and sending the element to the appropriate output. This is often more efficient and cleaner in intent, especially when you have many partitions or complex routing logic.

A Caution: The number of partitions is fixed at pipeline construction. If you need truly dynamic routing (varying number of output collections depending on data), Beam does not support that directly in a single pipeline; you would need to design around it, perhaps by using a single output with a key, and then splitting in receiving logic, or running separate pipelines per category.

Therefore, a common and practical workaround is to emit a routing key with each element and let the sink handle the dynamic fan-out. Instead of trying to create dynamic partitions inside the pipeline, you can produce elements in the form:

```
(route_key, value)
```

Then, you may write them to **dynamic destinations** based on that key. For example, in Beam you can write to files, databases, or message topics, where the destination is chosen at runtime from the key:

- **Files**: One directory or file prefix per **`route_key`**
- **Kafka**: One topic per **`route_key`**
- **BigQuery**: One table per **`route_key`**

Conceptually:

```
routed = pcoll | beam.Map(lambda x: (compute_route(x), x))
```

Then, use a sink that supports dynamic destinations, such as **`FileIO.writeDynamic()`** in Java or **`WriteToText/custom`** sinks in Python with routing logic.

Hence, this pattern keeps the pipeline static while allowing **unbounded routing flexibility** at the output layer. It is the standard Beam approach when the number of "partitions" is not known ahead of time, or depends on the data itself.

Now that we have covered how to transform individual elements and how to group or split data collections, we need to address a crucial aspect of Beam pipelines, which is how data is encoded and decoded during pipeline execution. This is where **coders** come into play.

Understanding Coders in Beam

When you run a Beam pipeline, the data in **`PCollections`** often needs to be moved between different machines, or persisted temporarily (especially during group-by-key operations which involve shuffling data). To do this efficiently, the Beam needs to serialize (encode) the elements of your **`PCollections`** into bytes, and deserialize (decode) them later. **Coders** are the components in Beam that define how to encode/decode each data type.

Think of a coder as the "serializer" for a specific type of element. For example, an integer coder knows how to turn an integer into a byte array and back, a string coder knows how to encode a string (Beam typically uses UTF-8 for strings), and so on. Every **`PCollection`** in Beam has an associated coder for its element type. If Beam does not know how to encode the elements of a **PCollection**, the code will not run, as the runner would not know how to shuttle the data around.

Therefore, Beam tries to automatically assign an appropriate coder for your **PCollection**'s type whenever possible:

- **For common simple types**, Beam has built-in coders. For example, Integer in Java uses **VarIntCoder** (which writes integers in a variable-length format), String uses **StringUtf8Coder** (for UTF-8 encoding), and so on. In Python, common types like int, float, and str, have default coders (often using variants of Pickle or simple native encodings).
- **For composite types (for example, a KV<String, Integer> or a Python tuple)**, Beam will construct a coder composed of coders for each part (for example, a KV coder made of a **StringUtf8Coder** and **VarIntCoder**).
- **For custom or unknown element types,** Beam will fall back to default **element coders** to encode data as it moves between transforms and workers. In Java, this is often **SerializableCoder** if the type implements Serializable (though it is usually not the most efficient choice). In Python, the default element coder for many arbitrary objects is typically **PickleCoder**, which uses Python's pickle-based serialization to encode *elements* in a **PCollection**.

  It is thus important to distinguish this from **user-code serialization**, which is how Beam distributes your pipeline logic (functions, lambdas, DoFns) to worker machines. Element coders determine how **data** is serialized on the wire and at rest, whereas user-code serialization determines how **your transform code** is shipped and reconstructed on workers. These are related but separate concerns; you might use **PickleCoder** for elements while your DoFn/function is serialized and transported using a different mechanism under the hood, depending on the runner and SDK internals.

These default strategies ensure that many pipelines run out-of-the-box without you having to worry about coders. However, there are important considerations:

- **Performance:** The default fallback coders (Java's **SerializableCoder** and Python's **PickleCoder**) are general but not the most efficient. Java serialization can be slow, and may produce large payloads. Python pickle is convenient, but it can be slower than needed for simple types, and might not produce consistent byte outputs for certain objects (thus not deterministic).
- **Determinism:** For key grouping (**GroupByKey/CoGroupByKey**), Beam requires that the coder for the key type is *deterministic*. Deterministic means that if two keys are equal, their encoded bytes are exactly equal every time. A simple way to reason about determinism is: **if k1 == k2, then encode(k1) must be exactly equal to encode(k2) byte-for-byte, across all runs and all workers.** This requirement is the reason why using complex objects such as

dictionaries, sets, or custom classes as keys is risky. Their serialized form may depend on internal ordering, memory layout, or implementation details that are not guaranteed to be stable, which can cause two logically equal keys to be encoded differently. When that happens, Beam cannot reliably group elements, leading to incorrect results or pipeline validation errors. Hence, for this reason, stable primitive types like strings, integers, or small tuples of primitives are the safest choices for keys.

- Non-deterministic coders might encode the same logical value in different ways (for example, a coder that encodes a Python dictionary might not preserve key order, leading to different byte sequences for the same dictionary in different runs). If a coder is not deterministic, the grouping transforms may not work correctly, or Beam might reject the pipeline. **`PickleCoder` is not deterministic** for all types (because, for instance, the order of dictionary iteration in Python is not guaranteed across pickling). **`SerializableCoder` in Java is also not guaranteed deterministic** (and generally is not). Thus, non-deterministic key coders are rejected by many runners, or can lead to incorrect grouping; this is why you must always use deterministic key encodings for grouping/joining.

How Beam Chooses a Coder: In Java, Beam uses a **`CoderRegistry`** that maps types to coders. It knows about standard types. You can query it (for example, **`pipeline.getCoderRegistry().getCoder(MyType.class)`**) to see the coder it would choose. In Python, there is a registry too (**`apache_beam.coders.registry`**), which by default will pick **`PickleCoder`** for unknown types. Hence, if you apply a **`beam.Map`** or other transform with type hints (in Python) or use Beam schemas, they can influence coder selection.

Custom Coders: Sometimes you have a custom data type (say a class in Java or a custom object in Python) and you want to control how it is serialized, either for performance or because Beam cannot handle it by default. Beam allows you to define custom coders in the following ways:

- In **Java**, you can create a class extending Coder<T> or more commonly extend **CustomCoder<T>**, and implement the encode and decode methods. You can then register this coder with the coder registry, or apply it to a **`PCollection`**. For example, if you have a Person class, you might create **`PersonCoder`** to encode a person to bytes (perhaps via JSON or via specific fields), and then do **`@DefaultCoder(PersonCoder.class)`** on the Person class. Therefore, the next time you use **`PCollection<Person>`**, Beam will use **`PersonCoder`**.

  Also, if your data can be represented by a well-known encoding like Avro or Protocol Buffers, Beam provides **`AvroCoder`** and **`ProtoCoder`**. Hence, using those (along with schema annotations, or by wrapping your data in an Avro/Proto type) can save you from writing custom serialization logic. This is because they tend to be more efficient than Java serialization.

You can also call **pCollection.setCoder(MyCoder.of())** in Java to set a specific coder for a **PCollection** if needed, or use methods like **withOutputType/ withCoder** on certain transforms.

- In **Python**, you can define a subclass of Coder (found in **apache_beam.coders** module) and implement encode and decode methods. You would then register it for your type. Python makes this easier with the concept of type hints and the coder registry. For instance, you can register a coder for a custom class by using **apache_beam.coders.registry.register_coder(MyClass, MyClassCoder)**. Additionally, Python Beam supports a **@DefaultCoder** decorator on a class to associate it with a coder (similar to Java's annotation). However, writing custom coders in Python is less common for beginners; majority of the times, just using Python built-in types or simple tuples (which Beam knows how to coder-ize) is enough.

Example: Suppose you have a custom Java class **MyData** with several fields, and you find that using it in a **PCollection** gives an error "**Unable to return a default Coder for MyData**". To fix this, you have options like:

1. **Make MyData Implement Serializable:** This way Beam will use **SerializableCoder**. However, as noted, this is not very efficient or deterministic.

2. **Write a MyDataCoder and Annotate MyData with @DefaultCoder(MyDataCoder.class):** Then, Beam will pick your coder whenever it sees **MyData**. In your coder, you could, for instance, encode the fields of **MyData** in a consistent way (for example, always in the same order, using known coders for each field).

3. **Use a Beam Schema** (since newer versions of Beam allow annotating classes with **@DefaultSchema** or auto-generating schemas): Beam can then create a coder based on the schema (often an efficient one).

4. **Use an Existing Structured Format** like Avro: Mark **MyData** with **@ DefaultSchema(AvroSchema.class)**, or simply convert **MyData** to a **GenericRecord** with **AvroCoder**, and so on.

For Python, if you had a complex object, you might instead use a dictionary or a tuple to represent it, because Beam knows how to handle those (or you rely on **PickleCoder** which will handle it, albeit with possibly less efficiency).

Deterministic Coders and Keys: As mentioned, if you are doing a **GroupByKey** or **CoGroupByKey**, ensure that the key's coder is deterministic. If you use strings or numbers as keys, you are safe because Beam's coders for those are deterministic. If you used a tuple as a key in Python, and if the tuple contains only simple types, it should also be deterministic (the **TupleCoder** will encode each element in order using deterministic coders). If you use a custom class as a key in Java, and you only provided **SerializableCoder** by implementing Serializable, you risk non-determinism. In such cases, it is better to provide a custom coder or use a structured key type. If a coder is not deterministic, Dataflow runner (for one) will actually raise an error at pipeline construction time for a `GroupByKey` step, while complaining that a deterministic key coder is required. Hence, this is a signal to the developer to switch to a deterministic coder.

In summary, **coders** are vital but often work behind the scenes. As a beginner:

- Rely on Beam's default coders for basic types.
- When using key-based operations, stick to simple key types (string, int, and so on) to avoid issues.
- Be aware that if you use complex objects in `PCollections`, you might need to help Beam by specifying a coder, or by converting the data to a simpler form for transmission.
- Efficient serialization can greatly affect your pipeline's performance, especially for large data volumes. We will discuss some optimization tips in the next section.

Optimizing Serialization with `PCollection` Coders

Now that you understand what coders do, let us discuss how to use them to improve your pipeline's efficiency and correctness. By default, your pipeline will run with whatever coders Beam assigns, but in some cases you can *override or customize* this to your advantage.

Here are some best practices and techniques for optimizing serialization with coders:

- **Use Appropriate Built-in Coders:** Whenever possible, use data types that have efficient built-in coders. For example, if you need to pass around a date/time, you might represent it as a Unix timestamp (long) or ISO string, rather than as a complex date object, as longs and strings have efficient coders. If you have binary data, use bytes in Python (which uses a `BytesCoder`) or byte[] in Java (uses `ByteArrayCoder`) rather than, say, encoding binary as a base64 string (which would bloat it). The Beam SDK provides many optimized coders (`VarIntCoder` for integers, `DoubleCoder`, `StringUtf8Coder`, and so on). Therefore, using simple types keeps the coder fast.
- **Avoid Generic Object Serialization for Hot Paths:** As mentioned, Java's `SerializableCoder` and Python's `PickleCoder` are convenience fallbacks, but are not optimal. They can be an order of magnitude slower than a well-designed custom coder. If your pipeline is processing a large number of elements (especially in `GroupByKey` or join, where data gets shuffled), the overhead of

default serialization can become a bottleneck. For Java, prefer using schema-based serialization (Beam's schema, Avro, Proto), or write a custom coder for frequently used custom types. For Python, where possible, break your data into basic structures (like lists, dicts of primitives) which Beam can handle with its optimized Coder (as Beam has optimized coders for common primitive types).

- **Annotate or Register Coders for Custom Types:** If you have a class that you will use in many places, define a custom coder and attach it. For Java, use **@ DefaultCoder** on the class or **call .setCoder()** on the **PCollection**. For example:

Java:

```
PCollection<MyType> data = ...;
data.setCoder(MyTypeCoder.of());

or
Java:
@DefaultCoder(MyTypeCoder.class)
public class MyType { ... }

This ensures that Beam uses your efficient coder. In Python, you
could use:
Python:
from apache_beam.coders import Coder, FastPrimitivesCoder
# use FastPrimitivesCoder for a custom type if it can be treated
as tuple of primitives
pipeline.get_coder_registry().register_coder(MyClass, MyClassCoder)
```

(The example is illustrative; the coder registry in Python can be accessed via **Pipeline().coder_registry**.)

If writing a custom coder is too much, consider if you can utilize something like JSON. For instance, a quick workaround in Python for a non-picklable object; convert it to a JSON string and use StrUtf8Coder. This sacrifices some performance for simplicity but yields a deterministic encoding. In Java, you might use **AvroCoder** by first defining an Avro schema for your object (or using reflections with **AvroCoder.of(MyClass.class)**, if compatible).

- **Ensure Determinism for Key Coders:** As emphasized before, if you have a custom key type for grouping, implement **Coder.verifyDeterministic()** properly in your coder. If you are using a composite key (like a KV of two values) in Java, ensure that each part's coder is deterministic, or use a structured approach. In Python, avoid using types like **dict** or **set** as keys (since their iteration order can vary; if you need a composite key, use a tuple of values instead of a **dict**). If you must use a non-deterministic structure as a key, you can convert it to a deterministic representation (for example, sort a `dict`'s items tuple to make a tuple key) before grouping.

- **Leverage Beam Schemas (Advanced):** Apache Beam has a concept of schemas that allow you to treat custom objects in a declarative way, somewhat like how databases treat rows. Therefore, if you annotate a Java class with `@DefaultSchema` or use the `SchemaCoder`, Beam can automatically generate coders for you that are often more efficient than Java serialization (they will encode it field by field). Similarly, in Python, Beam's use of type hints can allow it to use more efficient coders for known types (for example, a `NamedTuple` might get a schema-based coder). This is a more advanced feature, but it can greatly simplify coder management for complex types.
- **Memory vs. Speed Trade-Offs:** Some coders use compression or variable-length encodings to reduce size (for example, `VarIntCoder` compresses small numbers to fewer bytes). This can save network I/O and disk, but might use more CPU to encode/decode. Usually, the defaults are well-balanced, but if you know your data distribution, you might choose differently. For example, if you primarily have large integers (that do not benefit from `VarInt`), you might use a fixed 8-byte coder to decode faster. These micro-optimizations are rarely needed for beginners, but it is good to understand that coders have different performance characteristics.
- **Test and Monitor:** If your pipeline is running but you suspect coder overhead (maybe based on logs or just large data sizes), you can test by printing out coder info. In Java, you can do `pCollection.getCoder()` to see what coder is being used. In Python, `pcollection.coder` might be accessible in some contexts. Knowing that, you can override if it is not what you expect. Also, Dataflow's monitoring UI can show if a particular step (like a `GroupByKey`) is taking a long time; sometimes non-deterministic coder issues manifest as warnings in logs.

Example Scenario (Java): You have a pipeline grouping events by a complex key (say a combination of `userID` and `sessionID` stored in a custom class `Key(userId, sessionId)`). If you did not provide a coder, Beam might use `SerializableCoder` for Key. When running on Dataflow, the pipeline might actually fail to run, which will give the error that Key's coder is not deterministic. To fix it, you can implement `KeyCoder` (that encodes the `userId` and `sessionId` in a consistent byte order, maybe by writing `userId` as a fixed-length string or `VarInt` followed by `sessionId`). You then either annotate Key with `@DefaultCoder(KeyCoder.class)` or do `myPCollection.setCoder(KeyCoder.of())` after you create the `PCollection` of Key,Val pairs. Now, Beam knows to use `KeyCoder`, which is deterministic by design, and the `GroupByKey` can proceed. As a bonus, your `KeyCoder` might produce a smaller encoding than Java serialization (which might include a lot of metadata), so that your shuffle size is smaller and your pipeline will run faster.

Example Scenario (Python): Suppose you are using a Python tuple (**`user_id`**, **`session_id`**) as a key, where **`user_id`** is an int and **`session_id`** is an int. Beam's default for a tuple of ints will be a **`TupleCoder`** composed of two **`VarIntCoders`**. It is deterministic and efficient. Great. Now, suppose instead you used a custom object **`SessionKey(user, session)`**, and Beam defaulted to **`PickleCoder`**. It will work, but maybe slower. If performance is a concern, you could change your pipeline to use (user, session) tuple as the key (thus using efficient coders), or implement a custom coder for **`SessionKey`**. A quick fix might even be to convert **`SessionKey`** to a bytes or string representation as the key (like f"{user}:{session}"), and use that as key for grouping–this ensures determinism (string coder is deterministic). After grouping, you can parse the string back if needed.

In summary, **optimizing coders** boils down to these considerations:

- **Use the right type** for the job (choose a representation that Beam can coder-ize efficiently).
- **Provide Beam hints** when it cannot infer the best coder (through annotations or direct coder settings).
- **Mind key coder determinism** for correctness in grouping.
- **Be aware** of the cost of serialization in your pipeline's critical paths, and refactor if necessary.

Most beginner pipelines will not need heavy custom coder work, but understanding this layer will help you reason about pipeline performance, and also debug issues when they arise. Next, let us tie everything together with some example pipelines. We will also include instructions on how to run these pipelines both locally and on the cloud.

Example Pipeline Implementations

Let us build a few practical pipelines using the transformations and coders concepts we have learned. We will walk through them step-by-step. These examples will demonstrate how to combine multiple transforms to solve a task, and how to execute the pipeline on different runners.

Before running any example, ensure that your environment is set up:

- **Python:** Install Apache Beam (**`pip install apache-beam`**), and then choose a runner. For local runs, the **`DirectRunner`** is used by default. For cloud runs on Dataflow, you will need Google Cloud credentials, and also to specify pipeline options (explained in the following section).
- **Java:** Add the Apache Beam SDK to your project (Maven coordinate, for example, **`org.apache.beam:beam-runners-direct-java:2.x`** for **`DirectRunner`**, and **`...:beam-runners-google-cloud-dataflow-java:2.x`**

for Dataflow, or simply **`beam-sdks-java-core`** with runners as needed). Hence, you will create a Pipeline object with appropriate **`PipelineOptions`** in your main method.

Example 1: Word Count Pipeline (Python)

Word Count is a classic example that demonstrates reading data, transforming it, and aggregating results. We will create a simplified version that counts words from an in-memory collection of lines. This will use **`FlatMap`** to split lines into words, **`Map`** to create (word, 1) pairs, and **`GroupByKey`** (or a Combine) to sum up the counts per word.

Goal: Count the occurrences of each word in the input lines.

Steps:

1. **Create the Pipeline and Input `PCollection`**: We will use **`beam.Create`** to provide a list of lines of text.
2. **Split Lines into Words**: Use **`FlatMap`** with a split function to get individual words.
3. **Map Words to (word, 1)**: Prepare key-value pairs for counting.
4. **Group by Word and Sum Counts**: Use **`GroupByKey`** to collect all the 1s for each word and then sum them, while yielding (**`word, total_count`**).
5. **Inspect or Output the Results**: For demonstration, we will print the results. (In a real scenario, you might write to a file or database.)

Let us implement this now:

```
import apache_beam as beam

# 1. Define input data (could be from a file, but here we will
hard-code some lines)
lines = [
    "Apache Beam is great",
    "Beam unifies batch and streaming",
    "Streaming data is processed with Beam"
]

def split_words(line):
    # Split a line into words by whitespace
    for word in line.split():
        # Normalize the word by lowercasing and stripping
punctuation (basic cleanup)
        yield word.lower().strip(".,!?")
```

```
with beam.Pipeline() as pipeline:
    # Create a PCollection of lines
    lines_pc = pipeline | "CreateLines" >> beam.Create(lines)
    # 2. Split lines into words
    words = lines_pc | "SplitWords" >> beam.FlatMap(split_words)
    # 3. Map each word to a (word, 1) pair
    word_ones = words | "AddCountTuple" >> beam.Map(lambda w: (w,
1))
    # 4. Group by word and sum counts
    grouped = word_ones | "GroupByWord" >> beam.GroupByKey()
    word_counts = grouped | "SumCounts" >> beam.Map(lambda kv:
(kv[0], sum(kv[1])))
    # 5. Print the results
    word_counts | "PrintResults" >> beam.Map(print)
```

Let us break down what happens in the pipeline:

- We create a **PCollection lines_pc** containing three lines of text.
- **SplitWords Step**: For each line, the **split_words** function yields each word in lowercase. For example, the first line "**Apache Beam is great**" will produce "**apache**", "**beam**", "**is**", "**great**". **FlatMap** collects all words from all lines into the words **PCollection**.
- **AddCountTuple Step**: We convert each word into a tuple (word, 1). After this, if "**beam**" appeared 2 times, you will have ("**beam**", **1**) twice, and so on.
- **GroupByWord Step**: This groups the tuples by the word key. Now, we have for example (**"beam", [1, 1, 1]**), if "**beam**" appeared 3 times across all lines (in our input, "**beam**" appears in every line, so it should be 3 times). Other words like "**apache**", "**unifies**", "**streaming**", and so on, might appear once.
- **SumCounts Step**: We take each (**word, iterable_of_ones**) and sum the ones. This gives (**word**, **total_count**) for each word.
- Finally, **PrintResults** step prints each word and its count.

If we run this pipeline, we might see an output (the order might vary) like:

```
('apache', 1)
('beam', 3)
('is', 2)
('great', 1)
('unifies', 1)
('batch', 1)
('and', 1)
('streaming', 2)
('data', 1)
('processed', 1)
('with', 1)
```

Here, each tuple is a word and how many times it appeared. For instance, "beam" appears in all three lines (3 times), "**is**" appears in two lines (2 times), and so on.

Also note that the Beam provides a built-in transform **Count.perElement()** that could do steps 3-4 in one go. We did it manually to show how **GroupByKey** works. For example, we could replace **GroupByKey** and **Sum** with:

Python:

```
word_counts = words | beam.combiners.Count.PerElement()
```

We will get the same result (**Count.PerElement** replicates this pattern internally). However, it is good to understand the manual steps as we have implemented before.

Runner Considerations: Running this with the **DirectRunner** (locally) will print to the console as shown. If we wanted to run this on Dataflow, printing to console is not practical (it would print from remote workers to worker logs, however we could write **word_counts** to a text file using **beam.io.WriteToText("gs://<your-bucket>/output.txt")**. For brevity, we did not include file I/O here. Just knowing that printing is mainly for local debugging is enough. For production pipelines, printing is therefore not a practical way to observe results. You should always write outputs to proper sinks such as files, databases, BigQuery, or message queues. Logging should be used only for debugging and diagnostics, while real pipeline results must go to durable, queryable storage systems. We will cover how to run it on Dataflow in the next section.

Example 2: Partitioning a Dataset (Java)

For our second example, let us use the **Partition** transform in a scenario. Imagine we have a stream of numbers and we want to separate them into two categories: even and odd. After partitioning, we will perform a different operation on each category. This example is simple, but partitioning is often used for more complex branching logic.

Goal: Split a **PCollection** of numbers into evens and odds, then process each separately.

Steps:

1. Create a **PCollection** of integers.
2. Apply Partition with 2 partitions using a lambda that assigns 0 or 1 based on parity.
3. Extract the even and odd **PCollections**.
4. On evens, calculate the sum of even numbers. On odds, calculate the sum of odd numbers (just as an example of separate processing).
5. Print or output the results of each branch.

Let us implement this in Java:

Java:

```
import org.apache.beam.sdk.Pipeline;
import org.apache.beam.sdk.transforms.Combine;
import org.apache.beam.sdk.transforms.Create;
import org.apache.beam.sdk.transforms.MapElements;
import org.apache.beam.sdk.transforms.ParDo;
import org.apache.beam.sdk.transforms.Partition;
import org.apache.beam.sdk.transforms.Sum;
import org.apache.beam.sdk.transforms.DoFn;
import org.apache.beam.sdk.values.PCollection;
import org.apache.beam.sdk.values.PCollectionList;
import org.apache.beam.sdk.values.TypeDescriptors;

public class PartitionEvenOddExample {
  public static void main(String[] args) {
    Pipeline pipeline = Pipeline.create();

    // 1. Input data: numbers 1 through 10
    PCollection<Integer> numbers =
        pipeline.apply("CreateNumbers", Create.
of(1,2,3,4,5,6,7,8,9,10));

    // 2. Partition into evens and odds
    PCollectionList<Integer> partitions =
        numbers.apply(
            "PartitionEvenOdd",
            Partition.of(2, (Integer n, int numPartitions) -> (n
% 2 == 0) ? 0 : 1)
        );

    // 3. Retrieve each partition
    PCollection<Integer> evens = partitions.get(0);
    PCollection<Integer> odds  = partitions.get(1);

    // 4. Sum each partition (single element output per branch)
    PCollection<Integer> evenSum =
        evens.apply("SumEvens", Combine.globally(Sum.ofInte-
gers()).withoutDefaults());
    PCollection<Integer> oddSum =
        odds.apply("SumOdds", Combine.globally(Sum.ofIntegers()).
withoutDefaults());

    // 5. Format and print (good for local DirectRunner demos)
    evenSum
```

```
        .apply("FormatEvenSum", MapElements.into(TypeDescriptors.
strings())
            .via(sum -> "Sum of evens: " + sum))
        .apply("PrintEvenSum", ParDo.of(new DoFn<String, Void>() {
          @ProcessElement
          public void processElement(@Element String msg) {
            System.out.println(msg);
          }
        }));

    oddSum
        .apply("FormatOddSum", MapElements.into(TypeDescriptors.
strings())
            .via(sum -> "Sum of odds: " + sum))
        .apply("PrintOddSum", ParDo.of(new DoFn<String, Void>() {
          @ProcessElement
          public void processElement(@Element String msg) {
            System.out.println(msg);
          }
        }));

    pipeline.run().waitUntilFinish();
  }
}
```

Let us clarify a few things in this code:

- We use **`Partition.of(2, ...)`** with a lambda. The **`lambda (Integer n, int numPartitions) -> n % 2 == 0 ? 0 : 1`** returns 0 for even numbers and 1 for odd numbers. So, partition 0 will collect evens, while partition 1 collects the odds.
- We get the two partitions.
- We use the **`Combine.globally(Sum.ofIntegers())`** transform to sum all elements in each partition. This is a convenient way to get a total. **`withoutDefaults()`** is used because if a partition were empty, Beam by default would output a default value; we suppress that as it is not needed here (assuming both evens and odds have at least one element in 1–10, which they do).
- The resulting **`evenSum`** and **`oddSum`** are each a **`PCollection`** containing a single element (the sum). We then map those to a string message, and finally, print them.

If we run this pipeline, the expected output would be:

```
Sum of evens: 30
Sum of odds: 25
```

This is because evens (2+4+6+8+10) equal to 30, and odds (1+3+5+7+9) equal to 25.

Note: *Printing via* **`System.out.println`** *is primarily for local runs; on distributed runners (for example,* **`Dataflow/Flink`***), these statements appear in worker logs; this is why you must use a real sink (files, BigQuery, Kafka, and so on) for pipeline outputs.*

This example illustrates partitioning and independent processing. In a more realistic scenario, you might partition log messages by severity (info, warning, error) into 3 partitions, and then handle each differently. Or, partition transactions by region and send each partition to a different database.

Note: *In Java, printing from within the pipeline (especially using* **`System.out`** *in a DoFn) will work on the* **`DirectRunner`** *(it will print to your console). On Dataflow, those prints would appear in worker logs. For actual results, you would normally write to an output sink. We used printing here for demonstration.*

Example 3: Joining Two Collections (Python)

For the third example, let us use **`CoGroupByKey`** to perform a join. We will use a scenario with two small datasets, similar to the earlier explanation: one dataset of people and their ages, and another of people and their **`favorite colors`**. We will join these by person name to get a combined view of each person.

Goal: Join two **`PCollections`** on a key (person name) to combine their information.

Steps:

1. Create first **`PCollection`** of (**`name`**, **`age`**).
2. Create second **`PCollection`** of (**`name`**, **`favorite_color`**).
3. Apply **`CoGroupByKey`** on the two, tagging them appropriately.
4. Process the joined result to produce a cleaner output (**`name`**, **`age`**, **`color`**).
5. Print the results.

Let us implement this in Python:

```
with beam.Pipeline() as p:
    # 1. PCollection of names to ages
    ages = p | "Ages" >> beam.Create([
        ("Alice", 30),
        ("Bob", 20),
        ("Charlie", 25)
    ])
    # 2. PCollection of names to favorite color
    colors = p | "Colors" >> beam.Create([
        ("Alice", "Blue"),
```

```
        ("Bob", "Green"),
        ("Diana", "Red")
    ])
    # 3. Join the two PCollections by name
    joined = ({'age': ages, 'color': colors}
              | "JoinAgesColors" >> beam.CoGroupByKey())
    # 4. Process joined results
    def format_result(name_info):
        name, info = name_info
        ages_list = info['age']
        colors_list = info['color']
        # Get the single age or None if not present
        age = ages_list[0] if ages_list else None
        # Get the single color or None if not present
        color = colors_list[0] if colors_list else None
        return (name, age, color)

    formatted = joined | "FormatResults" >> beam.Map(format_result)
    # 5. Print the output tuples
    formatted | beam.Map(print)
```

Explanation:

- We have ages **PCollection**: **Alice->30**, **Bob->20**, **Charlie->25**.
- We have colors **PCollection**: **Alice->Blue**, **Bob->Green**, **Diana->Red**.
- **CoGroupByKey** with the **dict {'age': ages, 'color': colors}** will group by name. The result joined will have a dictionary of lists, as we have seen before.
- In **format_result**, for each (name, info):
    - **info['age']** is the list of ages for that name (could be empty or contain one or more entries).
    - **info['color']** is the list of colors for that name.
    - In our data, each name appears at most once in each input, so these lists will be either length 1 or 0. We will extract the first element, if it is present.
    - We return a **tuple (name, age, color)**, while using None, if one piece was missing.
- We then print the results.

Expected output (the order is not guaranteed, but let us reason it out):

```
('Alice', 30, 'Blue')
('Bob', 20, 'Green')
('Charlie', 25, None)
('Diana', None, 'Red')
```

Alice had both an age and color, Bob had them as well. Charlie had an age, but no color (so color is None). Diana had a color, but no age (so age is None). Hence, this matches an "**`outer join`**" behavior.

This example shows how **`CoGroupByKey`** can be used. Typically, you will have to write a little post-processing to merge the values. You could also output a string or a custom object. Therefore, if we were to write this to a file, we might format it as a CSV or JSON lines.

Runner Considerations: Running this locally will print the tuples. On Dataflow, as usual, printing is not directly visible except in logs. You would more likely write the formatted **`PCollection`** to an external sink (like a BigQuery table or a text file in Cloud Storage) to observe the results.

Running Pipelines Locally and on Google Cloud Dataflow

We have shown how to construct pipelines and apply transforms. To actually execute these pipelines, you need to run them on a Beam **runner**. The runner is what takes your pipeline definition and executes it, either on your local machine, or on a distributed service.

`DirectRunner` (Local Execution): The **`DirectRunner`** is Beam's built-in runner that runs the pipeline on your local machine (or wherever the code is running) in a single process (it can use multi-threading for parallelism). It is great for development, testing, and small scale jobs. By default:

- In **Python**, if you do not specify a runner in **`PipelineOptions`**, it uses the **`DirectRunner`**.
- In **Java**, if you create **`PipelineOptions`** without specifying a runner, it also defaults to **`DirectRunner`** (provided by Beam SDK).

Hence, to run a pipeline locally, you can just execute your pipeline script or main class without any special flags. For example:

- **Python**: Use python **`wordcount_pipeline.py`**. This will run with **`DirectRunner`** unless you changed the options.
- **Java**: If using the Beam examples archetype, you might run **`mvn compile exec:java -Dexec.mainClass=com.example.MyPipelineMain`**, and it will use **`DirectRunner`** by default.

Thus, when running locally, any output transforms (like **`WriteToText`** to a local file path, or prints) will produce output on your machine. You do not need a cloud project or any cloud resources.

Using the `DirectRunner` Explicitly: If you want to be explicit, you can set the runner to **`DirectRunner`**. In Python:

```
from apache_beam.options.pipeline_options import PipelineOptions,
StandardOptions
options = PipelineOptions()
options.view_as(StandardOptions).runner = 'DirectRunner'
p = beam.Pipeline(options=options)
In Java:
PipelineOptions options = PipelineOptionsFactory.create();
options.setRunner(DirectRunner.class);
Pipeline p = Pipeline.create(options);
```

However, it is usually not necessary to set it explicitly in code, since the default is fine.

Google Cloud Dataflow (Cloud Execution): Dataflow is a fully managed service for running Beam pipelines at scale. To run on Dataflow, you need to provide pipeline options that tell Beam to use the DataflowRunner and configure details like your project ID, region, temp file location, and so on You also must have your Google Cloud environment set up (that is, if Cloud SDK is installed or the application default credentials are available, and a Cloud project with Dataflow API is enabled).

Here is how to run a pipeline on Dataflow:

- **Python:** You specify Dataflow options via the **`PipelineOptions`**. Typically, you would pass command-line arguments, or construct the options in code. For example:

```
from apache_beam.options.pipeline_options import PipelineOptions

options = PipelineOptions([
    "--runner=DataflowRunner",
    "--project=<YOUR_GCP_PROJECT_ID>",
    "--region=<YOUR_DATAFLOW_REGION>",        # for example,
"us-central1"
    "--temp_location=gs://<YOUR_BUCKET>/temp",
    "--job_name=beam-wordcount-example"
])
p = beam.Pipeline(options=options)
```

In code, you can also do:

```
options = PipelineOptions()
options.view_as(StandardOptions).runner = 'DataflowRunner'
options.view_as(GoogleCloudOptions).project = 'YOUR_GCP_PROJECT_
ID'
options.view_as(GoogleCloudOptions).region = 'us-central1'
```

```
options.view_as(GoogleCloudOptions).temp_location = 'gs://YOUR_
BUCKET/temp'
options.view_as(GoogleCloudOptions).job_name = 'beam-wordcount
-example'
p = beam.Pipeline(options=options)
```

The result is the same. These options tell Beam to use the DataflowRunner, which will translate your pipeline into a Dataflow job, and then submit it. The **temp_location** is a Cloud Storage path where Beam can stage the job files and temporary data (you must have a GCS bucket created for this). The region is where the Dataflow service will run your job (for example, us-central1 or others available). **job_name** is optional, but it is good to set for identification (it must be unique for each run, or Beam can auto-generate one with a prefix).

Hence, when you run the script, instead of executing the pipeline locally, it will build and submit the job to Dataflow. You will see logs indicating it is uploading the job, then you can monitor it in the Google Cloud Console (Dataflow section).

Java: For Java, you use **DataflowPipelineOptions** (which extends **PipelineOptions**). The simplest way is via command-line **args**. For example, you could run your pipeline with:

```
--runner=DataflowRunner
--project=YOUR_GCP_PROJECT_ID
--region=us-central1
--tempLocation=gs://YOUR_BUCKET/temp
--jobName=beamWordcountExample
```

If you packaged your pipeline into a fat jar, you might run:

```
java -jar mypipeline-bundled.jar \
  --runner=DataflowRunner \
  --project=YOUR_GCP_PROJECT_ID \
  --region=us-central1 \
  --tempLocation=gs://YOUR_BUCKET/temp \
  --jobName=beamWordcountExample
```

If using Maven exec as in the examples:

```
mvn compile exec:java -Dexec.mainClass=com.example.MyPipelineMain \
    -Dexec.args="--runner=DataflowRunner --project=YOUR_GCP_
PROJECT_ID --region=us-central1 --tempLocation=gs://YOUR_BUCKET/
temp --jobName=beamWordcountExample"
```

In code, similarly execute:

```
DataflowPipelineOptions options = PipelineOptionsFactory.as
(DataflowPipelineOptions.class);
options.setRunner(DataflowRunner.class);
options.setProject("YOUR_GCP_PROJECT_ID");
```

```
options.setRegion("us-central1");
options.setTempLocation("gs://YOUR_BUCKET/temp");
options.setJobName("beam-wordcount-example");
Pipeline p = Pipeline.create(options);
```

- Then define your pipeline as usual. On calling **`p.run().waitUntilFinish()`**, it will submit to the Dataflow.

Important Dataflow Considerations:

- Ensure that the Dataflow API is enabled in your GCP project, and that you have the necessary permissions.
- The machine where you launch the job (your laptop or a VM) needs to have authentication set up (for example, run **`gcloud auth login`** and **`gcloud config`** set project **`YOUR_PROJECT`**, or set the **`GOOGLE_APPLICATION_CREDENTIALS env var`** to point to a service account key file).
- The GCS bucket for temp and any file output must exist beforehand.
- Dataflow jobs incur costs, so be mindful to cancel jobs when done (if they are streaming or stuck).

Once on Dataflow, Beam will handle deploying workers, and so on. If your pipeline had any print statements or **`System.out`**, those will be in the logs but not directly visible. Therefore, it is better to use Beam logging (**`beam.Log`** transforms, or the logging module in Python) for things you want to see in Cloud logs, or write results to sinks.

Running the Examples on Dataflow:

- **Word Count**: We would likely write results to a file. For instance, instead of **`beam.Map(print)`**, do **`word_counts | WriteToText('gs://YOUR_BUCKET/wordcounts/output')`**. Then run the pipeline with DataflowRunner, as highlighted above. After it is done, check the Cloud Storage bucket for the output file.
- **Partitioning**: We can similarly write the sums to a file or a log. Or, we might split the pipeline–one branch writes the even sum to one file, while the other branch writes the odd sum to another. On Dataflow, that will produce two output files.
- **Joining**: We can output the results to BigQuery or a text file. For example, use **`beam.io.WriteToText('gs://YOUR_BUCKET/joined_output')`** on the formatted **`PCollection`**.

Local vs. Dataflow Summary:

- Locally, you get quick iteration and can use print statements for debugging. It is limited by your machine's resources.

- Dataflow allows scaling to large datasets distributed across many workers, but you need to set up the options and environment. It is not instantaneous (job submission and startup takes a couple of minutes typically), so use it when you need to handle big data, or want a managed service to run continuously (for streaming pipelines).
- The Beam code (your transforms logic) largely remains the same regardless of runner. This is Beam's portability in action; you can develop it and test locally, then run it on the cloud by just changing pipeline options.

Finally, always remember to **shut down** or **cancel** your Dataflow jobs when they are no longer needed (especially streaming jobs) to avoid ongoing costs.

Conclusion

Thus, we conclude the chapter on using transformations and coders in Apache Beam. We explored how to transform individual elements with **`Map`**, **`Filter`**, and **`FlatMap`**, how to group and join data using **`GroupByKey`** and **`CoGroupByKey`**, how to branch pipelines with Partition, as well as how coders ensure correct and efficient serialization of data across distributed workers. Through runnable examples, we saw how these building blocks come together to form reliable batch and streaming pipelines, and how careful choices around grouping, partitioning, and key design directly affect correctness, scalability, and performance.

In the next chapter, we will build on these fundamentals and focus on making pipelines faster, cheaper, and more scalable. We will also examine topics such as minimizing shuffle costs, handling hot keys, choosing efficient coders, optimizing windowing and triggers, and understanding runner-level execution behaviors, so that your Beam pipelines perform well under real-world production workloads.

CHAPTER 6
Advanced Pipeline Optimization Techniques

Introduction

In this chapter, we will delve into advanced techniques for optimizing Apache Beam pipelines to handle large volumes of data efficiently. By now, you have learned how to construct basic Beam pipelines; the next step is to ensure those pipelines run **fast** and are **cost-effective**. Pipeline optimization is crucial for achieving high throughput and low latency, especially in production scenarios where even slight inefficiencies can escalate with big data. Without proper tuning, a pipeline may suffer performance issues or even fail under heavy load, and delay insights for any given enterprise. Hence, we will explore strategies to improve pipeline performance, using a consistent real-world example of an e-commerce data processing pipeline to ground these concepts.

E-commerce Example Context: Consider the example of an online retail platform that processes user events and orders. The Beam pipeline reads streams of events (page views, add-to-cart actions, purchases, and so on), and performs transformations to produce analytics–for example, computing total sales per product category, identifying peak traffic periods, as well as detecting any "hot" products that are generating an unusually high load.

Note: Although this scenario is described in a streaming context, some of the examples in this chapter will use bounded sources such as ReadFromText for simplicity and ease of execution. This allows us to focus on optimization techniques without requiring a full streaming infrastructure to be set up. Conceptually, you should think of these batch examples as stand-ins for streaming inputs.

In a real streaming deployment, the same pipeline would typically read from sources such as Apache Kafka, Google Pub/Sub, or Kinesis, and the pipeline would be executed in streaming mode (for example, by setting the appropriate streaming options in the runner configuration). The transforms, optimizations, and performance considerations remain the same; only the source and pipeline options change. We will explicitly point out where a batch source is being used for demonstration and describe the equivalent streaming source, so that the mental model remains firmly grounded in real-time event processing.

We will use this scenario throughout the chapter, while applying optimization techniques to this pipeline, so that it can handle high event rates and large order volumes efficiently. All examples will use Beam's native features and transforms (no third-party frameworks), and we will explain code snippets line-by-line to be beginner-friendly. By the end of this chapter, you will be able to understand how to design **efficient Beam pipelines** that scale to real-world data; how to troubleshoot common performance problems; how to benchmark and profile your pipelines, as well as how to use Beam and runner-provided tools to monitor pipeline health.

Structure

In this chapter, we will cover the following topics:

- Understanding Pipeline Execution and Bottlenecks
- Optimizing Join Patterns and Side Inputs
- Efficient Serialization and Data Formats (Coders)
- Optimizing Data Sources and Sinks
- Tuning Resource Utilization and Parallelism
- Monitoring Pipeline Performance with Metrics and Logs
- Benchmarking and Testing Pipeline Performance
- Troubleshooting Common Performance Pitfalls

Understanding Pipeline Execution and Bottlenecks

Before diving into specific optimizations, it is important to understand how Beam executes pipelines under the hood and where bottlenecks typically arise. Apache Beam pipelines run in parallel across distributed workers (machines or threads), coordinated by a runner (such as Dataflow, Flink, Spark, and so on). Beam's model breaks up the work into **stages** separated by data exchange boundaries (like **`GroupByKey`** operations). Within each stage, independent elements can be processed in parallel. However, certain patterns in pipeline design can limit parallelism, or introduce expensive operations (like data shuffles). Thus, to optimize a pipeline, we must recognize these factors:

- **Parallelism by Keys:** Many transforms group data by keys (for example

`GroupByKey`, `CoGroupByKey`, `CombinePerKey`). Under the hood, a key forms the unit of parallel processing–all the data with the same key is routed to the same worker for aggregation. If your data has only a few keys, you will not fully utilize a large cluster because work cannot be evenly split. Conversely, a very large number of keys can add overhead in bookkeeping.

Here, "overhead" refers to the extra operational work the runner must perform to manage a very large number of parallel tasks. When you have too many keys, the pipeline creates a huge number of small work units (one per key or small group of keys). This increases scheduling and coordination costs; the more threads there are to manage, the more context switching there will be. As a result, there is more bookkeeping for state and timers, and the runner will have to track more metadata. Hence, instead of spending time doing useful computation, the system spends more time orchestrating the work.

Operationally, this can show up in several ways:

- Increased task scheduling overhead, where workers spend noticeable time picking up and releasing tiny bundles of work
- Thread contention, as many small tasks compete for limited CPU cores
- Higher memory usage for tracking per-key state, timers, and metadata
- Slower overall throughput, even though plenty of parallelism "exists" on paper
- How you will notice this in practice:
- CPU utilization stays relatively low, even though there is a growing backlog of unprocessed data.
- The pipeline appears "busy" (many active tasks), but progress per second is poor.
- Monitoring dashboards show a very high number of small work items being scheduled.
- Latency increases because the overhead of managing work dominates the actual processing time.

Therefore, there is a balance to strike:

- Too few keys lead to poor parallelism and underutilized workers.
- Too many keys will lead to excessive scheduling and coordination overhead.

Hence, a good pipeline design aims for keys that distribute load evenly, while still allowing each worker to process sufficiently large chunks of data to amortize this management cost.

Therefore, you should aim for a balanced key distribution. Rather than targeting a fixed number such as "thousands of keys", it is better to treat key cardinality as something that must be **measured and tuned as per the runner and the workload**.

Different runners (Dataflow, Flink, Spark) have different execution models, bundle sizing strategies, and scheduling overheads; hence, the "right" number of keys varies.

In practice, you should:

- Observe how evenly work is distributed across workers (CPU usage, backlog, throughput).
- Check runner diagnostics for skew and hot keys (for example, Dataflow's hot key warnings and parallelism metrics).
- Look at bundle sizes–extremely small bundles indicate too many keys, while very large bundles indicate too few keys.

The goal is balance:

- **Too few keys**, which can lead to limited parallelism, idle workers, and poor utilization.
- **Too many keys**, which can result in excessive scheduling overhead, tiny bundles, and reduced throughput.

Hence, in our e-commerce example, if we key events by **`productCategory`** for aggregation, we should ensure that there are enough categories to distribute work (if not, perhaps include a finer-grained key like product ID, or another dimension to increase parallelism). We will discuss **hot keys** (popular keys causing imbalance) and their mitigation later.

- **Data Shuffling:** When Beam groups or joins data (for example a **`GroupByKey`** or a join), it triggers a **shuffle**–data is exchanged between workers, so that all elements with the same key end up together. Shuffling is an expensive operation–it involves network I/O, serialization of data, and disk I/O on some runners. Thus, minimizing how often and how much data you shuffle is a key optimization goal. The Beam runner will automatically perform *fusion* of operations to avoid unnecessary shuffles (merging consecutive steps into the same stage to eliminate intermediate data writes), which is beneficial in most cases. However, whenever your pipeline logic *requires* grouping or repartitioning data, a shuffle is unavoidable. For example, if we want to compute total sales per category, we must bring together all events for each category–this step will cause a shuffle. We will explore ways to reduce shuffle volume (for example, by combining data early).
- **Fusion and Stage Boundaries:** Beam's runtime optimizes pipelines by fusing adjacent transforms where possible. **Fusion** means that if you have a sequence of element-wise operations (like a Map followed by a **`ParDo`**), they may run in a single combined step, while avoiding writing intermediate results to the memory or the disk. This generally improves performance. However, an extremely heavy transform that produces a *massive fan-out* (for instance, one element expands into millions) can sometimes benefit from breaking

fusion to distribute work. However, fusion can hurt when it causes **one fused stage to become the bottleneck**. Common situations include: (1) A heavy or skewed DoFn, which makes certain bundles take far longer than others (stage stragglers), (2) An extreme fan-out, where a single input element expands into a very large number of outputs, and overwhelms memory/CPU within one stage, and finally, (3) I/O throttling, where a fused stage couples expensive computation tightly with a slow sink or source, which reduces overall pipeline concurrency.

You can confirm fusion-related issues by looking for signals such as sustained backlog growth even though workers are allocated, high variance in per-bundle processing time (a few bundles dominate wall-clock time), frequent out-of-memory/GC pressure in the same stage, or "hot" work items that repeatedly lag behind others in runner monitoring. When these symptoms appear, intentionally **breaking fusion** (for example, using Reshuffle, or an equivalent pattern) can help distribute work more evenly, and then decouple compute from I/O. The tradeoff here is that breaking fusion typically introduces **materialization/shuffle cost**–which means more network and disk I/O–therefore, it should be used as a targeted optimization after observing evidence that fusion is the limiting factor.

- **Transform Overhead:** Every transform (like a `ParDo` or Map) introduces some overhead like reading an element, invoking user code, and encoding/decoding data. Simple per-element functions are typically not the bottleneck, but complex processing in a DoFn can be. Expensive computations or external service calls per element can drastically slow a pipeline. For example, if our e-commerce pipeline calls an external inventory service for each order to check stock, doing that for thousands of orders per second will be a major bottleneck. Hence, we need to find ways to batch or reduce per-element overhead (we will cover this in **Optimizing External I/O** section).
- **Resource Constraints:** Sometimes a bottleneck is not in the code logic but in the available resources. For instance, a stage might be CPU-bound or memory-bound if workers are too small. Therefore, understanding how to choose worker types, how autoscaling works, and how to tune parallelism is important for optimization (we will discuss resource tuning later). For example, if our pipeline is CPU-heavy (say, it does image processing on product photos), using workers with more CPU, or increasing the number of workers can speed it up. On the other hand, if the bottleneck is reading from a database that allows only a few connections, adding more workers will not help, and can hurt instead by overwhelming the source.

Therefore, by keeping these execution details in mind, we can reason better about where to apply optimizations. Next, we will dive into specific techniques to optimize pipeline logic–starting with how we shape our data and transforms to minimize work.

Filtering Data Early to Reduce Volume

One of the simplest yet most effective optimizations is **filtering out unnecessary data as early as possible** in the pipeline. This concept is often phrased as "filter first" or *push-down filters*, which means that you should place any Filter or conditional logic at the front of your pipeline's DAG (directed acyclic graph) before doing expensive transforms on the data. The rationale is straightforward; the less data you carry forward, the less work needs to be done in subsequent steps (less network transfer, less processing per element, smaller state for aggregations, and so on).

In our e-commerce scenario, suppose that we are only interested in analyzing **completed orders** for revenue calculations. The raw event stream, however, might contain a mix of event types (page view, add to cart, checkout initiated, order completed, and so on). Hence, by filtering to keep only "order completed" events right after reading the input, we drop irrelevant events early. This prevents wasting resources on processing events that ultimately do not contribute to the final results.

Let us illustrate this with a code snippet. Assume that our input is a stream of JSON strings representing user events, and each event has a field "**`event_type`**". We only want events where **`event_type == "ORDER_COMPLETED"`**, which might look like:

```
python
import json
import apache_beam as beam

# Sample DoFn to parse a JSON event string into a Python dict
class ParseEventJson(beam.DoFn):
    def process(self, element):
        # element is a JSON string from the input
        record = json.loads(element)
        yield record

# Pipeline setup (assuming pipeline options are configured
elsewhere)
with beam.Pipeline() as p:
    # Read raw events from a source (could be a file or Pub/Sub
subscription in real scenario)
    raw_events = p | "ReadEvents" >> beam.io.ReadFromTex-
t("events.json")  # Input source

    # Parse JSON strings to dicts
    parsed_events = raw_events | "ParseJSON" >> beam.ParDo
(ParseEventJson())

    # **Filter early:** Only keep events that are completed
orders
```

```
    orders = parsed_events | "FilterCompletedOrders" >> beam.
Filter(
        lambda record: record.get("event_type") == "ORDER_
COMPLETED"
    )

    # Continue pipeline with only order events...
    # (For example, map to (product_category, order_amount) for
aggregation later)
    order_kvs = orders | "ToCategoryAmountKV" >> beam.Map(
        lambda record: (record["product_category"], record
["order_total"])
    )
    # ... further transforms ...
```

In the code example, we perform the filter (**FilterCompletedOrders**) as soon as we have the structured event records. The code is commented line-by-line to explain each step:

- We first read from text (this could be from a file containing JSON lines, or it could be from a streaming source; for simplicity we use **ReadFromText** here).
- We define **ParseEventJson** as a DoFn to convert each JSON string into a Python dictionary. This is done via **beam.ParDo(ParseEventJson())**. (We use a DoFn here to illustrate custom parsing logic; one could also use **beam.Map(json.loads)** as a shortcut.)
- **FilterCompletedOrders** uses **beam.Filter** with a lambda to keep only events where the "**event_type**" field equals "**ORDER_COMPLETED**". This will drop all other events (for example, page views).
- After filtering, we can transform each order event into a key-value pair (**product_category**, **order_total**) for later aggregation.

Hence, by filtering early, we can ensure that any downstream computation (like summing revenue per category) runs only on the relevant subset of data. If, for example, only 10% of events are completed orders, we just eliminated 90% of the data from further processing, which is a huge performance win.

This matters because early filtering reduces data volume, which cuts down on CPU usage and memory footprint in subsequent steps. It also reduces shuffle volume if the next step is a grouping by key; fewer elements to shuffle means faster grouping. This aligns with the advice to "place filter operations as high in the DAG as possible.

Thus, in practice, always look at your pipeline inputs and ask: *Can I drop anything I do not need upfront*? Sometimes filters are obvious (like filtering by event type or a date range). In other cases, you might derive a filter condition–for instance, if we only care about orders above a certain value (say high-value orders for a special analysis), we could include that in the filter too. The general principle stands: **do not process what you do not need.**

Combining Aggregations Early (Pre-Aggregate as Much as Possible)

Many pipelines involve aggregation operations–computing sums, counts, averages, or other composites over groups of elements. In Beam (and data processing in general), there are typically two ways to aggregate by key:

- **Group, then Aggregate:** Use **`GroupByKey`** to bring all values for a key together, then in a subsequent step (often a **`ParDo`** or Map), combine those values (for example, sum them).
- **Combine as You Go:** Use Beam's **`CombinePerKey`** (or specific combiners like **`Sum.perKey`**, **`Count.perKey`**) which *logically* does the same grouping and aggregation but with an optimization–it can **combine partial results locally before the shuffle**.

The second approach is usually more efficient, especially for large data, because it reduces the amount of data that needs to be shuffled across the network. A best practice is to **combine (aggregate) as early as possible** in your pipeline graph. This means that if you have a chance to reduce data by combining, you must do it sooner rather than later.

Let us apply this to our example. Suppose after filtering for completed orders, we want to compute the total revenue per product category. We could do it with a **`GroupByKey`** followed by summing, or directly with a combiner:

Approach A: `GroupByKey`, then Sum (Less Efficient)

```
# Continuing from the previous snippet where we have order_kvs =
(category, order_total)
# Approach A: Group then sum
grouped_by_category = order_kvs | "GroupByCategory" >> beam.
GroupByKey()
# Now each element is (category, Iterable[order_totals])
sums_per_category = grouped_by_category | "SumOrders" >> beam.
Map(
    lambda kv: (kv[0], sum(kv[1]))
)
```

Approach B: `CombinePerKey` to Sum (More Efficient)

```
# Continuing from order_kvs = (category, order_total)
sums_per_category = order_kvs | "SumOrdersByCategory" >> beam.
CombinePerKey(sum)
```

Both approaches produce the same final result: a **PCollection** of (**category**, **total_revenue**) pairs. However, the performance characteristics differ:

- In Approach A, **GroupByKey** will shuffle all **order_total** values for the same category to one worker, then the Map(sum) will add them up. If a category has 100,000 orders, one worker receives 100,000 numbers, and then sums them.
- In Approach B, **CombinePerKey(sum)** still involves a shuffle, but Beam will **pre-sum chunks of data on each worker** before sending an intermediate result over the network. For example, if those 100,000 orders were originally spread across 5 workers, each worker might sum its portion locally (say each sums 20,000 orders). Then only 5 partial sums need to be sent and added, instead of 100,000 individual numbers. This drastically reduces data transfer and central processing.

Therefore, Beam's combiner transform (**CombinePerKey**) is essentially the Beam equivalent of a "reduce" in MapReduce (as opposed to a full group). It can do hierarchical aggregation–first through a local combine, then through a global combine of accumulators. The difference might seem small, but it is critical for performance with big data. Hence, by combining early, we can cut down the data volume *during* the shuffle, and not later.

For more insight, remember that under the hood Beam's combine involves an **accumulator** data structure. Therefore, if you write a custom **CombineFn**, you can define how to create an accumulator, add one element into it, merge accumulators, and produce the final result. Beam uses these methods to merge values in a tree-like fashion (enabling that multi-level combining). Fortunately, for simple cases like summing or counting, Beam provides ready-to-use combiners (we used sum directly in Python, or one could use **beam.CombinePerKey(beam.combiners.SumCombineFn())** explicitly for clarity).

In summary, prefer **CombinePerKey** (or **CombineGlobally** for global aggregation) over a raw **GroupByKey** followed by manual combination. Not only is it less code for you to write, it also **scales better**. Grouping without combining can lead to a single worker handling huge iterables of values, which can become slow or even cause out-of-memory errors if the list is too large. Hence, using combiners alleviates this by splitting the workload. The Beam official documents note that while **GroupByKey** is a fundamental operation, it is often more efficient to use a Combine transform, when you actually want an aggregated result.

To reinforce this point: "*combine early*" is the motto for pipeline optimization. In our pipeline, we apply **CombinePerKey(sum)** at the earliest opportunity after we have key-value pairs. If we were doing more complex aggregations (like computing average order value per category and count of orders), we can use **CombinePerKey** with a custom **CombineFn**, or use tuple combiners. Therefore, the earlier we shrink data by aggregating, the less data will remain for later stages.

Line-by-Line Explanation for Approach B Code:

```
sums_per_category = order_kvs | "SumOrdersByCategory" >> beam.
CombinePerKey(sum)
```

- **order_kvs** is a **PCollection** of (**category**, **order_total**) pairs (output from the previous step).
- **CombinePerKey(sum)** tells Beam to group elements by key (category), and then apply the sum function to all values for that key. We label this transform "**SumOrdersByCategory**" for clarity.
- Beam can perform partial and distributed aggregation only when the combine function is associative (and preferably commutative). For operations like sum, this property holds; therefore, Beam can legally split, aggregate, and merge results across workers. For custom aggregations, developers must ensure that the combine logic is mathematically safe for hierarchical execution; otherwise, subtle correctness bugs may appear, even if the pipeline "runs successfully". It will produce the **PCollection sums_per_category**, where each element is (category, total).

In Java SDK, this would be done via **Combine.perKey(new SumInts())**, or by using predefined combiners. In our Python example, it is concise with the built-in sum function.

Finally, note that if you *did* use Approach A (**GroupByKey** then sum), Beam's runner would not automatically combine values for you–it would literally send all values, and then let your Map(sum) do the work in one shot on one worker. Thus, Approach B is strictly better for performance in virtually all cases of large-scale aggregation.

Managing Data Skew and Hot Keys

Even after filtering and combining, a pipeline's performance can be severely impacted by **data skew**, which is an uneven distribution of data across keys or workers. The most common culprit is the **hot key** problem–one or a few keys have far more data than others, which can one worker to do a disproportionate amount of work. Data skew can therefore lead to bottlenecks where one machine (processing the hot key) lags behind, and limit overall throughput and parallelism.

E-Commerce Example: Imagine a holiday sale on a particular popular product category, "**Electronics**". If 50% of all orders placd in a time period are electronics, then the key "**Electronics**" will have to aggregate a massive volume of records. If we naively combine per key, one worker might end up summing all those electronics orders, while other workers handle only light loads for other categories. Therefore, this **hot key** can slow down the entire pipeline, since the pipeline cannot finish until all keys are processed. In extreme cases, it can even cause out-of-memory errors if one key's data is too large to fit in memory on a single worker.

However, Beam provides a few ways to handle hot keys and skew, which are:

- **Avoiding Skew in the Key Design:** The first line of defense is to pick a key that naturally balances. If one category is too popular, maybe refine the key. For instance, use a composite key like (category, subcategory) or (category, hour-of-day), if the question allows it, to spread the load. However, this changes the meaning of the aggregation; hence, it is not always applicable. A trick specifically mentioned in Beam best practices is appending the window to the key (for streaming scenarios), so that the key is effectively **`{original_key, window}`**–this ensures that each window's aggregation is separate (which Beam does by default anyway; the keys are scoped to a window in streaming).
- **Random Key Salting (Manual Sharding):** A common technique to handle hot keys is to **shard the key** artificially. Beam does not have a built-in "salt" transform, but you can achieve it by altering the key in a **`ParDo`** before a shuffle. For example, if "Electronics" is hot, you could create N shards of it, produce keys like "Electronics:0", "Electronics:1", ..., "Electronics:N-1" for each record, with a random shard number. This distributes the electronics orders across N keys, so that N workers can handle the summing in parallel. After that, you would need one more step to combine those N partial sums for "Electronics" into a final sum (essentially, another combine of the N shards). This two-level combine (first by sharded key, then by original key) can eliminate the single-hot-node problem. The Beam Dataflow runner's documentation suggests this approach of "re-keying" data to avoid hot keys. However, doing this manually adds complexity to your pipeline.
- **Built-in Combiner Fanout:**

  Before resorting to manual sharding patterns, it is important to know that Beam already provides a built-in mechanism for handling hot keys in combiners. Hence, when using **`CombinePerKey`**, you can instruct Beam to internally parallelize the aggregation for a single key by specifying a *fanout*. This allows multiple partial combiners to run in parallel for the same key, and then merge their results.

In Python, this is done as:

```
result = (
    pcoll
    | beam.CombinePerKey(my_combine_fn).with_hot_key_fanout(5)
)
```

In Java, the equivalent is:

```
pcoll.apply(
    Combine.perKey(myCombineFn).withHotKeyFanout(5)
);
```

Conceptually, a fanout of 5 means the Beam will:

1. Split the values for a hot key into 5 parallel partial combines.
2. Aggregate each shard independently.
3. Merge the 5 intermediate results into a final value for the said key.

   This is the **recommended first approach** for hot keys when your workload is an aggregation, because:

   - It is simple and declarative.
   - It keeps your pipeline logic clean.
   - It is optimized by the runner.
   - It avoids introducing artificial shard keys into your data.

   Manual sharding should only be considered when:

   - You are not performing a combine (for example, you need raw grouped values, joins, or custom correlation logic).
   - You need fine-grained control over sharding strategy.
   - You are dealing with non-combine workloads, such as **`GroupByKey`**, joins, or stateful processing, where fanout is not applicable.

- **Reshuffle for Even Distribution:** Sometimes data skew is not about one key having all data, but upstream partitions being uneven. The **`beam.Reshuffle()`** transform (or simply a **`GroupByKey()`** followed by flatten hack) can randomly redistribute elements to balance load. This is more useful when you have a fixed number of upstream partitions (like reading from a few large files), and want to spread elements more evenly across workers before a heavy operation. In streaming, Reshuffle is primarily used to **break fusion and redistribute work more evenly across workers**. It introduces a materialization boundary that forces data to be rebalanced, which can help when one stage becomes a bottleneck, or when a single worker is overloaded and others are idle.

  Therefore, reshuffle itself is **not a deduplication mechanism**. It does not remove duplicates or detect repeated elements. Its purpose is execution control, and not correctness control. Hence, if you need deduplication, you must use an explicit pattern such as:

  - Key elements by a unique identifier
  - Apply windowing

- Use stateful processing (or a built-in deduplication pattern) to remember which IDs have already been seen within a time bound.

In general, if you see one worker overloaded and others being idle (and it is not due to a single key), injecting a reshuffle can help equalize distribution.

To strengthen your understanding, let us implement a simple strategy for a hot key in code. Suppose that we know the category "Electronics" is extremely frequent. We will shard that key into 5 buckets for intermediate combining in the following way:

```
import random

class ShardHotCategory(beam.DoFn):
    def process(self, element, hot_category, num_shards):
        category, value = element
        if category == hot_category:
            shard = random.randint(0, num_shards - 1)
            # Composite key avoids string parsing issues
            yield ((category, shard), value)
        else:
            ### Use a single shard for non-hot keys (optional,
but keeps key type consistent).If reproducibility matters, replace
random.randint(...) with a deterministic shard choice (for example,
hash(event_id) % num_shards), or explicitly seed random in a con-
trolled way. #####
            yield ((category, 0), value)

# ... inside the pipeline ...
NUM_SHARDS = 5
hot_cat = "Electronics"
# shard the hot category key into 5
sharded_kvs = order_kvs | "ShardHotKey" >> beam.ParDo(ShardHot-
Category(), hot_category=hot_cat, num_shards=NUM_SHARDS)

# First level combine on sharded keys
partial_sums = sharded_kvs | "CombineShards" >> beam.CombinePer-
Key(sum)

# Now combine shards back to original category by mapping the key
rekeyed = partial_sums | "UnshardKey" >> beam.Map(lambda kv:
(kv[0].split("_")[0], kv[1]))
# Second level combine by original category (this final combine
should be small since there are at most num_shards values per
category)
final_sums = rekeyed | "FinalCombine" >> beam.CombinePerKey(sum)
```

In this snippet:

- `ShardHotCategory` DoFn takes each (category, value), and if the category is the hot one ("`Electronics`"), it tags it with a random shard 0-4, yielding keys like "`Electronics_0`", "`Electronics_1`", and so on. Other categories pass through untouched.
- We then combine by these sharded keys. "`Electronics_0`"..."`Electronics_4`" each get their partial sum.
- Then we map the key back (split on underscore to get the category name), and do a final combine. Now "Electronics" has at most 5 values (one from each shard), which is trivial to combine.
- The result `final_sums` is the same format as before: (category, total) for each category, but we have effectively parallelized the combine for the hot category.

This manual sharding approach is verbose but demonstrates the principle. In practice, if the Beam SDK or runner provides a `.withHotKeyFanout(5)` option, it will do something similar internally, which is to partition the combine for that key.

General Skew Considerations: It is not just keys that can be skewed. If your pipeline involves a heavy CPU operation (like parsing or regex on each element), and the data size per element varies a lot, some elements (for example, a super large record) might take significantly longer, causing a straggler. Therefore, Beam's autoscaling and work-stealing (on some runners) try to mitigate stragglers, but not all scenarios are covered. Hence, whenever possible, design your data and transforms to avoid any single item or key from dominating the workload.

Also, remember the earlier note: if you have *too few keys overall*, you will not achieve good parallelism. For example, if our pipeline keyed everything by country, and we only operate in 3 countries, at most 3 workers would be busy during a group-by-country stage. This is a case of low fan-out. The solution would be to include a more fine-grained key (like city or user) for processing, and only aggregate to country at the very end, if needed. Beam metrics or runner UI can help detect this; if you see a stage where CPU usage is low and only a few workers are active, you might have an insufficient key spread.

In summary, **data skew and hot keys** can seriously hinder pipeline performance. However, you must be aware of your data distribution. Use **parallelism hints** like Beam's combiner fanout or manual techniques to break up oversized workloads for single keys. Therefore, by ensuring work is evenly spread, you keep all workers busy, and can avoid slowdowns caused by a single worker being overloaded.

Optimizing Join Patterns and Side Inputs

Many pipelines need to combine data from multiple sources (joins). For example, our e-commerce pipeline might enrich each order event with additional data; perhaps, a static product catalog to get the product's category or price, or a user database to get user demographics. Hence, how you implement joins in Beam can greatly affect performance.

In Beam, a full join between two large datasets typically involves a **CoGroupByKey** (or a pair of **GroupByKey** and a subsequent merge), which will shuffle both datasets by key. This is a heavy operation if both sides are big. However, an important optimization is recognizing when one side of the join is small enough to be used as a **side input** instead of a full shuffle join.

Here is a quick decision table you can use as a practical rule-of-thumb when choosing a join strategy in Beam:

Situation	Recommended Approach	Why It Is the Right Fit	Common Pitfall to Avoid
One side is a small "lookup" dataset (fits comfortably in memory per worker, but changes infrequently).	**Side input join** (broadcast the small side; AsDict / AsIter / View.asMap)	Avoids a full shuffle; each worker can look up matches locally.	Broadcasting a "not actually small" dataset can cause memory pressure and worker instability.
Both sides are large (need distributed join).	**Shuffle join** using CoGroupByKey (or Beam SQL join).	Both sides must be redistributed by key so matches can be co-located.	Expect this to be I/O heavy; reduce payload size *before* the shuffle.
Join keys are skewed / hot (few keys dominate volume).	**Hot-key mitigation and join** (fanout/ manual sharding, pre-aggregation, or salting strategies).	Prevents one worker from becoming a bottleneck, and running out of memory.	Treating a skew problem as "just add more workers" usually fails because the hot key still funnels to one place.

Table 6.1*: Decision Table on What Type of Join to Use in Beam*

Side Input Optimization: If you have one dataset that can fit in memory (or be partitioned into manageable chunks), you can use it as a **broadcast** via side inputs. Beam allows you to convert a **PCollection** into a side input (for example, as a dictionary, list, or iterable) that can be fed into a DoFn processing another **PCollection**. Therefore, each worker will get a copy of the side input data, and can look up values without needing to shuffle the main data.

In our example, imagine that we have a products table that maps **product_id** to category and other information. Rather than keying orders by **product_id** and doing a **CoGroupByKey** with the product information, we could read the product info as a **Pcollection,** and use it as a side input to the orders pipeline. That way, the orders (which could be millions) do not have to be shuffled by **product_id** at all; each order event can directly find its category via an in-memory lookup.

Let us demonstrate this pattern:

```
import apache_beam as beam
from dataclasses import dataclass
from datetime import datetime

# Example products.csv format (recommended):
# product_id,category,updated_at
# P123,Electronics,2026-01-10T08:15:00Z

def parse_product(line: str):
    parts = [p.strip() for p in line.split(",")]
    product_id, category, updated_at_str = parts[0], parts[1],
parts[2]
    # ISO-8601 parse; adjust if your timestamp format differs
    ts = datetime.fromisoformat(updated_at_str.replace("Z",
"+00:00")).timestamp()
    return product_id, {"category": category, "ts": ts}

def latest_record(a: dict, b: dict) -> dict:
    # "latest wins"
    return a if a["ts"] >= b["ts"] else b

with beam.Pipeline() as p:
    # Read & parse products
    products = (
        p
        | "ReadProducts" >> beam.io.ReadFromText("products.csv",
skip_header_lines=1)
        | "ParseProducts" >> beam.Map(parse_product)  # (product_
id, {"category":..,"ts":..})
    )

    # Deduplicate so each product_id has exactly one record
(latest wins)
    products_latest = (
        products
        | "LatestPerProduct" >> beam.CombinePerKey(latest_record)
# (product_id, {"category","ts"})
        | "ToLookupKV" >> beam.Map(lambda kv: (kv[0], kv[1]
["category"]))  # (product_id, category)
    )
```

```
    # Safe AsDict now (unique keys)
    products_side = beam.pvalue.AsDict(products_latest)

    # Example orders stream (for demo purposes we use Create, but
this could come from Kafka #/ PubSub in streaming)
orders = (
    p
    | "CreateOrders" >> beam.Create([
        {
            "order_id": "O1001",
            "product_id": "P123",
            "user_id": "U001",
            "amount": 1500.00
        },
        {
            "order_id": "O1002",
            "product_id": "P456",
            "user_id": "U002",
            "amount": 2300.00
        },
        {
            "order_id": "O1003",
            "product_id": "P999",  # product not in products.csv
            "user_id": "U003",
            "amount": 799.00
        }
    ])
)
    class AddCategory(beam.DoFn):
        def process(self, order: dict, products_lookup: dict):
            prod_id = order.get("product_id")
            category = products_lookup.get(prod_id, "UNKNOWN")
            # Avoid mutating shared objects; create a copy
            out = dict(order)
            out["product_category"] = category
            yield out

    enriched_orders = orders | "AddCategoryInfo" >> beam.
ParDo(AddCategory(), products_lookup=products_side)

    # For a real pipeline, write to a sink instead of print()
    # enriched_orders | beam.io.WriteToText("output/enriched_or-
ders")
```

In the code:

- We read products.csv to get a collection of product IDs and categories. We then map it to key-value pairs (**product_id**, **category**).
- We convert that **PCollection** to a dictionary side input with **beam.pvalue.AsDict**. This tells Beam to gather the entire **PCollection** into a single dictionary Side inputs can be deceptively expensive because they are typically replicated across workers (and, in streaming, may be materialized per window); therefore, avoid fixed size rules like "a few hundred MB"; instead, estimate **side_input_size × worker_count** (and × **number_of_active_windows**) to gauge total memory pressure, and if that footprint is too large, prefer alternatives such as a shuffle join (**CoGroupByKey**/Beam SQL join), an external key-value store for lookups, or designs that partition the lookup data, rather than broadcasting it everywhere.
- The **AddCategory** DoFn takes each order element from the orders Pcollection, and has access to **products_lookup**, which is the side input dict. We simply do a get on the dict to find the category for the order's **product_id**, and then add it to the order record.
- The output **enriched_orders** now contains order events with an extra field "**product_category**" populated from the side input.

This approach avoids a shuffle of the orders by **product_id**. The cost is that the product data is broadcast to all workers. In many cases, that cost is trivial compared to shuffling the big side (orders). Therefore, runners typically materialize side inputs for efficient lookup, but memory behavior varies by runner, and windowing strategyBeam handles the mechanics of sending side input data to workers.

Important Considerations for Side Inputs:

- **Size**: The side input must be reasonably sized. If it is huge (does not fit in memory), this method will not work or will cause thrashing. For large-but-not-huge side inputs, Beam might use disk or chunking, but performance will degrade. There is a threshold (runner-specific) beyond which side inputs are not advisable.
- **Side Input Type**: We used **AsDict** which materializes the entire **PCollection** as a dict. There is also **AsList** (as list), **AsIterable** (streaming iterable), and singleton for single values. Use the appropriate one. **AsDict** is convenient for lookup by key, as seen in our join case.
- **Windowing**: If both main and side input are unbounded (streaming), you need to consider windowing. Beam requires that side inputs in streaming have finite windows (since you cannot have an ever-growing global side input). Often, side inputs in streaming are either bounded datasets or periodic snapshots.

Hence, the general rule of thumb is that **if one side of a join is small enough, use a side input instead of a full join**. This is a classic optimization in distributed systems (sometimes called map-side join or broadcast join in Hadoop/Spark world). It can turn an O(n+m) shuffle into O(n) local lookups.

Back to our scenario, by using side inputs, we might:

- Broadcast a product catalog or exchange rates, and so on, to enrich events.
- Broadcast a small "VIP customer list" to tag orders from VIPs, without a shuffle.

If both sides are huge, and you truly need to join (for example, joining two big datasets by user ID), then you have to accept the shuffle cost. In that case, ensure that you have applied previous tips (filtering, perhaps partitioning by some domain if possible, and so on). Also, consider **bloom filters** or pre-filtering techniques; for example, if only 10% of users in dataset A appear in dataset B, maybe extract those keys first, and then filter dataset A by those keys via side input to reduce what goes into the heavy join. This is a more complex optimization pattern involving multiple steps.

In summary, *optimize your joins*. Use side inputs for small lookup datasets to avoid shuffles. If you must join two large **`PCollections`**, try to reduce their size first (filter, aggregate, and so on), and be mindful of skew (one key joining millions versus others joining few–the hot key issue can appear in joins too).

Efficient Serialization and Data Formats (Coders)

Apache Beam must serialize (encode) and deserialize (decode) elements as they are passed between transforms and especially when they are shuffled between workers. The choice of data encoding (controlled by **coders** in Beam) can influence performance. While this is a lower-level concern than algorithmic changes like we discussed above, it is worth noting for completeness in an advanced chapter.

In Beam, every **`PCollection`** has an associated *coder* that defines how its elements are serialized into bytes for transport and storage. Coders are chosen based on the **element type and type information**, and not on the semantic format of the data. For example, if your elements are JSON strings, Beam will use a string or bytes coder, not a special "JSON coder." Beam only uses structured coders such as Avro, Proto, or Row-based coders when your elements are explicitly modeled as structured objects (for example, using schemas, Avro records, or typed Java classes).

This distinction is crucial because coders operate on the *representation* of your data, not its meaning. Efficient coders produce compact byte representations, besides enabling faster I/O and shuffling. Inefficient coders, such as Java's default SerializableCoder, often generate large payloads and introduce CPU overhead during serialization and deserialization, which can significantly slow down pipelines, and also increase network and storage costs. Choosing the right coder is therefore a performance decision, and not just a correctness requirement.

For **Java** pipelines, a known best practice is to use a specialized coder like Avro, Proto, or Beam's KryoCoder instead of the default Java serialization, which is slow. If you are processing records, using Beam's Schema and letting it use an Avro-based coder, or directly using AvroCoder for a POJO, can improve throughput. For example, if your events are JSON strings, decoding and encoding JSON on each step is expensive, you might instead define a custom coder to handle your event objects more directly, or convert them to a binary format early on.

For **Python** pipelines, the default coder often is the Pickle coder (for arbitrary objects). Pickling in Python is not extremely fast. Where possible, use simpler types or Beam's native types, so that Beam can use the C-based FastCoder. For instance, if you can represent your data as a tuple of primitives or a Beam Row with a schema, do so; Beam might then use an optimized coder. Also, avoid unnecessarily large objects. If you have a very large blob of data, but only need part of it downstream, try to parse out only what you need (this relates to not carrying unnecessary data).

Here is an advanced tip–if your transform deals with a large blob (say a large text), but you only need a small piece of info from it, consider extracting that information as early as possible, instead of passing the whole blob through the pipeline. This reduces the serialization overhead per element.

In our e-commerce example, suppose each order event initially includes a big JSON with a lot of details, but ultimately, we only need a few fields (like **`product_id`**, **`user_id`**, **`amount`**). Hence, it would make sense to **flatten** the event to just those fields early on (perhaps in the same step where we parse JSON, we create a lightweight tuple (**`product_id`**, **`user_id`**, **`amount`**, **`category`**), rather than carrying the entire JSON dict forward). This lighter-weight element is faster to serialize, and takes less space in memory, as well as on the wire.

Here is another serialization tip: if you use Python and pass data to an external library or C extension, sometimes converting data structures can be costly. Beam allows using **Row** objects with schemas, which can integrate with pandas or other systems more efficiently. Hence, this is more relevant to advanced pipelines that mix Python and SQL transforms.

In summary, **while pipeline logic optimizations yield the biggest wins, do not overlook serialization overhead**. Use efficient coders whenever possible:

- In Java: Avro, Protobuf, or custom CombineFn accumulators that are small.
- In Python: Ensure that your data types are easily serializable, and are not larger than needed. When possible, rely on Beam's built-in coder for common types, instead of custom classes that require pickling.

Also, **compress data sources**: Reading compressed files (for example, gzip) is fine if you have many small files, but note that some compressed file formats cannot be split. For instance, if you have a 10GB single GZIP file, Beam cannot split that among workers–a single worker must read it fully, which eventually becomes a bottleneck.

A practical rule therefore is:

- If the source is splittable, Beam will be able parallelize reads.
- If the source is compressed in a non-splittable way, Beam is forced into single-worker reads.

Here is what you can do instead in production:

- Prefer many small compressed files, instead of a single large one. This allows parallelism at the file level.
- Use splittable compression formats whenever possible (such as BZIP2 in some runners, or columnar formats like Parquet/Avro with internal block structure).
- Preprocess large compressed files by decompressing and rewriting them into a splittable format before running Beam pipelines.
- For streaming or high-throughput batch workloads, consider storing data in native splittable storage formats, rather than in raw .gz logs.

Hence, for input data, consider format choices as part of optimization (this ties into both I/O and serialization). The Beam documents mention that *if you have very large compressed files, consider uncompressing them first, or use formats like compressed Avro that allow you to split them.*

Optimizing Data Sources and Sinks

The efficiency of your pipeline is also affected by how you read the input and write the output. Hence, we will cover some best practices for sources and sinks:

- **Parallelizing Input Reading:** If your pipeline reads from a data source, make sure that it can be read in parallel. For example, if reading from cloud storage, use a file pattern that matches multiple files (for example, gs://data/2025-01/*.json), rather than one huge file. This allows Beam to distribute the work across multiple workers. Beam's TextIO and other file-based IO connectors can split input into multiple read tasks **only if the underlying source is splittable**. Some formats or compression methods (for example, a single large `.gz` file) are not splittable; hence, they must be read entirely by one worker, which severely limits parallelism, and can become a performance bottleneck. Designing your storage layout with splittable formats and multiple files is therefore essential for scalable ingestion. You can also hint at desired sharding. For example, ReadFromText supports parameters such as:

```
beam.io.ReadFromText(
    file_pattern,
    compression_type=beam.io.filesystem.CompressionTypes.AUTO,
    min_bundle_size=0
)
```

Here:

- **`compression_type`** controls how compressed inputs are handled (and whether splitting is possible).
- **`min_bundle_size`** influences how large each work bundle should be when the source is splittable, which can affect how finely the input is parallelized.

However, even with these options, the dominant factor for parallelism is still:

- Having many input files instead of one large file.
- Using splittable formats and compression types (for example, uncompressed text, or splittable formats like Parquet or Avro).
- Avoiding single large compressed files such as .gz, which usually force a single worker to read the entire file.

  In our e-commerce case, if we have historical order logs by date, reading a whole month as one file is slow–it is much better to break the data into daily (or even hourly) files, so that Beam can distribute the read across many workers. This becomes even more critical if the data is compressed; a single large compressed file (for example, a .gz file) is usually *not splittable*, which means that only one worker can read it from start to finish, while completely eliminating parallelism. In contrast, many smaller compressed files can still be read in parallel, one per worker, and give better throughput and scalability.

- **Avoiding Single-Threaded Output:** Similarly, when writing output, avoid a single file or single connection unless the volume is tiny. If writing to files, use **`.WriteToText(..., file_name_prefix="output", num_shards=20`**) to output 20 files in parallel, instead of one giant file. If you are writing to a database, consider that many DBs have limits on connections or ingest rate; therefore, you might need to buffer and batch writes (Beam's built-in connectors like BigQueryIO handle a lot of this under the hood; for example, using load jobs for bulk write). For example, writing final category sales results to a small file is fine, but if you are writing millions of user records, you should use multiple shards. In Apache Beam's Java SDK, when writing to BigQuery, this is controlled through this API:

```
BigQueryIO.write()
    .to("project:dataset.table")
```

```
    .withMethod(BigQueryIO.Write.Method.FILE_LOADS)
```

Here, **`BigQueryIO.Write.Method.FILE_LOADS`** tells Beam to first write data to files (typically in Cloud Storage), and then load those files into BigQuery in bulk. This approach is optimized for large batch loads, as well as it provides much higher throughput and lower cost when compared to row-by-row inserts.

In contrast, **`BigQueryIO.Write.Method.STREAMING_INSERTS`** writes each element directly to BigQuery using the streaming API. This is appropriate for low-latency, real-time use cases, where data must appear in BigQuery immediately, but it is more expensive. Moreover, it has lower throughput limits.

As a rule of thumb:

- Use **`FILE_LOADS`** for large batch outputs and high-volume pipelines.
- Use **`STREAMING_INSERTS`** for real-time pipelines where freshness matters more than cost and maximum throughput.
- **External Service Calls:** If your pipeline calls external services (for example, an HTTP API, database, or microservice) for each element, this often becomes the bottleneck. External services might not be able to handle high QPS from all workers simultaneously; therefore, the network latency adds up. Although Beam cannot magically speed up an external RPC, you can optimize overall performance by batching requests to process multiple records in a single call. This typically increases throughput and reduces per-request overhead, but it also introduces a trade-off; larger batches mean higher latency for individual elements, since each element must wait for the batch to fill before the call is made. Hence, in practice, you should choose the batch size based on your SLA requirements, while balancing acceptable latency against the need for higher throughput and lower RPC cost. One practical way to reduce the cost of external RPC calls is to **batch multiple elements into a single request**. Instead of calling an address-validation service once per order, you can collect (for example) up to 50 orders, send them in one API call, and then fan the results back out as individual enriched records. In Python Beam, the cleanest (and officially supported) way to do this is to use **`BatchElements`** to form batches, and then apply a ParDo that performs the single batched call.

```
import apache_beam as beam

# Example external service call (replace with your real
implementation)
def call_address_api(orders_batch):
    """
    orders_batch: list[dict]
    returns: list[bool] (same length), where each bool indicates
validity
    """
```

```
        # Placeholder logic
        return [True for _ in orders_batch]

class ValidateAddressBatch(beam.DoFn):
    def process(self, orders_batch):
        # Make ONE API call for the whole batch
        validations = call_address_api(orders_batch)

        # Emit one enriched order per input order
        for order, is_valid in zip(orders_batch, validations):
            enriched = dict(order)  # avoid mutating input
references
            enriched["address_valid"] = is_valid
            yield enriched

# Example pipeline usage
with beam.Pipeline() as p:
    orders = p | "CreateOrders" >> beam.Create([
        {"order_id": "o1", "address": "1 Main St"},
        {"order_id": "o2", "address": "2 High St"},
        {"order_id": "o3", "address": "3 Lake Rd"},
    ])

    validated_orders = (
        orders
        # Batch into lists of elements (Beam chooses actual batch
sizes within these bounds)
        | "BatchOrders" >> beam.BatchElements(min_batch_size=10,
max_batch_size=50)
        # Call the external service once per batch
        | "ValidateAddressInBatches" >> beam.ParDo(ValidateAddress-
Batch())
    )

    validated_orders | "PrintForDemo" >> beam.Map(print)
```

This pattern is preferable because `BatchElements` handles batching safely and clearly, while the **`DoFn.process()`** method yields outputs directly (therefore, nothing is dropped). In streaming pipelines, this pattern also generalizes well; Beam will still form batches, but the effective batch size depends on arrival rate and runner behavior. Hence, you can tune **`min_batch_size/max_batch_size`** to balance throughput and latency.

This is an advanced optimization pattern, and should be used only when external service calls become a real performance bottleneck. Apache Beam runners **do not guarantee fixed bundle sizes, or stable bundle boundaries**. Hence, a bundle may end early due to memory pressure, checkpointing, autoscaling, or scheduling decisions.

Due to this, batching that relies purely on bundle lifecycle (such as accumulating elements inside a DoFn with **`finish_bundle`**) can be **inconsistent and unpredictable**.

For this reason, Beam provides the **`BatchElements`** transform, which is the **recommended and supported** way to batch elements. It expresses your batching intent declaratively, and lets the runner decide how to form batches safely and efficiently.

You should think of batching as **"best-effort size control"**, not as a strict contract. The real guarantee can be that:

- Batching reduces the number of RPC calls.
- It improves throughput.
- However, it may increase latency slightly.
- Exact batch sizes are dependent on runner and workload.

Use this pattern when you want to control QPS and amortize expensive remote calls, and not when you need exact batch sizing semantics.

The Dataflow runner specifically encourages batching RPCs via bundle methods to avoid backpressure on external systems.

- **Data Locality:** Where your workers run relative to where your data lives has a direct impact on latency, throughput, and cost. Therefore, moving large volumes of data across long network distances is expensive and slow, if compared to processing it close to the source.

  You should try to preserve data locality on runners where you manage the infrastructure yourself (such as Spark or Flink on-premises). For example, if your input data is stored in HDFS, schedule workers on nodes that host the data blocks. This minimizes network transfer, and allows the pipeline to read data at disk speed, rather than on the network speed.

  On fully managed runners like Google Cloud Dataflow, much of this placement is handled automatically, but locality still matters at a regional level. Hence, a simple and very important rule is to always run your Dataflow job in the same region as your storage systems (GCS, BigQuery, Pub/Sub, and so on).

  If your Dataflow job runs in us-central1, but your GCS bucket or BigQuery dataset is in europe-west1, every read and write will cross regions. This introduces:

  - Higher latency
  - Lower throughput
  - Additional network egress costs
  - Increased chance of transient network failures

For example:

- **Good:**
  - Dataflow Region: us-central1
  - GCS Bucket: us-central1
  - BigQuery Dataset: us-central1
- **Risky:**
  - Dataflow Region: us-central1
  - GCS Bucket: europe-west1
  - BigQuery Dataset: europe-west1

In hybrid architectures, locality becomes even more critical. If your pipeline reads from an on-prem database and writes to cloud storage, the network link between your data center and the cloud becomes the bottleneck. No amount of parallelism will be overcome physical distance and bandwidth limits. Hence, in such cases, you should:

- Run Beam workers as close as possible to the database (same data center or VPC).
- Or replicate data into the cloud first, and process it there.
- Avoid streaming large raw datasets over slow WAN links, whenever possible.

In short:

- Keep compute close to storage.
- Keep Dataflow jobs in the same region as GCS and BigQuery.
- Avoid unnecessary cross-region or cross-network traffic.
- Treat network distance as a real performance constraint, and not an abstract one.

Thus, good data locality often produces larger performance gains than any code-level micro-optimization.

- **Throttling**: If a sink (such as an external API or database) cannot handle high parallel request rates, avoid "funneling" traffic through a single key using **`GroupByKey`** as a throttle. This is because it often creates a hot key, forces a heavy shuffle, and can materialize large per-key state that leads to memory pressure. Instead, prefer batching primitives like **`GroupIntoBatches`** (keyed) or **`BatchElements`** (unkeyed), and pair them with **explicitly controlled concurrency** in the sink-writing DoFn (for example, limited worker threads/ connection pool limits), since rewindowing alone does not reliably throttle throughput without an intentional batching or a concurrency control mechanism. This is contrary to the usual goal of maximizing parallelism, but it is necessary to avoid overloading a system. For instance, if writing to an old system that can only handle 100 writes per second, firing 1000 workers at it will just cause failures. Therefore, you could reduce the number of workers for that transform by using `.rewindow()` or a `.GroupByKey()` to funnel things (effectively serializing), or use a custom transform that batches, and perhaps, uses a singleton key. Hence, this is scenario-specific.

In our e-commerce pipeline, let us say the final step is to write the category sales results to a database for the finance team. If it is a SQL database, we would want to batch those writes (Beam's JdbcIO allows writing in batches). If it is BigQuery, Beam will likely use load jobs for us if the data is large, which is efficient. Therefore, always leverage Beam's connectors that are optimized, as they often have built-in retries, batching, and parallelism control.

To conclude, **use parallel I/O** whenever possible, batch external operations, and keep the data close to where it is processed. This ensures that the pipeline's edges (input and output) do not become the choke points. A pipeline can only run as fast as its slowest link, and that link is often an I/O operation.

Tuning Resource Utilization and Parallelism

Beyond logical optimizations in the pipeline code, you can often improve performance by tuning how the pipeline uses resources. This includes setting the number of workers, worker machine types, and leveraging autoscaling or other runner-specific features.

- **Choosing the Right Worker Size:** Beam pipelines (especially on cloud runners) let you choose the machine type, or the amount of CPU and memory per worker. A common mistake is using too small workers that get overwhelmed, or using very large workers that stay underutilized. For instance, if each element in your pipeline needs 1 GB of memory to process (say it is a large image), and you choose workers with only 2 GB RAM, you will likely run into thrashing or OOMs. On the other hand, if your worker has 64 CPU cores, but your pipeline only efficiently uses 8 (due to limited parallelism in a step), the rest sit idle. So, match worker resources to your workload needs. Therefore, for our e-commerce pipeline, if we do simple computations, standard 4-core machines might suffice; if we were doing heavy ML inference on each event, maybe, we would want machines with GPUs or more CPUs.

  Deciding Worker Size

  CPU Pegged (Near 90–100% for Long Periods): It means that you are CPU-bound, and your transforms are doing heavy compute per element.

- **What To Do:**
  - **Scale out** (more workers) if you have plenty of parallelism (which means lots of independent elements/keys).
  - **Scale up CPU per worker,** if each worker/thread is saturated, and adding workers does not help much (for example, fixed parallelism due to a hot key, a single heavy stage, or limited downstream capacity).
- **Common Examples:** JSON parsing at scale, complex aggregations, heavy feature engineering, encryption/compression, and CPU-only inference

OOM Errors, Frequent GC Pauses, Spilling to Disk, "Thrashing": It means that you are memory-bound (working set per element/bundle exceeds RAM).

- **What To Do:**
  - **Increase memory per worker** (bigger RAM machine type).
  - **Add/Increase local disk,** if your runner supports spilling, and you see spill-related slowdowns (disk buys you stability, but can slow you down).
  - **Also consider reducing per-element footprint** (batching strategy, avoid materializing large objects, use streaming/iterators, and reshape bundles).
- **Common Examples:** Large images/documents per element, big joins/shuffles with large side inputs, and wide group-bys that produce huge intermediate state.

Low CPU Usage, but Still Slow Throughput: It means that you are likely **I/O bound** (waiting on network/storage/external services), or blocked on backpressure.

- **What To Do:**
  - **Increase Concurrency** (more workers, or more in-flight requests per worker) *if* the external system can handle it.
  - **Optimize I/O**: Bigger reads/writes, fewer round trips, connection pooling/keep-alive, compress where appropriate, colocate compute with data, and use bulk APIs.
  - **Check External Bottlenecks**: Database rate limits, API quotas, storage throttling, and sink write limits.
- **Common Examples:** Reading from remote object storage, calling a feature store / HTTP service per element, and writing to a slow sink, cross-region traffic.

- **Maximizing Parallelism:** Ensure that the pipeline can actually use multiple workers. This goes back to having enough keys or independent tasks. If you see that adding more workers does not speed up the job, check if you have a bottleneck step that is single-threaded, or is limited by small key space.

Sometimes, a transform like a global combine without parallelism or a doFn that is not distributed will limit scaling. Beam's runners usually execute many elements per worker thread in parallel, but you can also set hints. For example, Dataflow's autoscaling looks at how busy the CPUs are; if they are low because of limited parallelism, it may not scale out. In streaming jobs, **allowing autoscaling** is generally good; therefore, the runner can adjust worker count as data rate changes. In batch jobs, you might directly set a high number of workers (`--max_num_workers` in Dataflow) to finish faster, provided the work can actually be split.

- **Autoscaling and Throttling:** Google Cloud Dataflow has autoscaling which can add or remove workers based on pipeline backlog and CPU. This is great for cost, but sometimes, you want to fix worker count for consistent performance. If your job has consistent load, turning off autoscaling, and just using a fixed pool can avoid the overhead of scaling decisions. On the other hand, if your input size is unpredictable (say streaming with spikes), autoscaling ensures you handle peaks, but drop back down in idle times. There is also **vertical autoscaling** (changing machine size) in some runners. The key is to monitor your job, and see if it is CPU-bound, memory-bound, or I/O-bound, and adjust accordingly. For example, if the CPU is 100% on all workers, and the job is slow, you likely need more workers or bigger CPUs. If CPU is 10%, and the job is slow, maybe it is waiting on I/O, or stuck on something that is not parallelizing.
- **Splitting Work into Smaller Tasks:** If a source supports parallelism (like reading from a big query or a large file), ensure that Beam knows it can split. Some advanced configurations can be, for example, when BigQueryIO in Beam can use **Direct Read (storage API),** which splits input into many shards for parallel reading, as opposed to a single export job. Therefore, for very large tables, the storage API approach can be faster because it parallelizes the read. Features such as BigQuery Direct Read via the Storage API are **runner- and IO-connector specific**. They are not always enabled by default, and often require explicit configuration and permissions (for example, enabling the BigQuery Storage API, granting **`bigquery.readsessions.create`**, and using a runner that supports it). Without this setup, Beam may fall back to slower mechanisms such as export-based reads. Similarly, if you are reading from a database, you might split by key ranges manually, and read in parallel (Beam does not automatically split an SQL query; you might have to have multiple queries partitioned by key). Hence, consider if your data source is a bottleneck, and if you can parallelize it.
- **Avoid Over-Parallelizing Small Work:** The flip side of parallelism is overhead. If you have a very small amount of data, using dozens of workers might actually be slower due to overhead of coordination. For example, processing 1000 records does not need 50 workers, as the startup time and

coordination would dominate. Beam's autoscaling usually will not spin up many workers for trivial loads, but if you manually set workers, you must keep this in mind.

- **Pipeline Options (Persistent Disk, and so on):** Some runners let you configure things like disk size (for shuffle or spill). If your combines or groupings involve very large data, ensuring that enough disk space is allocated for shuffle (especially in Dataflow) can prevent failures. For example, **`--disk_size_gb`** in Dataflow options can be increased if you know you will shuffle terabytes of data. Also, **`--worker_harness_container_image`** can be used to specify a custom container with optimized libraries, if needed (for advanced tuning, for example, using a more efficient numpy version for some calculations).

Hence, tuning resource usage is often iterative: you run the pipeline, observe its metrics, and then adjust. For instance, you might find that the stage "**`SumOrdersByCategory`**" is stuck on one worker because Electronics is hot; therefore, you may implement fanout, or raise the worker memory. Or, you can see that your I/O read stage is only using one worker; at this point, you realize that you had one big file. So, you split it.

Here is a quick guide to tuning:

- Start with defaults (many times if they are good enough).
- If the job is slow, check runner UI or logs to determine if it is stuck on a few keys, and if all the CPUs are maxed. Additionally, check if there is lots of data that is spilling to the disk.
- Apply the relevant optimization; for example, add more workers for CPU saturation, or increase machine memory if OOM, or fix key distribution if one key is slow, and so on.
- Repeat until the performance is satisfactory, or till you hit the external limits.

Another tip is to use **metrics** to understand how many elements are going through, and use the runner's execution details. On Dataflow, the *execution details* and *job graph* show each stage's input size and timing. It can highlight if one stage is taking 80% of the time, or if one stage is not parallelized well. This information guides your tuning (maybe that stage is the grouping by country with only 3 keys, and hence, is the problem).

Monitoring Pipeline Performance with Metrics and Logs

To optimize effectively, you need insight into what the pipeline is doing. Beam provides a Metrics API that allows you to collect custom metrics (counters, distributions, gauges) during pipeline execution. Runners like Dataflow and others surface these metrics in their UIs or in logs, which can be invaluable for understanding performance, and also while verifying behavior.

Using Beam Metrics: For example, you might count how many orders were processed, or how many orders fell into each category, as sanity checks. You might measure the distribution of order values to detect skew. Here is a simple use of a counter metric in our pipeline:

```
from apache_beam.metrics import Metrics
class ProcessOrder(beam.DoFn):
    def __init__(self):
        # Define a counter metric
        self.order_counter = Metrics.counter("ecommerce",
"orders_processed")
        self.large_order_counter = Metrics.counter("ecommerce",
"large_orders")
    def process(self, order):
        # Increment counter for every order
        self.order_counter.inc()
        # If order total is large, count it separately
        if order.get("order_total", 0) > 1000:
            self.large_order_counter.inc()
        # (Do some processing on the order, for example, format
or validate)
        yield order

# Use the DoFn in pipeline
processed = orders | "ProcessOrder" >> beam.ParDo(ProcessOrder())
```

In this snippet, we defined two counters: "**`orders_processed`**" and "**`large_orders`**" under the namespace "ecommerce". Each order increments the first; orders above $1,000 increment the second. These metrics will be collected as the pipeline runs. On Dataflow's monitoring UI (or by querying the job via REST API, or in **`DirectRunner`** after pipeline completion), you can see the values of these metrics. This helps ensure that the pipeline is processing the expected number of orders, and what fraction of it are large orders–which could hint at skew, or special cases.

For performance, metrics like counters will not drastically slow your job (they are aggregated efficiently), but avoid extremely high-frequency logging or metric updates that are not needed. For example, using logging.info per element is strongly discouraged as it can flood logs, and slow down the pipeline. Instead, prefer **Beam Metrics** for counting, aggregations, and high-level visibility. If logging is necessary for debugging, use **sampled logging** (for example, log every Nth element), or log **only anomalies and errors**, rather than every record. Thus, metrics are a better alternative for counting occurrences, instead of logging each event.

Runner Monitoring Features: Different Beam runners provide ways to monitor pipeline performance:

- **`Google Cloud Dataflow`**: It has a rich UI in the cloud console. You can see the pipeline DAG, each transform's progress, system lag (for streaming), CPU, memory, and I/O graphs per stage, and autoscaling decisions. Dataflow even has specific diagnostics for issues like hot keys (it logs messages if it detects a key with a huge bundle of work, which points to **`hot_key_logger`**, as mentioned earlier). You can also set up alerts on metrics like backlog or errors. Dataflow's *Execution Details* tab can show how data is distributed across keys for groupings, which helps identify the skew.
- **`Apache Flink Runner`**: If running on a Flink cluster, you can use the Flink Web UI. Beam transforms appear as nodes in the Flink job, and you can see task statistics, throughput, and any accumulators (Beam metrics might surface as Flink accumulators).
- **`Apache Spark Runner`**: It can integrate with Spark's UI, where you see RDD jobs/stages corresponding to pipeline parts.
- **`Direct Runner`**: It is local, so not much of a UI, but if you run it in verbose logging mode, you can get some insight. For testing and debugging, `DirectRunner` can output counters after run. For example, **`res = p.run(); res.wait_until_finish(); res.metrics().query(...)`** can retrieve metric values in your code (this is useful in unit tests to assert that the pipeline did what you expected).

Using Metrics to Measure Performance: You can instrument your pipeline to measure things like:

- How long certain steps take (though you often rely on runner for that; still, you could record a timestamp at start and end if needed).
- Sizes of **`PCollections`** (count elements out of a transform).
- Rate of events (maybe a counter per second using a state and timer in streaming, but that is complex; it is easier on runner UI, which often shows elements/second).

In our context, we might track how many events we processed per category using:

```
class CategoryMetrics(beam.DoFn):
    def __init__(self):
        self.counters = {}
    def process(self, kv):
        category, value = kv
        # Lazily create a counter for this category
        if category not in self.counters:
            self.counters[category] = Metrics.counter("orders_by_
category", category)
```

```
            self.counters[category].inc()
            yield kv  # pass data through
```

If used, this DoFn would keep a separate counter for each category encountered. This is dynamic, and on some runners (Dataflow) the set of metric names has to be known; therefore, dynamic creation might not show up until some data is processed. However, it is a way to see distribution.

Logging: While heavy per-element logging is bad for performance, targeted logging for anomalies is useful. For instance, you might log a warning if an order's total is extremely high ("Order {id} has abnormally high total of $X"). These should be rate-limited or sample-based if possible, so that you do not log 10 million lines. The key is to use logs sparingly in hot code paths.

Debugging Performance with Logs: You can add log statements in **`startBundle`/`finishBundle`** to see when bundles start and finish on workers, which can hint at how data is being split. Dataflow provides "worker logs", where you can see if any errors occur, or GC thrashing messages, and so on, which can hint at memory issues.

In Dataflow, enabling **Dataflow Shuffle** (for batch) is a feature that uses an external service for shuffle operations. It can speed up shuffles and relieve worker memory pressure, all at the cost of additional service usage. Therefore, if you are using Dataflow and dealing with massive groupings, enabling this (it might be on by default in newer versions) can help. It is not something you control in code, but via the pipeline option flag.

Summary for Monitoring: Make liberal use of Beam's metrics to track pipeline health internally, and take advantage of runner-specific dashboards to observe CPU, memory, data volume, and parallelism. Often, the fastest way to find a bottleneck is to see which transform is taking the most time. Metrics and logs will guide you here; for example, a metric might show 1 billion elements went into a particular step. Maybe, it is higher than expected, and you realize that you missed a filter. Or, the logs might show "Combine had to spill to disk" warnings, indicating that maybe, a hot key caused a huge combine that did not fit in the memory.

Hence, by monitoring, you not only troubleshoot issues, but also verify that your optimizations (filtering, combining, and so on) are having the intended effect (for example, counters show a drop in elements after a filter. This means that the filter is working and cutting down data).

Benchmarking and Testing Pipeline Performance

After applying optimizations, it is wise to **benchmark** your pipeline—that is, measure its performance under realistic conditions. Benchmarking helps answer questions like: *Can my pipeline handle the required data volume within acceptable time/cost?*, or *Which version of my pipeline is faster?*

Here are some strategies for benchmarking Beam pipelines:

- **Use Synthetic Data Generators:** If you do not have access to production data at scale for tests, you can generate data. Beam even has a `GenerateSequence` transform (in Java), or you can use Python's beam. Create with repetition to produce large numbers of elements. For example, to test our e-commerce pipeline, we could generate 1 million fake orders (perhaps using a small DoFn to emit random orders), and then run the pipeline in a controlled environment (maybe `DirectRunner` or a small Dataflow run) just to measure throughput. Ensure that the synthetic data distribution resembles real data (for example, include a hot key, if that happens in reality).
- **Measure End-to-End Time:** The simplest benchmark metric for batch pipelines is the total elapsed time for a known input size. Hence, for streaming, you might look at steady-state throughput (elements per second), or end-to-end latency (time from event ingestion to result emission). You can run the pipeline with timers or external instrumentation. On Dataflow, you can see how long each stage took in the job details. Therefore, if you are comparing two approaches (say `GroupByKey` vs `CombinePerKey`), run the pipeline both ways on the same input size, and note the total job time, as well as any cost metrics.
- **Use Load Tests or the Nexmark Suite:** Apache Beam comes with **Nexmark**, which is a suite of streaming benchmarks (based on simulated auctions). It is more for advanced users, but you can adapt those patterns. Google Cloud has documented approaches to load testing Dataflow jobs using JUnit or integration tests. Essentially, you create a pipeline with a synthetic source that can pump data at a certain rate (Beam's `TestStream`, or an unbounded `GenerateSequence` can do this), and measure how the pipeline scales.
- **Profile Locally**: For certain code-heavy parts, you can profile them outside Beam, or with a direct run. For example, if a custom DoFn is suspected to be slow, you could run its logic in a normal Python loop with a large sample of data and profile CPU usage. Or use Python's `cProfile` with `DirectRunner` on a subset of data to see which functions are consuming time.
- **Benchmark in Isolation:** If possible, break your pipeline into parts, and test them separately. For instance, benchmark just the ingestion and filtering part (maybe by writing its output to a sink and measuring time), then benchmark the aggregation part with a pre-prepared dataset. This modular benchmarking can pinpoint slow segments.
- **Automate and Rerun:** Performance can vary run to run, especially in distributed systems due to noise. Therefore, if you can, run the pipeline multiple times,

and take average metrics. If you have a CI/CD setup, consider adding a performance test that runs a smaller version of the pipeline, and also checks that the throughput is above a threshold to catch regressions.

- **Costs:** While benchmarking on cloud, also consider cost metrics (like CPU hours, memory usage, and so on). Sometimes a faster pipeline might cost more (using more workers); therefore, you need to balance your goals. Beam's flexibility with runners means you could benchmark on your laptop for convenience, but ultimately the cloud run is what matters for real data. Therefore, some companies set up "performance pipelines" that run nightly on sample data to track any slowdowns.

For our running example, a simple benchmark might be to feed 1 million synthetic order events into the pipeline (perhaps by using a `beam.Create`, or reading a pre-generated file of that size). Run it with N workers, and measure how long until all results (say, total sales per category) are produced. If it finishes in, say, 2 minutes, that might be acceptable. If it takes 20 minutes, perhaps we need to scale out more, or we find that 1 worker was stuck on "Electronics" for too long. This confirms the existence of a hot key problem.

Another aspect of benchmarking is **stress testing**; therefore, you should push the pipeline to its limits. What happens if input doubles? Does runtime roughly double (linear scaling), or worse? If it is worse, look for bottlenecks that amplify with size (non-linear inefficiencies, like a poor choice of algorithm, or something that causes data to explode).

Tooling: There are third-party tools and frameworks (like PerfKit Benchmarker or Dataflow-specific load testing frameworks), but since we are focusing on Beam-native approaches, we will not consider those. Beam's own metrics, as well as some simple scripts often suffice.

Interpreting Results: Once you have the benchmark numbers, you might iterate by increasing shards or enabling a feature, and then monitoring the effect. For example, benchmark with fanout=1 versus fanout=5 for combine, and see if the hot key processing time drops. Or, you can test filter placement by running pipeline with an early filter versus with that filter removed (to see its impact on runtime).

Always be mindful of variance—a cloud VM might have a slow moment or a fast moment, so do not jump to conclusions from one run. Look for consistent trends.

In conclusion, treat pipeline optimization as an empirical process: apply best practices, and then measure. Use Beam's metrics and runner metrics to validate that change X improved the situation (for example, "combine early reduced shuffled data by 90%, and indeed job time went down proportionally"). Therefore, by benchmarking, you can ensure that your pipeline not only looks efficient in theory, but actually meets the performance requirements in practice.

Troubleshooting Common Performance Pitfalls

Even with all these techniques, you may run into performance issues. Hence, let us discuss some common problems in Beam pipelines, and how to troubleshoot them. Here is a **troubleshooting checklist** with symptoms, causes, and remedies:

- **Symptom:** Pipeline **running very slowly** overall, or taking longer than expected for a known data size.
    - **Possible Causes:** Insufficient parallelism (not using enough workers, or a bottleneck with too few keys); extremely large data volume hitting I/O limits, or a specific transform that is slow (like a heavy regex or external call).
    - **What to Check:** Look at runner UI. Is the CPU high on all workers? If not, maybe they are waiting on I/O or stuck. Check if one stage is straggling (for example, a group by with few keys). Also check if the autoscaling did not scale up enough (maybe it thought that it did not need more workers).
    - **Solution:** If CPU is low, but the job is slow, identify the bottleneck stage. Perhaps increase parallelism by adding workers (`--max_num_workers`), or ensuring that your keys are better distributed. If an external sink is slow, consider batching or another sink. If one transform is CPU-heavy (profile it), consider optimizing that code, or using a faster library. Make sure that no debug logs are printing per element, and slowing things down.
- **Symptom:** A specific pipeline **stage is stuck at 99%** (one worker taking much longer than others).
    - **Cause:** Likely a **straggler** due to a hot key or uneven partition. One worker might be processing a giant group or a large file split.
    - **Check:** If using Dataflow, the job logs might mention "hot key" with the key value identified. Also, stage progress in UI will show one worker still busy, while others are finished.
    - **Solution:** Implement hot key mitigation–for example, use combine with fanout, or manual sharding as discussed in *Managing Data Skew*. If it is a single large file causing a straggler in reading, consider splitting that file. For batch, sometimes enabling the Dataflow Shuffle service helps because it will auto-balance large key loads across more machines (since shuffle is external).
- **Symptom: Out of Memory (OOM) errors** on workers (seen in logs or as worker restarts)
    - **Cause:** It could be a single key with too much data (trying to buffer a huge

group in memory), or an execessively large dataset for the chosen worker memory, or a bug (like accumulating data unboundedly).

- **Check:** Logs might show a GC overhead warning or OOM around a `GroupByKey` or Combine. If it is always at a certain step, the step might be the culprit. Also, verify if you accidentally are using a global window in streaming without triggers, as that can cause infinite accumulation.
- **Solution:** For hot key OOM, do the hot key mitigation (fanout). For general memory issues, consider using larger machines or fewer threads per machine (sometimes too many threads, where each is handling data, can exhaust memory). If using Java, check if coder is bloating data (maybe switch to a more compact coder). In streaming, make sure tha the windows are set such that data eventually gets emitted and cleared. For example, if you had a global window on an unbounded source and never triggered, the system would hold all data forever. This is definitely not what you want for performance or memory.

- **Symptom: Excessive disk spill** (seen in logs, or just deduced by slow shuffle)
  - **Cause:** If a combine or group has to spill to disk (data does not fit in memory), it will slow things down. This often accompanies hot keys or very large overall group.
  - **Solution:** Break into smaller chunks via combiner, or increase memory via larger workers. Also, check if the runner has a shuffle service (Dataflow's external shuffle), and consider using it as it is optimized for disk IO.
- **Symptom: Autoscaling is not scaling up,** even though the pipeline is struggling (in Dataflow).
  - **Cause:** Possibly, the pipeline appears idle or limited from the autoscaler's perspective. For instance, if a single key is the bottleneck, from an autoscaler viewpoint, adding more workers does not help (because that key cannot be split), so it does not add workers. Or, you might have hit max workers limit.
  - **Solution:** If you identify this scenario, manual intervention is needed–fix the root cause (key distribution), so that autoscaler sees balanced load. Or, set a higher `max_num_workers`. Check autoscaling logs; Dataflow often notes why it is not scaling (for example, "CPU is low, not scaling up"). If CPU is low, but one key is the problem, autoscaling can be misled. That is why solving the data skew is the key.
- **Symptom: High system latency is observed in streaming** (events taking too long to get output).
  - **Cause:** Could be event backlog (pipeline cannot keep up), or waiting for watermark advancements (if using large windows). If using global window

  with default trigger, you will not see results until the pipeline finishes (which in streaming is never, so effectively nothing outputs).

  - **Check:** In Dataflow, look at "System lag" metric–if it is growing, you are falling behind. If backlog/lag is high, the pipeline is under-provisioned. If backlog is zero, but you see no output, maybe a trigger/window issue.
  - **Solution:** If under-provisioned, add workers, or see if some transform is slow. If it is windowing, consider using earlier triggers. For example, in streaming, use time windows (like hourly windows), so that results emit periodically rather than waiting forever. This is both correctness and performance, as holding data indefinitely is a memory risk.

- **Symptom: Checkpointing or downtime issues** (for stateful processing)
  - **Solution:** Make sure that you are not checkpointing huge state unnecessarily, and that timers/state usage is efficient. This is advanced, but keep the state small, or use aggregations instead.

One more category:

- **Symptom: Unexpected output or incorrect results under load**
  - **Cause:** Possibly, it can be caused by a bug in the pipeline logic that only surfaces with certain timing or volume. For instance, using a side input in streaming without windowing alignment can cause it to not show up as expected. Or, a combine function not being associative leads to wrong results at scale.
  - **Solution:** This goes beyond performance into correctness, but be sure that your optimizations have not broken the logic. Always test on smaller scale to ensure correctness before pushing it to the maximum scale.

Approach to Troubleshooting: When a pipeline misbehaves, start by simplifying. You may wonder if you can reproduce the issue with less data, or in a local environment. If not (only happens at scale), use metrics and logging at strategic points to narrow down where things diverge. The runner's diagnostic messages are very helpful here; for example, Dataflow might tell you "Stage X is stuck due to one slow shard", or "Worker lost contact", and so on.

For performance issues, the answer will most probably be among the topics we discussed:

- Did not filter enough -> Filter more.
- Did not combine early -> Add combiner.
- Hot key -> Mitigate it.
- Not enough resources -> Add workers, or bigger machines.
- External system slow -> Batch or throttle.

- Lots of waiting -> Maybe, there is blocking in code (for example, do a synchronous call per element; batch them, or do asynchronously, if possible).

Finally, do not hesitate to use Beam's community resources (mailing list, StackOverflow) when stuck. Often if you describe your pipeline pattern and the performance issue, someone might recognize a common pitfall.

Conclusion

Optimizing Apache Beam pipelines, therefore involves a combination of thoughtful pipeline design, careful handling of data, and tuning of execution parameters. In this chapter, we explored how early filtering and combining can drastically reduce data processing load, how to handle skew and hot keys to prevent bottlenecks, and how to use Beam's features like side inputs to avoid expensive operations. We also discussed best practices for interacting with sources and sinks–from parallel reads/writes, to batching external calls–and how to tune resources and parallelism for optimal throughput. Throughout, we used an e-commerce example to illustrate these concepts in a concrete way, while showing code snippets with detailed explanations.

It is worth emphasizing that optimization should not come at the expense of clarity unless absolutely necessary. We maintained the use of Beam-native transforms, and avoided premature optimization. The techniques here are meant to address real performance needs when basic pipelines (as introduced in earlier chapters) start to struggle with scale. Always start with a correct, simple pipeline, and then profile and optimize wherever needed. As a developer, you should approach performance systematically; apply best practices (like those in this chapter), use metrics to verify their impact, and iterate.

Thus, by following the strategies outlined, such as **minimizing data shuffles**, **combining data efficiently**, **balancing workload across keys**, and **monitoring your pipeline with metrics**, you can achieve significant improvements in Beam pipeline performance and scalability. Thus, whether you are processing a million events per second or terabytes of batch data, these optimizations ensure that your pipeline remains robust, fast, and cost-efficient.

Moreover, with these advanced techniques, you are now well-equipped to build pipelines that not only work, but work **well** at scale. In the next chapter, you might explore more specialized Beam features (like stateful processing and custom windowing), or dive into runner-specific tuning. However, the foundation you have now will serve you in any big data scenario. Happy optimizing, and may your pipelines always meet their SLAs!

CHAPTER 7 Deploying Apache Beam Pipelines on Different Runners

Introduction

In this chapter, we will learn how to deploy Apache Beam pipelines on various **runners** (execution engines). A runner is the component that translates your Beam pipeline into the API of an underlying distributed processing system or service. We will thus start with an overview of Apache Beam runners, and then provide step-by-step guidance for deploying pipelines on Google Cloud Dataflow, Apache Flink, and Apache Spark. We will cover both batch and streaming pipeline examples will be covered, with code samples in **Python** and **Java**. Additionally, we will discuss runner-specific considerations and best practices for cloud and on-premise deployments, which will help you to understand how to adapt your Beam pipelines to different environments with minimal configuration changes.

Structure

In this chapter, we will cover the following topics:

- Overview of Apache Beam Runners
- Deploying on Google Cloud Dataflow
- Deploying on Apache Flink
- Deploying on Apache Spark
- Runner-Specific Considerations and Differences
- Best Practices for Cloud and On-Premise Deployments

Overview of Apache Beam Runners

Apache Beam's motto is "*write once, run anywhere*". This is achieved through the use of different runners that execute your pipeline on various backends, without requiring you to rewrite your pipeline logic. In practice, this is the most accurate for **core pipeline logic and transforms** (such as **`ParDo`**, **`GroupByKey`**, windowing, and combiners), which are designed to be portable across runners. However, some aspects of a pipeline are **runner-specific**. IO connectors may have different capabilities or performance characteristics on different runners, the way metrics are exposed and monitored can vary by execution environment, and certain streaming semantics (such as checkpointing behavior, watermark propagation, and exactly-once guarantees) depend on the underlying runner. In Beam, you define your pipeline using the unified API, and the choice of runner determines **where** and **how** the pipeline runs. This decoupling allows you to develop your pipeline once, and then execute it on multiple processing engines or services such as Google Cloud Dataflow, Apache Flink, Apache Spark, and others.

Describing a Runner

A runner is essentially an adapter that translates the Beam pipeline into the native instructions of a specific processing engine. More importantly, this translation is not only syntactic, but **semantic**. The runner maps Beam's execution model into the underlying engine's concepts of event time, watermarks, windowing, triggers, state storage, checkpointing, and fault tolerance.

In other words, a runner does not just "convert" your pipeline into another API; it defines how Beam's guarantees are realized in practice. For example, how watermarks advance, how often state is checkpointed, how failures are recovered from, and whether exactly–once processing is achievable all depend on how the runner implements Beam's semantics on top of its execution engine. This is why pipelines can behave slightly differently across runners even when the code is identical.

Runner choice thus affects scaling, fault tolerance, and available connector. For example, the **Dataflow runner** submits the job to the Google Cloud Dataflow service, the **Flink runner** executes the pipeline on an Apache Flink cluster, while the **Spark runner** runs it on an Apache Spark cluster. Beam also provides a **`DirectRunner`** for local execution and testing on your machine (without a distributed backend), which is useful for development and validation, but is not meant for production deployment.

Available Beam Runners: Beam supports a range of runners, each corresponding to a different platform. Some of them are explained here:

- **`DirectRunner`:** Runs the pipeline locally on a single machine (primarily for testing and debugging)

- **`Google Cloud Dataflow Runner`:** Runs on the fully managed Google Cloud Dataflow service (serverless, autoscaling)
- **`Apache Flink Runner`:** Runs on an Apache Flink cluster (an open-source stream processing engine)
- **`Apache Spark Runner`:** Runs on an Apache Spark cluster (the popular batch/stream processing engine)
- **Others:** There are runners for other systems as well (for example, Apache Samza, Apache Nemo, Hazelcast Jet, and so on). However, this chapter will focus on Dataflow, Flink, and Spark, as they are among the most widely used runners.

One of Beam's core advantages is that you can switch runners by changing a few configuration options rather than rewriting your pipeline code. In practice, this means setting the **`--runner`** flag (or corresponding property in code), and providing any runner-specific options. For example, to run a pipeline on Dataflow versus Flink, you mostly just adjust pipeline options such as project IDs or master addresses, as we will see in the coming sections. This portability is possible because all runners implement the Beam Model's semantics for batch and streaming to the extent that the underlying engine supports them.

However, before you dive into each runner, ensure that you have the Apache Beam SDK installed or available for your chosen language (for example, the Python apache-beam package or the Beam Java libraries via Maven). We will not assume any prior cloud or cluster setup; instead, we will guide you through the minimal steps needed to get each environment ready. Now, let us explore each runner in detail, and also learn how to deploy Beam pipelines on them.

Deploying on Google Cloud Dataflow

Google Cloud Dataflow is a fully managed cloud service for running Apache Beam pipelines at scale. With Dataflow, you do not need to manage any infrastructure–the service will provision workers, auto-scale, and also handle fault tolerance. It is a serverless, pay-as-you-go model that allows you to easily process large amounts of data in a batch or streaming model. The Beam **Dataflow runner** integrates with this service, which simplifies deploying pipelines to Google Cloud.

Prerequisites: To deploy a pipeline on Dataflow, you will need the following:

- A Google Cloud Platform (GCP) project with billing enabled.
- The enabled Dataflow API in your project (this is usually done via the Cloud Console or the gcloud SDK).

- A Google Cloud Storage (GCS) bucket for staging and temporary files (for example, **`gs://your-bucketName`**). Beam will use this bucket to store pipeline code packages and intermediate data.
- The Google Cloud SDK (gcloud) should be installed and authenticated (to provide credentials to Dataflow). Alternatively, you can authenticate via other means (such as Application Default Credentials), if you are running the pipeline in a cloud environment.
- Apache Beam SDK should be installed in your development environment (for Python, **`pip install apache-beam[gcp]`**, as it ensures that GCP extensions are included; for Java, include the Beam runners Dataflow library in your project).

Note: *If you do not yet have a GCP account or project, you can sign up for a free trial on Google Cloud. However, it is not necessary to actually execute the examples to follow along; we will focus on how you would usually deploy to Dataflow.*

Dataflow Pipeline Options

When using the Dataflow runner, there are a few important pipeline options you must configure. These options tell the Beam pipeline where and how to run in Google Cloud. Hence, some common Dataflow options include:

- **`--runner=DataflowRunner`:** It specifies that the Dataflow service will execute the pipeline.
- **`--project`:** This is your GCP project ID where the Dataflow job will run.
- **`--region`:** The region for the Dataflow job (for example, us-central1). It is best to choose a region close to your data sources.
- **`--temp_location`:** A GCS path for temporary files (for example, **`gs://<your-bucket>/temp`**). This is required; Dataflow uses it for staging data, and also as a default for other storage needs.
- **Deployment Artifact Staging Path (Language-Specific Expression of the Same Concept):**
    - In **Java**, this is explicitly set using:
        - **`--staging_location`** → the GCS path where the pipeline JAR and dependencies are uploaded.
    - In **Python**, there is no separate **`--staging_location`** option by default. Instead:
        - Artifacts are automatically staged under **`--temp_location`**, unless they are overridden by advanced packaging options.

   - Beam builds a source distribution, and then uploads it to this staging area.
- **--output**: (this is not a built-in option, but we often pass an output path parameter for where the results should go in examples; this is pipeline-specific).
- **--streaming**: This is a flag to indicate streaming mode. You must set this to true for unbounded streaming pipelines. In batch pipelines (bounded data), this is not needed (as it defaults to false).
- Additional settings such as **--autoscalingAlgorithm**, **--numWorkers**, **--maxWorkers** can control worker scaling, but they have reasonable defaults. Hence, you can usually omit them for a simple deployment.

In Python, these options can be passed in a list to **PipelineOptions**, or you can use **argparse** to parse command-line flags. In Java, you typically use the **PipelineOptionsFactory** to create a **DataflowPipelineOptions** object. However, we will demonstrate both in this chapter. You must also remember that pipeline options should always be parsed from command-line arguments and treated as deployment-time configuration in the production phase. Hardcoding values is acceptable only for small demonstrations. Therefore, for reproducible and automated deployments, the same pipeline binary or script should be deployed to different environments simply by changing the runtime parameters.

Example 1: Batch Pipeline on Dataflow (WordCount)

Let us walk through deploying a simple **batch** pipeline (**WordCount**) on Dataflow. The **WordCount** pipeline reads text, counts occurrences of each word, and writes the results out. Therefore, we will show the code in both Python and Java, along with the required Dataflow options.

Python Example (WordCount on Dataflow):

```
import apache_beam as beam
from apache_beam.options.pipeline_options import PipelineOptions

# Define pipeline options for Dataflow
options = PipelineOptions([
    "--runner=DataflowRunner",
    "--project=YOUR_GCP_PROJECT_ID",
    "--region=us-central1",                # or your desired
Dataflow region
    "--temp_location=gs://YOUR_BUCKET/temp/",
    "--staging_location=gs://YOUR_BUCKET/staging/",
    "--job_name=wordcount-example",        # Dataflow job name
(lowercase required)
```

```
    "--save_main_session",              # for serialization of
session (if needed)
    # "--streaming" is not set because this is a batch pipeline
])

# Example pipeline: WordCount
input_file = "gs://apache-beam-samples/shakespeare/kinglear.txt"
# sample public data
output_path = "gs://YOUR_BUCKET/output/wordcounts"

with beam.Pipeline(options=options) as p:
    # Read a text file from GCS
    lines = p | "ReadLines" >> beam.io.ReadFromText(input_file)
    # Split lines into words
    words = lines | "Split" >> beam.FlatMap(lambda line: line.
split())
    # Count each word occurrence
    word_counts = words | "Count" >> beam.combiners.Count.
PerElement()
    # Format and write the results to GCS (as newline-delimited
text)
    formatted = word_counts | "Format" >> beam.Map(lambda wc:
f"{wc[0]}: {wc[1]}")
    formatted | "WriteResults" >> beam.io.WriteToText(output_
path, file_name_suffix=".txt")
```

In this Python code, we construct a **PipelineOptions** with the Dataflow runner and the necessary settings (project, region, and so on). The pipeline itself is the classic word count; therefore, you must read from a text source, do transformations, and then write to an output. The input in this example is a public sample file on GCS, and the output is written to your GCS bucket. After writing this script (for example, as **wordcount_dataflow.py**), you would run it from your terminal via:

```
python wordcount_dataflow.py
```

When it is run, this script will package your code and dependencies, upload them to the staging location, and submit a Dataflow job. You can then monitor the job in the Google Cloud Console's Dataflow section. The results will be written to the specified GCS path when the job is completed.

Tip: *In the preceding options, **--save_main_session** is used (without a value, which implies **True**). This option saves the state of the main Python session, which is useful if you define any functions or classes in your **__main__** module that need to be used on the workers. It ensures that they are pickled and sent to the Dataflow worker machines. It is often needed for pipelines defined in interactive environments or notebooks.*

Java Example (`WordCount` on Dataflow):

```
import org.apache.beam.sdk.Pipeline;
import org.apache.beam.sdk.options.PipelineOptionsFactory;
import org.apache.beam.runners.dataflow.options.DataflowPipeline
Options;
import org.apache.beam.sdk.io.TextIO;
import org.apache.beam.sdk.transforms.Count;
import org.apache.beam.sdk.transforms.FlatMapElements;
import org.apache.beam.sdk.values.TypeDescriptors;
import java.util.Arrays;

public class WordCountDataflow {
    public static void main(String[] args) {
        // Create Dataflow pipeline options
        DataflowPipelineOptions options = PipelineOptionsFactory.
create()
            .as(DataflowPipelineOptions.class);
        options.setRunner(com.google.cloud.dataflow.sdk.runners.
DataflowRunner.class);
        options.setProject("YOUR_GCP_PROJECT_ID");
        options.setRegion("us-central1");
        options.setTempLocation("gs://YOUR_BUCKET/temp/");
        options.setStagingLocation("gs://YOUR_BUCKET/staging/");
        options.setJobName("wordcount-example-java");
        // options.setNumWorkers(2); // for example, to specify
initial workers (optional)

        Pipeline p = Pipeline.create(options);

        // Read from a text source (for example, GCS file)
        p.apply("ReadLines", TextIO.read().from("gs://apache-
beam-samples/shakespeare/kinglear.txt"))
         // Split lines into words
         .apply("SplitWords", FlatMapElements.into(Type
Descriptors.strings())
                                             .via(line -> Arrays.
asList(line.split("\\s+"))))
         // Count each word
         .apply("CountWords", Count.perElement())
         // Format results as "word: count" strings
         .apply("FormatResults", FlatMapElements.into(Type
Descriptors.strings())
                                               .via(kv -> Arrays.
asList(kv.getKey() + ": " + kv.getValue())))
         // Write results to text files in GCS
```

```
            .apply("WriteResults", TextIO.write().to("gs://YOUR_
BUCKET/output/wordcounts-java")
                                                .withSuffix(".txt"));

        p.run().waitUntilFinish();
    }
}
```

Let us break down the Java code, as follows:

- We will use **DataflowPipelineOptions** to specify the runner and related configurations. We will also set the project ID, region, and Cloud Storage locations for temp and staging. Additionally, we will set a job name (must be in lowercase and unique for each run).
- The pipeline is constructed using the Beam Java SDK transforms: **TextIO.read()** to read an input text file from GCS, a **FlatMapElements** to split lines into words (using a simple whitespace split), **Count.perElement()** to count occurrences of each unique word, and **TextIO.write()** to write the output to GCS.
- We will then run the pipeline. The **waitUntilFinish()** call will cause the program to block until the Dataflow job completes (which might be some time, depending on the data size). In many cases, you might omit **waitUntilFinish()** to allow the Java process to exit after submission, unless you need to ensure completion, or get the result state.

Hence, to run this Java pipeline, you would compile it, and then execute it. If you are using Maven, ensure that you have the Dataflow runner dependency in your pom.xml (for example, **beam-runners-google-cloud-dataflow-java** as runtime scope). You can run it using Maven exec, or package it as a "**fat jar**". For example, one approach is:

- **Add Dataflow Dependencies**: In **pom.xml**, include:

```
<dependency>
  <groupId>org.apache.beam</groupId>
  <artifactId>beam-runners-google-cloud-dataflow-java</artifactId>
  <version>2.XX.0</version>  <!-- use the Beam version you are
using -->
  <scope>runtime</scope>
</dependency>
```

- **Compile and Run**: Use **mvn compile exec:java -Dexec.mainClass=your.package.WordCountDataflow -Dexec.args="--project=YOUR_GCP_PROJECT_ID --region=us-central1 --tempLocation=gs://YOUR_BUCKET/temp/ --stagingLocation=gs://YOUR_BUCKET/staging/"**. Maven will pass those args into **PipelineOptionsFactory.fromArgs(args)**. In our code, we used **PipelineOptionsFactory.create()** to set values programmatically for clarity. Alternatively, you could use **fromArgs(args)** to parse command-line arguments directly into the options.

- **Additionally**, packaging a self-executable JAR. Beam's documentation suggests using the Maven Shade plugin to create a fat jar (bundling all dependencies). After packaging, you could run: **`java -jar target/your-jar.jar --runner=DataflowRunner --project=... [other options]`** to submit to Dataflow. This might be useful if you need to schedule the job, or run it outside your development environment (for example, from a CI/CD pipeline).

Once the job is submitted, you can monitor it using the Dataflow Monitoring UI on GCPb. You will see a visualization of the pipeline steps, progress, and logs. Dataflow will handle splitting the work across multiple workers, and can automatically scale the number of workers based on data volume (for batch) or traffic (for streaming). Hence, now that we have seen a batch example, let us look at streaming on Dataflow.

Example 2: Streaming Pipeline on Dataflow

Streaming pipelines on Dataflow handle unbounded data (for example, data from messaging systems such as Pub/Sub, or real-time logs). Therefore, deploying a streaming pipeline is similar to batch, but there are a few additional considerations such as:

- You **must** specify **`--streaming=true`** in your pipeline options (otherwise Dataflow will treat it as a batch job, and will likely error out if you use unbounded sources).
- Streaming jobs on Dataflow run continuously until canceled; they do not "finish" on their own because the data stream is unbounded. This means that when you run **`pipeline.run()`**, it will submit the job, and then, you will **not have to** wait for it to finish because it would run indefinitely.
- You will need to use streaming-capable sources and sinks. Common sources include Google Cloud Pub/Sub (for ingesting messages), and sinks might be Pub/Sub, BigQuery, Cloud Storage (with windowing), or Bigtable, and so on. For simplicity, we will use Pub/Sub for both input and output in our example, as it is a convenient way to demonstrate streaming.

Python Example (Streaming Pipeline on Dataflow Using Pub/Sub):

```
from apache_beam.options.pipeline_options import PipelineOptions
import apache_beam as beam

# Pipeline options for Dataflow streaming
options = PipelineOptions([
    "--runner=DataflowRunner",
    "--project=YOUR_GCP_PROJECT_ID",
    "--region=us-central1",
    "--temp_location=gs://YOUR_BUCKET/temp/",
    "--streaming"
])
```

```
# Pub/Sub topic and subscription
input_subscription = "projects/YOUR_GCP_PROJECT_ID/subscriptions/
your-input-sub"
output_topic = "projects/YOUR_GCP_PROJECT_ID/topics/your-out-
put-topic"

with beam.Pipeline(options=options) as p:
    messages = p | "ReadPubSub" >> beam.io.ReadFromPubSub(
        subscription=input_subscription
    )

    transformed = (
        messages
        | "Decode" >> beam.Map(lambda b: b.decode("utf-8"))
        | "Uppercase" >> beam.Map(lambda s: s.upper())
        | "Encode" >> beam.Map(lambda s: s.encode("utf-8"))  #
Explicitly convert back to bytes
    )

    transformed | "WritePubSub" >> beam.io.WriteToPubSub-
(topic=output_topic)
```

Note: *Pub/Sub sources emit bytes, while Pub/Sub sinks expect bytes. Hence, even if your processing logic uses strings, you must explicitly encode them back to bytes before writing. Making this conversion visible in examples avoids subtle runtime failures, and also makes the data contract of the IO explicit.*

Therefore, in this Python streaming example, the pipeline will continuously read from a Pub/Sub subscription, convert each incoming message to uppercase, and then publish the result to another Pub/Sub topic. To actually run this, you would need to create the Pub/Sub subscription and topic in your GCP project beforehand (which can be done via the GCP Console or gcloud commands). When you run this script, it submits a streaming job to Dataflow. You will **not** see the job "finish" because it will keep running, while waiting for new messages. You can cancel the job via the Dataflow UI or CLI when you are done.

Thus, a few things to note while streaming on Dataflow are:

- **Windowing and Triggers:** In streaming pipelines, you often need to group data into windows (time-based or element count-based), and use triggers to control when the results are emitted. By default, Beam uses a global window with default triggers, but for most real use-cases, you would specify something like fixed-time windows (for example, compute every minute) for aggregation. In our example, we did not need windowing because we are just transforming each element independently. For example, suppose we want to count the number of messages arriving at **every minute. This is shown here:**

```
from apache_beam.options.pipeline_options import PipelineOptions
import apache_beam as beam
from apache_beam.transforms.window import FixedWindows
from apache_beam import window

options = PipelineOptions([
    "--runner=DataflowRunner",
    "--project=YOUR_GCP_PROJECT_ID",
    "--region=us-central1",
    "--temp_location=gs://YOUR_BUCKET/temp/",
    "--streaming"
])

input_subscription = "projects/YOUR_GCP_PROJECT_ID/subscriptions/
your-input-sub"
output_topic = "projects/YOUR_GCP_PROJECT_ID/topics/your-out-
put-topic"

with beam.Pipeline(options=options) as p:
    messages = p | "ReadPubSub" >> beam.io.ReadFromPubSub(
        subscription=input_subscription
    )

    # Decode bytes → string
    decoded = messages | "Decode" >> beam.Map(lambda b: b.de-
code("utf-8"))

    # Apply 1-minute fixed windows
    windowed = decoded | "WindowInto1Min" >> beam.WindowInto(
        FixedWindows(60)
    )

    # Count number of messages per window
    counts = (
        windowed
        | "AddDummyKey" >> beam.Map(lambda x: ("all", 1))
        | "CountPerWindow" >> beam.CombinePerKey(sum)
    )

    # Format output: "window_start → count"
    formatted = counts | "Format" >> beam.Map(
        lambda kv, ts=beam.DoFn.TimestampParam:
            f"Window starting {ts.to_utc_datetime()}: count =
{kv[1]}"
```

```
    )

    # Encode back to bytes for Pub/Sub
    encoded = formatted | "Encode" >> beam.Map(lambda s: s.encode
("utf-8"))

    encoded | "WritePubSub" >> beam.io.WriteToPubSub
(topic=output_topic)
```

- **Exactly-Once Processing:** Dataflow with Pub/Sub provides **at-least-once message delivery**. Beam's stateful processing, deduplication, and checkpointing allow pipelines to process each message in a fault-tolerant way, which can achieve *effectively exactly-once processing inside the pipeline.* However, end-to-end "exactly-once" behavior is not guaranteed by the runner alone. It depends on three factors, which are:
    - **Source Delivery Semantics**: Pub/Sub delivers messages at least once (with optional exactly-once delivery support in newer configurations).
    - **Pipeline Processing Semantics**: Beam ensures consistent state, replay, and recovery, so that each logical event is processed once per window when deduplication or state is correctly applied.
    - **Sink Semantics**: The final outcome depends on whether the destination system supports idempotent writes, transactional commits, or native exactly-once behavior.

  Hence, always assume that duplicates are possible at system boundaries for production pipelines. You must design sinks such that they are idempotent (for example, using upserts, unique keys, or transactional writes), or apply explicit deduplication in the pipeline to achieve reliable and effective exactly-once outcomes.

- In general, Dataflow's runner ensures strong consistency, and checkpoints the progress of the stream, so that if the job is restarted, it can continue where it left off without duplicating work for typical sources and sinks (for example, it uses unique IDs in Pub/Sub messages to avoid reprocessing).
- **Autoscaling:** Dataflow can autoscale streaming pipelines by dynamically adding, or removing workers based on throughput and backlog. This is a huge advantage of using Dataflow for streaming, as you can get elastic scaling without manual intervention.

Java Example (Streaming Pipeline on Dataflow Using Pub/Sub):

```
import org.apache.beam.runners.dataflow.options.DataflowPipeline
Options;
import org.apache.beam.sdk.io.gcp.pubsub.PubsubIO;
import org.apache.beam.sdk.transforms.MapElements;
```

```
import org.apache.beam.sdk.values.TypeDescriptors;
import org.joda.time.Duration;

DataflowPipelineOptions options = PipelineOptionsFactory.create()
    .as(DataflowPipelineOptions.class);
options.setRunner(DataflowRunner.class);
options.setProject("YOUR_GCP_PROJECT_ID");
options.setRegion("us-central1");
options.setTempLocation("gs://YOUR_BUCKET/temp/");
options.setStreaming(true);  // Enable streaming

Pipeline p = Pipeline.create(options);

// Define Pub/Sub I/O
String inputSub = "projects/YOUR_GCP_PROJECT_ID/subscriptions/
your-input-sub";
String outputTopic = "projects/YOUR_GCP_PROJECT_ID/topics/
your-output-topic";

// Read from Pub/Sub (as Strings)
PCollection<String> messages = p.apply("ReadPubSub",
    PubsubIO.readStrings().fromSubscription(inputSub));

// Transform each message to upper-case
PCollection<String> uppercased = messages.apply("Uppercase",
    MapElements.into(TypeDescriptors.strings())
              .via((String msg) -> msg.toUpperCase()));

// Write to Pub/Sub topic
uppercased.apply("WritePubSub", PubsubIO.writeStrings().to(out-
putTopic));

p.run();  // For streaming, typically do not waitUntilFinish
```

In the Java streaming example, we use **PubsubIO**, which is a built-in I/O connector in the Beam Java SDK for Google Cloud Pub/Sub. The pipeline reads strings from a subscription, transforms them, and then writes strings to a topic. We set **options.setStreaming(true)** to ensure the Dataflow runner knows that it is a streaming job. We then call **p.run()** without **waitUntilFinish()** because a streaming job will never complete on its own; you would have to stop it manually when needed (or use Dataflow's **drain** feature to finish processing buffered data, and then stop it).

Running the Java streaming pipeline is similar to the batch case, except that you must pass the **--streaming** flag if you use command-line arguments. For example:

```
mvn compile exec:java \
  -Dexec.mainClass=your.package.StreamingPipelineDataflow \
```

```
    -Dexec.args="--project=YOUR_GCP_PROJECT_ID --region=us-central1 \
                 --tempLocation=gs://YOUR_BUCKET/temp/ --streaming
=true"
```

Or, you may include **options.setStreaming(true),** just like we did in the code example. However, make sure that the Pub/Sub topic and subscription exist, and your GCP credentials have access to them.

Monitoring Streaming Jobs: When a Dataflow streaming job is running, the UI will show it as continuously running. You can observe elements in-flight, watermarks, and system lag in the Dataflow monitoring interface. This helps in tuning the pipeline (for example, if you see the watermark lagging, you might need to investigate bottlenecks, or adjust parallelism or windowing).

Stopping a Dataflow Job: If you want to stop a streaming job, you can cancel it from the UI, or you may use the command **gcloud dataflow jobs cancel <job-id>.** A **drain** option also exists, which tries to finish processing all pending data and then stop. This is useful for graceful shutdown of streaming pipelines (drain can be initiated via **gcloud dataflow jobs drain <job-id>,** or in the UI).

Dataflow Runner Considerations

The Dataflow runner has some unique features and considerations, which are:

- **Auto-Scaling and Dynamic Work Rebalancing:** In batch mode, Dataflow can split work and rebalance workloads across workers at runtime (called *dynamic work rebalancing*), which can speed up pipelines where some tasks take longer. In streaming, Dataflow's autoscaling will adjust workers based on the backlog.
- **Exactly-Once Sinks:** Dataflow ensures that built-in sinks such as BigQuery are exactly-once (through a two-phase commit or deduplication logic). Hence, when you are writing to external systems, always consider the idempotency of writes, as failures and retries can cause duplicates if they are not handled promptly.
- **Cost Considerations:** As Dataflow is managed, you pay for the worker time. The best practice is to use **resource hints** (such as choosing an appropriate machine type or number of workers) for large jobs to avoid excessive auto-provisioning, and to **monitor** the job to stop it if things go awry and avoid runaway costs.
- **Templates:** Dataflow has a feature to create templates (classic or Flex templates), which allows you to stage a pipeline, and run it later with different parameters. This is useful for production deployments. While it is beyond our scope to dive into templates, you must be aware that it is a deployment option which simplifies running recurring jobs.

- **Beam Version Compatibility:** The Dataflow service tries to maintain compatibility with multiple Beam SDK versions. It is generally recommended to use a relatively recent Beam SDK version to get the latest fixes and features on Dataflow.
- **Local Testing before Cloud:** A common workflow is to test your pipeline locally with the DirectRunner on a small subset of data, then switch to DataflowRunner for full scale. This catches errors early without incurring cloud costs, or waiting for a full job.

In summary, deploying to Dataflow is pretty straightforward: you set the pipeline options for Dataflow, ensure that you have the correct GCP setup, and then run the pipeline. The service handles the heavy lifting. Next, we will see how to deploy on Apache Flink, which is a different scenario as you deal with your own cluster.

Deploying on Apache Flink

Apache Flink is an open-source distributed processing engine known for its efficient handling of streaming data, while also supporting batch. The Apache Flink Runner allows Beam pipelines to execute on a Flink cluster. This is ideal for scenarios where you want to run Beam pipelines on your own infrastructure, or in an on-premise cluster (or even in cloud VMs or Kubernetes, but self-managed). Flink provides features such as high-throughput, low-latency processing, and an exactly-once state consistency, which Beam can leverage via the runner.

Unlike Dataflow, with Flink, you are responsible for managing the cluster (or at least having an environment where Flink is installed). Now, let us outline how to prepare for running Beam on Flink:

Prerequisites for the Flink Runner:

- An Apache Flink cluster or installation. You can download Flink from the Apache website and run it locally in **standalone mode** (for testing), or have a full cluster (Standalone cluster, YARN, Kubernetes, and so on). For a beginner, the easiest way is to run Flink locally:
    a. Download the Flink distribution (the version compatible with your Beam runner, for example, Flink 1.15+ or 1.16; we will elaborate the compatibility aspect shortly).

    b. Start a local cluster by running `bin/start-cluster.sh,` which launches a Flink JobManager and TaskManager on your machine. Hence, by default, the JobManager's REST interface will be at **http://localhost:8081**.

- Apache Beam SDK and **Flink Runner Dependency**:

  a. **Java:** Add the Beam Flink runner dependency to your project. For example, for Beam **2.X** and Flink 1.16, you might include:

```
<dependency>
  <groupId>org.apache.beam</groupId>
  <artifactId>beam-runners-flink-1.16</artifactId>
  <version>2.XX.0</version>
</dependency>
```

  The version of Flink runner should correspond to a Flink release; Beam's documentation lists runner artifacts for different Flink versions (for example, `beam-runners-flink-1.15, -1.16`, and so on).

  - **Add Python:** The Beam Python SDK supports Flink via the *portable Flink runner*. Typically, when you install `apache-beam`, it includes the necessary bits to run with Flink. You may need a Flink job server (which can run via a Docker container) for complex setups, but Beam can also start an embedded Flink for you. We will demonstrate a simple approach using the `FlinkRunner` option, which in newer Beam versions automatically uses the portable runner behind the scenes.
  - Ensure that Java is installed (Flink runs on the JVM; even for Python pipelines, the Flink cluster is JVM-based).
  - (Optional) Install Docker, if you plan to use the portable runner default Docker-based job server for Python. If you are running it in LOOPBACK mode (which means that the Python worker runs in the same process or a local machine), Docker is not strictly required. However, for more robust execution, the Python SDK may use a Docker container to execute user code on Flink.

Flink Runner Flavors (Classic versus Portable):

It is important to know that Beam's Flink runner comes in two distinct execution models, and they behave very differently when they are operational.

The **classic Flink runner** is Java-only. Your Beam pipeline runs directly inside the Flink JVM, and Beam transforms are compiled into native Flink operators. There are no extra services involved. The execution model is simple:

Beam Java Pipeline → Flink Operators → Flink Cluster

This is why the classic runner is usually easier to debug and more predictable; everything runs in one JVM ecosystem, with no container images, job services, or cross-language communication.

The **portable Flink runner**, on the other hand, is designed to support multiple languages such as Python, Go, and cross-language pipelines. It introduces additional runtime components such as:

Beam SDK (Python/Go/Java)

↓

Job Service (Translates Beam Pipeline to a Flink Job)

↓

Flink Cluster

↓

SDK Harness (Runs User Code, Often inside Docker)

Here are the key moving parts in the portable model:

- **Job Service**

  A service that receives the Beam pipeline definition, and then submits a job to Flink.

  This is why you might see references to "job endpoints".

- **SDK Harness**

  A separate process that runs your user code (for example Python DoFns). This often runs inside a Docker container unless you explicitly use LOOPBACK.

- **Execution Environment**

  This is controlled by options like:

  - `--environment_type=DOCKER`
  - `--environment_type=LOOPBACK`
  - **DOCKER**: It is production-style, isolated, reproducible, but requires Docker and the correct images.
  - **LOOPBACK**: It runs the user code in the same process for simplicity, and is useful for local testing, but not for production.

Therefore, this explains many "it worked locally, but it failed on the cluster" problems, which are articulated here:

Symptom	Root Cause in Portable Runner
Docker Not Found	The SDK harness expects containers.
Image Pull Failure	There is missing or blocked container registry access.

Classpath Errors	SDK harness and Flink cluster do not share dependencies.
Pipeline Runs Locally, but Fails Remotely.	LOOPBACK hid real execution constraints.

Table 7.1: *Common Issues and Root Causes in Portable Flink Runner*

Therefore, the distinction becomes:

Aspect	Classic Runner	Portable Runner
Language Support	Java Only	Java, Python, Go
Runtime Complexity	Simple	Multi-Component
Docker Required	No	Often Yes
Best for	JVM Pipelines	Multi-Language Pipelines
Debug Difficulty	Lower	Higher, but More Powerful

Table 7.2: *Aspect breakdown By Classic Runner Vs Portable Runner on Flink*

Running a Beam Pipeline on Flink

There are two main ways to run a Beam pipeline on Flink, which are:

- **Directly from Your Beam Code by Specifying `FlinkRunner` and Flink Master:** In this mode, you run your pipeline as a program (just like we did for Dataflow), and tell the Flink runner where the Flink cluster is (or use an embedded Flink). The Beam code will then submit the job to Flink.
- **Packaging the Pipeline as a JAR and Submitting via Flink's Command-Line (Flink Run):** In this mode, you treat your Beam pipeline like any Flink job jar. You use Flink's tools to run it on the cluster. This is common in Java scenarios.

We will explore the first approach in detail, as it is conceptually simpler for beginners (and closer to what we did with Dataflow). The second approach is just a deployment difference, but you would still need the pipeline jar that is produced by your build.

Example 3: Batch Pipeline on Flink (`WordCount`)

We will reuse the **`WordCount`** example, but this time, we will deploy it to Flink. For simplicity, we assume either that you have a Flink cluster already running at localhost:8081, or that Beam will start a local Flink job server for you. In the portable runner, Beam always executes the pipeline inside Flink; the difference is whether Flink is external or locally managed. Your Python code runs in a separate SDK harness (usually in Docker), unless you explicitly use **`--environment_type=LOOPBACK`**, which runs the user code in the same process for debugging.

Python Example (`WordCount` on Flink):

```
import apache_beam as beam
from apache_beam.options.pipeline_options import PipelineOptions

# PipelineOptions for Flink
flink_options = PipelineOptions([
    "--runner=FlinkRunner",
    "--flink_master=localhost:8081",  # Flink Master URL; assuming
local cluster.
    # If flink_master is not specified, Beam will start an embedded
Flink cluster.
    "--environment_type=LOOPBACK"     # (Optional) run Python
code on the same process for testing.
])

with beam.Pipeline(options=flink_options) as p:
    # We will do a simple word count on a small in-memory data
for demonstration
    lines = p | "CreateLines" >> beam.Create([
        "apache beam runners",
        "beam pipelines on flink",
        "flink runner execution"
    ])
    words = lines | "Split" >> beam.FlatMap(lambda line: line.
split())
    counts = words | "Count" >> beam.combiners.Count.PerElement()
    # Print results (in real Flink, prints go to worker logs; for
local run, it will output here)
    counts | "Print" >> beam.Map(print)
```

Let us discuss the preceding code here:

- We set **`--runner=FlinkRunner`** to use the Flink runner. We also provided **`--flink_master=localhost:8081`**, which is the default address of a local Flink JobManager's REST API. This tells Beam to submit the pipeline to that Flink cluster. If you had a remote cluster, you could put its host:port or a cluster identifier there. If you omit **`flink_master`**, the pipeline will start an **embedded Flink** instance within the Python process, and then run the job there. Hence, it can be convenient for quick tests (no external cluster needed), but for anything non-trivial, you would have to use a real cluster.
- We included **`--environment_type=LOOPBACK`**. This is a pipeline option specific to portable runners, which means to "run the SDK worker in the same process (no Docker)". We will use it here for simplicity, so that the Python transforms the execute in the local process. Without it, Beam might attempt to use a Docker container for the Python SDK harness by default. Therefore, using **`LOOPBACK`**

is fine for local testing, but you must note that it is not recommended for production, as it does not isolate the execution (it mostly exists for ease of use).

- The pipeline itself is similar to before, except that instead of reading from a file, we used a **beam.Create** transform with some in-memory data (a few example lines). This is just to make the example self-contained; in a real scenario, you could read from files or databases. We will then split the lines into words, count them, and print the counts.
- Printing within a Beam pipeline is generally done via a **beam.Map(print),** or a **beam.ParDo** with a DoFn that prints. Keep in mind that on a Flink cluster, the print statements in distributed workers write to each worker's stdout, which becomes part of the task manager logs. In production, this should not be treated as a debugging convenience, but as a part of your **observability strategy**. Therefore, logging in a distributed system has real cost, performance impact, and operational consequences. Printing or logging inside distributed Beam pipelines is an observability decision, not a debugging shortcut. Uncontrolled logging can flood log storage, increase costs, slow down workers, and make real issues harder to find. Pipelines that rely on per-element logging may be logically correct but operationally undeployable. Hence, in local execution, you will see the printouts in your console.

To run this Python pipeline, ensure that your Flink cluster is running (or be prepared for it to spin up an embedded one), and then simply execute the script via:

```
python wordcount_flink.py
```

If everything is configured correctly, you should see the word count results printed. On a local cluster, you can also open the Flink Web UI (http://localhost:8081) to see the job. It will appear as a job with a name auto-generated from the Beam job name (if not set, Beam generates one). Once the pipeline completes (it is a batch job, so it will finish after processing the bounded input), the job will disappear from the Flink UI, and the Python script will exit.

For a more realistic example, you could have **ReadFromText("input.txt")** and **WriteToText("output.txt")** in the pipeline. If you do that on Flink, make sure that the path is accessible by the Flink worker machines. In local mode, local file paths are fine; in a cluster, using a distributed filesystem (HDFS), or mounting shared storage might be needed.

Java Example (WordCount on Flink):

```
import org.apache.beam.runners.flink.FlinkPipelineOptions;
import org.apache.beam.runners.flink.FlinkRunner;
// (Other imports same as before for TextIO, Count, etc.)

public class WordCountFlink {
```

```
    public static void main(String[] args) {
        // Create Flink pipeline options
        FlinkPipelineOptions options = PipelineOptionsFactory.
create().as(FlinkPipelineOptions.class);
        options.setRunner(FlinkRunner.class);
        options.setFlinkMaster("localhost:8081");  // Flink
master (JobManager) address.
        options.setParallelism(2);                // Example: set
parallelism for Flink tasks.

        Pipeline p = Pipeline.create(options);

        p.apply("ReadLines", TextIO.read().from("input.txt"))
// adjust path as needed
         .apply("SplitWords", FlatMapElements.into(TypeDescriptors.
strings())
                                      .via(line -> Arrays.
asList(line.split("\\s+"))))
         .apply("CountWords", Count.perElement())
         .apply("FormatResults", MapElements.into(TypeDescriptors.
strings())
                                     .via(kv -> kv.getKey()
+ ": " + kv.getValue()))
         .apply("WriteResults", TextIO.write().to("word-
counts-flink-output").withSuffix(".txt"));

        p.run().waitUntilFinish();
    }
}
```

Here are the key points in the Java Flink example:

- We will use **`FlinkPipelineOptions`** (which is available when you include the Beam Flink runner dependency) to configure the pipeline. We will also set the runner to **`FlinkRunner.class.options.setFlinkMaster("localhost:8081")`** points to the Flink cluster's master. If we wanted to run this in embedded mode, we could have set it to "[auto]", or leave it unset (in which case Beam treats it as embedded). Here, "[auto]" is a special value that the Flink runner uses to denote an embedded Flink deployment. Hence, if you leave it null, it also defaults to embedded.
- We will explicitly set **`setParallelism(2)`** to show that you can control the degree of parallelism for the Flink execution (this corresponds to Flink's parallelism for tasks). If it is not set, Flink's default will be used (which might be 1 for embedded, or the cluster default for remote).
- The pipeline logic is identical to earlier **`WordCount`** examples. We read from "**`input.txt`**" (you would replace this with a real path, for example, a local file

path or an HDFS path if running on a cluster), and write to **`wordcounts-flink-output-*.txt`** files.

- After **`p.run()`**, we will call **`waitUntilFinish()`** to block until done (it will terminate, since this is a batch job).

Therefore, to run the Java pipeline on Flink, you have two choices:

- You can run it as a regular Java program (through your IDE or **`java -cp ... WordCountFlink`**). This will execute the main, which in turn submits to Flink. If it is a remote Flink cluster, your program will act as a client that sends the job to the cluster, and waits for it to finish.
- You may also package it as a JAR, and then use Flink's CLI. For instance, build a jar named **`wordcount-beam-flink.jar`**. Then, use this:

  ```
  $FLINK_HOME/bin/flink run -c your.package.WordCountFlink wordcount
  -beam-flink.jar
  ```
- This submits the job to a Flink cluster (it uses Flink's REST or RPC mechanisms). However, you note that if you do this, the pipeline's **`FlinkMaster`** should usually be set to [auto] (so, it uses the cluster you submit to). Moreover, if you leave **`FlinkMaster`** as "**`localhost:8081`**" and run Flink on a different host, it might try to connect to a local Flink that is incorrect. However, using Flink run inherently sends the job to the cluster you target, so that "[auto]" is appropriate.

After running, you can inspect the results (the output files or any logs). The Flink Web UI will show the job's DAG (which will correspond to the Beam pipeline graph), and you can view metrics such as throughput, task durations, and so on.

Example 4: Streaming Pipeline on Flink

For streaming on Flink, the process is similar, but there are a few Flink-specific considerations that you must keep in mind:

- Flink runner does not require a special **`--streaming`** flag; as it will automatically run in streaming mode if the pipeline has unbounded sources. (Beam's **`StreamingOptions`** flag is mainly for Dataflow; on Flink, a pipeline with an unbounded source is naturally streaming.)
- Flink provides **checkpointing** for state and watermarks. The Beam Flink runner will leverage Flink's checkpointing to persist snapshots of the pipeline state periodically. You might configure the checkpointing interval, or external checkpoint storage through Flink configuration if needed. Therefore, by default, Flink might checkpoint to memory or file; for a production streaming job, you would configure a durable state backend (such as RocksDB, as well as a filesystem for checkpoint files).

- In Beam, you would use unbounded sources such as Kafka, socket, or generate sequence, and so on, to simulate streaming input if needed. Commonly, Beam does not have a built-in "socket read" (like Flink's own examples do), but Beam **KafkaIO** is frequently used on Flink for streaming.

Let us demonstrate a simple streaming pipeline on Flink using a synthetic source (**GenerateSequence**) and a sink, which is shown here:

Java Example (Streaming on Flink with Synthetic Data):

```
import org.apache.beam.sdk.io.GenerateSequence;
import org.apache.beam.sdk.transforms.MapElements;
import org.apache.beam.sdk.transforms.ParDo;
import org.apache.beam.sdk.values.TypeDescriptors;
import org.joda.time.Duration;

// ... (FlinkPipelineOptions setup as before)
options.setRunner(FlinkRunner.class);
// We do not need to set a special streaming flag; unbounded
source triggers streaming mode.
options.setFlinkMaster("[auto]");  // use embedded or submission
cluster automatically
options.setParallelism(1);         // for demo, use parallelism 1

Pipeline p = Pipeline.create(options);

// Generate an infinite sequence of numbers (unbounded PCollec-
tion)
PCollection<Long> numbers = p.apply(GenerateSequence.from(0).
withRate(1, Duration.standardSeconds(1)));

// Map each number to a simple string and print it
numbers.apply(MapElements.into(TypeDescriptors.strings())
                        .via(num -> "Number: " + num))
       .apply("PrintToConsole", ParDo.of(new DoFn<String, Void>()
{
           @ProcessElement
           public void processElement(ProcessContext c) {
               System.out.println(c.element());
           }
       }));

p.run();  // For streaming, do not waitUntilFinish in this demo
```

In this Java streaming example, we use **GenerateSequence.from(0).withRate(1, Duration.standardSeconds(1))** to produce a new Long every second indefinitely. **GenerateSequence** is a handy Beam transform to create an unbounded stream of incremental numbers. This is useful for testing or simulating streaming data. We will then map each number to a string, and then print it. We use a **DoFn** to print because it is a side-effect (alternatively, one could use a logging framework).

When you run this on Flink, it will start a job that prints "**Number: 0**", "**Number: 1**", "**Number: 2**", and so on, once per second. If using an embedded Flink ([auto]), you will see the printouts in the console. On a real cluster, they would appear in the task manager logs. This job will run until canceled because the source is infinite. You can then cancel it via the Flink UI, or stop the program if running is embedded.

Python Example (Streaming on Flink with Kafka)

For a Python example, a realistic scenario might be reading from Kafka, and writing to some sink. Note that Beam's Kafka IO in Python is provided via cross-language transforms (the implementation is in Java). This requires starting an expansion service, or using the default expansion service that Beam can auto-start for you if you have the correct dependencies. Detailing the setup of Kafka is beyond our scope, but here is how a Python pipeline *could* look:

```
import apache_beam as beam
from apache_beam.options.pipeline_options import PipelineOptions
from apache_beam.io.kafka import ReadFromKafka, WriteToKafka

options = PipelineOptions([
    "--runner=FlinkRunner",
    "--flink_master=localhost:8081"
    # No need for streaming flag explicitly
])

with beam.Pipeline(options=options) as p:
    kafka_source = ReadFromKafka(
        consumer_config={'bootstrap.servers': 'localhost:9092',
                         'auto.offset.reset': 'earliest'},
        topics=['input-topic']
    )
    kafka_sink = WriteToKafka(
        producer_config={'bootstrap.servers': 'localhost:9092'},
        topic='output-topic'
    )
    # Read from Kafka topic
    messages = p | "ReadKafka" >> kafka_source
    # Process messages (for example, just convert value to
uppercase assuming UTF-8 bytes)
    processed = messages | "UppercaseValue" >> beam.Map(lambda
kv: kv[1].decode('utf-8').upper().encode('utf-8'))
    # Write to output Kafka topic
    processed | "WriteKafka" >> kafka_sink
```

In the preceding Python snippet (not executed here), we use **apache_beam.io.kafka.ReadFromKafka** and **WriteToKafka**. Each Kafka message is a key-value (KV<byte[], byte[]> in Beam's type system for Kafka. In this case, we ignore the key, as well as uppercase the message value. The pipeline will continuously consume from the **input-topic** and produce to **output-topic.** To run this, you would need a Kafka broker running at **localhost:9092** and the topics created. Beam will likely need the Kafka client libraries–in Java, we would add them as dependencies; in Python, since it is cross-language, Beam's expansion service would use the Java KafkaIO. This is an advanced scenario, but it demonstrates that Beam pipelines on Flink can connect to typical streaming sources in on-prem environments like Kafka.

For many beginners, a simpler approach to test streaming on Flink is to use a bounded source, but run the pipeline in streaming mode (to observe differences), or use **GenerateSequence** as shown in Java. Keep in mind that when using Beam's I/O connectors like Kafka on Flink, you should ensure your Beam **expansion service** (for cross-language) is available if using Python. The Beam Flink runner can automatically start a job server that includes expansion services for some IOs when you use **--flink_master,** and then run the pipeline (for example, it might use a combined job service container that knows about Kafka expansion).

Flink Runner Considerations

When you are deploying on Flink, here are some runner-specific considerations and best practices:

- **Flink and Beam Version Compatibility:** Check the Beam documentation for which Flink versions are supported by your Beam runner version. Thus, always verify compatibility using the official Apache Beam version matrix. The Flink runner is not "generically compatible" with Flink; instead, Beam publishes separate artifacts such as beam-runners-flink-1.16 or beam-runners-flink-1.17, each of which supports only a specific range of Beam SDK versions. Using a mismatched runner and Flink version will fail at runtime, or during job submission. Using a mismatched version could cause runtime errors. The Beam Flink runner artifact name often encodes the Flink major version (as we saw with flink-1.16). Therefore, you must always use the appropriate runner dependency for your Flink cluster's version.

  You may access the Official Beam compatibility matrix via this link: https://beam.apache.org/documentation/runners/flink/#flink-version-compatibility

- **Managing Dependencies:** If your pipeline uses additional connectors (such as KafkaIO, JDBC, and so on), you will need to include those in your jar (shadow jar) for Java. Flink's cluster classpath typically does not have Beam-specific connectors, therefore, it is the safest to **shade** all needed dependencies into your job jar. In our Java examples, if we wanted to use KafkaIO, we would add Beam's Kafka IO dependency, and then use the Maven Shade plugin to create a fat jar. Thereafter, Flink can distribute that jar to workers.

- **Parallelism and Resources:** Flink allows you to set a parallelism for the job or individual operators. We already showed you how to set a pipeline-wide parallelism. The Flink runner will map Beam `ParDo/GroupByKey`, and so on, to Flink operators. Ensure that your Flink cluster has enough Task Slots to accommodate the parallelism. For example, if you have a local cluster with 4 slots, and you have set parallelism to 8, the job will be queued, otherwise will not run fully due to insufficient slots.
- **State and Checkpointing:** If your Beam pipeline uses stateful transforms or timers (which are advanced features), Flink's exactly-once state model will ensure that it is consistent. You should therefore configure a checkpoint interval in Flink for streaming jobs (this can be done via Flink config, or programmatically by the Flink runner's options, for example, `options.setCheckpointingInterval(seconds)`, if it is exposed). The Flink runner exposes a checkpointing interval option in milliseconds (for example, `options.setCheckpointingInterval(60000)` for 60 seconds). If this option is not set, checkpointing is considered unset, and it thus relies on Flink defaults, or may be effectively disabled. There is no guaranteed built-in default such as "5–10 seconds" at the Beam layer. Therefore, for production, writing checkpoints to durable storage (such as a distributed filesystem or database) is crucial. You may also configure Flink's state backend (for example, the RocksDB state backend with the checkpoint directory on HDFS) for large-scale streaming.
- **Job Management:** Running Beam on a Flink cluster means that you will eventually use Flink's tools to manage the job. The Flink web interface or CLI can be used to cancel jobs. You can also take savepoints (which are Flink's consistent snapshots on demand) if you want to stop a job and resume later. Beam does not abstract that away; you would still use Flink's mechanisms directly.
- **Monitoring:** Use the Flink Web UI to monitor throughput, latency (if you are using event time windows, watermarks, and so on), and to view task logs. Beam's own metrics (Beam metrics API) should also integrate–they will be available via Flink's metrics system, or can be logged on completion.
- **Batch versus Streaming on Flink:** The Flink runner supports both batch and streaming pipelines. From Beam's perspective, the distinction is simple–pipelines with only bounded sources are batch pipelines, and pipelines with any unbounded source are streaming pipelines. Beam does not explicitly toggle Flink's execution mode. Instead, the Flink runner infers the mode from the

boundedness of the sources, and then submits the job accordingly. In modern Flink versions, batch and streaming share a unified execution model, where batch jobs are effectively treated as finite streams that terminate naturally. On the other hand, streaming pipelines will run until canceled. However, there is something you should note: If you run a batch pipeline on a Flink cluster, Flink may treat it as a streaming job with bounded sources by default. However, Flink has a concept of *execution mode* (streaming versus batch) that Beam does not explicitly toggle. Under the hood, newer Flink versions have a unified execution model. Hence, the Beam Flink runner chooses the execution mode based on whether the sources are bounded or unbounded.

- **`FlinkRunner` versus `PortableRunner` Usage:**

  For **Python pipelines on Flink**, both **`FlinkRunner`** and **`PortableRunner`** use Beam's **portable execution model** under the hood. The difference is mainly about *who starts and manages the job service.*

  In a portable model, here are the components that run and where do they run:

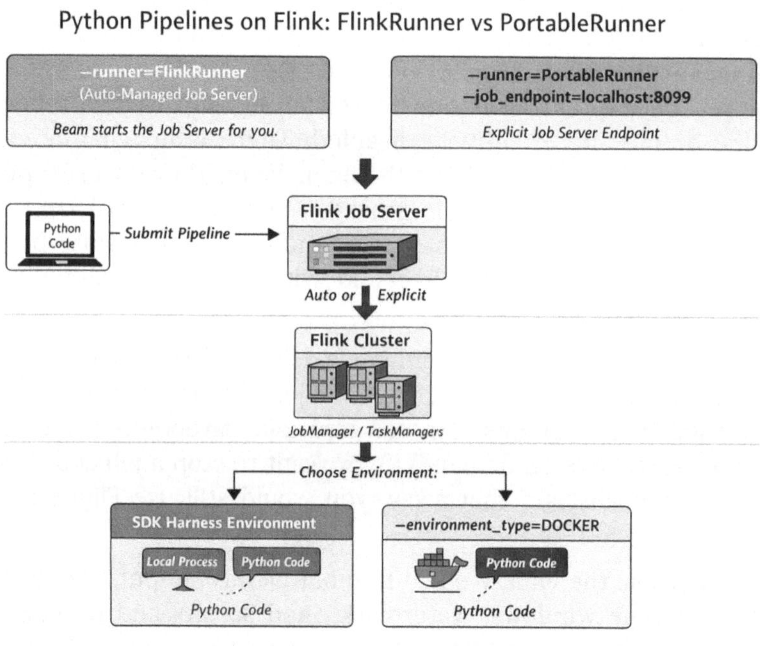

Figure 7.1: *FlinkRunner vs Portable Runner on Apache Flink*

What `--runner` Changes:

- **`--runner=PortableRunner --job_endpoint=host:port`**
  You explicitly point to a running Flink Job Server, and your client just submits the pipeline.

- `--runner=FlinkRunner` (Python)
  Beam typically **starts/manages the job server for you** (implementation detail), and then submits the pipeline through it. This can feel "simpler," but the same moving parts still exist.

  What `--environment_type` Changes (Where Your Python Code Runs):

- `--environment_type=LOOPBACK`
  The SDK harness runs in the same process/machine as the client environment. This is good for local debugging, but is not representative of production isolation.

- `--environment_type=DOCKER` (Common Default for Real Deployments)
  The SDK harness runs in a container image. This is production-like, but it introduces requirements such as Docker availability (or container runtime), image pull access, correct image versions, as well as networking between Flink workers and the harness.

  Operational Importance and Causes of Failure: Python-on-Flink can fail even when the pipeline code is correct because the deployment depends on container images, harness startup, job server connectivity (`--job_endpoint`), and network access from Flink TaskManagers to pull images, besides communicating with the SDK harness. Hence, understanding this chain prevents "it worked locally" surprises, and makes debugging systematic rather than have you guess it out.

- **Supported Features:** The Flink runner supports most of Beam's model, which includes windowing, triggers, state, and timers. The classic runner executes Beam pipelines directly inside the Flink JVM. The portable runner introduces an SDK harness boundary that enables multi-language support, but it adds serialization and interprocess communication costs. The magnitude of this overhead is dependent on the workload, and therefore must be measured for each pipeline. Performance should be validated empirically rather than assumed. Therefore, the Flink runner is known to provide exactly-once semantics in streaming when you are using proper checkpointing.

Thus, by deploying on Flink, you can exert more control over the environment by configuring the number of nodes, memory, and so on, which is great for on-premise scenarios. Next, we will look at Apache Spark, which is another common engine to run Beam pipelines.

Deploying on Apache Spark

Apache Spark is a widely used unified analytics engine, primarily for batch processing with its RDD and DataFrame APIs, and also for micro-batch stream processing with Spark Streaming or Structured Streaming. Beam's Spark Runner allows you to execute pipelines on a Spark cluster, while enabling integration with the existing Spark infrastructure. Spark is often chosen in organizations that already run big data pipelines on Spark and want to unify some processing with Beam's API.

However, it is worth noting that the Beam Spark runner has historically been more limited in streaming support compared to Flink or Dataflow. There are two main Spark runner implementations in Beam–the original RDD/DStream-based runner, a newer Structured Streaming runner (experimental), and the portable Spark runner for multi-language support. In this section, we will focus on the **Spark 3** runner (RDD/DStream based), which is stable for batch, and also supports streaming (micro-batch). Additionally, we will mention the portable usage for Python.

Prerequisites for the Spark Runner:

- An Apache Spark installation or cluster. This could be:
  - A local Spark setup, as Spark can run locally for testing using a local master URL like **local[4]** for 4 threads.
  - A Spark Standalone cluster, a YARN cluster, or Kubernetes, and so on. Spark is flexible in deployment. For simplicity, you can simulate a cluster by running Spark locally, or using something like Spark's Standalone mode.
- If you are using Java, include the Beam Spark runner dependency. For Spark 3, the artifact is **beam-runners-spark-3**. Ensure that the version matches your Beam SDK. For example:

```
<dependency>
  <groupId>org.apache.beam</groupId>
  <artifactId>beam-runners-spark-3</artifactId>
  <version>2.XX.0</version>
</dependency>
```

  From Beam 2.46.0 onward, the Spark runner supports Spark 3.x only, with the official compatibility being targeted at the Spark 3.2.x minor line. Spark 2.4 is no longer supported. However, the Beam–Spark compatibility is defined per minor version, so not all Spark 3.x releases (for example 3.0, 3.1, or 3.4) should be assumed to work, that is unless they are explicitly listed in the Beam compatibility matrix.

- If you are using Python, the Spark runner is only available via the portable approach. For Python, Spark execution is always portable. There are two supported deployment patterns, which are discussed as follows:

  a. Submit pipelines dynamically using **PortableRunner** and a Spark Job Server endpoint.

  b. Build an executable Spark job using **--output_executable_path**, and submit it with spark-submit.

The first approach favors interactive and service-driven execution, whereas, the second fits production CI/CD, restricted clusters, and environments where Spark is the only allowed entry point.

Requirement	Choose Job Server	Choose Executable JAR
Interactive Submission	Yes	No
CI/CD and Artifact Promotion	No	Yes
Locked-Down Spark Clusters	No	Yes
Minimal Runtime Infrastructure	No	Yes
Dynamic Orchestration Systems	Yes	No

Table 7.3: *When to Choose Job Server vs Executable JAR*

- A note on Spark Structured Streaming: The Beam runner for Spark Structured Streaming is still experimental, and only supports batch mode currently. Although Spark Structured Streaming is a streaming engine in native Spark, Beam's Structured Streaming runner does not implement Beam's streaming semantics. It cannot execute unbounded pipelines, does not support event-time processing, and does not provide continuous execution. Hence, it should be treated strictly as a batch runner. So, for streaming on Spark, Beam actually uses the DStream-based Spark Streaming under the hood if you use the default SparkRunner. This uses micro-batches with a default batch interval (1 second). Therefore, conceptually, Beam streaming on Spark works, but it has slightly different guarantees (Spark's streaming is often *at-least-once* in delivery).

Running a Beam Pipeline on Spark (Basic Concepts)

Beam's Spark runner can run in different ways such as:

- **Embedded in a Spark Driver (Local or Cluster)**: You run your Beam pipeline as a Spark job, typically by submitting via `spark-submit`. The Beam runner will create the necessary Spark RDDs or DStreams under the hood. If you run the pipeline in local mode (for example, via a main method and Spark local), it uses the Spark libraries on your machine.
- **Using a Job Server (Portable)**: You start a Beam Spark job server that communicates with a Spark cluster, and then run the pipeline with **`PortableRunner`** pointing to that server.
- **Bundling Python Pipelines**: Since Python does not run on the JVM, Beam provides a mechanism to bundle a Python pipeline into an executable Uber-

JAR containing a Spark job. This JAR can then be submitted to Spark like a normal Spark job.

We will illustrate typical usage for both Java and Python.

Example 5: Batch Pipeline on Spark (`WordCount`)

Java Example (`WordCount` on Spark):

```
import org.apache.beam.runners.spark.SparkPipelineOptions;
import org.apache.beam.runners.spark.SparkRunner;
// ... other imports ...

public class WordCountSpark {
    public static void main(String[] args) {
        SparkPipelineOptions options = PipelineOptionsFactory.
create().as(SparkPipelineOptions.class);
        options.setRunner(SparkRunner.class);
        options.setSparkMaster("local[4]");  // using local Spark
with 4 threads
        // options.setSparkMaster("spark://spark-master:7077");
// example for cluster master URL
        options.setAppName("BeamWordCountSpark");

        Pipeline p = Pipeline.create(options);

        p.apply("ReadLines", TextIO.read().from("input.txt"))
         .apply("SplitWords", FlatMapElements.into(TypeDescriptors.
strings())
                                            .via(line -> Arrays.
asList(line.split("\\s+"))))
         .apply("CountWords", Count.perElement())
         .apply("FormatResults", MapElements.into(TypeDescrip-
tors.strings())
                                            .via(kv -> kv.getKey()
+ ": " + kv.getValue()))
         .apply("WriteResults", TextIO.write().to("wordcounts-
spark-out").withSuffix(".txt"));

        p.run().waitUntilFinish();
    }
}
```

In the Java Spark example:

- We use **`SparkPipelineOptions`** (from the Spark runner library) to set up the pipeline. We also specify **`SparkRunner`** as the runner.
- We set **`SparkMaster`** to `local[4]`, which means that the job will run using 4

threads on the local machine (no external Spark cluster is needed). Hence, if you wanted to run on a Spark cluster, you would put the Spark master URL here, for example, **spark://host:port** for a standalone cluster, or yarn for YARN mode.

- The pipeline itself is again **WordCount**. There are no changes that you require in logic here.
- Running this is as simple as running the **main()** (through your IDE or **java -jar ...**). Since we specified **local[4],** it will start a local Spark context within the process, and will thus execute. Hence, if we specified a cluster master, the Spark runner would try to connect to that cluster, and then run the job there. In cluster mode, typically, you would submit via spark-submit, rather than running directly.

To deploy on an actual Spark cluster using this code, you would:

1. Package the application into a JAR (including Beam and runner dependencies). Use the Maven Shade plugin to create a fat jar if you plan to use **spark-submit**. The Beam Spark runner, your pipeline, and any connectors should be in that jar.
2. Use **spark-submit** to submit the job. For example:

   ```
   spark-submit --master spark://spark-master:7077 \
       --class your.package.WordCountSpark \
       /path/to/wordcount-spark-bundled.jar
   ```

   You would not include **--runner=SparkRunner** in **spark-submit;** this is because it is specified in the code. The Spark master is provided via the `--master` flag (which will override what you put in **options.setSparkMaster** if it conflicts). In practice, you might leave **setSparkMaster** out of the code, and rely on `--master` at submission time instead. The **SparkPipelineOptions** also has a **getSparkMaster()** property, which will default to local if it is not set.

Spark's output (if local) will just be files written to the path we gave. In a cluster, if using HDFS or another distributed FS, you would specify an appropriate path.

Python Example (WordCount on Spark):

Running Beam Python on Spark requires using the portable runner. A convenient method provided by Beam is to use the pipeline option **--output_executable_path** with **SparkRunner**, which packages the pipeline into an executable jar. This is demonstrated in Beam's documentation for running Python on Dataproc (Spark). We can emulate the approach as follows:

Suppose we have the Python wordcount pipeline in a file, or we use the built-in example **apache_beam.examples.wordcount**. Thus, we can execute:

```
# Command-line invocation to create an executable jar for the Py-
thon pipeline
python -m apache_beam.examples.wordcount \
    --runner=SparkRunner \
    --output_executable_path=wordcount_spark_job.jar \
    --spark_version=3 \
    --output=/tmp/wordcounts/result
```

Here is an explanation of the flags:

- **--runner=SparkRunner:** It tells Beam to use the Spark portable runner in "batch job bundling" mode, since we provided **output_executable_path**.
- **--output_executable_path=wordcount_spark_job.jar**: This tells Beam to bundle the entire pipeline (with a small harness) into the specified jar file. After running this command, you will get **wordcount_spark_job.jar**.
- **--spark_version=3**: It ensures that the jar is built targeting Spark 3.x, since Beam supports Spark 3, while Spark 2 is deprecated.
- **--output=/tmp/wordcounts/result**: This is a pipeline-specific option for the **WordCount** example, which indicates the output prefix for results. It is unrelated to runner configuration.

When you run this command, it will not actually execute the pipeline on Spark *at that time*. Instead, it produces the jar. You should see output logs indicating the jar was created.

Next, to run the pipeline on Spark, use spark-submit with that jar, as shown here:

```
spark-submit --master local[2] wordcount_spark_job.jar
```

This will run the Beam pipeline on Spark (in this case, it is local with 2 threads). If you have a Spark cluster, replace **--master** with your cluster's master. Whether **--class** is required depends on how the executable JAR is built. If Beam sets a Main-Class in the JAR manifest, spark-submit can run it directly. If not, you must specify the entry point explicitly. Do not assume that the manifest is always present unless you have verified it.

After it runs, check the output files in **/tmp/wordcounts/** (or wherever you pointed the output). You should see the word count results files.

This method is very useful for deploying Python Beam pipelines to Spark in production, as you can automate the packaging and submission. It essentially uses Beam's portability to generate a self-contained Spark job.

If you prefer not to produce a jar, another approach is to run a job server: for example, start the Beam Spark job server (**docker run apache/beam_spark_job_**

`server:latest --spark-master-url=spark://...`) and then run the pipeline with **`--runner=PortableRunner --job_endpoint=host:port --environment_config ...`** and so on. Hence, this approach is more complex, and therefore, the jar method is simpler for a beginner.

Example 6: Streaming Pipeline on Spark

The Spark runner is micro-batch based, and not record-by-record streaming. Hence, this affects latency, watermark behavior, and event-time semantics.

Semantic Differences to Consider

- **Latency is Batch-Bound.**

  Results are only produced once per micro-batch. If **`batchIntervalMillis = 2000`**, your pipeline has an inherent minimum latency of ~2 seconds, even if data arrives continuously.

- **Watermarks Advance in Steps, and Not Continuously.**

  In Spark, watermarks typically move forward at micro-batch boundaries. This means:

  - Event-time windows close later than in Flink/Dataflow.
  - Late data handling is coarser.
  - Trigger behavior is less fine-grained.

- **Event-Time Semantics are Approximated.**

  Spark's micro-batch model can emulate Beam's windowing and triggers, but it cannot match the precision of true streaming engines that process events individually.

Therefore, Spark Streaming provides fault tolerance through checkpointing and replaying micro-batches. This usually results in **at-least-once processing semantics**, but the end-to-end guarantees depend on three factors:

- The **Source** (Can it replay data deterministically?)
- The **Pipeline** (Does it deduplicate or manage state correctly?)
- The **Sink** (Are the writes idempotent or transactional?)

With the Spark runner, correctness is achieved by design, and not by default. Hence, the pipelines must assume that duplicates are possible at batch boundaries; therefore, it must make sinks idempotent, or explicitly deduplicate outputs.

Java Example (Streaming on Spark):

```
import org.apache.spark.SparkConf;
import org.apache.spark.streaming.Duration;
```

```
SparkPipelineOptions options = PipelineOptionsFactory.create().
as(SparkPipelineOptions.class);
options.setRunner(SparkRunner.class);
options.setSparkMaster("local[2]");
options.setBatchIntervalMillis(2000);  // 2-second micro-batch
interval
options.setAppName("BeamStreamingSpark");

Pipeline p = Pipeline.create(options);

// Simulate streaming data by generating numbers 0,1,2... every
second
PCollection<Long> numbers = p.apply(GenerateSequence.from(0).
withRate(1, Duration.standardSeconds(1)));

// Map to strings and log them (using a DoFn to avoid collecting
huge output)
numbers.apply(MapElements.into(TypeDescriptors.strings()).via(num
-> "Number: " + num))
      .apply("Log", ParDo.of(new DoFn<String, Void>() {
          @ProcessElement
          public void processElement(ProcessContext ctx) {
              System.out.println(ctx.element());
          }
      }));

p.run();  // do not wait, streaming job
```

Here are some important points to note:

- We set **batchIntervalMillis** to 2000 milliseconds (2 seconds). This means that the Spark runner will configure Spark Streaming to batch events in 2-second windows. The **GenerateSequence** is generating one element per second; therefore, each micro-batch will have 2 elements.
- We use **GenerateSequence** to simulate an unbounded source. This triggers the pipeline to be treated as streaming.
- We print each element. In a real streaming job, you might write to an external system instead (for example, append to a file or database). Writing to files in streaming on Spark is possible, but it requires using windowing and a proper sink.
- If we were reading from a real streaming source, Beam's I/O connectors could be used (for example, KafkaIO as with Flink). The setup would be similar, as the Spark runner would create a DStream under the hood to consume Kafka.

Hence, running this Java streaming pipeline will start printing numbers. If you are running it locally, you will see output in the console. This job runs indefinitely.

Therefore, you must stop it with a kill or Ctrl+C if running from a main program, or spark-submit termination if it is in cluster mode.

Spark Runner Considerations in Streaming

Here are some considerations you should factor in while setting up Spark runners:

- **At-Least-Once vs. Exactly-Once:** Classic Spark Streaming (DStream) provides at-least-once processing guarantees. It relies on checkpointing to potentially avoid reprocessing data on failure, but if a failure happens after output, duplicates can occur. The Beam Spark runner inherits this behavior. Thus, it may not achieve the same level of exactly-once as Flink or Dataflow for certain patterns.
- **Accumulation of State:** Spark's micro-batch model means that each window's results are computed per batch. Therefore, for long-running streaming, you must be mindful of state or memory usage. Use Beam's windowing to periodically drop state whenever required. Moreover, the `checkpointDir` option in `SparkPipelineOptions` can be set to allow Spark to checkpoint streaming state (like any Spark Streaming job).
- **Spark Structured Streaming (Experimental):** There is a runner that uses Spark's Structured Streaming API. It currently only supports batch pipelines (and not actual streaming), and is marked experimental. Therefore, for production streaming, you would prefer to stick to the default `SparkRunner` (DStream).
- **Deployment on Cluster:** For streaming on a Spark cluster, you would typically submit your job in cluster mode (like spark-submit with master URL, and possibly `deploy-mode = cluster`, so that the driver itself runs on the cluster). Therefore, you should ensure that the driver is configured to have enough memory if it is doing any heavy lifting (Spark drivers in streaming mainly coordinate, as most processing takes place on executors).

Spark Runner Considerations

Here are the important points you should consider when deploying Beam on Spark:

- **Compatibility:** Use Beam versions that support your Spark version. As of Beam 2.48.0+, Spark 3.2+ is supported, while Spark 2 is deprecated. Therefore, you must make sure that the `beam-runners-spark-3` library is the correct one.
- **Cluster Integration:** If using YARN, you can set `--sparkMaster=yarn` in `SparkPipelineOptions` or simply rely on `spark-submit --master yarn`. On Dataproc (Google's managed Hadoop/Spark service), you can use Beam on Spark as well (there are guides to run Beam jobs on Dataproc's Spark).

- **Resource Management:** Spark does not auto-scale like Dataflow. If you are running it on YARN or Kubernetes, you might have some elasticity, but generally, you can allocate a fixed number of resources for the Spark job. Therefore, you should plan the number of executors and their memory based on your pipeline needs.
- **Metrics and Monitoring:** You can use Spark's Web UI (usually on port 4040 for local or through the Spark History Server for cluster jobs) to monitor the pipeline. Beam metrics (counters, and so on) will be integrated, and can be thus viewed via Spark's metrics sinks, or in logs. Hence, you can enable Spark metric sinks via Spark configuration, if required.
- **Runner Feature Support:** The Beam capability matrix shows that the Spark runner supports core Beam transforms (**`ParDo`**, **`GroupByKey`**, windowing, and so on), but has partial support for some features like side effects, as well as some stateful processing in earlier versions. Over time, it has improved, but still, some advanced Beam features might not be as robust on Spark. Therefore, for beginner's pipelines (which typically do not go into custom timers or exotic triggers immediately), the Spark runner will work just fine.
- **Dependencies:** Just like Flink, if you use any connectors (such as JDBC, Hadoop InputFormat, and so on), include them in your job's classpath. Spark's `--jars` option can attach additional jars if you do not bundle them. For example, if reading from a JDBC in Beam, you will need the JDBC driver jar available to the Spark executors.

In practice, many Beam users choose Dataflow (for Google Cloud) or Flink (self-managed) for heavy streaming, and use Spark runner mostly for batch jobs or where they want to integrate Beam into a Spark-centric environment. Hence, your choice will depend on factors such as existing infrastructure, expertise, and specific feature needs.

Now that we have covered how to deploy on each runner, let us consolidate some **runner-specific considerations,** and then discuss best practices for deploying pipelines in cloud and on-prem environments.

Runner-Specific Considerations and Differences

We have seen how to deploy on Dataflow, Flink, and Spark. Thus, it is important to understand how these runners differ in behavior, capabilities, and configuration. Here is a summary of considerations for each:

- **Language Support:**
    - **Dataflow**: It supports Java, Python, and Go pipelines natively. Therefore, when you use DataflowRunner with any of these SDKs, the Dataflow service

spins up workers for the respective SDK (for example, Python workers for a Python pipeline) automatically. Multi-language pipelines (cross-language transforms) are supported, as Dataflow has full portability support.

- **Flink**: The classic Flink runner supports only JVM languages (Java/Scala). The portable Flink runner supports Python and Go as well. In practice, if you run a Python pipeline with `FlinkRunner`, Beam uses the portable runtime to execute Python on Flink. This requires the job server and SDK harness as discussed. Therefore, make sure that your environment can pull the required container images if they are not in loopback.
- **Spark**: Similar to Flink, the original Spark runner was Java only. The portable Spark runner allows Python (and other) support, but running it is more involved (as we did with the executable jar approach). Thus, Java pipelines run easily on Spark; Python pipelines require the extra bundling or a job server.

- **Pipeline Features and Beam Model Coverage:**
  - All three runners (Dataflow, Flink, Spark) support the core Beam model (batch and streaming transforms, windowing, triggers, state, timers to varying degrees). Dataflow and Flink have near-complete support for streaming features (such as timers, stateful processing, and watermarks) in production. Spark runner supports most features but historically had partial support for some streaming concepts (like it does not support the advanced Beam watermark propagation perfectly due to micro-batch nature, and stateful processing may be limited by Spark's capabilities).
  - Check the Beam Capability Matrix for details. The Beam Capability Matrix is the authoritative source for feature support, but it is most useful when paired with a clear deployment intent. If your pipeline relies heavily on advanced Beam features such as timers, stateful processing, or precise event-time semantics, Flink or Dataflow are the safest choices. If your workloads are primarily batch-oriented and already live in a Spark ecosystem, Spark is appropriate. Always validate runner choice against your pipeline's semantic requirements, and not just for convenience's sake.

  Therefore, if your pipeline needs:

Requirement / Feature	Prefer This Runner	Why
Heavy streaming with event-time semantics, low latency, precise watermarks	**Flink** or **Dataflow**	True record-by-record streaming, strong support for timers, state, and triggers
Stateful processing and timers in production	**Flink** or **Dataflow**	Most complete Beam model support

Exactly-once sinks (BigQuery, transactional DBs)	**Dataflow** (First) / **Flink** (with Care)	Strong built-in exactly-once integrations
Micro-batch streaming is acceptable.	**Spark (DStream runner)**	Uses Spark Streaming; higher latency, simpler ops
Python or multi-language pipelines	**Dataflow** or **Flink (portable)**	Native or well-supported portable execution
Java-only, maximum performance, simple deployment	**Flink classic runner**	No SDK harness, no containers, lowest runtime complexity
Batch pipelines on existing Spark clusters	**Spark runner**	Natural fit for Spark-centric organizations
Interactive / serverless-style deployment	**Dataflow**	Managed infrastructure, minimal operational overhead
Strictly on-prem or air-gapped environments	**Flink** or **Spark**	Full infrastructure control

Table 7.4: *Runner to be Used versus Requirement*

- **Performance and Scalability:**
  - **Dataflow**: It automatically scales for you. In a batch, it can autoscale up or down based on data size, while in streaming, it will autoscale based on throughput. Google continuously tunes Dataflow's performance (like using optimized shuffle implementations). Therefore, you typically get great performance out of the box, but you might pay more if your pipeline is not efficient (since it will scale to meet the demand).
  - **Flink**: You have more control over resources such as several TaskManagers, slots, and so on. Flink is designed for low-latency streaming, and can achieve very high throughput with low latency. You also need to manually size your cluster or use the Flink Kubernetes Operator or YARN for elasticity. Flink jobs can be optimized by configuring task buffers, network threads, and so on. The Beam Flink runner will use Flink's defaults unless you override via Flink's configuration. One notable aspect here is that Flink can perform **backpressure** –that is, if consumers are slow, it will signal the upstream to slow down to not overwhelm the system.
  - **Spark**: Spark is optimized for batch throughput. For streaming, micro-batch adds some latency (which is a minimum of 0.5-1 seconds, depending on batch interval). Spark does not natively auto-scale individual jobs, but if you are using YARN or Kubernetes, resources can be flexibly allocated according to the job. Beam on Spark inherits Spark's performance characteristics. Hence, it is excellent for batch (especially with optimized Beam transforms that can translate to Spark operations), and is also decent

for streaming. However, it has a potentially higher latency than Flink. Spark also, by default, materializes (caches) RDDs for certain Beam operations to avoid recomputation, which can be tuned.

- **Fault Tolerance:**
    - **Dataflow**: Provides fault tolerance by checkpointing and replay internally. If a worker crashes, Dataflow will restart it, and also replay any unprocessed bundles. Streaming Dataflow jobs use persistent state and exactly-once sinks to avoid duplicates. The service hides these details; you typically do not worry about it except to ensure that your pipeline is idempotent for external side effects.
    - **Flink**: Uses Flink's checkpointing mechanism. Flink can achieve exactly-once processing of stateful operations and sources that support replay (Kafka, for example) by storing checkpoints and, restoring state and replaying from the last checkpoint when any failure is encountered. With Beam on Flink, if your pipeline fails, you can restart from the last checkpoint/savepoint to resume without data loss. Hence, you should configure **`checkpointingInterval,`** as well as the state backend for production.
    - **Spark**: Spark Streaming can recover from failures using checkpointing (if enabled) for stateful transformations. However, if a driver fails and you have not checkpointed the streaming context, the streaming job will start again from scratch. In batch, Spark will recompute lost partitions on executor failure (standard RDD lineage). For exactly-once delivery in streaming, Spark's model does not guarantee it for all sinks (it is typically at-least-once). For example, writing to a file or database could have duplicates if a task is retried.
- **Scheduling and Execution:**
    - Dataflow is a managed service–you just submit a job, and it decides how to schedule it.
    - Flink uses its own job manager and scheduler. If multiple Beam jobs are submitted to the same Flink cluster, they will be queued or share resources depending on the cluster's slot availability. You might run a dedicated Flink cluster per pipeline, or share a cluster for multiple pipelines.
    - Spark can run one Beam pipeline per Spark application (job). You typically would not run multiple pipelines in one Spark application (unless you manually multiplex them), instead, you would submit separate jobs. On YARN or K8s, each Spark job is an application with its own set of executors.
    - If using Spark's **dynamic allocation** (on YARN or Kubernetes), Spark can acquire and release executors based on workload. Beam does not directly

control that, but it is something you should enable for variable workloads (though it is more effective for batch than streaming, since streaming has a steady allocation usually).

- **Monitoring and Debugging:**
  - On Dataflow, use the Dataflow UI and Cloud Logging. Also, Stackdriver alerts can be set on Dataflow metrics for automation.
  - On Flink, use Flink's Web Dashboard (which shows operator-level details, watermarks, as well as the throughput per task). You can also use Flink's CLI (bin/Flink list to see jobs, and so on). Debugging on Flink might involve looking at TaskManager logs, or using the web UI to download exception traces.
  - On Spark, use the Spark UI. For streaming, the Spark UI (or History Server) will show batches and processing times. Logging is through the Spark driver and executor logs (the stdout that we saw goes to those logs via print). You might integrate with a log aggregator to collect logs from the executors in a cluster.
  - Beam's internal logging (like logging from DoFns) will end up in the worker logs for all runners. For example, logging.info() in a Beam Python DoFn on Dataflow goes to Cloud Logging, on Flink to TM logs, on Spark to executor logs. Therefore, you must plan how to access such logs in each environment.
- **IO and Connectivity:**
  - If your pipeline reads/writes to specific systems, consider where that system is relative to the runner. Some of these considerations are mentioned here:
    - For example, Google BigQuery is easily accessible from Dataflow (within GCP, likely the same region), and there is a native sink. Therefore, you can still use BigQuery via Beam's IO (it will use BigQuery APIs over the internet) on Flink or Spark on-prem, but you would need network access and credentials on those machines, which implies that more setup will be involved.
    - Apache Kafka: On-prem Flink or Spark can directly consume from your local Kafka cluster (low latency). Dataflow can also read from Kafka (Beam has KafkaIO), but then your Kafka must be accessible from the cloud VMs (possibly over VPN, or a public IP). Additionally, you would need to provide the Kafka broker addresses that are reachable from the GCP.
    - Essentially, choose the runner that has good proximity to your data sources/sinks to minimize network bottlenecks. Beam provides you

flexibility, but the physical data location and network still matter for performance.

Therefore, while choosing a Beam runner, the physical proximity to your data sources and sinks is more important than the theoretical capabilities of the runner itself. Beam gives portability at the API level, but its performance is governed by network distance, bandwidth, latency, and egress costs. In practice, moving large volumes of data across networks is far more expensive and slower than moving computation to where the data already dwells. Runner selection is thus not only a software choice, but a deployment and infrastructure decision.

- For Dataflow, the best performance is achieved when your data is already in Google Cloud–native services such as Pub/Sub, BigQuery, and Cloud Storage. Hence, pipelines like Pub/Sub → Dataflow → BigQuery benefit from Google's internal network, which provides high bandwidth, low latency, and no egress charges within the same region. This makes Dataflow ideal for cloud-native architectures where both sources and sinks are already colocated in GCP.
- For Flink, especially in on-premises or private cloud deployments, the optimal scenario is when your data resides inside your own network. Pipelines such as Kafka (on-prem) → Flink → HDFS or an S3-compatible object store avoid WAN hops entirely. This eliminates cloud egress costs, minimizes latency, and gives you full control over network tuning and throughput. Therefore, Flink excels when tight integration with internal systems is required.
- For Spark, proximity matters most in batch-oriented data platforms. When data already exists in HDFS, Delta Lake, or Hive tables, running Beam pipelines through Spark allows you to take advantage of data locality and Spark's optimized batch execution. Here, Spark is a natural fit in organizations that already standardize on Spark infrastructure and storage formats.
- Moreover, portable runners and cross-language execution models require extra caution. If your runner is far from your data, every record must traverse wide-area networks. For example, Kafka on-prem feeding a portable Flink or Spark runner in the cloud introduces latency, bandwidth costs, and reliability risks. At scale, these costs dominate pipeline performance and operational expense.

Thus, as a rule of thumb, always colocate compute with your dominant data sources and sinks. Ideally, your runner should be in the same cloud provider, region, and private network zone as your data. Avoid cross-cloud movement unless it is unavoidable. Additionally, when boundaries must be crossed, use private connectivity such as VPNs, Direct Connect, or Interconnect rather than public internet paths.

    - Bandwidth and egress costs should be explicitly estimated during design. High-volume streaming pipelines magnify even small inefficiencies. Hence, a few milliseconds of added latency or a few extra megabytes per second can translate into significant monthly costs and unstable pipeline behavior.

    Therefore, in practice, the guiding principle is simple: move compute to the data, and not data to the compute. For most real-world pipelines, network placement dominates performance far more than the choice between Flink, Spark, or Dataflow.

- **Developer Experience:**
    - Dataflow requires a GCP account, and it might feel a bit opaque since you rely on Google's service (even though the UI is user-friendly). Therefore, debugging can sometimes mean checking Cloud logs and metrics after the fact.
    - Flink and Spark allow you to run everything locally for testing (which is great). You can step through some parts of the pipeline in local mode (especially with `DirectRunner` for unit tests, and then do an integration test with Flink/Spark local).
    - The iteration cycle might be slower on Dataflow (because of deployment overhead) than on a local Flink/Spark cluster. So, a common practice is to test with `DirectRunner`, then test with Flink/Spark in local mode, and then deploy to the Flink/Spark cluster or Dataflow for full scale.

Therefore, with these differences in mind, you can make an informed decision about which runner to use for a given scenario. Often, Dataflow is chosen if you are on GCP and want ease of use. If you need on-prem or multi-cloud flexibility, Flink is a strong choice for streaming, and Spark for batch or where integration with the Spark ecosystem (for example, using Spark MLlib or libraries) is desired.

Next, we will outline some best practices for deployments, while comparing cloud (managed) against on-premise (self-managed) scenarios.

Best Practices for Cloud and On-Premise Deployments

Deploying Beam pipelines in production requires attention not just to the pipeline code, but also to the runtime environment and configuration. Therefore, here are some best practices grouped by **cloud deployments** (using a managed service like Dataflow) and **on-premise deployments** (using self-managed Flink or Spark clusters):

Best Practices for Cloud Deployments (for example, Dataflow):

- **Leverage Autoscaling and Right-Size Resources:** An advantage of cloud services is autoscaling. Therefore, you should design your pipeline to take advantage of it. For batch jobs on Dataflow, use autoscaling (default) unless you have a good reason to fix the number of workers. For streaming, Dataflow autoscaling will handle growth in load. However, you must also consider setting a maximum worker count to control cost if there is a chance of an unexpected surge. Choose an appropriate machine type–Dataflow has options from smaller VMs to very powerful ones. Hence, if your pipeline is CPU-bound, a larger machine with more vCPUs might process more per worker (while reducing the overall workers that may be required).
- **Use Regional Settings Wisely:** Always run your pipeline in the same region as your data sources/sinks when possible. For example, if your data is in us-central1 (like BigQuery dataset or Pub/Sub topics in that region), run the Dataflow job in us-central1. This avoids cross-region data transfer, and it also reduces latency.
- **Manage Temporary and Permanent Storage:** Use Cloud Storage paths for temp and staging that are in the same region. Clear out temp directories after runs if they accumulate. If writing output to Cloud Storage, consider using **sharding** to produce multiple output files for large output, which Beam's **`WriteToText`** does by default. For very large outputs, consider writing to a database or BigQuery, which can handle large aggregated outputs more gracefully.
- **Avoid Hot Keys and Ensure That Data is Evenly Distributed:** This is a pipeline design issue, but is crucial in cloud (where you pay for more resources if one worker gets overloaded). For example, if using **`GroupByKey`** or Combine in Beam, make sure that you are not grouping everything by a single key (which would cause one worker to handle it). Hot keys (single keys that have enormous volume) can bottleneck and defeat parallelism. Hence, you must use techniques like pre-partitioning or combiner lifting (Beam automatically does some combiner optimization) to mitigate.
- **Take Advantage of Managed Services:** If using Dataflow, integrate with other Google Cloud services wherever appropriate in the following ways:
    - Use Pub/Sub for streaming ingestion, BigQuery for batch outputs or streaming sinks (Dataflow has a BigQueryIO that can do streaming inserts efficiently).
    - Use Dataflow templates if you need to run the same pipeline multiple times with different parameters, or on a schedule (Using a Cloud Scheduler and Dataflow template is a common pattern).
    - Use Cloud Monitoring: Dataflow jobs export custom metrics (such as

elements processed, user counters) to Cloud Monitoring. Therefore, you must put up dashboards or alerts on these metrics for production pipelines.

  - Use Cloud Data Loss Prevention or Encryption When Dealing with Sensitive Data: Dataflow can read from encrypted sources or use DLP APIs within a DoFn if needed, while keeping compliance in check.

- **Dependency Management for Cloud (Python Specific):** When running Python pipelines on Dataflow, if you use any external libraries, you need to provide them. Options include:
  - Using **`--requirements_file`** to have Dataflow install pip packages on workers
  - Using **`--setup_file`** to package your code and dependencies
  - Using container images (as Beam Python allows custom container via **`--worker_harness_container_image`**)
    Thus, you must ensure that your dependencies are correctly picked up on Dataflow. Nothing is worse than a job that fails after a few minutes because a module was not found on the worker.

- **Cost Optimization:** Monitor your pipeline's CPU, memory, and I/O usage. Dataflow has an optional feature called Flexible Resource Scheduling (**FlexRS**), which can use lower-cost spare capacity (preemptible workers) for batch jobs to reduce cost. Thus, if your batch job is not super urgent, consider FlexRS for 30-50% cost savings. You must also delete or drain streaming jobs that are no longer needed; an idling streaming job can still incur costs.

- **Robustness and Idempotency:** Design your pipeline to handle retries gracefully. Dataflow will retry failed bundles. If your DoFn writes to an external system, ensure that it should not cause inconsistent duplicates when it retries. For example, if you are writing to a database, perhaps write with upsert or de-dup on unique IDs, or use an external **deduplication** mechanism. Using Beam's **Checkpoints** (for stateful processing) or deduplicating with a time window (for example, using a combination of Combine with an accumulator that ignores duplicates by ID) can also help.

- **Testing in Cloud (Dry Runs):** For batch pipelines, you can run with a small input or sample of data on Dataflow by limiting the input (if possible), or using filtering. This "dry run" can catch issues that might not appear locally (such as permissions issues, missing dependencies). Hence, you might test for a short duration with test input topics for streaming.

- **Secure Your Pipeline:** If you are running it in a corporate environment, ensure that the service account running Dataflow has the least privileges it needs (access to read the input data sources and write to outputs, and nothing more). Dataflow can be run with a user-managed service account. Similarly, use encryption and VPC Service Controls to limit data egress.

In summary, you must treat a Dataflow pipeline as you would any cloud resource: monitor it, secure it, and use the tools available to maximize performance and minimize cost. Google Cloud's documentation provides an extensive list of Dataflow best practices, like how to structure pipelines for optimal performance.

Best Practices for On-Premise Deployments (For Example, Flink and Spark)

- **Provision Sufficient and Stable Resources:** Unlike managed services, on-prem or self-managed clusters require you to provision the right amount of resources. Therefore, you should ensure that your Flink or Spark cluster has enough CPU, memory, and disk for the pipeline's needs. It is better to have a bit of headroom than to run at the ragged edge (which can cause out-of-memory errors or prolonged GC pauses). Hence, for Flink, configure the taskmanager heap sizes appropriately, and consider using the RocksDB state backend for heavy stateful processing (with adequate disk space). For Spark, allocate executor memory and cores, while keeping in mind the data volume.
- **Enable Checkpointing and Savepoints (Flink):** For Flink streaming jobs, always enable checkpointing (for example, every 30 seconds or 1 minute, depending on your latency tolerance). This ensures that if a job fails, it can recover with minimal data loss. Also, plan a strategy for updating pipelines–Flink allows taking a savepoint (manual snapshot), and then starting a new job from that savepoint (by running a newer version of your pipeline jar). This can achieve zero-data-loss upgrades. Therefore, test the savepoint and restore the process in a lower environment to be comfortable with it.
- **Use Reliable Storage for State/Checkpoints:** Configure Flink to store checkpoints and savepoints in a distributed filesystem (HDFS, NFS, S3, and so on) that is accessible by all nodes. For Spark Streaming, if you use any stateful operations (like Beam's stateful `DoFn` or simply Spark's `updateStateByKey` indirectly through Beam state API), set a checkpoint directory to a durable location as well. This could be an HDFS path via `SparkPipelineOptions.setCheckpointDir()`. Hence, reliable storage ensures that if the driver goes down or the cluster restarts, you can resume the stream.
- **Logging and Diagnostics:** Ensure that logging from your Beam pipeline (which goes to the logs of the Flink/Spark executors) is captured. For example, in a YARN cluster, use the YARN `ResourceManager` UI or CLI to get logs; in a Kubernetes setup, check pod logs; with standalone clusters, as the logs might be on the VM's filesystem. Hence, it is good to integrate a centralized logging system (ELK stack or Splunk, and so on) to aggregate logs from your cluster for easier searching when something goes wrong.

- **Isolation and Dependency Management:** When running on your own cluster, be mindful of classpath issues such as:
    - **Flink**: It is often best to **shade (relocate)** Beam and dependencies in your job JAR to avoid conflicts with Flink's own classes. Flink's classpath already includes many common libraries (such as Netty, Guava, and so on), and version mismatches can occur. Using the Maven Shade plugin to relocate packages can prevent this. The Beam Flink runner is designed to work with certain versions of Flink libraries. However, shading your pipeline code remains a recommended best practice in Flink jobs.
    - **Spark**: Similarly, package dependencies carefully. Spark's classpath might have certain versions of libraries (for example, Hadoop client libraries). Therefore, if Beam needs a different version, shading might be needed. Also, if you are running multiple Beam pipelines in the same Spark cluster at different times, try to use the same Beam version for all to avoid needing different dependencies to be loaded (since Spark driver/executors might reuse JVMs or share classloader contexts across jobs; even though in practice, each Spark job is separate, but if you are using Spark's shell or an interactive session, conflicting versions could clash).
- **Avoid Overloading the Driver (Spark specific):** In Spark, the driver coordinates tasks and collects results for certain operations. Therefore, in a Beam pipeline, if you use .collect() or any operation that brings data to the driver, you must avoid it for large data. Beam generally does not encourage that, as it deals with **`PCollections`** distributed), but remember that any log or print will gather data on executors, and then send them to the driver (as printing a million lines will overwhelm the driver). Hence, you must use logging sparingly or output data to files/sinks, instead of printing in production jobs.
- **Tune Parallelism and Partitioning:** On Flink, the parallelism option we saw controls how many parallel tasks each step gets. You might tune this higher or lower based on cluster size. Also, Flink (and Spark) allow setting parallelism per operator (not directly via Beam API, but you could apply hints or use the runner's settings). For example, if one stage is slow, you could increase its parallelism if the runner API exposes it. Beam does not expose per-transform parallelism easily, but you could break your pipeline and run sub-components separately, if at all it is required (this is an advanced scenario).
    - On Spark, parallelism is determined by default by the number of partitions of RDDs/Dataframes. Beam likely decides an appropriate partitioning (for example, after a **`GroupByKey`**, the number of partitions might equal a default parallelism or number of keys). You can also influence it by setting

--parallelism in Spark runner, or through **.withNumShards()** on some Beam transforms (such as Write) to control output parallelism.

- **Manage Backpressure (Flink) and Batch Size (Spark):** In Flink streaming, if your sink is slow, Flink will propagate backpressure. Therefore, you must watch out for any alerts in Flink UI about backpressure. Moreover, you might need to scale out the sink (if possible) or increase resources if they are present. In Spark streaming (micro-batch), you will see a growing scheduling delay if batches start taking longer than the batch interval to process. This means that the system is falling behind. The solution is to either increase parallelism (more executors), or increase the batch interval (process bigger chunks less frequently, while trading latency for throughput). Beam does not directly expose the batch interval in pipeline code, but we have the **batchIntervalMillis** in options, which serves this purpose.
- **Plan for Maintenance:** On-prem clusters require maintenance (patching, scaling, and so on). For Flink, you must consider using the Flink Kubernetes Operator (if on K8s), as it can manage job lifecycles (as described in an Apache Beam blog for Beam on Flink on K8s). For Spark on YARN, leverage YARN's capacity scheduler to allocate resources, and reserve capacity for critical pipelines. Have a strategy for updating the Beam version, because that means updating your application JARs. Therefore, you must test the new Beam versions in a staging environment (Beam aims to maintain backward compatibility within a major version, but behavioral changes, performance differences, or updates in runners and dependencies may still affect existing pipelines. Therefore, new Beam versions should always be validated in a staging environment before upgrading production workloads.)
- **Combine Beam with Native API Whenever Necessary:** In some on-prem scenarios, you might want to mix Beam with native Flink or Spark code. For example, maybe you have a Spark SQL query that's complex, and you trust Spark's engine to optimize it. Therefore, you can incorporate that into a Beam pipeline by using Beam's external transform, or simply by splitting the pipeline (for example, run a Spark job to prepare data, then Beam for something else). Do not force everything into Beam if it is not a comfortable fit; Beam is flexible, but you can use the right tool for each sub-task in a pipeline. Therefore, playing to the strengths of your runner is a design philosophy that you can follow here. For example, Spark's cache and SQL optimizations, or Flink's native CEP library for complex event processing; you could potentially combine those with Beam by writing a custom transform that calls into those APIs (since Beam on Flink/Spark ultimately runs on those engines, you *could* interop, but it might be advanced).
- **Community and Support:** When running Beam on your own, you rely on the Beam community for support. Therefore, you must keep an eye on Beam's Jira or Stack Overflow for any known issues with the runner versions you use.

For example, certain Beam versions might have a bug on the Flink runner for specific features; therefore, upgrading or applying patches might be necessary. The advantage of Dataflow is that Google handles a lot of that under the hood, whereas with Flink/Spark, you have more control, but you also need to stay updated.

Finally, whether on cloud or on-prem, a best practice is **observability**—build into your pipeline ways to observe its behavior. Use Beam's metrics (Counters, Distributions, Gauges) to track key indicators (such as the number of events that are processed, as well as the errors you encountered). All runners will report these metrics (Dataflow shows them in the UI, Flink can be configured to log or send metrics to Prometheus, and Spark can log them). Therefore, by monitoring metrics and logs, you can detect issues early (such as data skew, high error rates in parsing, and so on) and tune your pipelines accordingly.

Conclusion

In this chapter, we explored how Apache Beam enables the same pipeline logic to be executed across different runtimes by selecting an appropriate runner. We also examined Google Cloud Dataflow as a fully managed, serverless option, Apache Flink as a high-performance and highly controllable engine for streaming workloads, and Apache Spark as a natural extension point for organizations that have already invested in the Spark ecosystem. Through configuration examples and code samples in both Python and Java, we showed how runner selection is primarily an operational choice driven by infrastructure, performance requirements, and data locality, instead of changes in business logic. While Beam abstracts the execution layer, each runner brings its own operational model, strengths, and constraints that must be understood to build reliable and efficient pipelines.

Hence, the key takeaway is that Beam offers architectural flexibility, but production success depends on aligning runner choice with deployment realities such as scalability, fault tolerance, streaming semantics, network proximity to data, and operational maturity. Dataflow favors simplicity and automation, Flink favors fine-grained control and streaming precision, and Spark favors integration with existing big data platforms. Therefore, by understanding these tradeoffs, teams can treat runner selection as an engineering decision, instead of considering it a purely technical configuration step.

In the next chapter, we will focus on monitoring, debugging, and tuning Apache Beam pipelines. We will look at how to observe pipeline behavior in production, interpret metrics and runner dashboards, diagnose failures and performance bottlenecks, as well as apply systematic tuning techniques to make pipelines reliable and cost-efficient.

CHAPTER 8
Monitoring, Debugging, and Tuning Apache Beam Pipelines

Introduction

Building an Apache Beam pipeline is only the first step in a long process. Therefore, once a pipeline is running, especially in a production environment, you need to **monitor** its health, **debug** issues that arise, and **tune** it for optimal performance and cost efficiency. Hence, in this chapter, we will explore how to monitor Beam pipelines using metrics, how to debug pipeline problems, how to employ Apache Beam's metrics for observability, the techniques for tuning and optimizing pipeline performance, and the strategies for managing costs in cloud deployments. The focus here will be to provide beginner-friendly, practical guidance which is applicable to both **Python and Java SDKs**, with particular attention to running pipelines on **Google Cloud Dataflow** and **AWS** (for example, using Apache Flink on Amazon's managed service). Throughout this chapter, we will use clear explanations and simple code examples (in both Python and Java) to illustrate the concepts.

Structure

In this chapter, we will cover the following topics:

- Monitoring Pipelines with Metrics
- Monitoring on Google Cloud Dataflow
- Monitoring on AWS and Other Runners
- Establishing Alerts and Dashboards
- Debugging Pipelines
- Using Apache Beam Metrics for Observability

- Tuning and Optimizing Pipeline Performance
- Choosing the Right Worker Size

Monitoring Pipelines with Metrics

When a Beam pipeline is running (either a batch job that eventually completes or a streaming job that runs continuously), you should keep an eye on several aspects:

- **Pipeline Health and Completion:** It addresses if the job is still running, if it has been completed successfully, and the probable errors, if it failed.
- **Throughput:** It addresses the number of elements or records that are being processed per second by the pipeline. This indicates if the pipeline is keeping up with input data, which is important for streaming.
- **Latency:** It addresses the time it takes for data to travel through the pipeline (end-to-end), especially for streaming. Metrics such as **processing latency** or **system lag** show up if the pipeline is falling behind in real-time.
- **Resource Usage:** It addresses CPU utilization, memory usage, and I/O usage on worker nodes. These indicate if the workers are overloaded or underutilized.
- **Backlog and Watermarks:** In streaming pipelines, you must monitor the **backlog** (unprocessed data waiting) and **watermark** progress (which indicates event time progress). A growing backlog or stalled watermarks may signal that the pipeline cannot keep up. Backlog and watermarks measure two different aspects of a streaming pipeline, and hence, they should not be treated as the same signal. Backlog is source and runner specific, and represents how much unprocessed data is waiting to be consumed. In Pub/Sub this appears as subscription backlog, in Kafka as consumer lag, in Kinesis as iterator age, and in Spark as micro-batch delay. A growing backlog means that the pipeline cannot ingest or process data as fast as it arrives, usually due to insufficient compute, slow sinks, I/O bottlenecks, skewed keys, or limited parallelism. Therefore, it is primarily a throughput and capacity issue.

  A watermark, on the other hand, is the runner's estimate of event-time completeness. It indicates the event-time timestamp at which most data has already arrived as per the system. It also controls when the windows can close, and when the results can be emitted. Watermarks are not a measure of how much data is waiting; they are an indicator of how confidently the system can reason about event time. Therefore, a pipeline can have low backlog, but it can still have a stalled watermark.

  Watermarks typically stalled when the runner cannot safely advance its event-time estimate. This happens if events do not have proper timestamps, if timestamps are all the same or invalid, if large amounts of late or out-of-order data are arriving, or if the source does not provide a mechanism to advance watermarks. In these cases, the pipeline may be processing data quickly, but it cannot finalize windows because it does not know whether the earlier data might still arrive. Therefore, monitoring backlog and watermarks together gives a more clear picture of pipeline health. A growing backlog with a moving watermark indicates performance or scaling issues. A stalled watermark with a small backlog indicates the existence of problems in event-time handling, timestamp assignment, or source behavior. Only when both are understood separately can you correctly diagnose whether a pipeline is failing to keep up with data volume, or if it is failing to reason correctly about the event time.

- **Error Counts:** This addresses the number of errors that are occurring during processing (This can be tracked via custom metrics or error logs.).

Monitoring on Google Cloud Dataflow

When running on Google Cloud Dataflow (the fully managed Beam runner on GCP), you will have many out-of-the-box monitoring tools, which are:

- **Dataflow Monitoring Interface:** Google Cloud Dataflow provides a web UI for each job. In the Dataflow console, you can view the **job graph**, which is a visual representation of your pipeline's transforms (steps). Each step shows metrics such as how many elements it has processed, its input/output sizes, and how long it is taking. The UI also highlights any slow or stuck stages, which is helpful in identifying bottlenecks.
- **Metrics and Charts:** Dataflow exposes metrics through two related but distinct layers: **Dataflow job metrics** and **Cloud Monitoring metrics**, and it is important to understand the difference between them. Dataflow job metrics are shown directly in the Dataflow UI and are tightly coupled to the pipeline execution. These include pipeline-level metrics such as element counts, step throughput, system lag for streaming jobs, watermark progression, and any custom Beam metrics (counters, distributions, and so on) that are defined in your code. These metrics help you understand how the logical pipeline is behaving, and whether individual transforms are processing data as expected.

  Cloud Monitoring metrics, on the other hand, focus more on infrastructure and resource behavior. These include worker-level metrics such as CPU utilization, memory usage, disk I/O, network I/O, and VM health. They are collected from the underlying compute resources running your Dataflow workers, and are used to understand whether your pipeline is constrained by hardware resources or scaling limits. These metrics are visible in Google Cloud Monitoring dashboards, and can be used to build alerts and long-term performance trends.

However, not all metrics are available in both places, and the naming conventions differ. For example, system lag and watermark metrics are typically associated with Dataflow job metrics, while CPU and memory utilization are Cloud Monitoring metrics. Some Beam metrics appear in the Dataflow UI but may show up in Cloud Monitoring under different metric namespaces. This separation can be confusing if it is not made explicit; therefore, it is useful to think of the Dataflow UI as "pipeline behavior" and Cloud Monitoring as "infrastructure behavior."

It is also important to note that metric availability can vary depending on job type and SDK harness. Batch jobs expose fewer streaming-specific metrics, such as watermarks or system lag. Streaming jobs provide richer event-time and backlog-related signals. Similarly, some metrics may behave differently between Java and Python pipelines, especially with different runner versions or SDK harness implementations. Therefore, when relying on metrics for tuning or alerting, you should always verify which metrics are actually exposed for your specific pipeline configuration.

- **Logs:** Each worker node in Dataflow streams logs to **Cloud Logging**. You can view logs for your job (with severity levels such as **`INFO`**, **`WARN`**, and **`ERROR`**). If an error occurs in processing, it often appears in the logs. Dataflow also surfaces **worker error count** metrics, and can show aggregated error messages in the UI. Hence, you should check the *Job Logs* in Dataflow's interface for any exceptions or warnings.
- **Dataflow Job Metrics Tab:** In the Dataflow UI, there is typically a section that lists custom **user-defined metrics** (Beam metrics such as counters) that your pipeline is reporting. This allows you to see, for instance, how many errors have been counted, or any other application-specific metric you defined.
- **Data Sampling:** A newer feature on Dataflow is *data sampling*, which allows you to inspect a sample of elements at each step of the pipeline for debugging purposes. This can be extremely helpful if you suspect that data at a certain stage is malformed, or if it is causing issues–you can peek at actual values that flowed through a transform, without needing to modify your pipeline. This feature is accessible in the Dataflow UI for running or recently finished jobs, and should be used instead of excessive per-element logging.

Tip: *Use meaningful names (labels) for your transforms. When building a pipeline, you can label each transform with a name (in Java, the string you pass to* ***`apply()`****, and in Python by using the | "Name" >> syntax). For example,* ***`p.apply("ReadFromSource",`*** ***`ReadFromText(...))`****. Good labels make the Dataflow job graph easy to understand, as those names will appear in the monitoring UI. If you see a step named "****`ReadFromSource`****" taking a long time, you will immediately know which part of your code it corresponds to. Make sure that each label is unique in your pipeline, as this practice greatly simplifies monitoring and debugging.*

Monitoring on AWS and Other Runners

If you run Beam on AWS, you likely use the **Apache Flink runner** (for streaming or batch on Amazon EMR or Amazon Kinesis Data Analytics, now known as Amazon Managed Service for Apache Flink), or possibly the **Apache Spark runner** (for batch on Amazon EMR or Glue). Hence, monitoring in these environments will be different from Dataflow, but equally important, as explained here:

- **Flink Web Dashboard (For Self-Managed Flink):** If you deploy a Beam pipeline on an Apache Flink cluster (say on EMR or an EC2 cluster), Flink's own dashboard provides metrics. You will be able to see each operator (transform) in the Beam pipeline as a node in Flink's execution graph. The Flink UI shows statistics such as records processed per second per operator, current throughput, and task CPU loads. It also highlights busy or backpressured operators (if an operator cannot keep up, Flink marks it as backpressured).
- **Amazon Managed Service for Apache Flink:** When running Apache Beam on AWS, the typical setup is Beam using the **Flink runner** on **Amazon Managed Service for Apache Flink** (formerly Kinesis Data Analytics). Unlike Google Dataflow, there is no Beam-native monitoring console. Your operational view is entirely built from three components: the Flink metrics exposed by the application, Amazon CloudWatch metrics, and application logs. Therefore, in practice, you are monitoring a Flink application that happens to be executing a Beam pipeline, not a Beam job directly.

  CloudWatch receives infrastructure and Flink-level metrics such as CPU utilization, heap and JVM memory usage, task throughput, records in and out, checkpoint duration and failures, and backpressure indicators. These tell you whether the Flink cluster is healthy, whether tasks are overloaded, and whether your pipeline can keep up with incoming data. Beam's own metrics (like counters and distributions) only appear if they are properly forwarded through Flink's metrics system, so they are secondary to Flink's native operational metrics in AWS.

  Therefore, day to day, what you actually look at is not "Beam metrics", but Flink and CloudWatch signals:

  - **CPU Utilization and Memory Usage**: They show whether the job is resource-bound or underutilized.
  - **Records in vs. Records out/Throughput**: They show if data is flowing normally or if the pipeline is falling behind.
  - **Checkpoint Duration and Checkpoint Failures**: These are critical for streaming stability and exactly-once guarantees.
  - **Backpressure Indicators**: They show the operators that are slowing down the pipeline.

   - **Application Logs (in CloudWatch Logs)**: They are used to inspect exceptions, serialization errors, failed DoFns, or crashes.

  Therefore, this makes the AWS operational model fundamentally different from Dataflow. On GCP, Beam is the first-class citizen and Dataflow provides a Beam-aware UI. On AWS, Flink is the first-class citizen and Beam is an abstraction layered on top. Monitoring therefore happens at the Flink and CloudWatch level, and not through a Beam-specific interface. Hence, understanding this early prevents confusion, and sets the right expectations for how production support is done on AWS.

- **CloudWatch Dashboards and Alarms:** On AWS, you can create CloudWatch dashboards to monitor your pipeline's key metrics (for example, CPU or records processed) over time. Setting up CloudWatch Alarms is a good practice to get notified if, say, the CPU stays too high (meaning that your pipeline is straining), or if the number of records in a source Kinesis stream's iterator age is growing (meaning that your pipeline is falling behind).
- **Logs on AWS:** If using the Flink runner, your pipeline logs will typically end up in CloudWatch Logs (for the managed service), or in log files on EMR nodes. Ensure that you have a way to access and search these logs for errors or warnings. In Amazon's managed Flink, each application has a log group in CloudWatch Logs where you can see the output (including any **`Beam Log.info()`** or print statements from your code, and exception stack traces, if things fail).

Thus, regardless of the runner, the goal of monitoring is to catch issues early. A well-monitored pipeline will tell you if it is healthy or if it is struggling, which will allow you to take action (such as scaling up resources or investigating a bug) before the data is lost or deadlines are missed.

Establishing Alerts and Dashboards

In a production scenario, it is not enough to manually watch metrics; you should set up automated alerts:

- On GCP Dataflow, you can use **Cloud Monitoring alerts**. For example, you might set an alert if **`system_lag`** exceeds a certain threshold (indicating your streaming pipeline is falling behind in processing), or if the pipeline's estimated cost or CPU usage goes beyond your expected budget. Likewise, alert any custom error counters in your pipeline that suddenly spike.
- On AWS, use CloudWatch Alarms for similar conditions. For instance, an alarm on a high CPU, or on a custom CloudWatch metric that counts error events.
- Create dashboards that aggregate the key metrics of your pipeline in one view. On GCP, a dashboard might include the elements processed per second,

system lag, watermarks, and user metrics. On AWS, a dashboard might show records in/out and resource utilization (KPU usage for the Flink application, and so on).

Hence, by proactively monitoring metrics and setting alerts, you can ensure that your Apache Beam pipelines remain healthy and meet their Service Level Agreements (SLAs) for throughput and latency.

Debugging Pipelines

Even with good monitoring, pipelines can encounter issues that require debugging. Debugging a distributed data pipeline can be challenging because problems might only manifest at scale or over time. In this section, we discuss strategies for debugging Apache Beam pipelines in both local and cloud environments.

Debugging Locally with Direct Runner

One of the advantages of Apache Beam's model is that you can often run the same pipeline locally for testing using the **DirectRunner**. This is extremely useful for debugging because you can use standard debugging techniques (such as breakpoints, print statements, or interactive analysis) on your local machine:

- **Unit Tests with TestPipeline:** Apache Beam SDKs provide testing facilities (for example, the `TestPipeline` class in Python or JUnit rules in Java) that allow you to write unit tests for your transforms or small pipelines. Hence, by crafting tests for your pipeline logic, you not only verify correctness, but also effectively debug logic in isolation. If a test fails, you can investigate the cause just like any other unit test.
- **`PAssert` and Matchers:** In tests, Beam's `PAssert` (available in Java and Python) can be used to assert that a `PCollection` contains the expected output. This helps catch logical errors. For example, you might have a test that feeds a known input into a small pipeline, and uses `PAssert` to verify the output. If the assertion fails, you know that there is a bug in your transformations.
- **Local Execution and Breakpoints:** You can execute your pipeline with a small sample of data using the `DirectRunner`. If using an IDE (for Java or Python), you can set breakpoints inside your user-defined functions (such as the `DoFn.processElement` method in Java or the process method of a Python `DoFn`). When you run the pipeline locally in debug mode, you can step through the code just like normal single-threaded code. Keep in mind that the `DirectRunner` executes the pipeline possibly in multiple threads, and may not preserve ordering strictly, but it works for debugging a single element's processing.

  Local execution with the `DirectRunner` is extremely useful for validating pipeline logic and debugging individual transforms. It allows you to set breakpoints inside your DoFns, inspect variables, and step through the processing of elements in a familiar IDE environment. This makes it ideal for catching functional bugs, verifying business rules, and ensuring that the transformations behave as expected on small datasets.

However, the **DirectRunner** should be understood as a *functional correctness tool*, not a full simulation of production behavior. It does not accurately represent how a pipeline will behave in a distributed environment. Concepts such as stage fusion, parallel execution across many workers, checkpointing, retries, watermark advancement, and backpressure are either simplified or absent. Ordering guarantees, execution timing, and failure semantics can differ significantly from runners like Dataflow or Flink.

Due to this, a pipeline that works perfectly on the **DirectRunner** may still exhibit issues in production, such as performance bottlenecks, incorrect windowing behavior, unexpected late data handling, or retry-related side effects. The **DirectRunner** confirms *what* your pipeline does, but not *how well* it will do it at scale.

- **Logging and Print Statements:** For quick insight, you can insert logging statements in your transforms. For example, in Python, use the logging module, and in Java, use a logger (**LoggerFactory.getLogger(...)**) to log debug info. Even when you are running locally with the **DirectRunner**, it is better to use proper logging instead of print or **System.out.println**. Print statements have a habit of surviving into production code, where they can create excessive, unstructured, and expensive logs that are hard to filter or analyze. Hence, using a logging framework from the start encourages cleaner debugging practices, and makes it easier to control what appears in logs as the pipeline moves from development to production. For instance, if you want to see what an element looks like at a certain stage, you might write a DoFn that logs **LOG.info("Element at stage X: " + element)** or similar. Just remember to remove or disable verbose logging once done, especially before deploying to a production runner.

Example (Python): Using **PAssert** in a test to debug and verify pipeline logic.

```
import apache_beam as beam
from apache_beam.testing.test_pipeline import TestPipeline
from apache_beam.testing.util import assert_that, equal_to

def double_numbers(nums):
    """A simple pipeline that doubles a list of numbers."""
    with TestPipeline() as p:
        input_collection = p | beam.Create(nums)
        output_collection = input_collection | beam.Map(lambda x:
x * 2)
```

```
        # Assert that the output is each input multiplied by 2
        assert_that(output_collection, equal_to([x * 2 for x in
nums]))

# This test will pass if the pipeline logic is correct, or raise
an AssertionError if not.
double_numbers([1, 2, 3, 4])
```

Remote Debugging and Troubleshooting in the Cloud

Sometimes, issues only show up when running at scale or with the specific environment of a cloud runner (Dataflow, Flink, and so on). Here are strategies for debugging in those scenarios:

- **Examine Error Messages:** If a pipeline fails on Dataflow, the Dataflow UI will often show an error message or exception stack trace. Always start by reading the error carefully; it might point directly to the issue (for example, a **`NullPointerException`** in a specific DoFn, or a serialization error for a certain class).
- **Pipeline Failure versus Data Error:** Determine if the pipeline is failing entirely (which could be due to a bug that throws an exception not caught within your code), or if it is processing, but is giving incorrect results (a logical error). For the former, the cloud logs/consoles are key. For the latter, you may need to sample data, or add instrumentation to figure out where the logic goes wrong.
- **Using Dataflow's Debugging Tools:** On Google Cloud Dataflow, take advantage of features such as:
    - **Data Sampling**: as mentioned, you can inspect sample data at each step through the Dataflow UI. If you suspect a transform is misbehaving, look at a sample of its output to see if it looks as expected.

      However, sampling is not a replacement for deterministic debugging. In practice, sampling may be **unavailable or insufficient** depending on factors such as pipeline shape (some transforms or sources may not be sample-friendly), very high throughput (samples may be sparse relative to total volume), or organizational privacy/security policies that restrict inspection of raw payloads. Sampling also will not reliably catch rare edge cases, because the problematic record might not appear in the sample window.

      When sampling is unavailable or does not reveal the issue, fall back to controlled, production-safe techniques. A common approach is to implement a **dead-letter path** (side output) for records that fail parsing/validation, and writing them to a quarantined sink (for example, Cloud Storage, BigQuery, or a secure bucket) for later inspection. Another approach is **targeted logging** with a sampling rate or conditional filters–log only one in N records, or only records matching a specific key/correlation ID, or failing a specific rule. These fallbacks give you repeatable evidence and better coverage while keeping cost and log noise under control.

  - **Execution Details**: Dataflow's "`Execution Details`" view can show how many elements were output by each step, and if any step is straggling. If one step outputs far fewer items than expected, maybe it is dropping data due to a bug (for example, a filter that filters too much).
  - **Worker Logs**: Use Cloud Logging to search for any ERROR or WARNING logs from your job. For instance, search for `"Exception"` or specific log messages you might have added. Dataflow gives each job an identifier you can filter logs by.
- **Flink Web UI (for Flink Runner):** If running on Flink (self-managed or Amazon's service), the Flink dashboard can show if tasks are failing (and how many times they have been retried). If a task in Flink keeps failing, Flink might retry it multiple times and then give up, causing the job to fail. The Flink UI typically provides the exception that caused the task failure. You can also access the logs for the task manager (worker) who had an issue to see the stack trace.

Common Issues to Check:

- **Serialization Problems:**

  Serialization problems occur because Beam must serialize user-defined functions (DoFns) and, in many cases, the data they reference, in order to ship them to worker processes. In Java, a common failure is the **`NotSerializableException`**, which usually means a DoFn has captured a non-serializable object such as a database connection, file handle, HTTP client, or thread pool. These objects cannot be safely serialized and sent to workers. The correct pattern is to avoid capturing such state in the DoFn constructor or as normal fields, and instead initialize them inside the @Setup method.

  It is important to understand that @Setup is executed once per DoFn instance, not once per JVM or per job. Each worker may create multiple DoFn instances, and each instance may be used by different threads depending on the runner. This means that resources created in @Setup are not automatically thread-safe or globally shared. If a resource (such as a database connection or HTTP client) is not safe to use concurrently, you must either protect it with synchronization, create one per thread, or create and close it at a finer granularity such as per bundle.

  For resource cleanup, **`@Teardown`** should be used. Any connections, sockets, or external resources created in @Setup should be closed in **`@Teardown`** to avoid leaks and resource exhaustion, especially in long-running streaming jobs where workers may be recycled over time. This makes the lifecycle of external resources explicit and predictable.

In Python, serialization issues appear differently because Beam relies on pickling and closure capture. Problems often arise when a DoFn captures non-picklable objects such as open file handles, database connections, or complex client objects. On portable runners (including Dataflow and Flink), these issues may surface as pickling errors or mysterious runtime failures. The same principle applies: create external resources lazily inside the **`setup()`** method of the DoFn, not in the constructor or global scope; you can then clean them up in **`teardown()`**.

In both Java and Python, the rule of thumb is:

Do not serialize live connections or heavy objects. Create them inside the worker, manage their lifecycle explicitly, and assume they are not thread-safe unless it is proven otherwise.

This avoids serialization failures, prevents subtle concurrency bugs, and ensures that your pipeline behaves correctly when scaled across many workers.

- **Incorrect Windowing/Triggering**: Incorrect windowing and triggering is a common source of logic bugs in streaming pipelines, but the issue is more specific than simply "not windowing unbounded data". Unbounded data can safely be processed in the global window when the pipeline is doing per-element operations, or writing directly to sinks that emit records one by one. The real problem arises when you apply grouping or aggregation operations such as **`GroupByKey`**, **`Combine`**, or **`Count`** on unbounded data in the global window while using the default trigger. In that case, the runner will wait indefinitely for the window to close, which never happens, causing the results to be buffered forever, and potentially leading to memory pressure or no output at all. For streaming aggregations, you must either define finite windows (such as fixed, sliding, or session windows), or explicitly define triggers that emit results periodically in the global window. Windowing controls *how data is grouped in time*, and triggering controls *when results are emitted*. Without one of these, the pipeline has no safe point at which to produce aggregated output.

  If you accidentally keep everything in the global window without triggers, Dataflow will buffer data indefinitely (potentially causing out-of-memory or simply no output until the job finishes which never happens for streaming). If your streaming job shows no output, ensure that you have windowed the data (for example, into fixed windows or sessions), or if you are using a global window, that you have set a trigger to emit results periodically. Therefore, debugging this might involve checking the watermarks–if the watermarks are stuck and no results are published, it could be waiting for a watermark advance that never occurs due to missing event time information, or late data handling.

- **Hot Keys (Skew)**: If your pipeline appears to hang or run extremely slowly at a certain stage, it could be due to data skew (one key having an enormous amount of data causing one reducer to be slow). The symptom might be one worker doing most of the work. Hot keys (data skew) happen when one or a few keys receive a disproportionately large share of the data. In pipelines that use **`GroupByKey`**, **`Combine.perKey`**, joins, or other key-based shuffles, this can create a "straggler" where one worker (handling the hot key) does far more work than the rest. The overall stage can look like it is hanging or moving extremely slowly because the job cannot complete until that one overloaded key finishes processing.

  A practical way to **confirm skew** is to instrument the pipeline with lightweight metrics. For example, you can track an (approximate) distribution of "records per key" by sampling keys and incrementing counters, or by using a Distribution metric to record group sizes once you have grouped (or record batch sizes per key if you pre-batch). Even approximate signals are useful; if most keys have counts in the hundreds, but one key shows counts in the millions, you have a clear skew problem.

  For **mitigation**, there are two common patterns:

  - **Hot Key Fanout (Recommended for Combines/Aggregations):** Instead of combining everything for a hot key in one place, you split the combine work across multiple partial combines, and then do a final combine. Beam supports this directly in many cases (for example, **`Combine.perKey().withHotKeyFanout(N)`** in the Java SDK). This spreads the load for a single hot key across multiple workers, and then removes the straggler bottleneck.
  - **Key Sharding (Salting):** You deliberately "shard" the hot key into multiple sub-keys (for example, append a random shard suffix like key#0..key#N), perform the grouping/aggregation on the sharded keys to distribute work, and then merge the partial results back to the original key in a final step. This works for more cases than fanout (including some joins), at the cost of extra logic.

  Together, these additions make the guidance actionable; you must identify skew with per-key count signals, and then fix it using fanout or sharding, so that one key cannot dominate an entire stage.

- **Using Side Outputs for Debugging:** A useful pattern for debugging in Beam is to route questionable data to a side output (also called a dead-letter output). For instance, if you have a parsing transform that sometimes fails for certain records, you can catch the exception and output the raw record to a separate **PCollection** (a dead-letter **PCollection** for bad records), instead of letting the exception crash the pipeline. This way, the pipeline continues for good data, but you can capture the bad data for further analysis. You can even count them. We will see an example of this pattern with metrics.

Example: Handling and Inspecting Bad Data (Java)

Consider a pipeline step that parses JSON messages into a Java object. Some messages might be malformed JSON. We want to **debug** and handle this gracefully, as shown here:

```
import com.google.gson.Gson;
import com.google.gson.JsonSyntaxException;
import org.apache.beam.sdk.metrics.Counter;
import org.apache.beam.sdk.metrics.Metrics;
import org.apache.beam.sdk.transforms.DoFn;
import org.apache.beam.sdk.values.TupleTag;

public class ParseJsonDoFn extends DoFn<String, MyRecord> {
    // Output tag for bad records:
    public static final TupleTag<String> DEADLETTER_TAG = new
TupleTag<String>(){};
    private final Counter malformedCounter = Metrics.
counter(ParseJsonDoFn.class, "malformed_json_count");
    private transient Gson gson;  // transient so it's not
serialized each time

    @Setup
    public void setup() {
        gson = new Gson();
    }

    @ProcessElement
    public void processElement(ProcessContext c) {
        String json = c.element();
        try {
            MyRecord record = gson.fromJson(json, MyRecord.
class);
            c.output(record);  // output to main output if
successful
        } catch (JsonSyntaxException e) {
            // JSON was malformed
            malformedCounter.inc();
            // output the raw JSON to the dead-letter output for
debugging
```

```
                c.output(DEADLETTER_TAG, json);
            }
        }
    }
```

In this Java example:

- We use a Counter metric (`malformedCounter`) to count how many bad JSON strings we have encountered.
- We have a side output (`DEADLETTER_TAG`) for the raw JSON of any record that failed to parse.
- The pipeline can be constructed to handle two outputs from this `ParDo`: the main output (`MyRecord` objects) and a `PCollection` of bad JSON strings. We could write the bad JSON to a file or a logging system for later inspection.
- This approach ensures that the pipeline does not fail just because of some bad data, and it gives us a path to debug those bad records after the fact.

When running on Dataflow, you would be able to see the value of the `malformed_json_count` metric (for example, in the Dataflow metrics UI or Cloud Monitoring) to know if there were any malformed records. You could direct the dead-letter `PCollection` to a sink such as Cloud Storage or BigQuery to examine the bad data.

For Python, a similar pattern can be applied using `apache_beam.Partition` or multiple outputs via `beam.DoFn.process` yielding `pvalue.TaggedOutput`. For brevity, the idea is the same: catch exceptions, increment a counter, and send problematic data to a side path.

Tips for Effective Debugging:

- **Reproduce with Smaller Data:** If a pipeline fails on a 1TB dataset, try to isolate a subset of data that can reproduce the issue. Perhaps a particular input triggers the bug. Use filtering or sampling to narrow it down, and then run locally if possible.
- **Use Version Control and Rollbacks:** When deploying a new pipeline version, if issues arise, having the ability to roll back to a known good state is crucial. This is more operational, but it saves debugging time if you can bisect the code change that introduced a problem.
- **Consult Runner Documentation:** Each runner has nuances. For Dataflow, Google provides extensive troubleshooting docs, and common error messages are documented. For Flink, understanding its own error messages (such as out-of-memory errors or misconfiguration issues) is useful. Do not hesitate to search error logs on Stack Overflow or community forums; often someone else might have hit the same issue.

- **Patience and Methodical Approach:** Debugging distributed systems can be tricky. Therefore, you must approach it methodically–check metrics (is it a performance issue or a crash?), check logs (what exceptions or warnings appear?), isolate components (maybe one transform at a time), and use Beam's tools (metrics, asserts, side outputs) to narrow down the problem.

Therefore, by combining local debugging techniques with cloud-based troubleshooting and good coding practices (such as defensive programming with metrics and side outputs), you can diagnose and fix issues in your Beam pipelines effectively.

Using Apache Beam Metrics for Observability

Apache Beam's model provides a built-in metrics API that allows you to collect custom metrics from within your pipeline code. These metrics serve as a powerful observability tool, as they help you understand what is happening inside your transforms in ways that simple external metrics (such as CPU or throughput) may not capture. Beam metrics can count events, track distributions (such as min/max/avg of values), and gauge instantaneous values.

Types of Beam Metrics

Beam supports three primary types of metrics, which are:

- **Counter:** This is a simple count of occurrences (for example, number of errors, number of records processed, and so on). You can increment or decrement a counter.
- **Distribution:** This records a distribution of numeric values, providing aggregated statistics such as count, min, max, and mean. Use this for things like sizes of processed elements, time taken for an operation, and so on.
- **Gauge:** This holds an instantaneous value (typically the latest value set). For example, you could use a gauge to set the current queue size at some point, or the last timestamp seen.

Thus, it is crucial to note that not all runners support all metric types equally and support varies by runner. For instance, Google Cloud Dataflow at the time of writing fully supports counters and distributions in its UI, whereas gauges may not be visible. Still, using these metrics in your code is runner-agnostic; you just might retrieve or view them differently, which depends on the runner.

Defining and Using Metrics in Pipeline Code

The way to use metrics is similar in Java and Python, with some syntax differences:

In Java: Metrics are typically defined as static or instance fields in your DoFn or transform class, while using the Metrics utility. For example:

```
public class MyDoFn extends DoFn<ElementType, OutputType> {
    private final Counter processedCount = Metrics.counter(MyDoFn.
class, "processed_count");
    private final Distribution lengthDistribution = Metrics.dis-
tribution(MyDoFn.class, "element_length");

    @ProcessElement
    public void processElement(ProcessContext c) {
        ElementType element = c.element();
        // Do some processing...
        processedCount.inc();  // increment counter for each
element seen
        int length = element.toString().length();
        lengthDistribution.update(length);  // record the length
of the element
        // ... output results, and so on
        c.output(transform(element));
    }
}
```

In this snippet:

- We create a counter metric named "**processed_count**" and a distribution metric named "**element_length**", both under the namespace of **MyDoFn.class** (the namespace is typically your class, or a string to logically group metrics).
- Each time **processElement** is called, we increment the counter, and update the distribution with the element's length.
- These metrics will automatically be collected by the Beam runner. On Dataflow, for example, you could see the "**processed_count**" metric in the Dataflow UI (under custom metrics), and then track how it increases. The distribution would show you min/max/mean element lengths.

In Python: Metrics are provided by the **apache_beam.metrics** module. You typically define them at the class level, or within the DoFn's **__init__**:

```
import apache_beam as beam
from apache_beam.metrics import Metrics

class MyDoFn(beam.DoFn):
```

```
    def __init__(self):
        # Define a counter and distribution metric
        self.processed_count = Metrics.counter(self.__class__,
'processed_count')
        self.length_distribution = Metrics.distribution(self.__
class__, 'element_length')

    def process(self, element):
        # Increment counter and update distribution
        self.processed_count.inc()
        self.length_distribution.update(len(str(element)))
        # yield the processed result
        yield transform(element)
```

Here, we use **`Metrics.counter(namespace, name)`** and **`Metrics.distribution(namespace, name)`**. We use **`self.__class__`** as the namespace (which will use the class name in the metric), but you could also provide a custom string namespace like **`"MyPipelineMetrics"`**.

Important: Beam metrics are intended for lightweight instrumentation. They are aggregated periodically by runners, not after every single element (to avoid overhead). So, using metrics will not significantly slow down your pipeline, but the heavy use of metrics can incur more costs. However, it is far more efficient than logging each element.

Observing Metrics at Runtime

Defining metrics is half the story; the other half is retrieving and viewing them:

- **Google Cloud Dataflow:** Beam user metrics are visible in the Dataflow job UI, but how they appear in Cloud Monitoring is more nuanced than simply considering that "each metric becomes a custom metric". In Cloud Monitoring, Beam metrics are most commonly exported under Dataflow-specific metric types such as **`dataflow.googleapis.com/job/user_counter`** and **`dataflow.googleapis.com/job/user_distribution`**. Your actual counter or distribution name is not the metric type itself; instead, it is stored as a label (along with labels such as the pipeline step or transform name). This means that you usually find your metric by selecting the Dataflow user metric type first, and then filtering by labels like the metric name and the emitting transform.

  This label-based model is the recommended and most reliable way to locate Beam metrics in Cloud Monitoring. It avoids creating a large number of separate custom metric types and scales well as your pipeline grows. Practically, it means that when searching for a metric, you should think in terms of "Dataflow user metrics filtered by labels", rather than "searching for a metric type named after my counter".

For backward compatibility, Dataflow can also export Beam metrics under metric names such as **custom.googleapis.com/dataflow/<metric-name>**. In this mode, each counter or distribution becomes its own custom metric type. While this can feel more intuitive, it has important implications, as Google Cloud enforces quotas on custom metrics, and excessive cardinality can increase monitoring costs and management overhead. For this reason, the label-based dataflow.googleapis.com/job/user_* approach is generally preferred for production systems

- **Beam's PipelineResult (For Batch Jobs):** If you run a batch pipeline and want to get metric results programmatically after completion, you can use the **PipelineResult** object. In Java:

```
PipelineResult result = p.run();
result.waitUntilFinish();
MetricResults metrics = result.metrics();
MetricQueryResults counters = metrics.queryMetrics(MetricsFilter.
builder()
                                        .addNameFilter(Metric-
NameFilter.named(MyDoFn.class, "processed_count"))
                                        .build());
for (MetricResult<Long> counter : counters.getCounters()) {
    System.out.println("Total processed: " + counter.getCommit-
ted());
}
```

In Python:

```
result = p.run()
result.wait_until_finish()
metrics = result.metrics().query({'namespace': 'MyDoFn'})
# filter by namespace or name
for counter in metrics['counters']:
    name = counter.key.metric.name
    value = counter.committed
    print(f"Metric {name}: {value}")
```

This allows you to fetch final metric values after a job is completed (for example, in a unit test or in some automated pipeline runner script).

- **Flink Runner/AWS:** When running on Flink, Beam's metrics integrate with Flink's metrics system. For example, Beam counters become Flink counters. When running Apache Beam on the Flink runner, Beam metrics are first emitted into Flink's own metrics system. They do not go directly to CloudWatch. This means that Beam counters, distributions, and other metrics only become visible in AWS monitoring tools if Flink itself is configured to export its metrics. Without this explicit configuration, Beam metrics may exist internally inside

Flink, but they will not appear anywhere in CloudWatch, which can easily give the impression that metrics are "not working".

In Amazon Managed Service for Apache Flink, the operational control point is the Flink application configuration, not Beam. Metrics reach CloudWatch only through Flink's metrics reporting mechanism. Beam does not have a native integration with CloudWatch; it relies entirely on Flink to forward metrics. As a result, Beam metrics appear in CloudWatch only if the Flink application has a CloudWatch metrics reporter enabled, a namespace defined, and sufficient IAM permissions to publish metrics.

At a minimum, this wiring involves enabling a CloudWatch metrics reporter in the Flink configuration, choosing a CloudWatch namespace, while granting the application role permission to publish metrics, and then verifying if Flink metrics are visible in CloudWatch. Only after this should you expect Beam counters to appear, and even then they usually show up as Flink-style metrics associated with operators and tasks, and not as Beam-labeled metrics or transform names.

Due to this indirection, Beam metrics on AWS should be treated as runner- and platform dependent. On Google Cloud Dataflow, Beam metrics are first-class, and are directly visible in the Dataflow UI and Cloud Monitoring. On AWS, Beam metrics are secondary, and are mediated through Flink. Monitoring is therefore Flink-first and CloudWatch-first, with Beam metrics appearing only as a part of the Flink metrics stream.

A useful mental model is that Beam writes metrics into Flink, and Flink writes metrics into CloudWatch only if you configure it to do so. There is no automatic or Beam-native path from a Beam pipeline to CloudWatch. Therefore, understanding this avoids the common assumption that Beam metrics will "just show up" in AWS monitoring without additional setup.

- **Other Runners:** For Apache Spark runner, metrics might integrate with Spark's metrics. Runners vary, but Beam's abstraction ensures that you can use the same metric API in your code, regardless of runner.

Use Cases for Custom Metrics

Using Beam metrics makes your pipeline more observable and self-monitoring. Some common use cases:

- **Counting Errors or Specific Events:** As shown earlier, count how many parsing errors occurred, how many records were dropped due to filtering, how often a certain condition was met, and so on. This can serve as a health indicator (for example, if error count > 0, something is wrong).

- **Data Quality Metrics:** Count, or compute the distribution of, things such as input record sizes, value ranges, and so on. For example, you might use a distribution metric to track the distribution of a numeric field in your data. Unusual spikes or ranges could indicate data issues upstream.
- **Performance Metrics:** Within a DoFn, you could time how long an operation takes (capture timestamp at start and end), and also record it in a distribution metric. This could tell you if a particular transform is taking unusually long for some elements. (even if it is for heavy profiling, one might use external profilers; still, metrics can give a high-level view of it).
- **Gauge Current Values:** Perhaps in a long-running streaming pipeline, you maintain some state (like the size of a cached dataset, or the number of live user sessions seen). A gauge metric could be updated to reflect the current count. Hence, monitoring this gauge over time can be useful to see trends or sudden changes.

Note: *In streaming pipelines, metrics are typically reported continuously. However, in some runners, you might only get the final aggregated values when the job finishes (which for streaming might be never cancelled). Dataflow streams metrics actively for streaming. Make sure to check the runner's documentation. For long-running jobs, using the runner's monitoring integration (such as Dataflow's UI or CloudWatch for AWS) is better for real-time observability.*

Example: Metric for Observability (Python)

To illustrate, let us add a custom metric to monitor data quality in a Python pipeline. Suppose that we have a transform that processes user event data, and we expect user IDs to be present. We want to count events that have missing user IDs, such as:

```
class ValidateEventDoFn(beam.DoFn):
    def __init__(self):
        # Counter to count events missing user_id
        self.missing_user_counter = Metrics.counter
("EventQuality", "missing_user_id")

    def process(self, event):
        # event is a dict with possibly a 'user_id' field
        if 'user_id' not in event or event['user_id'] is None:
            self.missing_user_counter.inc()
            # We could choose to filter out or tag this event
            # For this example, let us drop it (not outputting
it)
            return
        # If user_id is present, output the event
        yield event
```

```
# Usage in a pipeline:
events = p | beam.io.ReadFromText("events.json") | beam.Map(json.
loads)
valid_events = events | beam.ParDo(ValidateEventDoFn())
```

Here, we defined a counter metric "**missing_user_id**" under namespace "**EventQuality**". Every time an event with no **user_id** is seen, we increment the counter and choose not to emit that event further (thus, effectively dropping it from **valid_events**).

Now, if the pipeline is run on Dataflow, you could monitor **EventQuality:missing_user_id** in the metrics. If you see that counter increasing, it means that a lot of events are missing user IDs (which might signal an upstream data issue). If it stays zero, it means that all events had user IDs as expected.

This kind of inline observability—the pipeline reporting on the data that it is processing—is extremely valuable for trust in your data processing. It turns the pipeline into a watchdog for data correctness and processing health.

In summary, **Beam metrics** give you a window into the pipeline's inner workings. Therefore, by thoughtfully using counters, distributions, and gauges, you can create a pipeline that not only transforms data but also emits important signals about its operation. Moreover, when metrics are combined with external monitoring systems (Cloud Monitoring, CloudWatch, and so on), you gain a comprehensive observability toolkit.

Tuning and Optimizing Pipeline Performance

Once your pipeline is correct and observable, the next step is ensuring that it runs efficiently. Tuning Apache Beam pipelines can involve optimizing your pipeline code, adjusting how the runner executes the pipeline, and sometimes changing the pipeline's design to handle data more smartly. In this section, we will discuss various strategies to optimize performance, which is applicable to both batch and streaming pipelines, and both Python and Java SDKs.

Performance optimization in Beam often boils down to two broad areas:

- **Efficient Pipeline Logic and Data Handling**: This involves making sure that your transforms are written in an optimal way, and your data is handled in a parallel-friendly manner.
- **Resource and Runner Configuration**: This ensures that the runner has the right resources (workers, threads, and so on), and the settings to execute the pipeline optimally.

Now, let us go through the key considerations and best practices.

Pipeline Design and Data Transformation Best Practices

How you write your pipeline (the DAG of transforms) greatly influences performance. Therefore, here are some best practices for effective pipeline design:

- **Filter Early:** If possible, remove unnecessary data as early as you can in the pipeline. For example, if only 10% of input records are useful and you can determine that with a filter predicate, filter it at the beginning. This way subsequent expensive operations only deal with that proportion only, and not the entire dataset.
- **Combine (Aggregate) Early:** Similar to filtering, if you can reduce data volume by combining elements, do it early on. For instance, if you are summing values by key, doing a partial combine before grouping all data can reduce the amount of data shuffled across the network. Beam offers combiners (such as `Combine.perKey`, or simply using aggregating transforms), which should be leveraged instead of doing a heavy **GroupByKey,** followed by manual summation. Therefore, combiners are optimized to be more efficient.
- **Avoid Large GroupByKey Wherever Possible:** Grouping by key (or joining on a key) causes a shuffle of data that can be expensive, especially if one key has a huge amount of data (creating a "hot key" scenario). If you have a scenario like joining a large dataset with a small dataset, consider using **side inputs** for the small dataset, instead of a full join. Side inputs allow you to broadcast a small dataset to all workers, while avoiding a shuffle.
- **Manage Hot Keys (Data Skew):** If your data has skew (some keys are extremely popular), the work for those keys can become a bottleneck (one worker handling the key's group, while others sit idle). There are strategies to mitigate this:
    - Use Beam's built-in **combiner fanout** (in Java, **`Combine.PerKey.withHotKeyFanout(...)`**), which spreads the combine for a single key across multiple machines before final aggregation.
    - Manually "Salting" Keys: For example, append a random prefix to the hot key to distribute it, and then remove the prefix after grouping. This essentially tricks the system into treating it as multiple keys to parallelize the processing.

      For example, if key "USA" is super-hot, you can emit keys "USA_1", "USA_2", ... randomly, group by those, process, and finally combine those partial results for "USA". This requires extra code, but it can alleviate stragglers.
- **Optimize Windowing Strategy:** For streaming, choose window sizes that balance latency and overhead. Very large windows mean results are held longer

(increasing latency and memory use), while very small windows mean more frequent handling (increasing overhead). If using sessions or sliding windows, consider their impacts–a sliding window with a small interval, but a large size could produce many duplicate computations. Sometimes, introducing an earlier fixed window aggregation before a sliding window can reduce repeated work.

- **Fusion Optimization and Breaking Fusion:** Beam runners will fuse together sequential operations for efficiency (to avoid unnecessary data materialization). This is good in most cases. However, if you have a heavy operation followed by a light one, and they are fused into the same stage, the heavy one might single-handedly dictate the pace and parallelism. In rare cases, it might help to break fusion by inserting an artificial boundary (such as **`beam.Reshuffle(),`** or materializing to an intermediate sink and source), so that the heavy operation runs independently, and the light one can run in parallel after it. This is an advanced move; therefore, you must use it only if you have evidence (from the UI or metrics) that fusion is causing an issue (for example, the runner did not parallelize where it could have).
- **Use Efficient Data Coders:** Serialization and deserialization of data (to send between transforms, or between machines) can be a major overhead. Beam uses **coders** to encode/decode elements. By default, Beam will pick a coder for your data type (for example, for Java POJOs it might use Java's Serializable coder if nothing else is specified, which is slow). Therefore, whenever possible, use more efficient coders such as:
    - In Java, prefer using Beam's **`AvroCoder`** or **`ProtoCoder`** for complex objects instead of **`SerializableCoder.`** If you use Apache Avro or Protocol Buffers for your data schema, you get a big performance boost in serialization.
    - If using Python, Beam uses pickling (cloudpickle) by default for objects. This is generally okay, but if you can stick to simple types (integers, floats, strings, tuples, and so on), or Beam's native types, as it is faster.
    - Avoid encoding large objects as a single element if you can break them up. For example, instead of one element containing a huge blob of data, try to process it in smaller chunks if it is logically possible.
- **Use Batch Operations for External I/O:** If your transform is interacting with an external system (database, web API, and so on), doing it one element at a time can be slow, and also end up overloading that system. Therefore, it is often better to batch multiple records in a single external call:
    - In Java, you can accumulate elements in **`@FinishBundle,`** use the **`BundleFinalizer`**, or use libraries that provide bulk I/O transforms.

- In Python, you might accumulate in memory, and only actually call the external service every N elements, or every T seconds. The Beam transform **`GroupIntoBatches`** can help; it groups a **`PCollection`** into batches of a given size (which is useful before a writing transform).

  Example: Rather than calling a web service 1,000 times for 1,000 records, group them into 10 batches of 100, and then call 10 times. This drastically reduces overhead.

- **Parallel Reads and Writes:** Use Beam's I/O connectors that support parallelism. For instance, if reading from a file system, use **`FileIO`** or text I/O that splits the file into chunks for parallel reading. If you are writing to a database, see if there is a Beam sink that parallelizes writes, or consider writing to storage (such as cloud storage or S3), and then loading them to the database in bulk.

Resource Configuration and Runner Optimizations

Optimizing the pipeline code is the first part; the second part is ensuring that the runner is configured to execute it efficiently:

- **Autoscaling (On Dataflow):** By default, Google Cloud Dataflow will auto scale the number of worker VMs for your job (both batch and streaming, using different algorithms). Autoscaling is usually beneficial, as it adds workers when the load increases, and removes them when not needed. This achieves a balance of speed and cost. However, for very short jobs, autoscaling might not react fast enough to be useful. In such cases, you might disable autoscaling, and just start with an optimal number of workers. Always consider your pipeline's profile: long-running streaming jobs benefit hugely from autoscaling, while short-batch jobs might as well run with a fixed small cluster to avoid the overhead of spinning up and down.
- **Worker Machine Type and Parallelism:** The default worker type on Dataflow might not always be the best for your workload. For CPU-intensive tasks (for example, heavy data transforms or encryption/compression), a machine type with more CPU, or even attached GPUs (Dataflow supports GPU for certain workloads) could finish faster. Conversely, if your tasks are light, but you have a massive volume, then using smaller machines might be better. You can set the machine type via pipeline options (for example, **`--workerMachineType=n1-standard-4`** in Dataflow options to use 4 CPU machines). Also, consider the number of threads per worker; Dataflow by default can use multiple threads per worker (it uses something called "worker harness threads" for parallelism on one machine). Therefore, if you know that your transform is CPU-heavy and single-threaded, you might reduce the number of worker threads to

avoid contention; if it is I/O heavy, you might increase threads. Dataflow even has **dynamic work rebalancing** and **dynamic thread scaling**, which usually manage this automatically.

- **Initial and Maximum Workers:** You can configure the pipeline's start and max number of workers. For example, `--numWorkers=5 --maxWorkers=50` (Dataflow) to start with 5 and allow scaling to 50. If you know you have a huge job, starting with too few might waste time scaling up slowly; you could start with a higher number. On the other hand, capping max workers can control costs. In streaming, max workers prevent runaway scaling on unbounded workloads (which could cost too much).
- **Locality of Data:** Ensure that your workers are in the same region as your data sources/sinks. For instance, if your input data is in Google Cloud Storage `us-central1`, run your Dataflow job in `us-central1`. If your AWS Flink job reads from Kinesis in a certain region, run the job in that same region. This avoids cross-region network latency and egress costs, and improves performance.
- **Pipeline Options for Performance:** There are pipeline options that can impact performance:
    - **Dataflow Shuffle and Streaming Engine:** Dataflow has a feature called the **Dataflow Shuffle** (for batch) and **Streaming Engine** (for streaming). Dataflow Shuffle moves the heavy shuffle operation off the worker VMs into service, while speeding up large shuffles, and also reducing worker memory needs (at an additional service cost). It is enabled by default for batch, and is highly recommended. Streaming Engine similarly offloads state and shuffle for streaming pipelines to the Dataflow service, which can greatly improve throughput, and lower the per-worker load. It is usually enabled via an option `(--enableStreamingEngine).`
    - **Fusion Optimizations:** Dataflow automatically tries to optimize the pipeline graph (fusion, and so on). Generally, trust the runner, but you can use techniques (like `reshuffle()`) to tweak, if required.
- **Flink-Specific Tuning (For AWS or Self-Managed):** If using Flink, you might need to tune parallelism and memory in the following ways:
    - Set a proper parallelism for the job (how many parallel subtasks). This is equivalent to the number of CPU cores used. If parallelism is too low, the job will be slow; if it is too high, the overhead might dominate, or you might exceed the cluster capacity.
    - Flink allows different operators to have different parallelisms (if one stage is heavier, you can give it more parallel instances). This is advanced and not directly exposed via Beam's simple pipeline API, but if absolutely needed, one could incorporate Flink-specific configuration.

  - Ensure that the JVM memory settings are sufficient (**`OutOfMemory`** errors in Flink means that you need either more memory per machine, or distribute the load more).
  - Managed Flink on AWS can auto scale based on metrics like CPU. Hence, you should enable autoscaling, if it is available, so the service adds Kinesis Processing Units (KPUs) when needed.
- **Processing Timeouts:** Some runners might have timeouts for processing elements (especially in streaming with checkpointing). If you have a DoFn that might take a long time for one element (maybe calling a slow API), it could trigger timeouts. In such cases, consider reworking that DoFn to be faster per element, or increase the timeout settings if possible. Usually, breaking work into smaller chunks is the solution.

Example: Setting Pipeline Options for Dataflow (Python)

To illustrate how you might apply some of these settings, here is a snippet using the Python SDK to configure a Dataflow pipeline for a large batch job:

```
from apache_beam.options.pipeline_options import PipelineOptions,
GoogleCloudOptions, StandardOptions, WorkerOptions

# Set up PipelineOptions for Dataflow
options = PipelineOptions()
google_cloud_options = options.view_as(GoogleCloudOptions)
google_cloud_options.project = "my-gcp-project"
google_cloud_options.region = "us-central1"
google_cloud_options.job_name = "beam-performance-example"
google_cloud_options.staging_location = "gs://my-bucket/staging"
google_cloud_options.temp_location = "gs://my-bucket/temp"
options.view_as(StandardOptions).runner = "DataflowRunner"

# Tune worker options
worker_options = options.view_as(WorkerOptions)
worker_options.machine_type = "n2-standard-4"      # a machine
type with 4 CPUs
worker_options.num_workers = 5                     # start with 5
workers
worker_options.max_num_workers = 20                # autoscale up
to 20
worker_options.disk_size_gb = 50                   # disk size per
worker, if needed for shuffle or buffering

# Enable some Dataflow features
google_cloud_options.enable_streaming_engine = True  # if this
were a streaming pipeline
```

```
# (For batch, Dataflow Shuffle is on by default, no flag needed in
newer Beam versions)
```

In Java, similarly, you could do:

```
DataflowPipelineOptions options = PipelineOptionsFactory.create().
as(DataflowPipelineOptions.class);
options.setProject("my-gcp-project");
options.setRegion("us-central1");
options.setJobName("beam-performance-example");
options.setStagingLocation("gs://my-bucket/staging");
options.setTempLocation("gs://my-bucket/temp");
options.setRunner(DataflowRunner.class);

// Tuning:
options.setMaxNumWorkers(20);
options.setNumWorkers(5);
options.setWorkerMachineType("n2-standard-4");
options.setDiskSizeGb(50);
options.setEnableStreamingEngine(true); // for streaming jobs
```

These options will influence how the Dataflow runner executes your pipeline. For example, using a **`n2-standard-4`** machine (which has 4 vCPUs) might handle CPU-intensive tasks faster than the default (often n1-standard-1 or similar), at the cost of a higher per-worker hourly rate, but you might need fewer workers or finish quicker, as it is a trade-off to experiment with.

Testing and Iterating for Performance

Performance tuning is often an iterative process, and consists of:

- **Load Testing:** Try your pipeline on a smaller scale of data first to gauge performance, and then ramp up. If you plan to process 1TB, first test on 100GB, and then see how long that takes before adjusting it accordingly.
- **Metrics for Bottlenecks:** Use metrics (as above) to find where the time is being spent. If you have a distribution metric around a certain operation's latency, and it shows that some calls take 5 seconds, while most take 0.1 seconds. In that case, you have found a culprit for variance. If your counters show that one branch of a **`ParDo`** processes 90% of data, and another processes only 10%, splitting the pipeline differently could aid parallelism.
- **Profile, If Possible:** Google Cloud Dataflow offers a profiler (Cloud Profiler) integration to profile the CPU usage of your job. If you have access to that, it can pinpoint hotspots in code (for example, a particular library call using a lot of CPU). On your local machine, you could do a sample run, and then use profilers (such as VisualVM for Java, cProfile for Python) on the **`DirectRunner`**

to get some insight. However, keep in mind that the results may differ in a distributed setting, but they can still highlight inefficiencies in code.

- **Avoid Over-Engineering:** It is easy to dive deep into micro-optimizations. Hence, you should always ask: is this actually affecting my pipeline's end-to-end performance or cost? For example, spending a day to optimize a function that takes 1% of the total job time is not as fruitful as optimizing one that takes 50%. Therefore, you should use monitoring data to prioritize.
- **Stay Up-to-Date:** Newer versions of Apache Beam often include performance improvements and new features. For instance, the Beam Python SDK introduced a new optimized Dataflow runner (the "Runner v2") that improved performance for Python pipelines significantly by using portable architectures. Therefore, you should ensure that you are using a recent Beam SDK version, and are keeping an eye on release notes for performance-related changes.

Therefore, by following these tuning tips, you can significantly speed up your Beam pipelines, which not only meets business requirements faster, but often also saves cost (since many cloud charges are per resource consumed per time). Hence, performance and cost are closely related, which leads to our final topic, that is, cost management.

Cost Management in Cloud Deployments

Optimizing performance often goes hand-in-hand with optimizing cost, but there are specific considerations when it comes to **cloud deployment costs**. Therefore, in this section, we will discuss strategies to manage and reduce the cost of running Apache Beam pipelines in the cloud, while focusing on Google Cloud Dataflow and AWS environments.

Running data pipelines at scale can incur significant costs, if not managed. Costs come from the compute resources (CPU, memory), storage, and any additional services used during processing. The good news is that both GCP and AWS provide tools and best practices to help control these expenses.

Cost Optimization on Google Cloud Dataflow

Google Cloud Dataflow pricing is usage-based: you are billed for the total **worker vCPU time**, memory, the storage consumed, as well as any additional services such as Shuffle and Streaming Engine usage. Here is how to keep those costs in check:

- **Optimize Pipeline Performance:** As noted earlier, a more efficient pipeline often costs less because it uses fewer resources or runs for a shorter duration. If your job finishes in 30 minutes instead of 60 due to optimizations, you roughly halve the cost. So, all the tuning tips in the previous section (filtering early, avoiding hotkeys, and so on) also pay dividends in cost. A faster pipeline leads to fewer hours of VM usage.

- **Right-Size Worker Resources:** Choose the smallest worker machine type that can handle your job effectively. For example, if n1-standard-1 (1 vCPU) can handle the per-worker load, do not use n1-standard-8. On the other hand, if your job is CPU-bound and runs slowly on small machines, moving to a machine with more CPU (or more memory for memory-bound jobs) might let you use fewer workers overall. Dataflow charges by the CPU-hour; therefore, 1 machine for 4 hours and 4 machines for 1-hour cost roughly the same in terms of CPU, but there might be differences in overhead. Therefore, it is often worth experimenting. Generally, start with default, and adjust if needed.
- **Use Autoscaling and Max Workers:** Allowing Dataflow to autoscale can ensure that you are only paying for extra workers when needed. If the pipeline throughput needs to increase, autoscaling adds workers (cost goes up but you get the job done). When throughput is low, it downscales (reducing cost). Set a `max_num_workers` to put an upper bound on how many workers (and thus, the cost) the job can stretch to accommodate. This is critical in streaming jobs which might otherwise scale up indefinitely under a surge; therefore, a cap ensures that you will not bankrupt your project if something goes awry. You can always receive an alert and intervene, if the cap is hit regularly.
- **Streaming Engine and FlexRS:**
  - For streaming pipelines, **Streaming Engine** offloads work from workers, which can reduce the number of workers you need, which indirectly saves cost, even though Streaming Engine itself has a small per GB-second charge. In many cases, it improves throughput enough that the net cost is similar or lower for the same workload.
  - For batch pipelines, if your job is not urgent, consider using **Flexible Resource Scheduling (FlexRS)**. FlexRS (a feature of Dataflow) will schedule your job to run in a cost-optimized way, often by using preemptible VMs (which are much cheaper than regular VMs), and possibly waiting for a time with available capacity. Preemptible instances can be 70-80% cheaper, though they can be terminated (Dataflow will retry them). FlexRS essentially trades off some latency (the job might wait a bit to start, or might take slightly longer due to possible restarts) for lower cost. To use it, you set the pipeline option `--flexRSGoal=COST_OPTIMIZED`.
- **Avoid Wasting Resources on Idle Time:** If you have a streaming pipeline that is not needed on weekends, **shut it down** during that period. Dataflow charges as long as a job is running (even if it is just idling with 1 worker who is doing almost nothing, you still pay for that worker). Therefore, you might design pipelines to be restartable or drainable, so that you can turn them off when they are not in use. For batch, this is less of an issue (jobs run and finish).

- **Combine Small Jobs:** There is an overhead to starting a Dataflow job (spinning up VMs, and so on). If you have many tiny pipelines (say 100 pipelines each processing 1GB daily), the overhead might dominate costs. If feasible, combine work into larger pipelines to amortize the startup cost over more data. Each job has a minimum cost just to exist (for example, a job that runs for 1 minute on 2 workers still uses 2 minutes of worker time plus setup/teardown). Hence, combining could mean reading multiple input sources in one pipeline, and processing them in parallel branches, rather than in separate pipelines.
- **Use Cost Monitoring Tools:** GCP provides a **Dataflow Job Cost** estimate in the monitoring interface for running jobs, which updates as the job runs. Keep an eye on it to catch any anomalies (for example, a job's cost skyrocketing due to unexpected scale-up). Also, export billing data to BigQuery (GCP's Billing Export feature) to analyze your Dataflow spend over time. You can break down the cost by the job, by time of day, and so on, to find patterns (maybe certain job versions cost more, or certain times of month have a heavy load).
- **Storage and Intermediate Data:** Dataflow uses Cloud Storage for staging and temp files. While usually negligible in cost, do not forget to clean up temp files if a job fails. Also, if your pipeline materializes large data to Cloud Storage (maybe using FileIO or similar), that storage cost will persist until you delete the data. Therefore, a part of cost management is ensuring that you only keep what you need in storage or data sinks.
- **Take Advantage of Pricing Options:** If you have steady usage of Dataflow, you could consider **commitment plans** (like Committed Use Discounts on GCP). Google offers committed use discounts for Dataflow where you commit to a certain amount of resource usage (for example, a certain number of vCPUs for a year) in exchange for a lower price. This only makes sense if you know you will use Dataflow continuously at a certain level.
- **Network Egress:** Ensure your Dataflow workers are not accessing data across regions or clouds unnecessarily. Cross-region network egress can incur additional charges. For example, reading from an API or database hosted in another cloud or region might cost network fees. If your pipeline must do that, consider the cost, or find ways to minimize data transfer (filtering data before it leaves the source, and so on).

Cost Optimization on AWS (Apache Flink on Amazon Kinesis Data Analytics or EMR)

On AWS, Beam pipelines might run on different services, but a common scenario is to use Amazon's **Managed Service for Apache Flink** (which we will refer to as KDA for Flink) for streaming, or running on EMR for batch (using Flink or Spark). Cost considerations for AWS include instance hour costs, Kinesis/DynamoDB, or other service costs if they are used, and data transfer as well:

- **Amazon Managed Service for Apache Flink (KDA):** This service charges in **Kinesis Processing Units (KPUs)** for streaming apps. 1 KPU includes 1 vCPU, as well as some memory. There is a minimum of 2 KPUs for any application. You are billed per KPU hour. To optimize cost:
    - Right-size the parallelism (KPUs) for your stream. Do not allocate 10 KPUs if 2 can handle the throughput. Start small and scale up if the pipeline cannot catch up.
    - Use the **auto-scaling** feature of KDA: it can automatically add KPUs if CPU usage goes above a threshold (and remove them when load decreases). This is similar to Dataflow's autoscaling, and also helps in control cost by adapting to the load.
    - If your pipeline is idle for long periods, consider whether you need it to run 24/7. KDA has a threshold of at least 2 KPU, even if it is doing nothing. Therefore, if downtime is acceptable, you might stop the application and restart when needed (though, unlike batch, streaming state needs to be handled; you could snapshot state, and then shut it down).
    - KDA charges for running time; therefore, you must ensure that your pipeline is as efficient as possible (all the earlier tips about code efficiency apply–less wasted CPU means potentially fewer KPUs needed).
    - If your streaming job can tolerate some data loss or lag, and the cost is critical, you could potentially run Flink on spot instances, or a cheaper environment, but KDA itself abstracts that. On EMR, you can use spot instances for the Flink cluster to save cost (but with the risk of interruption).
- **EMR or Self-Managed Clusters:** If you are running Beam on a cluster you manage (EMR, Kubernetes, and so on), follow these tips:
    - Choose cost-effective instance types (for example, on EC2 consider using **spot instances** for task nodes which can drastically cut cost if your job can handle interruptions, or if you checkpoint state frequently in streaming).
    - Use auto-scaling groups with your cluster if possible to scale the number of nodes with the workload.
    - Shut down cluster nodes when jobs are done (do not leave an EMR cluster running idle–EMR costs accrue as long as instances are up).
    - If using EMR, be aware of EMR's own cost (EMR has a surcharge on top of EC2 costs). If you run many pipelines, EMR can be more cost-effective than Dataflow for very large constant usage, especially if you use spot instances, but it requires more management.

- **Data Transfer and Other Services:** If your Beam pipeline on AWS reads from or writes to AWS services (such as S3, Kinesis, DynamoDB, and so on), the cost of such services also matters. Hence, you must know that:
    - Reading from Kinesis has a cost per shard-hour and per volume of data retrieved. If your pipeline lags and has to catch up on a lot of Kinesis data, you might incur high GET records costs. Therefore, keeping the pipeline efficient (not falling behind) saves costs.
    - Writing to S3 is cheap per request, but if you write tiny files, the PUT request costs can add up. Hence, it is better to batch data into larger files (this is both a performance and a cost tip).
    - DynamoDB reads/writes cost money; hence, if you use Beam to write to DynamoDB, consider using DynamoDB's batch write APIs and provisioned capacity wisely to avoid extra throughput charges.
    - If your pipeline connects out to external APIs (outside AWS), note that the data egress from AWS might cost.
- **Monitoring for Cost on AWS:** AWS Cost Explorer or CloudWatch billing alarms can be set up to alert you if costs exceed certain thresholds. This can catch a pipeline gone wild (for example, stuck in a loop writing tons of data unintentionally). Also, CloudWatch metrics for KDA (such as milliseconds behind the latest for Kinesis, or CPU usage) indirectly indicate if your resources are under/over allocated, which eventually ties to cost.
- **AWS Savings Plans or Reserved Instances:** If you run Beam jobs on EC2 (EMR or self-managed) continuously, AWS Savings Plans or Reserved Instances can significantly reduce cost (up to 30-50% depending on commitment). This is analogous to GCP's committed use discounts. With KDA (Managed Flink), AWS does not currently have specific reserved pricing for KPU usage, but Savings Plans that cover EC2/Fargate might not apply to that fully managed service (KDA pricing is separate). Therefore, always check the latest in AWS offerings, as they evolve continuously.

Balancing Performance and Cost

Sometimes the fastest pipeline is not the cheapest (for example, you throw a huge number of workers to finish quickly, but the pipeline could instead run with fewer workers for a longer duration, which may lower the total compute cost.). Therefore, you can strike a balance in the following manner:

- If your pipeline is time-sensitive (needs results by a deadline), you may have to spend more to scale it up to speed.
- If it is cost-sensitive and time is not as critical, you might deliberately run it on fewer resources to save money, while accepting a longer processing time.

Apache Beam (and Dataflow) give you knobs to adjust this balance:

For example, Dataflow's autoscaling for batch tries to optimize for speed by default. Thus, if you wanted to optimize for cost, you might cap max workers, or even turn off autoscaling, and run in a smaller fixed cluster (so that it will not scale up and charge more, but it will take longer). Dataflow's FlexRS explicitly is a cost-optimization mode at the expense of time. Hence, you must choose it based on your objectives.

To conclude, effective cost management is about awareness and proactive control: monitor your jobs, understand how pipeline changes affect the cost, use platform features (such as autoscaling, preemptible workers, and committed discounts), and continually refine. Therefore, by designing efficient pipelines and running them intelligently, you can process large volumes of data on Beam without breaking the bank.

Conclusion

In this chapter, we covered the full lifecycle of running Apache Beam pipelines in production. This includes **monitoring** them for health and performance, **debugging** issues when things go wrong, **instrumenting with metrics** for observability, and **tuning both performance and cost** to meet your requirements.

The next chapter moves from these principles to practice. Through real-world case studies, we will examine how Apache Beam is used in production across different industries and workloads. These examples will show how the concepts from this chapter—monitoring, debugging, metrics, tuning, and cost optimization—come together in actual systems. You will also see how teams design pipelines for streaming analytics, batch processing, data enrichment, and large-scale transformations, how they diagnose real production failures, and how they evolve their pipelines over time to meet growing performance and reliability demands.

Key Takeaways

- Leverage built-in tools on your runner (Dataflow's UI, Cloud Monitoring, Flink's dashboard, and so on) to keep an eye on pipeline execution. Metrics such as throughput, latency, and custom counters are your friends for monitoring.
- Use systematic debugging approaches such as local testing with DirectRunner and PAssert for logic bugs, and cloud debugging with logs, data sampling, and defensive coding (like try/except in DoFns with side outputs for errors) for runtime issues.
- Apache Beam's metrics API (Counters, Distributions, Gauges) empowers you to make the pipeline introspect itself, and also report vital signs. Use it to track things that matter in your pipeline (error counts, data sizes, and so on), as it

will provide you deep insights, and also strengthen your confidence in what the pipeline is doing.

- Write pipelines with performance in mind. Avoid unnecessary work, maximize parallelism (but handle skew), and use efficient data encoding and batching. Small changes such as an early filter or using a combiner instead of a GBK can have a huge impact on speed.
- Adjust runner settings to fine-tune execution. Autoscaling, worker types, number of threads, and features like Streaming Engine can all influence both speed and cost.
- For cloud cost management, always consider the trade-off between faster results and lower spend. Therefore, you must use platform-specific cost-saving features (preemptible workers on GCP, spot instances on AWS, or autoscaling on both), and keep jobs only running when needed. Monitor costs just like you monitor pipeline metrics.

CHAPTER 9

Case Studies: Apache Beam in the Real World

Introduction

Apache Beam is an open-source framework that provides a **unified programming model** for processing both batch and streaming data. Hence, this "write once, run anywhere" approach lets developers focus on business logic without worrying about underlying execution details. Beam pipelines can run on multiple engines (called *runners*), such as Apache Flink, Apache Spark, or Google Cloud Dataflow, which allow for flexibility and avoid vendor lock-in. Due to this versatility, Apache Beam has been adopted across many industries such as finance, healthcare, media and advertising to solve real-world data processing challenges.

Therefore, in this chapter, we will explore several real-world case studies where companies in various domains leveraged Apache Beam for batch and streaming workloads. Each case study will outline the company and industry, the problem or use case they addressed, the architecture of their Beam solution, the challenges faced, and the lessons learned from it. The examples span illustrations from finance, healthcare, media, advertising technology, and energy to demonstrate the versatile applicability of Beam's unified model across diverse scenarios. The explanations focus on key takeaways, so that reaaders will be able to understand it without running into complicated jargon. Thus, new developers considering Apache Beam will be able to see how its concepts translate into real-world success, and how organizations achieved reliable, scalable data processing pipelines with relative ease.

Structure

In this chapter, the following topics will be covered:

- Finance| Credit Karma: Real-Time Financial Insights
- Healthcare| Moorfields Eye Hospital: Accelerating Medical Research with Batch Pipelines
- Media| Spotify: Large Scale Audio Date Processing Pipelines
- Advertising Technology| Booking.com: Optimizing Ad Bidding at Scale
- Energy| Accenture/Sustainable Power: Unified Batch and Streaming Pipelings

Finance| Credit Karma: Real-Time Financial Insights

Company and Industry: Credit Karma is a personal finance technology company with over 140 million members. They provide free credit scores and financial recommendations. The finance industry deals with sensitive data and demands timely insights (for example, detecting fraud, or updating credit recommendations in real-time).

Problem/Use Case: Credit Karma needed to deliver real-time financial insights and personalized recommendations to its users, which required processing streams of financial transactions quickly and reliably. Their previous system was built on in-house tools (Akka Streams on Kubernetes), and became insufficient for new requirements. However, they specifically struggled to **partition incoming data into time windows for analysis**, to **maintain state efficiently** (for example running totals for fraud detection), and to **reduce development time** for new pipeline features. Uptime was also an issue–the old pipelines had only around 80% uptime, which caused frequent outages in data-driven services.

Architecture and Solution: Credit Karma migrated to Apache Beam to unify their batch and streaming needs. They implemented streaming pipelines using **Apache Beam with the Google Cloud Dataflow runner**, as they extensively used Google Cloud Platform. Beam's model allowed them to handle streaming data with features like **windowing, stateful processing, and triggers** for event handling. For instance, one pipeline aggregates transaction features in real time for fraud detection; it ingests transactions (from sources like Pub/Sub and BigQuery), groups them into sliding time windows, updates state (for example running averages), and uses both event-time triggers (to output aggregated features quickly) and timer triggers (to evict old state)–all within a single job. Triggers decide when results are emitted, while timers support state lifecycle actions (for example, cleanup) that are keyed by event/processing time. This design was more complex than a typical streaming job, but Beam's API supported combining event-driven and time-driven computations in a single pipeline. Batch use cases (like periodic large-scale ETL for analytics) were also implemented with Beam by using the same codebase and concepts as streaming. The **execution environment** for most of these pipelines was Google Cloud Dataflow, which is a fully managed service for Beam that provided features such as autoscaling, built-in monitoring. Dataflow manages durable state and checkpointing for streaming pipelines. Thus, using Dataflow freed the team from managing their own streaming infrastructure, and let them focus on pipeline logic.

Use Case	Beam Primitive
Real-Time Streams of Financial Transactions	PubSubIO
Grouping Events by Time	Windowing (Sliding / Fixed Windows)
Maintaining Running Fraud Metrics	Stateful DoFn
Emitting Early and Final Results	Triggers
Cleaning up Old State	Timers
Persisting Results	BigQueryIO

***Table 9.1**: Use Cases and Beam Primitives Used in the Credit Karma Example*

Challenges and Resolutions: Some challenges for Credit Karma included migrating existing logic to the Beam model, as well as ensuring low latency. Beam's learning curve was eased by its clear abstraction that separates business logic from execution details, and also by the fact that Beam supports familiar languages (Credit Karma's teams use both Java and Python). Thus, ensuring low end-to-end latency (on the order of milliseconds) was critical for real-time features. Beam on Dataflow was able to meet strict latency requirements thanks to its efficient streaming engine. Another challenge was to implement complex trigger logic (combining immediate results with delayed cleanup of state); Beam's flexible trigger API made this possible, whereas their old system could not easily mix time-based and event-based triggers. Operationally, moving to Dataflow greatly improved reliability–the pipeline uptime jumped to ~99%, up from ~80% before. This was a big win for maintaining always-on financial data services.

Lessons Learned and Benefits: By adopting Apache Beam, Credit Karma achieved notable improvements in their data platform. They saw the **reliability rates escalate**, with 99% uptime for critical pipelines (versus 80% previously). This implied fewer incidents and less manual intervention. Additionally, development became faster and more efficient, as one key streaming pipeline was delivered by a single engineer in one quarter, whereas it was originally estimated to take a team of three engineers two quarters to build on the old stack. This represents a dramatically **faster time-to-market** for new features. Beam's unified approach also enabled **Machine Learning (ML) on streaming data**. These features, that were once only updated in batch, can now be computed continuously, while improving the freshness of ML models. The team also managed to **reduce on-call load** (fewer alerts), as well as improve the modularity and reuse of their pipelines. They even integrated an external service for data tokenization via Beam with relatively low effort. Therefore, the key takeaway for new developers from this case study is that Apache Beam can simplify the creation of **stateful, windowed streaming pipelines** that would be hard to implement from scratch. It provides out-of-the-box building blocks for complex streaming needs (like session windows, triggers, and stateful transforms), which **speeds up development** and ensures robust handling of real-time data. For Credit Karma, Beam's capabilities translated into **real-time financial insights** for users and a more agile data engineering process. Therefore, this case study demonstrates the value of Beam in the finance domain.

Citation: https://beam.apache.org/case-studies/creditkarmainsights/

Healthcare| Moorfields Eye Hospital: Accelerating Medical Research with Batch Pipelines

Company and Industry: Moorfields Eye Hospital is a leading ophthalmic hospital in the UK, known for world-class eye research. In healthcare, integrating and analyzing data (like medical images and patient records) is crucial for research and clinical insights, but data privacy and security remain the paramount consideration for hospitals like Moorfield.

Problem/Use Case: Moorfields had **millions of eye scan images** spread across about 40 different imaging systems, each with proprietary formats. The patient data was siloed: some images existed on local machines or shared drives, while others were stored in various clinical systems. Researchers who wanted to study, say, a certain eye condition had to manually gather data from multiple systems, **de-identify patient information by hand**, and get numerous approvals. This manual process to assemble a research dataset could take up to **9 months**. The hospital wanted to leverage this trove of images for groundbreaking Artificial Intelligence (AI) research (for example, predicting disease progression from scans), but needed a faster, more scalable way to prepare data—all while ensuring strict patient confidentiality.

Architecture and Solution: With the help of a software engineering firm, Moorfields built a **cloud-based data platform** on Google Cloud that automates data ingestion, processing, and anonymization. Apache Beam (with Cloud Dataflow) was a key component for the data processing pipelines. Although new medical images arrive continuously from clinical systems, the processing model is **incremental batch (micro-batch)** rather than fully event-driven streaming. In practice, Apache Beam pipelines running on Cloud Dataflow are triggered at fixed intervals (for example, every 15–30 minutes) to process all the newly arrived images since the previous run. Each micro-batch reads the latest files from cloud storage, converts them into standardized open formats, separates the image data from patient-identifiable metadata, and applies anonymization before loading the results into the research platform. Metadata such as patient age, diagnosis, and scan attributes is written to BigQuery, while the anonymized images are stored in a centralized image repository. Metadata (like patient age, diagnosis, and so on) is then stored in BigQuery, which is Google's analytics database, to enable rich queries. The use case here is largely **batch processing**, which includes ingesting large volumes of files, transforming them, and loading them into a database/catalog for researchers. Apache Beam was used to orchestrate this ETL (Extract, Transform, Load) at scale. Hence, by using **Beam's parallel processing**, the team could **massively speed up** the transformation of images and data compared to sequential or manual methods. In fact, they report that heavy parallelization with Apache Beam "*substantially reduced processing time*" for preparing datasets. The execution environment was Google Cloud Dataflow, which allowed the pipelines to scale out on many workers for faster throughput, and to integrate easily with other GCP services (Cloud Storage for images, BigQuery for metadata, and so on).

Challenges and Resolutions: A major challenge in this project was **data governance and privacy**. Therefore, handling sensitive medical data requires careful anonymization at every step. The team addressed this by designing the system with multiple secure perimeters and by using Beam pipelines to enforce transformations that strip or tokenize personal information. Raw images and metadata first land in a restricted "secure intake zone" in Cloud Storage that is accessible only to the ingestion pipeline. The Beam pipeline then executes a de-identification step where patient identifiers (such as hospital IDs, names, or timestamps that can re-identify individuals) are either removed, or are replaced with pseudonymous tokens.

Tokenization keys are managed in a secure key management system, and are never embedded in pipeline code, or stored in analytics systems. Only the pipeline has temporary access to these keys at runtime. After transformation:

- **De-identified metadata** (like age, diagnosis, scan attributes, pseudonymous patient ID) is written to BigQuery.
- **Original identifiers and token mappings** remain isolated in a secure, access-controlled system, and are not accessible to researchers.

As data flows through the pipeline, patient identifiers are removed or replaced with pseudonymous IDs, and only de-identified data enters the research database. Apache Beam itself provided the processing muscle, while security was handled via GCP's controls and careful pipeline design. Another challenge was to deal with **many data formats and sources**. Beam's I/O connectors and transformation logic were used to read from various sources and convert different image formats into a common format. The complexity of merging data from more than 40 systems was high, but by using

Beam pipelines orchestrated in Cloud Dataflow, Moorfields achieved a unified data flow that replaced manual steps.

Lessons Learned and Benefits: The resulting platform drastically **reduced the time to prepare research datasets**; what once took up to 9 months can now be done in a matter of days, or even minutes for certain queries. This acceleration meant that researchers could iterate faster, and also tackle larger studies than before. For instance, Moorfields can now create de-identified datasets with tens of thousands of patients, while unlocking AI research that previously was not feasible. Apache Beam's role in this success was to enable *scalable batch processing*. Hence, a key takeaway is that Beam is not only for streaming data; it is equally powerful for large-scale batch jobs like image processing. Thus, by leveraging Beam on Dataflow, Moorfields processed over **20 million images** into a structured repository. They achieved this with a relatively small team, thanks to the productivity of Beam's high-level SDK (in Python and other languages), instead of writing custom distributed code. Moreover, using Beam on a managed service meant they did not have to maintain servers or worry about parallelization details—the system could simply scale out when more images need processing. From a beginner's perspective, this case highlights Beam's ability to handle **complex ETL in a privacy-sensitive context**, as it demonstrates how Beam can be used to build data platforms in healthcare that are both fast and compliant. The resultant benefit is **faster scientific breakthroughs** (as researchers get data quicker), as well as the trust that data is handled correctly. In summary, Moorfields' case shows how Apache Beam enabled a *"bespoke, automated data platform"* for medical research that **transformed a laborious pipeline into an efficient, governed process**.

Citation: https://www.softwire.com/case-study/a-new-cloud-data-platform-to-enable-ground-breaking-healthcare-research/

Media: Spotify| Large-Scale Audio Data Processing Pipelines

Company and Industry: Spotify is a leading music and audio streaming company (pertaining to media and entertainment). Beyond streaming music to users, Spotify invests heavily in audio analytics and ML by analyzing songs and podcasts to drive features like recommendations, audio search, and ads. Therefore, this creates unique data processing needs on large volumes of audio files.

Problem/Use Case: Spotify's platform deals with an enormous library of audio content, which spans over **60 million songs (growing by ~40,000 tracks per day)**, as well as an ever-expanding catalog of podcasts. On any given day, a single audio file (like a song) might be processed in **a hundred different ways**—for example, by detecting their tempo, finding the language of lyrics, identifying segments (beats or silence), computing loudness, or even separating vocals from background music. These analyses support features like playlist generation, content moderation, and audio-based recommendations. Hence, the challenge was not only the **scale and variety** of these audio processing tasks, but also that **hundreds of teams** across Spotify needed to process audio files concurrently for different purposes. This led to duplicated efforts and complex pipelines, especially since dealing with large binary files (audio/video) in distributed systems was not at all trivial. The existing approaches (ad-hoc scripts or single-use pipelines) were hindering collaboration and slowing down product innovation. Therefore, it was hard for research teams to get their audio processing jobs running efficiently at scale.

Architecture and Solution: To solve this, Spotify created a framework called **Klio**, built on top of Apache Beam for Python. Klio provides a standardized way to construct data pipelines that ingest and process **media files** (audio, video, or images) by using Beam as the underlying engine. In essence, Klio leverages Beam's ability to handle both batch and streaming in one model–it treats the arrival of an audio file as an event in a streaming pipeline. Klio is designed as a **long-running streaming pipeline**, and not as a system where a new Beam job is launched for each uploaded file. The typical architecture therefore is: whenever a new audio file is available (say, uploaded to cloud storage), a message is sent to a pub/sub system (Google Cloud Pub/Sub in this case) to trigger processing. A Beam pipeline (encapsulated by Klio) then reads the audio file from cloud storage, performs a series of transformations/analyses on it (for example, runs it through an ML model for genre classification or calls libraries like FFmpeg/Librosa for audio features), and finally writes the results out (perhaps to another storage bucket or a database). Since it is built on Beam, this pipeline can be run in **streaming mode** (processing each file as it comes) or in batch (processing a collection of files), and it can scale out to handle many files in parallel. The execution environment often used here is Google Cloud Dataflow (since Spotify collaborated with Google Cloud engineers on this), which provides managed scaling. Klio also added conveniences like supporting Directed Acyclic Graphs (DAGs) of jobs (so that one processing job can trigger dependent jobs in sequence), and abstracting some of the Beam details. This made the interface simpler for audio specialists to use. Essentially, Spotify provided their teams with a Beam-powered toolkit that **simplifies and standardizes pipeline creation** for audio processing.

Challenges and Resolutions: Processing audio at this scale posed several challenges. One was to handle **large binary data** in a pipeline. Beam's model normally handles data element by element, but huge files needed careful handling (like downloading file chunks, processing, then uploading results). Klio addressed this by making the pipeline treat each media file as an element–with Beam managing parallel workers that each handle different files, and reading/writing from cloud storage efficiently. Another challenge was the **duplication of effort** and the lack of standard tools; before Klio, different teams wrote similar code to process audio. Hence, by building a common Beam-based framework, Spotify enabled code reuse and easier maintenance. So, if a library or method is updated, all the pipelines benefit from it. Additionally, ensuring that these pipelines were running reliably in production was critical (since they feed user-facing features). Therefore, using Apache Beam with Dataflow gave Spotify reliability and autoscaling out-of-the-box, which meant that researchers did not have to become experts in distributed computing, or worry about provisioning resources; they could focus on the audio logic. Finally, integrating ML (like TensorFlow models for audio) into data pipelines was streamlined by Beam's support for Python, and also by Spotify's customizations. For example, some Spotify teams use Klio to run TensorFlow models over audio files for tasks like audio **fingerprinting**, or generating short previews of podcasts. Beam can easily incorporate such model inference as a transform in the pipeline, and Dataflow can manage the heavy compute in parallel.

Lessons Learned and Benefits: The adoption of Apache Beam via the Klio framework yielded significant benefits for Spotify. It **dramatically improved efficiency and collaboration**. Now, teams across the company use a unified approach to process audio, while avoiding one-off solutions. This has sped up the development of new audio-driven features because engineers and researchers can plug into an existing pipeline framework, instead of reinventing it. According to Spotify, Klio (on Beam) allows them to process the massive audio catalog "*easily and at scale*", while letting users concentrate on their specific goals, rather than on the data plumbing. Therefore, for beginners, an important takeaway from this case is how Beam's model can be extended to niche domains–even working with binary media files is possible, which shows Beam's flexibility. The case also highlights that Beam can be used in an **event-driven architecture**; here, the event of a file upload triggers a pipeline run, blending batch (file processing) with streaming (continuous arrival of files). The result for Spotify is a future-proof, scalable system supporting audio R&D. They even open-sourced Klio, which means that others can leverage this Beam-based solution for their own media processing needs. In summary, Spotify's case demonstrates that Apache Beam is not just for text logs or numeric data; it can handle **rich media data** in production, while unifying various processing tasks into one consistent pipeline model. The benefit is faster innovation in audio features, because processing several tasks on millions of files became much simpler with Beam. However, working with media introduces a few important practical considerations; instead of passing large raw audio bytes through the pipeline graph, it is better to pass file URIs, and then stream the content directly inside workers; worker memory and disk must be sized carefully because audio files can be large, and any external libraries used for audio decoding or ML inference (such as FFmpeg, Librosa, or TensorFlow) must be packaged and tested with the worker runtime environment. Hence, these I/O and runtime constraints are often the hardest parts of building media pipelines, and are as critical to success as the Beam code itself.

Citation: https://cloud.google.com/customers/spotify

Advertising Technology| Booking.com: Optimizing Ad Bidding at Scale

Company and Industry: Booking.com is a major online travel company (hospitality industry), but here, we will focus on their **marketing technology/Ad Tech** operations. Booking.com runs large-scale advertising campaigns, especially pay-per-click (PPC) search ads on platforms like Google. The ad tech domain involves processing huge volumes of data (search queries, bids, and click feedback) and doing so quickly to adjust advertising strategies in real time.

Problem/Use Case: Booking.com's performance marketing team manages **massive PPC ad bidding** globally. They have to generate and update bids for millions of keywords, so that their ads appear to the right audience. They must also adjust those bids based on performance feedback. The scale is enormous, as the system handles **billions of search events per day** (from people searching travel terms), besides integrating data from many sources (analytics databases, transactional systems, external ad networks). In 2022, Booking Holdings (the parent company) spent nearly $6 billion on marketing, with Booking.com being a leading advertiser. Initially, their ad bidding processing was built as a custom batch system: the data was stored in MySQL, while scheduled jobs (cron) and scripts were stored in Perl to implement business logic. Over time, this setup hit a wall. It became a **performance bottleneck**, as it could not keep up with the growing volume of ad data and the need for faster bid optimizations. Bids were not always updated in time for auctions, and represented several lost opportunities. Moreover, maintaining this complex, home-grown pipeline (with multiple rewrites over the years) was costly and inflexible. Hence, the team realized they needed a more scalable and efficient solution to reliably process ad events, and also optimize bids in near real-time.

Architecture and Solution: The PPC team turned to Apache Beam for a new implementation of their ad bidding infrastructure. They designed a system where Apache Beam pipelines form the core data processing layer, using Google Cloud Dataflow as the runner. The solution needed both **batch and streaming components**. For instance, one pipeline might do a daily batch analysis of historical ad performance (scanning large datasets in BigQuery for analytics), while another pipeline handles streaming ingestion of real-time ad click feedback and cost data via Pub/Sub. Apache Beam's unified model allows them to use the same framework for both. In practice, the team built pipelines in **Java** (one of Beam's supported SDKs) to process ad data. They utilize Beam's connectors to integrate with Google Cloud services like reading from BigQuery, writing to Cloud Spanner and Firestore, and ingesting or publishing messages via Pub/Sub. This replaced the old cron and Perl batch jobs with more continuous and reactive data flows.

Crucially, Apache Beam provided powerful primitives for **parallel processing**. The new pipelines could process over **1 billion events daily** at the peak rate of thousands of messages per second. They scanned more than **2 PB of analytical data plus terabytes of fresh transactional data** each day. Beam's model of dividing data into **PCollections** and applying transforms in parallel let them scale out the workload easily across many machines. This was something that was very hard with the previous system. In addition to this, Beam's support for **stateful processing and timely processing** was used for certain aspects like maintaining counters for ad budgets or handling late-arriving data. The pipelines were deployed on **Google Cloud Dataflow**. This implied that the team did not have to manage servers or worry about scaling, as Dataflow automatically provisioned VMs and could autoscale the pipeline based on data volume. This let the team focus on the logic of bidding optimization (such as how to calculate optimal bids using ML models and performance data), rather than on infrastructure.

Challenges and Resolutions: Transitioning from a legacy system to Beam required careful planning. One challenge was **team buy-in and learning**, as the engineers had to become familiar with the Beam model. They overcame this by attending community events like Beam Summit and Beam College, and also learning from the Beam community. The simplicity of Beam's model helped them, as the team found it *straightforward to introduce the idea to the rest of the team* because Beam cleanly separates business logic and lets you think in terms of data flows, rather than low-level threads or cron jobs. Another challenge was ensuring that the new pipeline truly outperformed the old one. This was achieved convincingly; by piloting a prototype pipeline (in Java) to download ad performance reports, the team experienced a **multi-factor speed-up in development time**, and delivered that pipeline in 3 weeks, instead of an estimated 3 months on the old stack. This quick success built their confidence. On the technical side, they needed to ensure **exactly-once or reliable processing** of ad events. Using Beam with Dataflow thus provided them strong delivery guarantees and built-in checks that gave them the reliability they required. Rather than relying on global or end-to-end message ordering, their correctness was anchored in Beam's **keyed processing model**. Moreover, by grouping events by a campaign or keyword ID, the pipeline used **per-key state, windowing, and timers** to ensure that all updates for the same campaign were processed consistently and deterministically, even if events arrived out of order. Late or duplicate events were handled through Beam's windowing semantics and stateful logic, along with accurate budget tracking, bid updates, and performance aggregation without having to depend on strict message ordering from the underlying infrastructure. This approach guaranteed *per-key correctness*, instead of fragile assumptions about event sequence. They also leveraged Beam's stateful processing to handle scenario-specific logic like coordinating with external ad network APIs within the pipeline. Tuning and optimizing the pipelines was another area–the Dataflow runner offers tools to monitor pipeline performance, and the team used these to identify bottlenecks and adjust resource settings as needed. Overall, any challenges in adopting Beam were offset by the immediate gains in throughput and simpler pipeline maintenance.

Lessons Learned and Benefits: The move to Apache Beam resulted in a **drastically more efficient ad bidding system**. One standout metric was that the streaming pipelines which used to take around 6 hours to process certain cycles, could now be completed in **about 10 minutes**, while recording a **36× speed improvement** in processing time. This near-real-time processing of ad data meant that Booking.com can respond to market changes (like a sudden spike in travel searches) much faster, while optimizing the bids and the budget spend promptly. The new infrastructure could handle scale comfortably, while supporting over 1 million ad queries per month, and driving over 2 million customer nights booked daily via ads. The development agility also improved–the team noted that time from design to production release of a new pipeline was up to **4× faster**. This was due to Beam's abstraction that made pipeline code more concise, as well as eliminating the need to manage infrastructure (using Dataflow). Costs were optimized as well; Beam's efficient parallelism and Dataflow's autoscaling led to better resource usage. Thus, combined with the improved performance, it delivered significant cost-per-processing reduction.

For new developers, Booking.com's experience underscores a few key takeaways. First, **Beam's unified model can replace a patchwork of older systems** (like cron jobs and custom scripts) with a cleaner, maintainable approach. This reduces complexity and technical debt in the long run. Second, using a managed Beam runner (like Dataflow) can offload a lot of DevOps overhead; this is valuable for small teams that need to do big things. Third, Beam's ability to seamlessly scale and handle both batch and streaming in one framework enabled the team to combine what were previously separate pipelines. In fact, Booking.com is planning to unify several batch and streaming workflows into single pipelines using Beam, which would simplify their architecture further. The benefits of the approach are less code duplication and a consistent view of data processing. Lastly, the case highlights how Beam empowered the team to focus on **business logic**, since the framework handled parallelization and integration concerns. A quote from their engineers captures it well: "*Apache Beam serves as an effective abstraction for our data infrastructure... we do not need to worry about maintaining the runtime and storage infrastructure*". In summary, Apache Beam helped Booking.com build a **reliable, high-performance ad tech pipeline** that scales to massive data volumes, while significantly accelerating processing and development, and ultimately contributing to better marketing outcomes.

Citation: https://beam.apache.org/case-studies/booking/

Energy| Sustainable Power Analytics (Accenture): Unified Batch and Streaming Pipelines

Company and Industry: In the energy sector, we will look at a case study from Accenture Baltics, which is a regional branch of the global consulting firm Accenture. They implemented Apache Beam for a client who is a **global leader in sustainable energy**. The energy industry often involves processing data from IoT sensors (for example smart meters, turbines), transactional systems, and analytics for forecasting and optimization.

Problem/Use Case: The Accenture team was responsible for managing data workflows for their energy client, including **transforming, cleaning, and preparing data** for various teams like data scientists, finance, and operations. The client had diverse data sources: transactional data (for example energy sales or meter readings), sensor data (for example, IoT readings from equipment), and analytical data. They needed to provide *democratized* access to this data, meaning that even team members without a data engineering background should be able to get insights (often via SQL queries on a data warehouse). Before Beam, data processing might have involved multiple tools or manual steps, and the challenge was to create a robust infrastructure that could handle **real-time streaming data as well as periodic batch jobs**. For example, one use case was ingesting a live feed of energy transactions (to quickly spot issues or update dashboards), and another was running a**n ML model batch job** for classification on stored data. They also faced typical data engineering challenges: handling complex data transformations, ensuring data quality (deduplicating records, error handling), and routing data to different storage targets based on content.

Architecture and Solution: The solution was built on **Apache Beam running on Google Cloud Dataflow**, which the team had been using for about five years. Dataflow was chosen because it provides a fully managed execution environment with automatic scaling, built-in monitoring, and tight integration with Google Cloud's security and data services, including native connectors for Pub/Sub and BigQuery, as well as seamless use of IAM for access control. This allowed the team to focus on pipeline logic and bidding algorithms instead of managing clusters, capacity planning, or operational reliability, which would have been required with self-managed runners such as Flink or Spark. The architecture comprises multiple pipelines (they have around 12 distinct pipelines in production) that together form the data platform. Key components include Google Pub/Sub (for streaming ingestion), BigQuery (as a data warehouse), Cloud Storage (for batch output), and even Apache Airflow for orchestration. Here is an example of how it works: A **streaming Beam pipeline** listens to a Pub/Sub topic where transactional events are published in real time. As messages arrive (say a new energy usage record), the pipeline performs ETL; it cleans the data, augments it with reference information, and then writes the results into BigQuery tables for immediate use by analysts. Simultaneously, a **batch Beam pipeline** is scheduled (possibly via Airflow) to run an ML evaluation job. For instance, once a day it could read a batch of data, apply a pre-trained binary classification model to predict some outcome (maybe predicting equipment failure or classifying customers), and then write the results to Cloud Storage or BigQuery. Both pipelines use Beam transforms written in Python, and by using Dataflow as the runner, they enjoy features like auto-scaling, managed pipeline execution, and easy integration with GCP services. The team uses relatively modest Dataflow settings (n1-standard-2 or n1-standard-4 workers, scaling up to 5 workers typically) to handle their workloads, which shows that even a small cluster can process a lot with Beam's efficiency.

Challenges and Resolutions: Some challenges addressed by Beam in this scenario included **data accessibility** and **complex transformations**. Beam helped **democratize data access** by enabling pipelines that feed a BigQuery data warehouse, where users can simply use SQL to query fresh data. In other words, Beam is doing the heavy lifting under the hood, but the end users only see the results in an easy form. This meant data scientists and even finance analysts could get up-to-date information without always needing a data engineer's help, which is a big win for the client's agility. Another challenge was implementing robust **error handling and data quality checks**. The pipelines need to deal with possibly malformed messages or duplicates (especially in streaming). The team used Beam's features to implement solutions–for example, using Beam's ability to route data, they send any **failed transaction records to a separate BigQuery table** for later analysis. They also use Beam transforms to deduplicate Pub/Sub messages (in case the same event is received twice), and to catch JSON parsing errors, which prevents bad data from crashing the pipeline. Beam's programming model made it feasible to build these safeguards directly into the data flow. Monitoring was another area; the team integrated Google Cloud's monitoring with Grafana dashboards to keep an eye on pipeline health, and set up notifications for anomalies. Since Beam pipelines on Dataflow emit metrics and logs, hooking these into Grafana was straightforward, which gave the team more visibility into throughput, latency, and error rates.

Lessons Learned and Benefits: The outcome of using Apache Beam for this energy client was a **streamlined, reliable data infrastructure** that served multiple needs. They have 12 pipelines in total, which cover streaming and batch, and have achieved both **scalability and efficiency** in handling the client's data. One measurable result is that their streaming pipelines comfortably process approximately 10,000 events/second as mentioned, and their batch pipelines handle the monthly volume (several GB of data) with ease. Therefore, by leveraging Dataflow (Beam runner), the team ensured the solution scales as needed and remains stable, which is important for an industry where downtime or data lags can impact operational decisions. The use of Beam also led to **improved data governance**. Since all data flows are defined in Beam pipelines, it is easier to audit and understand how data is transformed and where it goes, which is valuable when dealing with regulatory or compliance concerns in energy data.

For new developers, this case study illustrates how Apache Beam can serve as a **general-purpose ETL and streaming tool in enterprise settings**. A key lesson is the benefit of having one model for both batch and streaming; the team did not need separate frameworks for real-time vs. nightly jobs, which reduced the technology footprint. It is noted that using *Dataflow with Beam is a natural choice for both streaming and batch data processing* for their workloads. Additionally, Beam empowered not just the engineers, but also end users; by making fresh data available in BigQuery, even non-engineers could access it with SQL, while fulfilling the goal of data democratization. The **error-handling patterns** (like using Beam to route bad data to a quarantine) demonstrate Beam's flexibility in building resilient pipelines. Finally, the partnership of Beam and a managed service (Dataflow) showed that even a small team can manage a fairly complex data ecosystem without a huge operations burden. As they reported, *"Apache Beam has proven to be a highly effective solution for orchestrating and managing the complex data pipelines...achieving scalability, reliability, and efficiency in handling large volumes of data"*. In other words, the energy sector case confirms that Apache Beam can reduce friction in data engineering, besides handling both **real-time streams and scheduled jobs** in one system, and delivering trustworthy data to drive critical decisions.

Citation: https://beam.apache.org/case-studies/accenture_baltics/

Conclusion

Across these case studies from sectors like finance, healthcare, media, ad technology, and energy, a common thread is how Apache Beam enabled organizations to build **robust, scalable data pipelines** that unify batch and streaming processing. Each company faced a different problem, from real-time fraud detection, to processing medical images or optimizing ad spend, yet Beam's flexible model was able to address their needs.

Thus, for a beginner, the practical takeaway is that **Apache Beam simplifies complex data processing tasks** by providing a high-level framework. Developers can write logic once and run it in different environments without rewriting code, and also leverage advanced features (windowing, state, triggers, connectors to various systems) without having to reinvent them. The real-world benefits observed include dramatic improvements in processing performance, improved reliability and uptime of data pipelines, as well as easier maintenance and faster development cycles.

Moreover, Beam often acts as an enabler for **innovation**; as we saw, it allowed Spotify to roll out new audio analysis features; it helped Moorfields accelerate medical research breakthroughs, and let Intuit and Lyft bring machine learning into real-time decision-making in their products. The "write once, run anywhere" nature of Beam also future-proofs applications–teams like Intuit is appreciate that Beam's runner-agnostic design will let them migrate, or use new execution engines over time without rewriting pipelines.

In conclusion, Apache Beam's real-world use proves that it is a **powerful tool for building data infrastructure**. It abstracts away much of the complexity of parallel and streaming computation, and lets beginners and experts alike focus on actual data transformations. Therefore, by studying these case studies, new developers can gain confidence that Beam is not just academically interesting–it is battle-tested in production across industries. Whether your data challenge is a batch ETL job or a low-latency streaming system, Apache Beam provides a clear path to implement a solution that is **scalable, portable, and maintainable**. The experiences of these companies highlight best practices (like combining batch and stream logic, using managed services to simplify operations, and building error-handling into pipelines) that can guide beginners in their own Apache Beam journeys. Hence, with this knowledge, you can approach your next data processing project with insight into how Beam might help you achieve similar success in the real world.

Index

A

C

D

E

F

G

L

M

O

P

U

V

W